DIALOGUE

DIALOGUE
Theorizing Difference in Communication Studies

Edited by

Rob Anderson
Saint Louis University

Leslie A. Baxter
University of Iowa

Kenneth N. Cissna
University of South Florida

SAGE Publications
International Educational and Professional Publisher
Thousand Oaks ▪ London ▪ New Delhi

For information:

Sage Publications, Inc.
2455 Teller Road
Thousand Oaks, California 91320
E-mail: order@sagepub.com

Sage Publications Ltd.
6 Bonhill Street
London EC2A 4PU
United Kingdom

Sage Publications India Pvt. Ltd.
B-42, Panchsheel Enclave
Post Box 4109
New Delhi 110 017 India

Printed in the United States of America

Library of Congress Cataloging-in-Publication Data

Dialogue : theorizing difference in communication studies / Rob Anderson, Leslie A. Baxter, and Kenneth N. Cissna, editors.
    p. cm.
Includes bibliographical references and index.
ISBN 0-7619-2670-4 (Cloth) — ISBN 0-7619-2671-2 (Paper)
    1. Dialogue analysis. 2. Communication-Philosophy. I. Anderson, Rob, 1945-
II. Baxter, Leslie A. III. Cissna, Kenneth N.
P95.455.D54 2004
302.3´46—dc21

2003011937

Printed on acid-free paper

03   04   05   06   07   08   09   10   9   8   7   6   5   4   3   2   1

Acquiring Editor:	Margaret H. Seawell
Editorial Assistant:	Alicia Carter
Production Editor:	Claudia A. Hoffman
Typesetter:	C&M Digitals (P) Ltd.
Copy Editor:	Edward Meidenbauer
Indexer:	Molly Hall

Contents

About the Editors

Rob Anderson, professor of communication and professor of international studies at Saint Louis University, teaches and learns about dialogue in campus settings, interpersonal relationships, and media institutions. His articles on these topics have appeared since 1972 in journals from a variety of disciplines. A vigorous advocate of the dialogue of coauthorship, Rob's ten books include texts in communication theory and interviewing, as well as scholarly studies of public dialogue in contemporary journalism and intellectual history: *The Conversation of Journalism* (Praeger, 1994), *The Reach of Dialogue* (Hampton Press, 1994), *The Martin Buber-Carl Rogers Dialogue* (SUNY, 1997), and *Moments of Meeting* (SUNY, 2002). He believes the following to be therapeutic: Quiet dinners with Dona, sitting on the porch, watching soccer, Miles Davis on the stereo, and classes that talk back.

Leslie A. Baxter is F. Wendell Miller Distinguished Professor of Communication Studies at the University of Iowa. She teaches and conducts research on communication in personal and family relationships, as well as on qualitative and quantitative research methods. She is the recipient of the 1995 Berscheid/Hatfield Award for Mid-Career Achievement by the International Network on Personal Relationships and the 2002 Legacy Theory Award by the Communication Theory Interest Group of the Central States Communication Association. *Dialogue* is her third book in the past decade on dialogic approaches to communication, the first of which, *Relating: Dialogues and Dialectics* (with Barbara Montgomery; Guilford, 1996), received the G. R. Miller Distinguished Book Award from the Interpersonal Communication Division of the National Communication Association.

Kenneth N. Cissna is professor of communication at the University of South Florida. He is the author (with Rob Anderson) of *Moments of Meeting: Buber, Rogers, and the Potential for Public Dialogue* (SUNY, 2002) and *The Martin Buber-Carl Rogers Dialogue: A New Transcript with Commentary* (SUNY, 1997) as well as a monograph on "The Rhetoric of Public Dialogue" in *Communication Research Trends* (also with Meghan Clune, 2003). His edited book *Applied Communication in the 21st Century* (Lawrence Erlbaum, 1995) won the Outstanding Book award from the Applied Communication Division of the National Communication Association. He edited the *Journal of Applied Communication Research* and the *Southern Communication Journal,* and is past president of the Florida Communication Association. Currently, he serves as Vice President Elect of the Southern States Communication Association.

About the Contributors

Ronald C. Arnett, professor and chair in the Department of Communication and Rhetorical Studies at Duquesne University, is past editor of the *Journal of Communication and Religion* and president of both the State Communication Association of Pennsylvania and the Religious Communication Association. His books include *Communication and Community: Implications of Martin Buber's Dialogue* (SIU, 1986), for which he won the Religious Speech Communication Association Book Award; *Dialogic Education: Conversations About Ideas and Between Persons* (SIU, 1992); *Dialogic Civility in a Cynical Age: Community, Hope, and Interpersonal Relationships* (SUNY, 1999); and *The Reach of Dialogue: Confirmation, Voice, and Community* (which he coedited with Rob Anderson and Kenneth N. Cissna; Hampton Press, 1994). He received the Religious Communication Association Article Award in 1979 and 1999.

Laura Black is a doctoral student at the University of Washington. She is interested in dialogue theory and in the ways in which dialogue occurs in and is understood by members of groups and organizations. Her current research examines the training in dialogue that a manufacturing company provides its employees and describes how profound learning occurs even when dialogue is taught as a set of tools or skills. She is also studying how newcomers learn organizational cultures through stories and how collaborative storytelling can be used in small groups facing divisive moral conflicts.

Stanley Deetz is professor of communication at the University of Colorado, Boulder, where he teaches courses in organizational theory, organizational communication, and communication theory. He is the author, coauthor, or editor of *Leading Organizations Through Transition* (Sage, 2000), *Doing Critical Management Research* (Sage, 2000), *Transforming Communication, Transforming Business* (Hampton, 1995), *Democracy in an Age of Corporate Colonization* (SUNY, 1992), and eight other books. He has published 100 essays in scholarly journals and books regarding stakeholder representation, culture, and communication in corporate organizations. He has served as a consultant on culture, diversity, and participatory decision making for several major corporations in the U.S. and Europe. He is a Fellow of the International Communication Association and served as ICA President, 1996–97.

H. L. Goodall, Jr., is professor and head of the Department of Communication at the University of North Carolina at Greensboro. He is the author or coauthor of 18 books and over 100 articles, chapters, and papers on communication and culture. As an ethnographer on the American scene, his work with dialogue began as a practical matter with *in vivo* explorations of self, others, and contexts in diverse settings—high tech cultures, rock and roll bands, political campaigns, and alternative spiritual communities. More recently, he has developed an interest in the dialectical tensions and ritual forms that characterize dialogic experiences, and the long-term effects of the presence of those tensions along with the absence of dialogue in families defined by secrets.

Leonard Clyde Hawes is professor of communication at the University of Utah. He is the author of a series of articles on dialogue, power, conversation, and politics in such journals as *Text and Performance Quarterly, Communication Theory,* and *Communication Yearbook.* His current book project addresses the problems of ethics and pragmatics when North American conflict resolution theory and practice are deployed in ethnically diverse, identity-based conflicts. He divides his time between the University of Utah, where he pursues the Mormon/secular division; the University of Aalborg, where he works on the Danish/"immigrants of color" division; and the University of Copenhagen, where he contributes to the Tibet Conflict Resolution project.

Michael J. Hyde is the University Distinguished Professor of Communication Ethics at Wake Forest University and a Fellow of the W. K. Kellogg Foundation. His research on the dialogic nature of human existence has appeared in many scholarly journals and books. His *The Call of Conscience: Heidegger and Levinas, Rhetoric and the Euthanasia Debate* (University of South Carolina Press, 2001) won the National Communication Association's Diamond Anniversary Book Award and the Marie Hochmuth Nichols Award. He is also the recipient of the Scholar Award for Communication Excellence in Ethics Education for the Mind, the Heart, and the Soul given by the Communication Ethics Center, Duquesne University. Currently, he is completing a book on *The Life-Giving Gift of Acknowledgment.*

Peter M. Kellett is associate professor of communication and Director of Graduate Studies at the University of North Carolina at Greensboro. He is the author of *Managing Conflict in a Negotiated World: A Narrative Approach to Achieving Dialogue and Change* (with D. G. Dalton; Sage, 2001) and several chapters and articles that explore the theory and practice of dialogue in analyzing, understanding, and managing human conflict. Currently, he is interested in how people learn to create more peaceful relationships from understanding their conflict experiences.

Sheila McNamee is professor of communication at the University of New Hampshire and holds the university's Class of 1944 Professorship. Her work focuses on dialogic transformation within a variety of social and institutional contexts, including psychotherapy, organizations, education, health care, and communities. She is the author of several books, including *Relational Responsibility: Resources for Sustainable Dialogue* (with Kenneth Gergen; Sage, 1999) as well as numerous articles and chapters on social constructionist theory and practice. She actively engages constructionist practices in a variety of contexts to bring communities of participants with diametrically opposing viewpoints together to create livable futures. She is a cofounder and Board member of the Taos Institute (*www.taosinstitute.net*), and she lectures and consults regularly.

Mark L. McPhail is professor of interdisciplinary studies in the Western College Program at Miami University. His research interests include rhetorical theory and epistemology, language and race relations, and visual communication. He is the author of *Zen in the Art of Rhetoric: An Inquiry Into Coherence* (SUNY, 1996), *The Rhetoric of Racism Revisited: Reparations or Separation?* (Rowman and Littlefield, 2002), and *Double Consciousness in Black and White: Identity, Difference, and the Rhetorical Ideal of Life* (Van Zelst Lecture, Northwestern University, 2001). His scholarship has been published in the *Quarterly Journal of Speech, Critical Studies in Mass Communication*, and the *Howard Journal of Communications*, and his creative work has appeared in *Dark Horse Magazine* and the *American Literary Review*.

John Pauly is professor of communication at Saint Louis University. His research on the history and sociology of mass communication has appeared in a variety of journals, including *Communication, Journalism and Mass Communication Monographs, Journalism and Mass Communication Quarterly, Media Studies Journal*, and *American Quarterly*. He has written extensively about public journalism and has participated in discussions of the movement at the Poynter Institute, American Press Institute, Kettering Foundation, and Stanford University. He is currently writing a book about the cultural and literary consequences of the New Journalism of the 1960s.

Kimberly A. Pearce is professor of speech communication at De Anza College, located in Cupertino, California. She is also cofounder of the Public Dialogue Consortium and Pearce Associates. She recently completed a training manual titled *Making Better Social Worlds: Engaging and Facilitating Dialogic Communication* (Pearce Associates, 2002). In addition to offering training in dialogic communication on three continents, she helped initiate, design, and facilitate a six-year public dialogue and community-building process for the city of Cupertino.

W. Barnett Pearce is professor in the School of Human and Organization Development at the Fielding Graduate Institute. He is a communication theorist involved with the development of the theory of the coordinated management of meaning. In addition, he is a founding member of the Public Dialogue Consortium and coprincipal of Pearce Associates, organizations through which he facilitates and offers training in the skills of dialogic communication. His publications include *Moral Conflict: When Social Worlds Collide* (with Stephen Littlejohn; Sage, 1997) and (with Kim Pearce) "Combining Passions and Abilities: Toward Dialogic Virtuosity" (*Southern Communication Journal*, 2000), "Extending the Theory of CMM through a Community Dialogue Process" (*Communication Theory*, 2000), and "Going Public: Working Systematically in Public" (*Pluriverso*, 2000).

John Shotter is professor of interpersonal relations in the Department of Communication, University of New Hampshire. His long-term interest is in the social conditions conducive to people having a voice in the development of participatory democracies and civil societies. He is the author of *Social Accountability and Selfhood* (Blackwell, 1984), *Cultural Politics of Everyday Life: Social Constructionism, Rhetoric, and Knowing of the Third Kind* (Open University, 1993), and *Conversational Realities: The Construction of Life Through Language* (Sage, 1993). In 1997 he was an Overseas Fellow at Churchill College, Cambridge, and a visiting professor at the Swedish Institute of Work Life Research, Stockholm, Sweden.

Jennifer Simpson is Coordinator for Student Affairs and lecturer in the Departments of Communication and Honors at the University of Colorado, Boulder. Her work bridges the theoretical and practical dimensions of dialogue. Believing in the importance of engaged scholarship, she uses her administrative experience to inform and enrich her teaching and scholarship, and in turn, her academic life informs and infuses her many other responsibilities on campus. A politically responsive, constructionist theory of communication is both informed by and informs her campus work on building community and multicultural development. She is a founder of the CU Dialogic Network, a group of faculty and staff members committed to using principles and practices of dialogue to inform and enrich campus conversations.

John Stewart is Vice President for Academic Affairs at the University of Dubuque. Since the 1970s, he has been learning and teaching dialogue philosophy and practice—for 32 years at the University of Washington. Since his 1978 article on the "Foundations of Dialogic Communication" in the *Quarterly Journal of Speech*, his scholarly and instructional writings have attempted to clarify the insights of dialogue philosophers and extend them to enhance dialogue practice in families, friendships, classrooms, and organizations. In recent years, John has coauthored all his professional writing in order to open a space for dialogue in this part of his life. He is also committed to dialogue practice outside the academy.

Mary S. Strine is professor of communication at the University of Utah, where she teaches and conducts research in cultural studies, interpretive and critical theory, and performance studies. Her articles on modern critical theory, performance theory and criticism, and the relationship between American literature and culture (published in *Text and Performance Quarterly, Western Journal of Communication,* and various edited books) rely heavily on dialogic theory as their animating center. Her current research focuses on the cultural work of artistic representations and practices, specifically on the ways that aesthetic performances create a distinctive sphere of dialogic encounter by actively engaging and molding their audiences, and on the ways that such aesthetically framed "dialogues" contribute to racial, ethnic, and national identity formations.

James R. Taylor is emeritus professor of communication at the University of Montreal, and the author or coauthor of several books on the communication theory of the foundations of organizations, including *The Emergent Organization: Communication as its Site and Surface* (Lawrence Erlbaum, 2000) and *The Computerization of Work: Organization, Communication and Change* (Sage, 2001) as well as articles in such journals as *Communication Theory, Communication Review,* and others. In his writing on the topic, dialogue figures as the central mechanism for the construction of coorientation, the basis of all organization.

Julia T. Wood is the Lineberger Professor of Humanities and professor of communication studies at the University of North Carolina at Chapel Hill. She teaches and conducts research on personal relationships; intimate partner violence; and intersections between gender, communication, and culture. She has written 15 books and edited 8 others, published more than 70 articles and book chapters, and presented over 100 papers at professional conferences. She has received ten awards for teaching and eleven for her scholarship. She lives with her partner, Robert Cox, who is also a professor of communication studies at the University of North Carolina at Chapel Hill.

Karen E. Zediker is a full-time lecturer at the University of Washington. Her dissertation developed a theoretical framework for understanding dialogue and how it concretely looks and sounds in classroom interaction. Her article with John Stewart, "Dialogue as Tensional, Ethical Practice," in the *Southern Communication Journal* (2000), reflects her focus on the ways that ethical communicative choices reflect theoretical insights and practical decisions, and the centrality of moral judgment in dialogic encounters. She is committed to the processes of engaging in, teaching about, and facilitating dialogue in her professional and personal life.

Foreword

Entering Into Dialogue

Julia T. Wood

The month of January takes its name from Janus, the Roman god whose two faces simultaneously look backward at the past and forward to the future. Like Janus, *Dialogue: Theorizing Difference in Communication Studies* looks backward at foundational and recent dialogical scholarship and peers forward to consider future challenges and opportunities for theory and praxis. Its Janus-like quality makes this volume an important marker of how our understandings of dialogue have developed and how they may evolve in the years to come.

In their introduction, editors Rob Anderson, Leslie Baxter, and Ken Cissna explain the organization of this book, preview the content, and discuss the book's broad themes. I will not repeat that coverage here. I would add, however, that *Dialogue: Theorizing Difference in Communication Studies* is unique in being the first collection of original essays on the theory and praxis of dialogue in the broad field of communication studies. The chapters presented here are uncommonly informed and informative, which is not surprising, as contributors to this volume include some of the most distinguished scholars in the field.

Chapter authors not only discuss, but also embody a dialogic approach to communication, knowledge, and identity. They do so by bringing dialogic thinkers into dialogue with one another and by asking how dialogic theories mutually form and inform one another and the process of communication. In exploring different currents within dialogue studies, this volume demonstrates that dialogic theory and praxis is not monolithic. Like other vibrant intellectual traditions, dialogue studies include different positions, some of which are in tension. For example, some dialogic theorists emphasize prescriptive attitudes and actions to improve the quality of communication, whereas other dialogic theorists adopt a broader view of dialogue as inherent in all of social life. These differences add to the richness of dialogue studies and underline this volume's importance in bringing together distinct views of dialogue as theory and praxis.

To complement the editors' introduction, I use this Foreword to look backward and forward. I first follow the volume's backwards gaze, which sketches humanistic, critical, and poststructural-postmodern branches in the family tree of dialogic theories and shows how these inform theory and praxis in diverse spheres of communication. Picking up on contributors' discussions of generative possibilities for future work, I then look forward to consider ways of amplifying dialogue's critical impulses by further engagement with other intellectual traditions.

Part I, Exploring the Territories of Dialogue, traces the intellectual history of dialogic theory and introduces readers to key people and ideas that have shaped understandings of dialogue as a unique way of knowing and meeting others in conversation. John Stewart, Karen Zediker, and Laura Black lead off by delineating relationships among dialogic philosophers. Following this, Barnett Pearce and Kimberly Pearce sketch a specifically communication perspective on dialogue, asking not what dialogue is, but how it is *made* in communication. Ron Arnett draws on the work of Buber and Levinas to describe a communication ethic centered on a responsive I that is defined more by responsiveness than self-expression. The responsive I, the I-in-relation, also inspires Michael Hyde's meditation on being and acknowledgment and Sheila McNamee and John Shotter's discussion of how "we create possibilities moment by moment in dialogue with others."

Despite variations among theorists, central to dialogue is the idea that any utterance or act is always responding to and anticipating other utterances and acts. Genuine dialogue depends less on self-expression and other transmissional aspects of communication than upon responsiveness. As Bakhtin (1981) insists, "each word tastes of the context and contexts in which it has lived its socially charged life" (p. 293). Yet it is not enough to say that response is central to dialogue. Response—or, more precisely, responsiveness—arises out of and is made possible by qualities of thought and talk that allow transformation in how one understands the self, others, and the world they inhabit. These qualities of thought and talk include willingness to risk change in one's own perspective and commitment to embracing and struggling with others whose worldviews may be radically different from and threatening to one's own. In signifying a hope for a particular kind of praxis, dialogue presupposes and means other things as well.

- It means that communication is not linear, nor even merely interactive. Instead, it is a fluctuating, unpredictable, multivocal process in which uncertainty infuses encounters between people and what they mean and become. As

Leslie Baxter notes in her chapter, social life and dialogue are fragmented and definitely, if not always obviously, disorderly. Dialogue is emergent (rather than preformed), fluid (rather than static), keenly dependent on process (at least as much as content), performative (more than representational), and never fully finished (rather than completed).

- It means that interlocutors are immersed in a process that shapes and forms them even as they shape and form it and one another in ways that are not entirely predictable or finalizable. Addressing this in his chapter, James Taylor emphasizes that identity emerges in and through communication. Whoever we are before we enter into dialogue, those are not the selves that exist during, after, and because of dialogue. Just as language has no independent life apart from the world in which it participates, selves have no independent life apart from the world that arises in interaction. In this sense, dialogic engagement predates selfhood, both of which are fluid and continually remade. The I that I take myself to be is (co)authored continuously in relation to others with whom I interact. In other words, dialogic communication is productive, or constitutive, rather than reproductive of previous experiences and ways of interpreting and assigning meanings to them. Each communicator is implicated in a particular historical-social-political discursive context, which frames and, in turn, is framed by communicators and what happens between them. In dialogue, communicators order each other and allow themselves to be ordered. They simultaneously voice and risk their perspectives.

- It means that tension is inherent in and integral to dialogue. Tension may be of many sorts: tension between the perspective one holds at a given moment and the perspective of an other(s); tension between possible views and versions of self; tension between alternative ways of ordering and acting in the world. We enter into dialogue with perspectives—beliefs, opinions, values, assumptions, interests, and so forth—on ourselves, others, and the world. Yet we hold these perspectives provisionally, if dearly. We allow—perhaps even embrace—tension between our perspectives and those of others, which may challenge and change our own. In conversation, we resist tendencies to reconcile or synthesize perspectives, much less to choose between them. Instead, we wrestle with the discomfort that comes from lack of closure and lack of unquestionably right answers.

- It means that dialogue does not necessarily idealize or seek common ground. The search for (and belief in) common ground may thwart, rather than facilitate, genuine dialogue, because almost inevitably the dominant culture defines what ground is common or legitimate. Rather than the reproductive goal of finding "common ground" or "resolving differences," dialogue allows differences to exist without trying to resolve, overcome, synthesize, or otherwise tame them. In the words of Cervenak, Cespedes, Souza, and Straub (2002), "If we begin by embracing conflict and contradiction for what they can teach us, the elusive goal of unity becomes less important than the process of learning to listen" (p. 352). Listening without being driven to find common ground opens the possibility of creating new ground—new ways of understanding self, other, and the social, symbolic, and material world. By extension, this means that dialogue does not necessarily preclude standing one's ground firmly, but it does require that in doing so one remain open to the call of the other.

• It means that we are realized in the *process* of dialogue. Points of view, relationships, and selves are not static. Rather they are fluid processes that are continuously open to being (re)formed, largely through interaction between people. For this reason, we are compelled to rethink familiar interpersonal concepts and the meanings and functions that actors and researchers assign to them. For example, rather than being a revelation of a preformed, preexisting self, self-disclosure is understood to be an authoring, or coauthoring—a coming into being in the process of conversation with an other.

Building on the philosophical foundations of Part I, the chapters in Parts II and III show that dialogue applies theoretically and pragmatically to communication in the public sphere, organizations, cultural and intercultural spaces, and performance venues—in short, to human communication in the range of contexts it inhabits. The chapters in Part II, Personal Voices in Dialogue, interrogate the possibilities for dialogue in personal, organizational, and group contexts. In her chapter, Leslie Baxter provides a remarkably rich discussion of dialogic work on personal relationships and interpersonal interaction. James Taylor explores the value of dialogic theory and praxis in building and sustaining coorientation in organizations. Working with the complementarity and tension between critical hermeneutic and postmodern conceptions of dialogue, Stanley Deetz and Jennifer Simpson develop a politically responsive constructionist theory of communication that emphasizes responsiveness to the demands of others in organizational life. H. L. Goodall and Peter Kellett offer an account of the process and outcomes of their own dialogic engagement with each other, signaling the potential of dialogue to open us to new ways of understanding and acting in our scholarly activities. Concluding Part II is Leonard Hawes's chapter, which contemplates both the difficulties and the importance of dialogue in situations that are marked by power relations that give birth to strong emotional responses.

Concern with dialogue in the civic sphere is the focus of Part III, Public Voices in Dialogue. Here Kenneth Cissna and Rob Anderson illuminate the potential of dialogue to improve public conversation; Mark McPhail interrogates the possibilities of dialogue about race; Mary Strine draws connections between dialogue, performance, and civic engagement; and John Pauly asks why dialogue and media studies have so seldom crossed paths and how greater rapprochement with dialogic traditions might alter media's view of its role and function in civic society. Contributors to Parts II and III eschew conservative views of dialogue as interaction between preformed and relatively autonomous selves who simply need to be revealed, or performed, and understood by an other. Contributors point out that genuine dialogue in personal and public settings demands more than response to preformed selves and a preordered common ground that tends to exclude all that is outside of it.

In place of this limited view, contributors encourage us to embrace a richer understanding of dialogue that takes into account social, historical, political, material, and linguistic contexts that shape meanings, selves, perspectives, and communication. Several contributors draw on the work of critical scholars such as Gadamer and Habermas, who focus on interaction as a site of meaning and endeavor to develop phenomenological conceptions of reason that are congenial with dialogic theory. Expanding this inclination, some authors attend to postmodern theorists such as Derrida and Foucault, who assume that selves are radically indeterminate and unstable, and they highlight otherness and the productive role of conflict in transforming the social world and those who live, work, and communicate within it.

In embracing critical and postmodern impulses, this volume points toward lines of future dialogical work aimed at theorizing possibilities for transformation of individuals, relationships, and the social world. For example, in his chapter on race, McPhail reminds us—as do critical theorists such as Fraser (1992) and Mouffe (2000)—that genuine dialogue is not always possible in the social world as it is currently constituted. Ensconced power hierarchies and the inequities to which they give rise sometimes undermine normative conceptions of communication such as Habermas's (1990, 1992) ideal speech situation and Buber's I-Thou dialogue. Sharing McPhail's concern about the reach of dialogue, Deetz and Simpson note that the call for dialogue is a *hope*. Hope is not a guarantee that dialogue can happen. In addition to hope, there must be a concerted, committed effort to cultivate conditions that foster, or at the least allow, dialogue between people—not just people who have polite differences, but also people who hold profoundly different perspectives that are born of locations in radically uneven social, material, and symbolic circumstances.

The social world is infused by power differences that have implications for the possibilities of dialogue. Why should a CEO engage in dialogue with a line worker who wants better working conditions but cannot afford to risk her or his job? Why should middle-class citizens on pristine property enter into dialogue with disadvantaged citizens who are angry that their neighborhood has been chosen as the site for a toxic waste dump? Why should men enter into dialogue with women who resent the fact that even in two-worker families, childcare and homemaking responsibilities are still primarily assumed by women? In short, not everyone wants or needs to enter into dialogue. Those who enjoy power and privilege often feel no motivation to interact dialogically with those who do not benefit from the same status and advantage. As Mouffe (2000) bluntly notes, "No amount of dialogue or moral preaching will ever convince the ruling class to give up its power" (p. 15). Yet for dialogue to be possible, people—particularly those who enjoy relative privilege—must take responsibility for identifying and reducing socially determined asymmetries that dictate who gets to speak, what forums and forms of speech are deemed legitimate, whose speech counts, and to whom it counts. It is difficult to imagine what might motivate such efforts on the part of those who are comfortable within current social structures, but precisely this kind of imagining is needed.

The critical possibilities of dialogue lie in its refusal to privilege any single voice, perspective, or ideology. It insists on the superiority of multivocality. But how does this insistence translate into praxis? What can prompt dialogic engagement from those who are not already inclined toward it, those whose social locations do not motivate them to risk their material well-being or their comfortable conceptions of self and social life? If people who enjoy power and privilege choose not to engage in dialogue, does this leave those who seek dialogue vulnerable to being silenced, frustrated, or exploited by those who do not? This seems to be McPhail's tentative conclusion, at least when dialogue attempts to deal with issues of race and racism. On a more hopeful note, Leonard Hawes suggests that discourse has the capacity to redistribute human subjectivity and agency. Pursuing this idea, it will be fruitful to theorize the possibilities and limits of dialogue, understood as inherent in the character of all social life, as a way to redistribute human subjectivity, as well as human locations and privilege.

In opening *The Dialogic Emergence of Culture,* Tedlock and Mannheim (1995) state that spoken words would "hardly be worthy of the name 'language' unless they were addressed to someone, and unless that someone had the capacity to reply" (p. 8). I agree, yet note that the meaning of "the capacity to reply" is not transparent. What is entailed in "the capacity to reply" or respond? Does it imply only the ability to respond within structural boundaries legitimized by and comfortable for dominant groups? Or might the capacity to respond be understood to allow for, perhaps encourage, responses that fall outside of interaction—both content and form—familiar to and favored by those at the center of cultural life?

To make the point another way, allowing different voices into conversation is not sufficient to foster responsiveness and possibilities for transformation.

We must also be open to changing what we consider open, responsive communication to be—that is, what forms it may take. We must be willing to open the conversation not only to different voices, but also to different ways of enacting voice. Critical scholarship has done much to document the unequal value assigned to different ways of communicating in Western culture. Cox (2001) recounts instances in which the normative procedures of government agencies defined the voices of low-income citizens as "indecorous" and discounted their discursive standing in allegedly public hearings about environmental health and safety. Conventionally feminine ways of enacting voice are still not regarded as equal to—that is, not as strong, persuasive, legitimate, or effective as—traditionally masculine modes of enacting voice. Vernacular Black English and traditional African American communication styles are still regarded by many as substandard to White, middle-class diction and style. Feminist scholars (Harding, 1991; Minister, 1991; Spender, 1985) and critical-race scholars (West, 1993b; Williams, 1992) note that whereas members of marginal groups often learn to communicate in the ways approved by dominant culture, the converse seldom occurs. How can people enter into dialogue on equal bases if the preferred communication style of only some participants is regarded as legitimate?

The risks entailed in genuine dialogue are unlikely to be embraced without confidence that one's self can remain whole and functional even if one's worldview is shaken. In her critique of conventional Western science, Keller (1985) resoundingly criticized the modernist idea(1) of autonomy in both scientific enterprises and everyday interactions. Modernist autonomy entails a rigid separation between researcher/self and object of research/other. To preserve scientific objectivity and the integrity of self in everyday life, a scientist/self must be radically independent of objects of research/others. Finding this view of autonomy inaccurate and unproductive, Keller proposed dynamic autonomy as an alternative. The scientist/self who develops dynamic autonomy understands that the scientist/self and objects of research/other are simultaneously connected and distinct, at once interdependent and independent. Thus, the scientist/self can be open to influence from the object of research/other, confident that such influence will not erase or colonize the self. This kind of confidence seems to be what Anzaldúa (2002) has in mind when she urges "honoring people's otherness in ways that allow us to be changed by embracing that otherness rather than punishing others for having a different view, belief system, skin color, or spiritual practice" (p. 4). Concepts such as dynamic autonomy might contribute to efforts to theorize what is necessary for individuals to take the risks of engaging in dialogue.

Dialogic theory will also be enriched by its growing engagement with critical-cultural traditions. For example, as Deetz and Simpson note, feminist standpoint theory might inform dialogic theory's efforts to deal with power differences between actual or potential interlocutors. Feminist standpoint theory is centrally concerned with the relationship between epistemic locations and power, opportunities, and perspectives on social life (Collins, 1986, 1998, 2000; Haraway, 1988; Harding, 1991, 1998; Hartsock, 1983; Smith, 1987). Standpoint theorists insist that profound differences in perspective can be appreciated and, to some extent, known. Entering into unfamiliar standpoints requires commitment and struggle, to be sure, but it is possible. This must be the case if either standpoint theory or dialogic theory is to be useful in recognizing, challenging, and changing inequities in personal, interpersonal, and public life.

Other critical-cultural traditions also seem congenial with dialogic theory. In questioning some of the most dearly held assumptions about selfhood, queer theory (Butler, 1999; Kirsch, 2001; Sedgwick, 1990) invites us to rethink what it means to be male, female, gay, lesbian, heterosexual, bisexual, transsexual, and transgendered. As categories of identity that have been assumed to be stable are claimed to be fluid, new understandings of self and others become possible. Critical race theory (Crenshaw, Gotanda, Peller, & Thomas, 1996; Delgado & Stefancic, 1997) advances important insights pertinent to dialogue. Understanding and engaging in dialogue requires a reflexive understanding of self, which critical race scholars' interrogation of Whiteness attempts to provoke in Whites. Performance ethnography might also be a productive ally for dialogical theory. In addition to Anna Deavere Smith, whose remarkable work Strine highlights, ethnographic performance work by Boal (1985), Conquergood (1988, 1991, 1992, 1998), and Madison (1999, in press) calls attention to the importance of embodied knowledge—bodily knowledge—as a means of gaining deeper understanding of those who differ from us.

In addition to theorizing conditions that foster dialogue, we should also ask when dialogue is a preferred option for productive, transformative human interaction. Are there times and issues for which nondialogic modes of action and interaction may be more productive—and productive might be defined in various ways—than dialogue? Nondialogic modes of action include strategic, rhetorical, and confrontational communication, all of which can foment transformation in individuals and social perspectives. Those who historically have been denied voices may reasonably believe that in some circumstances nondialogic alternatives are more empowering and have greater potential than dialogue to compel members of the dominant group to recognize and respond to them. Certainly Rosa Parks and Mother Jones relied on nondialogic communication to mobilize others who were able to contain or constrain dominants and ultimately force dominants to respond. The same may be said of the Crown Heights Riots and Stonewall, which gave voice to marginal groups whose efforts to gain a hearing in other ways were ignored.

Nondialogic forms of communication have been well recognized, even centered, in a field that historically has championed communicative forms such as debate, persuasion, and public address. What yet needs to be done is to define when these forms of communication are appropriate and likely to be effective and when dialogue is likely to be appropriate and effective. In other words, specifying hospitable contexts and conditions would clarify the theoretical and pragmatic scope of dialogue. I suspect that this kind of specification will be most productive if it draws not on dialogic traditions that aim to produce principles for improving communication, but rather on those that regard dialogue as an inherent, inescapable, and pervasive feature of all social life and interaction.

Like dialogue itself, the ideas in *Dialogue: Theorizing Difference in Communication Studies* are not finalized or finalizable. In providing a superb rendering of the intellectual history, current state, and future possibilities of dialogue, this landmark volume makes a major contribution to communication research, theory, and praxis that aim to include and respect multiple voices and ways of voicing.

1

Texts and Contexts of Dialogue

Rob Anderson, Leslie A. Baxter, and Kenneth N. Cissna

I t is one thing to assume that the primary purpose of communication is to get a message across, to shape up others' behavior, or to teach new information, as dominant traditions of teaching and research about the topic often appear to suggest. Yet it is quite another matter to recognize that at times these functions can be limiting or destructive even when they can seem most efficient. Understanding the potential for dialogue complicates any study of communication, because it necessarily widens our conversation about value, ethics, relation, reflexivity, mutually engaged performance, community, and responsibility.

Once we take dialogue seriously, it becomes harder to treat language as a compendium of labels, as a vocabulary-with-structure, or as a set of handy tools with which we accomplish our real human work of thinking and persuading. And once we take dialogue seriously, it becomes harder to treat people merely as encapsulated and isolated selves competing for recognition and material rewards. Two of us once observed that "dialogue implies more than a simple back-and-forthness of messages in interaction; it points to a particular process and quality of communication in which the participants 'meet,' which allows for changing and being changed. In dialogue, we do not know exactly what we are going to say, and we can surprise not only the other but even ourselves . . ." (Cissna & Anderson, 1994b, p. 10). Of course, the meanings and definitions for "dialogue" will often vary significantly from scholar to scholar as they adapt the term to various topics ranging from the social-psychological processes of developing a sense of self in the interpersonal setting to the political processes of achieving consensus in civic and cultural forums. As the chapters in this book demonstrate, any basic definitional starting point is insufficient for understanding the extraordinarily complex and specific definitions that evolve in different research programs. Yet, in most of these works, the quality of dialogue is conceived as emergent and transitory; it does not seem helpful to characterize certain kinds of relationships or special techniques as inherently either "dialogic" or "nondialogic." Rather, dialogue's seemingly protean nature offers a useful metaphor for how language, learning, research, and ethical decision making are enacted in all of life's arenas.

Theorists are actively approaching dialogue in new ways and in unprecedented numbers; this interest not only acknowledges interdisciplinary bridges but also helps to chart how this concept is related to the broad discipline of communication studies. Emphasizing dialogue is a helpful and theoretically rich trend, but it hardly represents a fad. The conceptual turn toward dialogue recasts and amplifies earlier interests of communication specialists in interesting ways, and suggests clear implications for future research and criticism.

In this introduction, we discuss both texts and contexts of dialogic traditions in communication studies. First, by identifying early touchstone *texts*—most of them articles and textbooks—we trace how communication scholars developed their curiosity about dialogue, especially in the 1970s and 1980s. In doing so, we hope to clarify its historical role within the discipline and its conceptual significance among scholars. We highlight four theorists who influenced early communication scholarship in dialogue, although more recent scholarship has broadened and to some extent shifted the range of the discipline's theoretical perspectives. We then identify signal publications of disciplinary importance. As we show, the history of dialogue studies in communication generally paralleled the interest of other academic traditions in Martin Buber, Hans-Georg Gadamer, Jürgen Habermas, and, most recently, Mikhail Bakhtin.

Second, by examining contemporary sites for intellectual inquiry—what we will term *contexts*—we explore the major stimuli for dialogue studies that have developed more recently under a broadly qualitative or naturalistic rubric. Communication-based studies of dialogue in the 1990s matured so rapidly in so many subfields that a comprehensive review of relevant articles would take us far beyond the space available for this chapter. Therefore, this section of the introduction concentrates selectively on scholarly books published since about 1990, and on interdependent research contexts important for our contributors—face-to-face talk in personal and work relationships, public political life, cultural life and otherness, and mediated/technological life.

Texts and Influences:
Alerting the Discipline to Dialogue

TOUCHSTONE THEORISTS
FOR COMMUNICATION SCHOLARS

Readers surveying the historical literature on dialogue within communication (in interpersonal communication, rhetoric, and media studies especially) encounter four names with special regularity: Buber, Gadamer, Habermas, and Bakhtin. Although these theorists started from somewhat different perspectives, their appreciation for dialogue seemed compatible in many ways to communication scholars. Due to space limitations, of course, we cannot begin to explore the richness of their ideas in a few paragraphs, but brief introductions should be helpful.[1]

Buber (1958, 1965a, 1965b) considered his intellectual contribution to be a form of "philosophical anthropology," an attempt to study the elemental aspects of human experience as they are grounded in meeting and relation. He consistently equated authentic human life with dialogic *meeting:* As we probe what most makes us human, we discover the central roles of speech and dialogue. Buber believed that even the self, which is so often experienced psychologically as a packaged or unitary thing, an "it," is a relational phenomenon; Buber's *I-Thou,* for instance was not two words, but one "primary word" in that the *I* does not develop apart from its link with an acknowledged other, a *thou* or *you,* toward whom the *I* turns with attention. Listening, in all its dimensions, became a critical communication function for Buber.

Gadamer (1976, 1982) considered his role to be a learner, teacher, and spokesperson for a philosophical hermeneutics. In his writing, especially *Truth and Method* (1982), he was interested in fresh applications for textual interpretation—the traditional purview of hermeneutics. Gadamer asserted that the truth of textual meaning is not preset by an author's intent, nor is it neatly captured, contained, or buried within the text, waiting to be excavated. Conversation partners are not bound in allegiance to each other's imagined intentions. Rather, for Gadamer, understanding is a dialogic and reciprocal experience of questioning texts and remaining open to being questioned by them. Truth cannot be disclosed by applying a simple method, but emerges through a complex process of understanding texts in the contexts of their history, their language, and their audiences. Communicative understanding to Gadamer, in other words, is less a matter of reproducing or apprehending prior meanings than it is a process of producing new and fresh meanings by which to test emerging truths. Gadamer's contribution to dialogue, therefore, was to imagine it as the human ability to read relationships and culture processually.

Habermas (1971, 1975, 1979, 1984, 1987), whose disagreements with Gadamer have been well documented (e.g., Warnke, 1987, pp. 107–117), nudged dialogue scholars in argumentation, public rhetoric, political communication, and media studies in a somewhat different direction. He sought to investigate the ground on which public dialogue became legitimized, and how those who structure public contexts might more successfully invite people and groups with divergent opinions into the argumentative mix. Many of Habermas's contributions that have been important to communication scholars focus on how situations might be structured procedurally for dialogic decision making. Habermas is not the only scholar to offer a discourse-based ethic for social communication, but he has pursued its implications as much as anyone in recent intellectual life. His concept of the *ideal speech situation* (Habermas, 1984, 1990, 1992) has been especially influential for theorists seeking ways to reconcile pluralistic viewpoints with possibilities for consensus—most recently, in the public journalism movement.

Bakhtin (1981, 1984, 1986) thought of himself primarily as a literary and social critic with a responsibility to point out the pervasiveness of dialogue in language and human history. His work emerged from relative obscurity, in North America at least, during the last three decades of the 20th century, and has made a remarkable impact on the interdisciplinary climate in dialogue studies. One turning point was a particularly influential 1981 issue of *Critical Inquiry* in which authors from many disciplines applied the Russian thinker's work to problems of inner speech, the novel, authorship, dialogic speech genres, and the threats of a monologizing society. For Bakhtin, society is inherently and forever multivocal and unfinalizable, and such insights seemed dangerous to the Soviet officials in power during his lifetime. Although Bakhtin thought of Buber as the foremost philosopher of the age (see Emerson, 1997, p. 74), his own approach to dialogue took a different, and in many ways a more linguistic and social/critical, turn.

SIGNAL PUBLICATIONS IN
COMMUNICATION STUDIES: EARLY YEARS, 1970–1990

The discipline began to solidify its interest in dialogue through a series of exploratory studies in the 1960s, 1970s, and 1980s. Our selective account of articles and books, of course, is only one kind of interpretation; interested readers should consult the sources themselves to explore further.

Early Articles. Before 1970, when communication scholars studied *dialogue* they tended to focus on the content of *dialogues;* that is, the term was probably most often used to apply to the Socratic dialogue form used by Plato to explore dialectically the nature of human experience and reason (e.g., Hyland, 1968).

This was reasonable and important (both Gadamer and Bakhtin heard dialogic resonances in Plato and imported these ideas into their work), but was in some ways limiting in stressing dialogue primarily as a model for rhetorical inquiry generally, or for teaching in particular.

In the 1970s, a series of seminal articles announced new ways of thinking about the mutual involvement of speakers and listeners, writers and readers. Blending older rhetorical traditions with newer approaches to interpersonal meeting, these articles were undoubtedly responding in part to the humanistic psychology movement of the 1960s and beyond (e.g., Sillars, 1974), which introduced fresh expectations and expansive styles of communication in the work of such theorists as Carl Rogers (1961), Sidney Jourard (1971), Abraham Maslow (1964), Jack Gibb (1961), Joseph Luft (1969), and other writers such as John Powell (1969), a priest whose writings on love and communication were popular with many interpersonal communication instructors.

Yet the interest in dialogue transcended humanistic psychology and should not be associated solely with it. Dialogic concepts also were essential for a wider landscape of ideas that appealed to philosophers, theologians, and social critics of the time, and the tone of their writing influenced scholars in communication. In particular, the 1957 publication of Tournier's dialogically oriented *The Meaning of Persons,* and 1967's *The Human Dialogue,* edited by Matson and Montagu, energized some in our discipline, as did a somewhat more superficial but still influential book, Howe's (1963) *The Miracle of Dialogue.* These works were widely publicized in the popular media and surely helped to shape the approaches laid out in Keller and Brown's (1968; Keller, 1981) conception of dialogic ethics and Johannesen's (1971) groundbreaking early essay in the *Quarterly Journal of Speech,* in which he identifies dialogue as an "emerging concept" for the discipline and charts its prominent characteristics.

Buber, with his concepts of "the between" and the I-Thou relation, had the most impact on the discipline's early work in the philosophy of dialogue, and this influence was evident in Johannesen's article as well as in some other publications that built on it and explored new territory in succeeding years (Clark, 1973; Poulakos, 1974; Smith & Douglas, 1973; Stewart, 1978; Thomlison, 1975). These scholars clarified how Buber's philosophy did not advance complete openness as a goal, nor did it overlook the normative limits of dialogue in rhetorical situations (as Hart & Burks, 1972, among others, had suggested). A scholarly colloquy from the 1980s focused on similar issues, including the assumptions of expressive openness and the limitations of roles, as it compared the dialogical approaches of Buber and the dialogically oriented psychotherapist Carl Rogers (Anderson, 1982, 1984; Arnett, 1981, 1982, 1989; Arnett & Nakagawa, 1983; Cissna & Anderson, 1990). In a slightly different vein, DeLima and Christians (1979) explored the work of Paulo Freire, a

Brazilian educator working in the same dialogic tradition as Buber, but with a strong political dimension.

Yet Buber was only one important touchstone for the discipline's newfound interest in the concept of dialogue. Researchers and critics also examined Gadamer's philosophical hermeneutics with its implications for everyday communicating (Chen, 1987; Deetz, 1973a, 1973b, 1978; Hawes, 1977; Hyde & Smith, 1979), as well as Heidegger's phenomenology (Deetz, 1973b; Smith, 1985). This scholarship regarded language as socially and historically situated and dependent upon relational meanings developed within immediate interpretive contexts. Clearly, meanings were not transmitted, carried in acts of linear transportation, as the discipline's earlier appropriation—and gloss—of information theory might have suggested. Rather, from Gadamer's account, meanings emerged in often unforeseen processes of playfulness and even prejudice. In other words, meanings were not *reproduced* by "receivers" but *produced* collaboratively and dialogically by communicators who are simultaneously and prototypically speakers and listeners questioning the nature of shifting "texts."

Scholars in the 1970s and 1980s also generated new interest in the problems of the public sphere, perhaps in part because of a wavering trust in government (consider Vietnam and Watergate) and other political factors in the industrialized West. This interest was seen especially in the work of rhetoricians (Beatty, Behnke, & Banks, 1979; Bormann, 1980; McGuire & Slembeck, 1987) and argumentation theorists. The latter turned to Habermas, the German social theorist, for an intellectual model that grounds public talk in dialogic assumptions, normatively and in some ways constitutively. As one communication historian (Hardt, 1992) put it, Habermas offered "a communicative rationality freed from the limitations of individualistic approaches of social theory," and an "understanding meant to achieve an agreement that ends in mutuality and intersubjectivity" (p. 163). To media critic Daniel Hallin (1985), this form of critical theory situated all human communication within the "elementary structure of dialogue" (p. 142). Habermas was the subject of the entire issue of the Fall 1979 *Journal of the American Forensic Association,* featuring articles by Thomas B. Farrell, Joseph Wenzel, Susan Kline, James Aune, Brant Burleson, and Donald Cushman and David Dietrich. Burleson and Kline (1979) also coauthored a longer "critical explication" of Habermas's theory of communication in the flagship *Quarterly Journal of Speech.* Later articles explored the relevance of Habermas's project for public argumentation (Goodnight, 1982), for the epistemology of power (Jansen, 1983), and for rhetorical criticism (Francesconi, 1986).

The discipline's interest in Bakhtin developed somewhat later, as his books first appeared in English in the 1970s and 1980s, for the most part, and the most important secondary literature on his work became widely distributed and discussed in the 1980s and 1990s. Communication scholars were impressed with Bakhtin's appreciation for the multivocal constitution of human experience, and his especially rich and fresh explanations of ideas that the discipline previously had associated with empathy, process, context, and language. Here was an interdisciplinary thinker who put the complexities of dialogic human speech at the very center of his project. Theorists responded in the 1980s by applying Bakhtin's and similar ideas to mass communication (Newcomb, 1984), to performance studies (Conquergood, 1985, 1991; HopKins, 1989; Park-Fuller, 1986; Strine, 1988), and to theorizing feminist approaches to literature and creativity (Strine, 1989).

Textbooks. Scholarship in the discipline of communication is a shared heritage with our pedagogy. We are proud of how research is translated readily for the classroom, and we consistently minimize the distinctions (sometimes valorized in other disciplines) between theory and practice, and between research and application. It is not surprising that an important aspect of communication's early encounter with dialogue is reflected in prominent textbooks from the 1970s and 1980s.

The surge of interest in interpersonal communication in the late 1960s and early 1970s led to a number of engagingly written and popular texts that, if they did not offer sophisticated analyses of dialogue in the philosophical sense, certainly were in tune with many of its assumptions. Books such as Keltner's (1970) *Interpersonal Speech-Communication* (with its focus on what he termed *engagement* and *availability*), Giffin and Patton's (1970) *Fundamentals of Interpersonal Communication,* and Patton and Giffin's (1974) *Interpersonal Communication,* with their eclectic mix of social science and humanistic resources, demonstrated that concepts of interpersonal communication quality can be presented rigorously. This emphasis on interpersonal appreciations and skills, despite its chilly reception from some sectors of the discipline, set the stage for more overt dialogic analyses to come.

Stewart's (1973) reader, *Bridges Not Walls,* stressed that dialogic assumptions are necessary for a full appreciation of interpersonal relationships. Buber's themes were showcased from the opening quotation to the concluding essay; Stewart tells readers that Buber is "the most profound thinker represented in this book" (p. 284). Stewart followed the success of this anthology with an interpersonal text that also mirrored assumptions of dialogue (Stewart & D'Angelo, 1975). These books eventually appeared in several editions, as did some others in this discussion—in fact, *Bridges Not Walls* has consistently been the standard by which readers in interpersonal communication are judged and, as of this writing, is in its eighth edition.

Two other texts expressly intended to emphasize the interpersonal dimensions of dialogic theory also advanced a commitment to dialogue in the

1970s—Brown and Keller's (1973) *Monologue to Dialogue,* and Rossiter and Pearce's (1975) *Communicating Personally: A Theory of Interpersonal Communication and Human Relationships.* Perhaps the most overtly dialogue-oriented interpersonal textbook, however, was Thomlison's under-appreciated 1982 work, *Toward Interpersonal Dialogue,* which extended his earlier research linking the concepts of Buber and Carl Rogers (Thomlison, 1975).

Dialogue would also become prominent in other courses in the speech communication curriculum, although in some cases this seemed to reflect a trend in terminology more than a substantive shift in pedagogical focus. Makay and Brown (1972) published *The Rhetorical Dialogue: Contemporary Concepts and Cases,* which integrated interpersonal concepts into a broad introductory text that stressed a social approach to rhetorical skill. Some communication theory teachers used Darnell and Brockriede's (1976) creative text-reader, *Persons Communicating,* to integrate a wide variety of social, philosophical, and rhetorical theories, including Buber's dialogue. Others used Fisher's influential *Perspectives on Human Communication* (1978), which included a section on dialogic theory within its social science focus on general systems, transactional, and organizational information approaches. Through this organizational mix, Fisher surely persuaded many students and faculty that these newer social science ideas could be reconciled with dialogic approaches. The first edition of our most popular general text on communication ethics, Johannesen's *Ethics in Human Communication* (1975), built on the author's 1971 article on dialogue as an emerging concept. During this time, scholars also published a number of books designed to help teachers clarify the philosophical assumptions guiding their classroom practices; several of these advocated dialogic concepts in one form or another, without necessarily focusing on Buber or other systematic philosophers of dialogue (e.g., Brown & Van Riper, 1973; Friedman, 1978). An early intercultural communication book, Prosser's (1978) *The Cultural Dialogue,* used dialogue as a metaphor for cross-cultural communication; the author mentions in one section that he has been "attracted and influenced by religious existentialists such as Martin Buber, Gabriel Marcel, Paul Tillich, Karl Jaspers, etc." and that their "central idea is that existence is communication—that life is dialogue. . . . Communication is dialogue, and dialogue, I-Thou meeting, is not just in the sense of two people talking, but of real efforts at mutual understanding, mutual acknowledgement, and mutual respect" (p. 227).

Scholarly Books. Communication scholars in the 1970s and 1980s were exploring dialogue in other ways, as well, although it might be fair to say that these decades mostly demonstrated our willingness to import, adopt, or adapt ideas from the work of other disciplines into our classes and research. Journal articles introduced readers to important theorists of dialogue, but most authors were evidently not yet ready to take on book-length scholarly projects of their own. Buber, Gadamer, Habermas, Bakhtin, and other thinkers were appreciated and their concepts applied, but few scholarly books in communication developed their ideas in significant ways. Yet there were notable exceptions.

Arnett's (1980) Buber-inflected *Dwell in Peace: Applying Nonviolence to Everyday Relationships* was followed in 1986 by perhaps his best-known work of philosophical synthesis, *Communication and Community: Implications of Martin Buber's Dialogue*. Schrag, a philosopher with close ties to communication scholars and departments, published several important books that clarified the importance of dialogue for a philosophy of communication; his *Experience and Being* (1969) and *Communicative Praxis and the Space of Subjectivity* (1986) were especially noteworthy. Pilotta (1982; Murphy & Pilotta, 1983; Pilotta & Mickunas, 1990) also pursued phenomenologically oriented work on dialogue that had implications for communication theory and research methods, as did Lanigan (1977, 1984, 1988).

In rhetoric and media studies, Fisher's (1987) important work on the narrative paradigm, *Human Communication as Narration,* defined dialogic-quality communication using Buber's concepts of I-Thou, juxtaposed it with various conceptions of dialectic, and proceeded to show how a fundamentally dialogic narrative impulse helps us understand and account for human experience at deeper levels. In addition, Haiman (1981) published a definitive work in free speech theory, *Speech and Law in a Free Society*—a book that explored the viability of "marketplace of ideas" assumptions in the public arena. A third rhetorical strain in dialogue was the work of Asante in Afrocentric theory—a fundamentally dialogic appreciation of cultural energy and diversity. Especially in *The Afrocentric Idea* (1987), Asante argued that this concept should not displace European ideas in multicultural settings, but would instead seek to coexist dialogically with them. Finally, the works of Carey (1988, 1989) and others (Jensen, 1990; Real, 1989) associated with American approaches to cultural studies have been influential in grounding social analysis in the dialogic and conversational social philosophies of pragmatists and neopragmatists such as Dewey (1927), Rorty (1979), and West (1993a), as well as in the media theories of Ong (1958, 1967, 1982).

Contexts: Advancing Dialogue in the Discipline

The contemporary interest in communication as dialogue, which, for purposes of this essay, we will trace somewhat arbitrarily to work done since about 1990, is broad, deep, lively, and increasingly influential. Perhaps the best news in this trend is that communication scholars are fully participating in, not just acknowledging or analyzing, a wider scholarly conversation. The idea's momentum can be traced to a number of especially important social and intellectual contexts that, it could be argued, have achieved more importance and centrality in the years since the late 1980s. Before we describe what we consider to be some especially important contributions from communication scholars, we highlight some of these social and intellectual contexts that cultivated the contemporary reception of dialogic theory.

Some of the most important social and intellectual changes that alerted us to new contexts for studying dialogue were previewed in the late 1980s in the widely read "Paradigm Issues" volume of the *Rethinking Communication* books sponsored by the International Communication Association (Dervin, Grossberg, O'Keefe, & Wartella, 1989). The stimulus essays of this book (Craig, 1989; Giddens, 1989; Hall, 1989; Krippendorff, 1989; Rosengren, 1989) made it clear that the hold of older traditions of researching and theorizing communication was giving way to newer and fresher definitions. Qualitative and interpretive research approaches were not just one kind of option among many research strategies but had become vital for understanding any communication practice in which meanings are fluid and emergent.

Qualitative and interpretive approaches ask researchers to recognize how reality is not unitary and given, but pluralized and constituted through communication practices themselves. The "how" of that constitutive nature naturally became an object of interest and concern, and dialogue was one key concept that helped some scholars guide their research with more constructionist epistemologies. Qualitative, interpretive, and hermeneutic methods, we were reminded, are not designed to supplant more traditional forms of social science research, but to supplement them in the task of "getting at" processes of meaning-making and sense-making that seemed inaccessible otherwise. In *Rethinking Communication*, the media theorist Rosengren (1989) critiqued the tendency to see qualitative methods as unsystematic, and the sociologist Giddens (1989) described the "emerging synthesis" of research in the social sciences; in doing so, they were referring to a realistic welcoming of plural methods if—and the "if" is very important to them—researchers developed suitably rigorous criteria for understanding such concepts as Giddens's "mutual knowledge" (p. 60). Mutual knowledge is what allows social actors to collaborate in producing meaningful and sensible acts and interpretations apart from the internalized states of individuals; another way to say this is that mutual knowledge is what constructs and sustains cultures.

Giddens (1989) and others noted that a new cultural awareness had begun to pervade intellectual life in the final decades of the 20th century. As we began to ground the concept of self, this task was not merely a call to study how we can become "better" selves as communicators, but a call to understand how selves necessarily develop uniquely in distinctive cultural settings. The discipline's newfound cultural focus was inextricably linked with media concerns. Hall (1989), writing in the same *Rethinking Communication* volume, wanted to theorize communication itself as what he referred to as a *cultural field* —which is "the arena in which the modern mass media intersect directly with the constitution and transformation of the field of culture, that is, of our conceptions of the world" (p. 41). Acknowledging the place of an other is to make contingent one's own place, a central insight of some postmodern theorists (Bauman, 1992; Lyotard, 1984)—and from such recognitions spring dialogic impulses. A sophisticated or "cosmopolitan" communication sense of globalization (to use Pearce's [1989] notion) depends on a simple dialectic premise: Without knowing the other, knowing the self is a futile exercise; without a self-position to know from, the other is inaccessible. Dialogue manages the seeming impasse. As Krippendorff (1989) concludes of the worlds we build together,

> communication is central to all of these worlds, not in the sense of control, which a positivist ontology naturally favors, but in the sense of dialoguing an ongoing process that respects the autonomy of different reality constructions, enables each participant to interrogate his or her own history and grow beyond it. Dialogue probably is the most noble form of human interaction and communication scholars should be the first to appreciate its outstanding human qualities. (p. 94)

Noble or not, dialogue has emerged as a fulcrum concept of the human sciences, one that bridges interpersonal, rhetorical, cultural, and mass media studies. With it, we can better address processes of communication that are not well explained by linear, conduit-based, positivistic, or excessively individualistic and agentic accounts of human action. With it, communication studies can become even more of what Craig (1989) called a "practical discipline," stimulating meaningful theoretical critique in addition to suggestions for better or more effective actions.

Which recent studies of mutualized cultural dialogue have been most influential for communication scholars as we expand our horizons? We find them in overlapping contexts of everyday life, public political life, cultural life, and media life.

EVERYDAY LIFE: FACE-TO-FACE CONTEXTS

The resurgence of dialogue has been especially powerful in the areas of interpersonal, group, and organizational life, and many works in this tradition from other disciplines have influenced communication scholars. Prominent books have explored the dialogic bases of mind (Billig, 1987; Wertsch, 1991; Wold, 1992), conversation (Markova & Foppa, 1990; Tannen, 1989; Stone,

Patton, & Heen, 1999), therapy (Anderson, 1997; Hycner, 1991; Maranhao, 1986), group creativity (Bohm, 1996), organizing (Ellinor & Gerard, 1998; Isaacs, 1999; Senge, 1990), cybernetic systemic approaches (Maturana & Varela, 1980), education (hooks, 1994; Palmer, 1983, 1998; Witherell & Noddings, 1991b), ethics (Noddings, 1984; Taylor, 1991b), and interactive and interpretive research methods (Mishler, 1986). In addition, the writings of Friedman (e.g., 1974, 1983a, 1985, 1992, 1996), which cut across many of these boundaries and, indeed, other literary and theological traditions as well, have served to ground much contemporary thinking in Buber's dialogue.

Communication scholars have added to this intellectual mix by publishing important scholarly books that develop dialogic conceptions of personal and organizational relationships. In interpersonal communication, works by Baxter and Montgomery (1996), McNamee and Gergen (1999), Pearce (1989, 1993), Penman (2000), Rawlins (1992), Shotter (1993a), and Stewart (1995, 1996) have displayed, explicitly or implicitly, a dialogic orientation. Similarly, in education, Arnett (1992) has taken a dialogic stance, describing education as "conversation about ideas and between people." Organizational communication has developed its own dialogic communication tradition, represented by works of Deetz (1992, 1995), Goodall (Goodall, 1991, 1994), and Taylor (1993). Eisenberg and Goodall (1993) published a dialogue-oriented text that generated many conversations among scholarly theorists in organizational studies; it has since been republished in multiple editions. Advocates of dialogic approaches to research practices include Ellis and Bochner (1996), Denzin (2002), and Montgomery and Baxter (1998a). Additionally, editors of one anthology collected relevant interdisciplinary materials about dialogue and framed them specifically for communication scholars (Anderson, Cissna, & Arnett, 1994).

POLITICAL LIFE: PUBLIC CONTEXTS

Recent political theorists and critics have demonstrated strong interest in the concept of dialogue, sometimes building on the work of Habermas (1979, 1984, 1990) or Hannah Arendt (1959), but more often developing their own distinctive systems of thought. Their books range from the work done in the tradition of Barber's "strong democracy" (1984, 1988), to explorations of the dialogic problems of the public sphere (Ackerman, 1980; Chevigny, 1988; Evans & Boyte, 1992; Fraser, 1989; Kingwell, 1995; Mathews, 1994; Yankelovich, 1999), to emerging developments in deliberative democracy (Bohman, 1996; Fishkin, 1991, 1992; Gutmann & Thompson, 1996), to the communitarian movement (Etzioni, 1993; Glendon, 1991), to the discussion of how to manage political conflicts of power and identity (Caspary, 2000; Colker, 1992; Saunders, 1999; Smith, 1997; Tannen, 1998; Young, 1990).

A number of books written by communication scholars have added to this tradition of exploring public dialogue, including the historical case studies developed by Anderson and Cissna (1997; Cissna & Anderson, 2002); Arnett and Arneson's treatment of *Dialogic Civility in a Cynical Age* (1999); Kaid, McKinney, and Tedesco's (2000) study of the 1996 U. S. presidential campaign; Pearce and Littlejohn's (1997) study of moral conflict and its consequences; Kellett and Dalton's (2001) book on dialogical approaches to conflict management; and Spano's (2001) account of the Public Dialogue Consortium's action-based program of public dialogue in Cupertino, California.

CULTURAL LIFE: CONTEXTS OF OTHERNESS

The pervasive multicultural awareness of the past several decades has encouraged new emphasis on dialogue across the disciplines. Bakhtin's and Gadamer's ideas, of course, are central for many—but not all—scholars as they consider this emergent sensitivity. Of course, one discipline intimately connected with the study of culture, anthropology, has a well-respected tradition of dialogue studies (Crapanzano, 1990; Maranhao, 1990; Marcus & Fischer, 1986; Schultz, 1990; Tedlock, 1983; Tedlock & Mannheim, 1995; Tyler, 1987). Yet much of the significant work on multicultural dialogic awareness has come from other disciplines, too. Psychologists have made strong contributions to our appreciation of how dialogue and culture are interdependent. Gergen's (1991, 1994) work on social constructionist theorizing, Bruner's (1990) narrative approaches to a self that is transactional and "dialogue dependent" (p. 101), and especially Sampson's (1993) *Celebrating the Other: A Dialogic Account of Human Nature* have reminded us of this connection, although only the last work seems thoroughly explicit in its dialogic orientation. Black feminist thought in literary studies and elsewhere also has taken a dialogic turn (Collins, 1990; hooks, 1994).

In recent years, most communication scholars have assumed culture to be an essential part of our discipline; this, unfortunately, was not always the case, to which Oliver (1973) and other cross-cultural scholars in the discipline's early history might attest. In addition to Asante's (1987) Afrocentric theory, mentioned previously, a number of recent communication books have adopted overtly cultural approaches to dialogue. Communication scholars were influential in producing a then-definitive collection of essays in the emerging interdiscipline of cultural studies—Grossberg, Nelson, and Treichler's (1992) *Cultural Studies*. McPhail's (1996) meditation on racism is another excellent example of dialogic cultural criticism and theorizing, whereas Shotter's (1993b) contribution is to extend the dialogic concept of culture to concrete interpersonal relations in everyday life. Another application to everyday experience, Drew's (2001) ethnographic exploration of karaoke culture, is a striking example of creative writing emerging from a dialogic engagement of "researcher" and "researched."

MEDIA LIFE: TECHNOLOGICAL CONTEXTS

Some decades ago, such proponents of dialogue as Ellul (1964, 1985) and Ferrarotti (1988) bemoaned how modern mass media—television, radio, print—had depersonalized human experience by removing or discouraging opportunities for genuine conversation. In recent decades, however, with the exception of Peters (1999b)—about whom, more later—scholars appear to have shifted their attention to examining the potential of new media to create different forms of conversation and dialogue.

Interdisciplinary theorists in history (Poster, 1990, 1995), literary criticism (Snyder, 1996), and philosophy (Taylor & Saarinen, 1994) have explored the dialogic possibilities of computer-mediated communication, including the implications for personal identity in a radically dialogized online/database culture. In addition, the broadly interdisciplinary reach of cultural studies has energized the study of popular culture as a dialogic matrix profoundly influenced by media practices (Ferguson & Golding, 1997; Grossberg et al., 1992; Kellner, 1995).

Research in media studies supports our theorizing about dialogue in a number of ways. For example, Grossberg (1992) has traced implications for public dialogue, broadly defined, in such popular culture venues as rock music. Further, the tradition that Meyrowitz (1994; see also Meyrowitz, 1985) calls *medium theory* has examined the tendency for media to change the ways we perceive and therefore to change the ways we expect to interact. One crucial aspect of media analysis since the contributions of McLuhan (1964) and Ong (e.g., 1967) has been to attempt to explain how electronic media have increased our expectations for, and abilities to effect, highly interactive communication (Farrell, 2000; Gronbeck, Farrell, & Soukup, 1991). Jones (1995), Markham (1998), and others have used dialogic assumptions and concepts to examine the premises of online culture, including how the new forms of computer-mediated interactivity have shifted our expectations for community and dialogue.

Another strain of recent communication theorizing has developed in what has come to be known as public journalism or civic journalism; researchers and critics have suggested, at times controversially, that newspapers and other journalistic outlets should accept more responsibility to facilitate dialogue within local communities. Dialogic approaches to journalism are clearly advocated, for example, in Carey's (1989) extensions of Deweyan democracy; in Christians, Ferré, and Fackler's (1993) communitarian ethics for the press; in Rosen's (1999) and Charity's (1995) spirited evocations of public journalism tenets; and in Anderson, Dardenne, and Killenberg's (1994) description of the interpersonal and conversational dimensions of journalistic practices.

Conclusion

Peters's (1999b) first chapter from his history of communication studies begins with a claim about how "in certain quarters dialogue has attained something of a holy status. It is held up as the summit of human encounter, the essence of liberal education, and the medium of participatory democracy" (p. 33). If the language of this comment sounds somewhat derisive ("holy," "summit"), it is because its author evidently intends a certain dismissiveness. Later, he asserts that dialogue is not the sole goal of communication, that it "can be tyrannical," that ignoring assumptions of dialogue also allows us to achieve many important social goals, and that the "strenuous standard" of dialogue "can stigmatize a great deal of the things we do with words" (p. 34). "Dialogue, to be sure," he summarizes, "is one precious part of our tool-kit as talking animals, but it ought not to be elevated to sole or supreme status" (p. 34).

Peters believes that the concept is being sold uncritically to a gullible public—an assertion that may be true in some quarters (platitudes from political campaigns and self-help books come to mind) but that is not, by all indications, applicable to academic theories of dialogue. We have not found in the scholarly literature the kind of uncritical dogma of dialogue Peters describes. The communication literature we survey here does not elevate dialogue uncritically to "a sole or supreme status"; rather, it typically presents dialogue (as Buber does) as an opportunity hard-won in daily life or (as Gadamer and Bakhtin do) as a concrete mode of human linguistic experiencing. Dialogue scholars tend to acknowledge, with Buber, that this phenomenon exists in moments rather than extended states, that it cannot be lionized, that it cannot become business as usual, and that it cannot be planned precisely or made to happen. Further, life presents many situations that do not demand dialogic responses, and a faith in dialogue will not necessarily lead to rosy results. Most theorizing about dialogue in fact downplays techniques of information or message transmission, concentrating instead on the extent to which human thinking, speaking, and listening can be appreciated as social and cultural intersubjective processes, rather than simply as individualistic, organism-centered acts. However, this suggests neither that dialogue is the only valid model for communication, nor that message dissemination techniques are inappropriate or unworthy of study.

We are wise to be skeptical about dialogue, but unwise to be dismissive. Dialogue matters, not as the only model for effective communication—in this we agree with Peters—but as an especially crucial one. Therefore, in this introduction, we have let our analysis be guided realistically by both historical and conceptual criteria. To our knowledge, for example, the discipline has never had an adequate history of the development of its concern with dialogue; in some small way, we hope to have contributed to that end. In the first section, we examined texts and influences that have shaped contemporary understanding of the concept, both from without and within the discipline. Communication theorists from the 1970s through the 1990s highlighted four thinkers—Buber, Gadamer, Habermas, and Bakhtin. Explications of their work laid the groundwork for more vigorous theorizing about dialogue. In recent years, as subsequent chapters in this volume will suggest, communication scholars have kept the work of Bakhtin and Buber in the foreground, with Gadamer receiving somewhat less attention. Attention to Habermas seems to be reflected primarily in the work of scholars in media studies and argumentation.

Our second section dealt with the contexts for recent theorizing. Here, although recognizing the artificiality and overlapping of categories, we chose to highlight work done in four general domains: face-to-face contexts, public/political contexts, cultural contexts of otherness, and media/technology contexts. Space limitations made it necessary to omit many recent influential articles and monographs. Therefore, we have concentrated on book-length contributions to indicate the emergent maturity of communication theorizing about dialogue.

Dialogue: Theorizing Difference in Communication Studies collects original contributions from many of the discipline's most important theorists of dialogue. Because we asked authors to summarize their current research programs with an eye to the future, their chapters collectively create a state-of-the-art survey. They also suggest exciting innovations and predict alternate futures for dialogue studies. Instead of attempting to fit these scholars' current concerns into the historical patterns summarized in this introduction, we note that the essays' topics and goals appeared to sort themselves into three basic divisions. Although all the contributors theorize and organize the study of dialogue in fresh conceptual contexts, some chapters emphasize a particular definitional goal especially prominently. Included in the first major section, *Exploring the Territories of Dialogue,* are chapters from John Stewart, Karen E. Zediker, and Laura Black; W. Barnett Pearce and Kimberly A. Pearce; Michael J. Hyde; Ronald C. Arnett; and Sheila McNamee and John Shotter. Other chapters focus on personalized social contexts in dyadic, group, and organizational life. This section, *Personal Voices in Dialogue,* offers chapters by Leslie A. Baxter; James R. Taylor; Stanley Deetz and Jennifer Simpson; H. L. Goodall, Jr. and Peter M. Kellett; and Leonard C. Hawes. Finally, a third section, *Public Voices in Dialogue,* examines the spaces for discourse in more expansive public, intercultural, and mediated settings through chapters from Kenneth N. Cissna and Rob Anderson; Mark McPhail; Mary S. Strine; and John J. Pauly. Finally, we pull together disparate implications, threads, and new directions in a dialogue-inspired conclusion.

Note

1.   Actually, a far wider range of theorists of dialogue has influenced communication scholars over the years. Most notably, as authors in this book will suggest, David Bohm, Martin Heidegger, and Emmanuel Levinas have become increasingly central to contemporary research programs in such areas as organizational communication (Bohm) and communication ethics (Heidegger and Levinas [see Hyde, 2001a]). Other important dialogic concepts have informed communication studies by way of these theorists: Michael Billig, Vincent Crapanzano, Jacques Ellul, Paulo Freire, Helmut Geissner, Kenneth Gergen, bell hooks, Edmund Husserl, Karl Jaspers, Alasdair MacIntyre, Tullio Maranhao, Gabriel Marcel, Maurice Merleau-Ponty, Fr. Walter Ong, Paul Ricoeur, Carl Rogers, Richard Rorty, Eugen Rosenstock-Huessy, Ragnar Rommetveit, Edward Sampson, Calvin Schrag, Alfred Schutz, Charles Taylor, Lev Vygotsky, and Ludwig Wittgenstein. In addition, John Dewey, George Herbert Mead, and others working within the tradition of American pragmatism and the symbolic interactionist perspective have contributed directly to theorizing social communication in the public and private spheres.

Part I

*Exploring the
Territories of Dialogue*

2

Relationships Among Philosophies of Dialogue

John Stewart, Karen E. Zediker, and Laura Black

Although the term *dialogue* has been commonly used in dramatic and literary theory and practice, philosophy, and ordinary language since at least Plato's time, it took on special meaning in the last part of the 20th century. Near the end of the century, Cissna and Anderson (1998b) introduced an important article about dialogue with 117 citations on this topic, 92 of which had been published since 1990. This proliferation of works across the human studies contributed to Penman's (2000) experience at a 1999 international communication conference during which she "attended every session with the word *dialogue* in its title and discovered that there were almost as many different usages of the word as sessions held" (p. 83).

Stewart and Zediker (2000) tried to bring some order to these multiple conceptions of dialogue by distinguishing between *descriptive* and *prescriptive* approaches. The former, we argued, use the term dialogue to label a pervasive and defining feature of humanity that, according to proponents, has too little been noticed and appreciated—namely, the irreducibly social, relational, or interactional character of all human meaning-making. From this perspective, all human life is inherently "dialogic." Mikhail Bakhtin (1981, 1986; Volosinov, 1973[1]) often used dialogue in this sense, and a similar interpretation surfaces in many social constructionist works (e.g., Gergen, 1994; Shotter, 1993a). Prescriptive approaches to dialogue, on the other hand, agree that all human meaning-making is inherently *relational,* but they reserve the term dialogue for a particular quality or type of relating. Martin Buber (1965a, 1965b, 1970, 1973) is the most prominent prescriptive theorist, and his description of

I-Thou relating sets the standard for those who treat dialogue prescriptively. One value of the descriptive–prescriptive distinction is that it prompts reflection about the role of epistemological and ethical considerations in dialogic theory and practice. Roughly, prescriptive approaches make ethics central whereas descriptive ones focus more on epistemological issues than on axiological ones.

Yet, our continued study of dialogue, especially as it is treated in the philosophical writings of Buber, Bakhtin, David Bohm, Paolo Freire, and Hans-Georg Gadamer, leads us to see as many similarities as there are differences among these programs. Especially because dialogic philosophers themselves emphasize connections, we want to balance our earlier effort to distinguish among approaches to dialogue with a consideration of what might have led all of these theorists to label their central interest with the same term. We focus on these five writers primarily because they are among the most frequently referenced philosophers of communication whose works foreground the term dialogue as fundamental to human being-in-the-world. Other influential writers, such as Martin Heidegger, Jürgen Habermas, and Emmanuel Levinas, comment extensively on human contact but not directly on dialogue. For example, some have characterized Levinas's influential writings on communication ethics as dialogic. Levinas's primary project, however, is a sustained critique of western philosophy's suppression of the *Other*. His main subtopics include "infinity," "the ethical," "the face," "exteriority," "subjectivity," "saying," and "the said" (Davis, 1996; Hand, 1989; Levinas, 1969, 1981). Thus, Levinas's meditations are clearly relevant to conversations about dialogue, but we do not understand him to be primarily or explicitly a theorist of dialogue in the same way as the five authors discussed in this paper.[2] Similar points could be made about Heidegger's and Habermas's primary interests (Habermas, 1993, 1998; Heidegger, 1962, 1971a; Risser, 1997).[3]

By contrast, we believe that Buber, Bakhtin, Bohm, Freire, and Gadamer are philosophers of dialogue who write from experiential bases and habits of mind that are more similar, even across decades and cultures, than they are dissimilar. Thus, the main goal of this chapter is to identify relationships among these primary philosophical sources. Because the literature by and about these authors is extensive, we will be able only to outline commonalities here. But, to the degree that this effort succeeds, it should facilitate increasingly coherent, collaborative, and synergistic dialogue theory and practice.

Before we begin to support this claim, we want to sketch what we mean by "experiential bases" and "habits of mind." We take experiential bases to be events lived-through by these writers, formative experiences in their personal or professional careers that, it is plausible to infer, materially influenced their ways of being-in-the-world.[4] As one philosophical biographer argues, there are reasons why each philosopher approaches topics as he or she does, and "some of those reasons can be extracted from biography" (Postel, 2002, quoting Carlin

Romano, p. A18). We notice events in the lives of each of the five, for example, that appeared profoundly to limit their commitments to certainty and closure and to strengthen their commitments to openness and indeterminacy.

By "habits of mind" we mean characteristic inclinations toward framing important topics, issues, or questions and typical approaches to problems. We identify two primary habits of mind that are common to these philosophers of dialogue: holism and tensionality. As a habit of mind, holism is the character-istic inclination to approach a topic or problem broadly rather than narrowly, as much as possible as a totality, rather than divided into its parts. There are varieties of holistic habits of mind, including summative, synergistic, and ten-sional ones. A summative holism attempts to catalogue all the elements, facets, or features of a problem exhaustively or comprehensively. On the other hand, if holism is synergistic, the emphasis is not just on comprehensiveness but also on the ways the whole is greater than the sum of its parts. Systems theory is a well-known version of this synergistic kind of holism (Senge, Kleiner, Roberts, Ross, & Smith, 1994; von Bertalanffy, 1968).

We notice that these authors' holism is tensional, and this feature is impor-tant enough that we identify it as a second habit of mind. By tensionality we mean the tendency to understand whatever is of interest ("reality," "the world," "human beings," and especially "communication") dynamically and dialecti-cally rather than as a static construct. It is possible to adopt a tensional orien-tation that is not holistic, such as Plato's account of the dialectic of question-and-answer that constitutes philosophy. But, as we will argue, these five authors approach their work both holistically and tensionally.

The evidence we cite about these writers' experiential bases and habits of mind come from their writings and biographies or autobiographies. These works sub-stantiate our claim that, despite their manifest differences, these philosophers' understandings of dialogue are as similar, in several specific ways, as they are dif-ferent. In this chapter, we review their shared commitments to holism and ten-sionality, briefly sketch some biographical commonalities, clarify how each focused on communication, and then review how all of them treated communication as dialogue. Our goal, again, is to underscore relationships among these programs.

Holism

All five of these philosophers of dialogue initially approach their subject matter holistically rather than analytically; each emphasizes the sum that is greater than its tensional parts. Each author developed a broad and context-dependent perspective, and each urged his readers to balance Enlightenment tendencies toward analysis, separation, and categorization with attempts to be aware of and understand a totality, a whole.

David Bohm was the most explicit about his commitment to holism. An American physicist and colleague of Albert Einstein, Bohm was driven out of the U.S. by McCarthyism and spent most of his career as professor of theoretical physics at Birkbeck College, University of London. Although he published widely cited works titled *Quantum Theory* (1951), and *The Special Theory of Relativity* (1966), he also taught and wrote about dialogue for the last 25 years of his life. In one of his primary treatises in physics, *Wholeness and the Implicate Order* (1980), Bohm wrote,

> I would say that in my scientific and philosophical work, my main concern has been with understanding the nature of reality in general and of consciousness in particular as a coherent whole, which is never static or complete but which is an unending process of movement and unfoldment. (p. ix)

Biographer Will Keepin (1993) explains that Bohm "postulates that the ultimate nature of physical reality is not a collection of separate objects (as it appears to us), but rather it is an *undivided whole* that is in perpetual dynamic flux" (p. 2). In his major work on dialogue, Bohm's (1996) analysis of thought centrally features warnings about "fragmentation" which involves breaking things up into bits "as if they were independent. It's not merely making divisions, but it is breaking things up which are not really separate. . . . Things which really fit, and belong together, are treated as if they do not" (p. 49). The physics of Bohm's holism and its implications for quantum theory are intriguing and consequential. His holistic habit of mind as a physicist is influential in his philosophy of dialogue as well. He argues that dialogue must be understood as a holistic process enveloping interlocutors, rather than as the sum of interactions between fragmented participants.

Martin Buber's commitment to holism is also explicit and pervasive. As perhaps the most widely known 20th-century philosopher of dialogue, Buber understood his primary life-project to be a philosophical anthropology, responding to Kant's fourth question "What is [the hu]man?,"[5] which Kant raised in his *Handbook* to his lectures on knowledge.[6] Buber (1965a) strongly criticized Kant, because "The *wholeness* of [the hu]man does not enter into this anthropology" (p. 120). In his definitive monograph, "What is Man?" Buber leveled this same criticism against many other philosophical anthropologies, and in the final section of this essay, he identified his own project as "a consideration of [the question] in the wholeness of its essential relations to what is" (p. 199). Friedman (1965) emphasizes the importance of holism to Buber in his introductory essay to the collection of Buber's (1965b) writings called *The Knowledge of Man*. Further, early in the first essay, Buber writes,

We may characterize the act and the work of entering into relation with the world as such—and, therefore, not with parts of it, and not with the sum of its parts, but with it as the world—as synthesizing apperception, by which we establish that this pregnant use of the concept involves the function of unity: by synthesizing apperception I mean the apperception of a being as a whole and as a unity. . . . The conception of wholeness and unity is in its origin identical with the conception of the world to which [the hu]man is turned. (pp. 62–63)

Throughout his corpus, Buber's focus on holism is consistent and consequential.

Bakhtin's commitment to holism is evident in his criticism that previous treatments of language in philosophy and linguistics are too narrow. *Marxism and the Philosophy of Language* (Volosinov, 1973; see note 1) chides Dilthey, Leibnitz, and especially Saussure for failing to attend to the whole event of living speech communication that Bakhtin calls "the utterance." The primary feature of this event is *responsiveness;* it consists not just of a speech act but what might be termed an event of speech-contact-in-context. As Volosinov (Bakhtin) writes,

our study of the forms of verbal communication and the corresponding forms of whole utterances can shed light on the system of paragraphing and all analogous problems. As long as linguistics continues to orient itself toward the isolated, monologic utterance, it will remain devoid of any organic approach to all these questions. (1973, p. 112)

Bakhtin (1986) evidenced a similar commitment in his later writings to "the *whole* of the utterance" (p. 60), "the actual whole of speech communication" (p. 68), and "the standpoint of the *whole* utterance" (p. 81; cf. p. 86). For Bakhtin, the study of the utterance is the study of the whole of a dialogic encounter.

Brazilian philosopher of education and dialogue Paulo Freire was similarly inclined toward holism. Freire focused much of his energy on the praxis of what he termed a "pedagogy of the oppressed" (1990). But his philosophy of education emphasizes holistic themes and his view of dialogue, indebted as it is to Buber, is similarly holistic. Freire insisted that liberation achieved by individuals at the expense of others is an act of oppression and that personal freedom and individual development can only occur in mutuality with others. He advocated liberatory education as a component of a liberatory praxis that seeks to transform the social order. This education consists of both critical consciousness and the development of appropriate competencies. Heany (1995) explains that Freire's conception of critical consciousness is holistic in that it

> is a level of consciousness characterized by depth in the interpretation of problems, through testing one's own findings with openness to revision, attempting to avoid distortion when perceiving problems and preconceived notions when analyzing them, receptivity to the new without rejecting the old because it is old. (glossary, para. 8)

This consciousness, as we note below, is achieved through negotiating tensions in dialogue rather than the oppressor imposing his or her view or the oppressed relinquishing his or hers. Thus, Freire's holism is apparent in his emphases on mutuality, community, transformation of macrostructures, and inclusiveness of contexts, perspectives, and individuals.

In many philosophical works, a commitment to holism surfaces in the prominence of the term *world* in such constructions as "the human world," "worlds of meaning," and "being-in-the-world," and in accounts of relationships between language and world.[7] Hans-Georg Gadamer's philosophical hermeneutics embodies this aspect of these programs; as he put it, "What I am describing is the mode of the whole human experience of the world. I call this experience hermeneutical" (1976, p. 15). Gadamer focused on language because, he argued,

> language is not just one of [the hu]man's possessions in the world; rather, on it depends the fact that [the hu]man has a *world* at all. . . . Language has no independent life apart from the world that comes to language within it. (Gadamer, 1989b, p. 443)

From the last section of *Truth and Method*, which he completed in 1960, through the essays he wrote until near his death in 2001, Gadamer argued that humans are basically understanders and that understanding is accomplished in verbal/nonverbal articulate contact, which is to say that "language" (read "communication") constitutes and achieves a human world. Or, as Stewart puts it—admittedly awkwardly—worlding happens in verbal/nonverbal talk (Stewart, 1995, pp. 123–124). Gadamer's holism is apparent each time he essays these topics.

In short, one basic habit of mind that animates these five philosophers is holism. Each developed a broad and context-dependent perspective, and each urged his readers to balance Enlightenment tendencies toward analysis, separation, and categorization with attempts to be aware of and understand a totality—for Bohm the "implicate order," for Buber the wholeness of human being, for Bakhtin the whole of speech communicating, for Freire the wholes of critical consciousness, and for Gadamer the whole of the relation between the human and his or her world.

Tensionality

As we noted, the holism embraced by these authors is not simply summative or synergistic. A distinctive feature of their holistic habits of mind and a second defining element of their philosophies of dialogue is *tensionality*, the sense that the whole each essayed is centrally marked by both a complementary and con-tradictory quality that renders it inherently fluid and dynamic.

Our primary understanding of this tensional feature or quality comes from the writings of philosopher of history Eric Voegelin (1987; Webb, 1981). In over 50 years of published works, Voegelin argued that philosophy is not a set of ideas but the most reflectively conscious phase of an existential process. Webb explains that in this process,

> one experiences and freely yields oneself to what Voegelin has come to call the "tension of existence" . . . the pull at the core of the philosopher's being toward a goal that will remain always mysterious but which draws him with imperative force. (Webb, 1981, p. 7)

This pull drew Voegelin to the conviction that humans live fundamentally in what Plato called a *metaxy*, an "in-between reality" (Sandoz, in Voegelin, 2000, p. 16).

Voegelin argued that across history, reflective humans have recognized this pervasive, ultimate tension as they have acknowledged the undeniability of both immanence and transcendence, that to be human is to live in-between these poles. Humans are immanent in that if cut, we bleed and if unsupported, we fall. *And* humans are transcendent insofar as there is more to us than cor-poreality, whether it is understood as *spirit, soul, psyche,* or something else. Human life is lived in-between these poles and several others, such as movement-and-rest, growth-and-deterioration, unity-and-multiplicity, purposiveness-and-randomness. As Voegelin put it in his last book, "The truth of existence in erotic tension . . . is not an information about reality but the event in which the process of reality becomes luminous to itself" (2000, p. 17). When humans understand our reality, he argued, it is an understanding that is tensional, and attempts to overcome or to end this tension with formulations that exclusively highlight one pole (immanence or transcendence) distort this feature of human reality.

Because Bakhtin's writings most clearly embody this elemental sense of ten-sionality, we begin with his work. Holquist (1990) coined the term *dialogism* as a label for Bakhtin's philosophy in order to preserve the "dynamic heterogeneity of his achievement" (p. 15), and Bakhtin (1990) described his study as moving "in spheres that are liminal, i.e., on the borders of all the aforementioned disci-plines, at their junctures and points of intersection" (p. 281). His well-known characterization of language as a battle between "centripetal and centrifugal" forces manifests this tensional orientation, as do his discussions of *heteroglossia,* his treatment of *chronotope,* a term that captures space–time relationships, and his insistence on the utterance as *responsive,* always-already implicated in the discourse context that frames it (Bakhtin, 1981, 1986). Baxter and Montgomery

(1996) and Montgomery and Baxter (1998a) foreground this quality when they appropriate Bakhtin to explain how communicators manage what they term "the both/andness" of such movements as privacy and disclosure across the timeline of a relationship. For Montgomery and Baxter (1998a) this feature "implicate[s] a kind of in-the-moment interactive multivocality, in which multiple points of view retain their integrity as they play off each other" (p. 160). Tensionality was unquestionably one of Bakhtin's dominant habits of mind.

This is also clearly a defining feature of Buber's program, beginning with his central constructs *I-It* and *I-Thou*. Buber argued that these terms label a single "twofold attitude" that characterizes humanity (1970, pp. 54, 82), and that each part of this one "attitude" or "orientation" (Stewart, 1994) is itself tensional. At one level, the feature of tensionality is evident in Buber's argument that humans orient to the world as relaters. Although we are distinct physical beings, Buber argued that it is not the case that humans exist and then enter into relations but that, *as* we relate and *in* our relating, our humanity is realized. A second level of tensionality exists between the two ways of relating Buber claimed are open to humans, I-It and I-Thou. Buber argued that prior accounts of human understanding as subject–object are incomplete because the human orientation includes both subject–object and what might be termed subject–subject relating.[8] Human life moves dialectically between these ways of relating, as at one moment we may meet a horse, hammer, or husband as an object or instrument (I-It) and others as an intersubjective partner (I-Thou). Partly because of its intensity, partnered (I-Thou) relating occurs only in moments (Cissna & Anderson, 1998b), but whoever might live completely without this quality of relating "is not human" (Buber, 1970, p. 85).

Freire's tensional orientation is evident in his arguments that humans are intersubjective, echoing Buber's discussion of I-Thou relating. "Neither objectivism nor subjectivism, nor yet psychologism is propounded here, but rather subjectivity and objectivity in constant dialectical relationship" (Freire, 1990, p. 35). Within the context of his own agenda of liberation, Freire argued that all humans struggle with the tension between oppressor and oppressed. Although some individuals may be identified as oppressors and others the oppressed, he maintained that each human experiences both sides of this tension, and "the solution of this contradiction is born in the labor which brings into the world this new [hu]man: no longer oppressor nor longer oppressed, but [a hu]man in the process of achieving freedom" (pp. 33–34). Freedom is achieved by engaging the tension in dialogic encounters.

David Bohm's version of tensionality is a feature of his understanding of reality. He postulated, as we noted, that the ultimate nature of physical reality is not a collection of separate objects but rather an undivided whole, and, as Keepin (1993) notes, "This undivided whole is not static but rather in a constant state of flow and change" (p. 2). Like the ebb and flow of the tide, Bohm wrote that in this flow, "mind and matter . . . are different aspects of one whole and unbroken movement" (Bohm in Keepin, 1993, p. 2). A concrete version of Bohm's tensionality surfaces in his discussion of a way of thinking he called *suspension*. Suspension for Bohm is a mode of awareness critical to the development of dialogue. For dialogue to emerge, a participant neither accepts his or her beliefs and opinions as reality nor rejects them completely. Rather, the interlocutor observes that he or she is experiencing beliefs and opinions and suspends judgment on them in order to examine the ways they shape his or her perspective and one's ability to experience and respond to others in dialogue. Bohm (1980) wrote,

> If we can all suspend carrying out our impulses, suspend our assumptions, and look at them all, then we are all in the same state of consciousness . . . a common consciousness. It may not be very pleasant. . . . But if people can share the frustration and share their different contradictory assumptions and share their mutual anger and stay with it . . . then you have a common consciousness. (p. 33)

For Bohm, the process of holding perspectives in tension rather than rushing to resolve them is imperative for dialogue to occur and be sustained.

Gadamer's philosophical hermeneutics is an extended meditation on understanding, and his work is most fundamentally tensional in that he conceives of understanding as occurring in events of conversation, lived as verbal-nonverbal to-and-fro or *play*. Gadamer's project is hermeneutical because it focuses on interpretation or understanding; it is philosophical because it takes understanding to be the human's way of being-in-the-world; and it is tensional because he conceives of understanding happening in context-dependent, always-unfinished, events of articulate contact (Risser, 1997; Stewart, 1995). Considerably like the Wittgenstein (1963) of the *Philosophical Investigations*, Gadamer viewed language holistically through the metaphor of play (1989b, pp. 101–110) and argued that the fundamental event of understanding is tensional in that it "is always the fusion of . . . *horizons supposedly existing by themselves*" (1989b, p. 306). At the end of *Truth and Method* (1989b), he characterized the discipline of hermeneutics as one of "questioning and inquiring," tensional discursive events that, when well-managed, can prompt "truth" (p. 491).

Experiential Bases

The tensional habit of mind that we find manifested in these authors' works affirms the necessity, for anything to be what it is, of its *other* or counterpart. Their tensional thinking understands that any identity requires or entails difference and that any quality must be defined by its complement or negation, as exhaling complements and negates inhaling, male is defined in part as not-female, and immanence and transcendence co-constitute humanity.

We believe that these five philosophers' relational-tensional habits of mind can plausibly be understood as emerging from formative experiences each had that negated the wisdom of any claims to certainty and closure. In other words, their existential situations and lived experiences made a mockery of stability and security and their philosophies of dialogue reflect this quality. This is not to say that "the meaning" of any of these—or other—philosophers' texts rests in the author's biography. Meaning emerges as readers interpret texts from, and in, their own contexts. It is simply to say, as we noted, that biography materially affects philosophy; in other words, all texts, including philosophical ones, reflect the lived experiences of their authors. Although there is only space here to sketch this claim, we believe that, in these five cases, formative experiences with similar features materially affected the authors' philosophies of dialogue.

For example, David Bohm "experienced a difficult childhood" (Pruyn, 2000) not only because he was a Jew living in America but also because of his mother's mental illness. After a promising start as an intellectual (Caltech, Berkeley, an appointment in physics at Princeton), he was driven into exile by McCarthyism, and despite his friendship with Einstein, was ignored or ridiculed by many colleagues for his mysticism. Buber's parents were divorced, his precociousness made him "odd" as a child, he was driven from his Austrian home by the Nazis, and he lived in continuous conflict with xenophobic and anti-Arab leaders in Israel (Friedman, 1981, 1983b, 1983c; Gordon, 1988). As for Freire, the 1929 market crash meant that "the precarious stability of Freire's middle-class family gave way and he found himself sharing the plight of 'the wretched of the earth.' This had a profound influence on his life as he came to know the gnawing pangs of hunger" (Shaull, 1990, p. 10). Freire dedicated his life to a philosophy of education that was responsive to the existential crisis he experienced and saw before him.

Simply to survive, Gadamer and Bakhtin had to cope with two of the 20th century's most repressive political regimes, Nazism and Stalinism. Gadamer experienced "living a single life in a historical sequence of four German states, with the corresponding social and psychological challenges this posed to the unity of that life" (Sullivan, in Gadamer, 1985, p. viii). "The carnage of the First World War, the normative disorientation of the Weimar period, . . . the threatening atmosphere of the early Nazi years," Allied bombing, and post-war guilt and prosperity all unfolded in Gadamer's long life (p. viii). By his own account, Gadamer survived Nazism mainly by being unobtrusive, but he also suffered along with many others from wartime deprivation and, sometimes uniquely, from hostile and personalized scholarly politics (Gadamer, 1997).

Bakhtin's life was even more complicated and precarious. He was an intellectual of 23 when the Russian revolution completely overturned his society and culture. His thinking was strongly influenced by the both-objects-and-mind constructivism of neo-Kantianism and relativity theory as it was developed by Planck and Einstein. Physically crippled by polio and politically suspect, he lived through the early 1920s in Petrograd "on the earnings his wife eked out by making stuffed animals from old rags" (Holquist, 1990, p. 7). He was arrested in 1929 and exiled to Kazakhstan, barely escaped the great purge of 1937, and then suffered through the German occupation. After World War II, his fortunes, like Gadamer's, changed dramatically, but by then his philosophy was already well-developed.

Of course, millions of others who matured during the first half of the 20th century experienced similar instability and upheaval. But not all dedicated themselves, as did these five, to reflecting on and working out the implications for human meaning-making of their life-experiences. We believe that it is of more than passing interest that all of these prominent philosophers of dialogue lived lives in which negotiating political, economic, social, personal, and religious tensions was a way of life, and that from each of their lives emerged coherent philosophies that privileged the relationship between uncertainty, context-dependence, and dynamic change, and their counterparts.

Communication Focus

It is also obviously important that all five of these dialogic thinkers, each for different reasons, turned their primary philosophical attention to human communication. While their philosophical contemporaries, following Einstein, Marx, Freud, Kant, and Darwin, reflected on such topics as relationships between space and time, power in politics, the psyche and its analysis, social evolution, and economics and social class, these five reflected primarily on the human-defining and culture-constituting events of meaning-making that occur in verbal-nonverbal language.

Why were they focally interested in communication? This is another interesting question that we can only sketch a response to here. The so-called "linguistic turn" in philosophy and the other human sciences (e.g., Rorty, 1967) had to have influenced each, given that it emerged as an intellectual force in the West early in the 20th century and continues to the present day. To some degree these five also read similar works—and each other's. Friedman (2001) emphasizes the close intellectual relationships between Buber and Bakhtin. In addition, Buber, Gadamer, and Bakhtin were all influenced by Kant and the neo-Kantianism of the Marburg School in Germany. Bakhtin, Gadamer, and Freire studied and cited Buber. Bohm and Bakhtin were strongly influenced by Planck and Einstein; Gadamer and Buber reacted—in different ways—to aspects of Heidegger's writings; and all five philosophers responded, again in different ways, to Marx. Ultimately, however, their strong desires to improve human understanding and praxis, combined with their holistic and tensional habits of mind, led them to focus on local events of human meaning-making as they are negotiated in discourse. Thus, in at least a major part of their professional activities, they became philosophers of communication.

Communication as Dialogue

All five of these philosophers used the same term to label the kind of communication they took most seriously: dialogue. As each encountered the term, it already had a life of its own. It meant conversation—especially in novels and plays—and, as we noted, it still does. In philosophy, the term identified a discursive form favored by Plato and those who wished to develop ideas similarly, a form that Gadamer (1980) argued embodies the content of Plato's philosophizing. But as each of the five appropriated the term, he imbued it with special significance.

As the chronologically senior member of this group, Buber's appropriation of this label has been most influential. Importantly, the word *dialogue* does not appear in his seminal work, *I and Thou*. Six years after he completed that book, Buber published an essay designed to respond to questions from its readers and, as he put it, "clarify the . . . principle presented in *I and Thou*" (Buber, 1965a, p. xi). The name Buber gave his central insight is "the dialogical principle" and hence this interpretive essay is titled, "Dialogue."

As we noted, the "principle of human life" that Buber presented in *I and Thou* is a description of the relationship between the world and what Buber calls the human's "twofold" orientation. Buber lays out this principle in the first two stanzas of this work (Stewart, 1994), and by his own account (Buber, 1967b) all his voluminous writings after the publication of *I and Thou* were designed, in one way or another, to develop and apply this principle. Especially when *I and Thou* first appeared in 1923, the principle was philosophically newsworthy because it denied the adequacy of the dominant claim that the human's orientation to the world is "onefold." At least since the Enlightenment, western philosophy had understood humans to relate to what they encounter in one or another kind of subject–object way; in Dallmayr's (1984) words, "the Cartesian *ego cogito* has served as a central metaphysical pillar of the modern era" (p. ix). Buber's central claim was that there is another mode of encounter that exists as a counterpart to, and in tension with subject–object (I-It) relating, and this is the I-Thou encounter. The purpose of *I and Thou* is to explain this twofold orientation as it is embodied in meetings with nature, other humans, and God. Because a central and crucial feature of this orientation is that it "is twofold in accordance with the two basic words [humans] can speak" (Buber, 1970, p. 53), Buber's explanation constitutes a philosophy of speech.

The essay, "Dialogue" (Buber, 1965a), begins its illumination of the meaning of this term with two concrete cases, the first a recurrent dream that Buber reported and the second a hypothetical example about two strangers seated together in silence, one historically shackled by "reserve" and the other more open. For some reason, the spell of closure and hiding is broken for the one and, without speaking, "he releases in himself a reserve over which only he himself has power." The other "receives it unreservedly as he receives all genuine destiny that meets him." Here, "even wordlessly . . . the word of dialogue has happened sacramentally" (p. 4).

This is the first of Buber's uses of the word *dialogue* as a label for a quality of contact that is characterized, as he clarified in *I and Thou,* by speaking-and-listening in which the communicators mutually manifest senses of uniqueness, presentness, immeasurability, evanescence, and ineffability (Buber, 1970, pp. 82–85). This quality of contact happens at least paradigmatically—and perhaps exclusively—between two persons. Although "sacramental" to human being, it is not an esoteric, mystical, or even extremely unusual quality of contact. Opportunities for it exist routinely, Buber insisted, on the shop floor, in the bus, in the classroom, in the office of the physician or counselor, at home, and in the air raid shelter. He was motivated to write about this quality of contact—or, more accurately, about this quality and its counterpart—because it had been effaced by modern instrumental rationality and the patterns, structures, and systems of human relating that it spawned (Buber, 1967b, p. 704).

In short, *dialogue,* for Buber, is the label for a quality of contact that exists for humans in tension with instrumental and objective contact. This quality is the birthright of every human being; many human inventions and institutions place obstacles in the way of this kind of contact; yet, it remains the site of human becoming. If appropriately facilitated, this quality of contact can enhance understanding, learning, medicine, family life, business, politics, and recreation.

Freire's understanding of dialogue is very close to Buber's. For Freire, speech communication is the identifying feature of humanity, as it is for Buber (Freire, 1990, p. 76). Speech that is monologic, which might involve slogans, instructions, and communiqués, is partial, oppressive, and limits authentic praxis. Freire (1990) wrote,

> if it is in speaking their word that [humans], by naming the world, transform it, dialogue imposes itself as the way by which [humans] achieve significance as [humans]. Dialogue is thus an existential necessity. And since dialogue is the encounter in which the united reflection and action of the dialoguers are addressed to the world which is to be transformed and humanized, this dialogue cannot be reduced to the act of one person's "depositing" ideas in another, nor can it be a simple exchange of ideas to be "consumed" by the discussants. (p. 77)

For Freire, the quality of contact he called dialogue requires love, humility, and faith. "Faith in [the hu]man is an *a priori* requirement for dialogue," but not a naive one. "The dialogical [hu]man is critical" and yet also optimistic (p. 79). "Only dialogue, which requires critical thinking, is also capable of generating critical thinking. Without dialogue, there is no communication, and without communication there can be no true education" (p. 81). In Freire's philosophy, dialogue serves primarily to transform education and empower the oppressed. He did not limit its occurrence to two people, but he did argue that there must be two perspectives or tensional positions represented, such as those of student/teacher or oppressor/oppressed.

As we noted, Freire's treatment of dialogue was in the service of his transforming praxis; his primary goal was to equip people for dialogic encounters that would help them name their worlds. As an educator, he found that as persons became better able to speak their truths, their worlds were transformed and they were unwilling to be viewed or to view others simply as objects (Freire, 1998). Participants in dialogue engage praxically *with* one another, not *for* or *about* the other. For Freire, the goal of dialogue is not to persuade the other but, through understanding of another as other, to transform the issue and the quality of contact between those in a similar or common struggle.

Bohm also used the term *dialogue* to label a quality of human contact, even though he drew on sources very different from Buber's and Freire's and described some features of this contact differently. Whereas Buber's tendency to offer two-person examples influenced interpreters to conceive of dialogue as primarily a dyadic event, Bohm argued that "any number of people can engage in Dialogue . . . but the sort of Dialogue that we are suggesting involves a group of between twenty and forty people seated in a circle talking together" (Bohm, Factor, & Garrett, 1991, para. 13). Bohm (1996) emphasized that the *dia* in the word dialogue means "through," not "two." *Logos*, he noted, means (among other things) "meaning," and thus

> the picture or image that this derivation suggests [for the term "dialogue"] is of a *stream of meaning* flowing among and through us and between us. This will make possible a flow of meaning in the whole group, out of which may emerge some new understanding. . . . And this shared meaning is the glue or cement that holds people and societies together. (p. 6)

Bohm argued that this quality of contact occurs when persons practice "suspension," which, as we noted earlier, permits them to transcend the fragmentation of thought learned throughout their lives and participate through dialogue in a common consciousness. Thus, in dialogue, each person does not attempt to *make common* certain ideas or items of information that are already known. To attempt this would be to reduce human communication to message-transmission-and-reception. "Rather, it may be said that the two people are making something *in common,* i.e., creating something new together" (Bohm, 1996, p. 2).

For Bohm, the payoff for this effort is the energy or power of a "common consciousness" (1990, p. 33), and this power comes from making a group's communicating congruent with the whole and ordered nature of ultimate reality itself, as this reality is understood by theoretical physics. This power can be harnessed to promote organizational and individual transformation.

Despite Gadamer's prominence as a philosopher of dialogue, the term itself is not as prominent in his corpus as in works by the other four. His one work with dialogue in its title is a collection of Plato studies (Gadamer, 1980), and his comments about I-Thou relating, for example, in *Truth and Method,* appropriate a good deal of Buber's analysis without either citing him or characterizing the topic as dialogue (Gadamer, 1989b, pp. 250, 358–361, 506, 535). Gadamer's concerns with *phronesis* (i.e., practical wisdom) and situated, discursive meaning-making, however, echo important parts of the central foci of Buber, Bohm, and Freire. For example, part of Gadamer's Plato project was to demonstrate that Plato did not use logically rigorous arguments to establish philosophical theses. Plato employed conversations— dialogues in the traditional sense—to demonstrate that "a live discussion is not at all to be measured by its logical rigor but by its effectiveness in bringing the essence of the subject matter to light to the extent that the limited conditions of any discussion permit" (Smith, in Gadamer, 1980, p. x). Another feature of Plato's dialogues that Gadamer illuminated is that they do not have their origin simply in human agents making "speech acts." Instead, they have the structure of play, a patterned-yet-always-new dynamic that people enter, influence, and are subject to and guided by. Part of what makes Gadamer a philosopher of dialogue, in other words, is his conviction that human truth is finite and emergent: It emerges in the address-and-response of focused conversation and is as context-dependent and dynamic as living conversations themselves.

Gadamer also appropriated the sense that Buber and other writers gave to "a Thou" to describe the quality of discursive engagement that best moves toward truth. As he wrote, "it is clear that the *experience of the Thou* must be special because the Thou is not an object but is in relationship with us" (1989b, p. 358). One approach to the experience of discursive engagement attempts to discover typicalities and make predictions about others; this "is the method of the social sciences, following the methodological ideas of the eighteenth century and their programmatic formulation by Hume" (p. 359). But the highest "type of hermeneutical experience" is open to the Thou truly as a Thou—i.e., not to overlook his[or her] claim but to let him[or her] really say something to us. . . . Without such openness to one another there is no genuine human bond. . . . When two people understand each other, this does not mean that one person "understands" the other. . . . Openness to the other, then, involves recognizing that I myself must accept some things that are against me, even though no one else forces me to do so.

This is the parallel to the hermeneutical experience. I must allow tradition's claim to validity. . . . This too calls for a fundamental sort of openness. (1989b, p. 361)

Gadamer's account of I-Thou relating thus served his hermeneutical project that was focused on written texts. He offered a description of what this essay calls a dialogic quality of discursive contact as a close analogue to how one reads a text for understanding in pursuit of truth. Gadamer was not a philosopher of interpersonal communication, but his is a philosophy of communication-as-dialogue, because, for him, *language,* the site of human understanding, consists of events of discursive engagement in the to-and-fro (play) of question and response between "Thous."

Bakhtin's conception of dialogue emerges out of the tradition of literary criticism that influenced his work. In "The Problem of the Text," Bakhtin (1986) differentiated between dialogue in a "semantic" sense and dialogue "with a Thou." The former highlights the fact that all utterances are responsive in some ways to the discourse that frames them. When dialogue is used in the second sense, it highlights the relationship between two unique "languaging" beings.

Bakhtin's focus on what he calls the *authoring function* of the human echoes aspects of Freire's analysis of dialogue and literacy. For Bakhtin, the authoring function is interpersonal, not social. Dialogue, as the central activity of human beings, requires active involvement with responsive others. Clark and Holquist (1984) argue that Bakhtin's repeated use of the prefix *co-* emphasizes the collaborative construction of meaning. For Bakhtin, the social or relational nature of existence does not emphasize either individualism or socialism, because both "fail to understand the dialogic of the self and other" (Jung, 1990, p. 86). Self and other are always interdependent, an interdependence characterized by Bakhtin as *we.* Each person of the we is unique, and at the same time, they are coauthors of, and active co-participants in the ongoing movement of the we (Jung, 1990, p. 88). As Clark and Holquist summarize,

the key feature of Bakhtin's thought is its attempt to make dialogue possible. Dialogue is understood not merely as the obvious sense of two people conversing. . . . Dialogue is more comprehensively conceived as the extensive set of conditions that are immediately modeled in any actual exchange between two persons but are not exhausted in such an exchange. Ultimately, dialogue means communication between simultaneous differences. (1984, p. 9)

These five authors' accounts of communication as dialogue serve different ends. Buber, Freire, and Bohm urged their readers to practice dialogue as a way of communicating interpersonally with others; Gadamer and Bakhtin promoted dialogic conceptions of understanding. Yet each distinguished dialogue as a quality of contact crucial to his philosophical enterprise.

Conclusion

Scores of authors in many disciplines have described and encouraged dialogue, and this chapter investigated commonalities among five of the most prominent. We have drawn from the lives and works of Buber, Bakhtin, Bohm, Freire, and Gadamer in order to identify habits of mind, conceptual commitments, and experiential bases that they share and that contribute to their philosophies. Our description of commonalities obviously covers over many very important historical, cultural, stylistic, and pragmatic differences among these five philosophers' conceptions of dialogue. These five sets of works demonstrate that writers can come to dialogue along paths leading through philosophical anthropology, education, physics, literary theory, and hermeneutics, and out of cultures that are predominantly Jewish, South American-Marxist, scientific-mystical, German philosophical, and Russian-literary.

And these paths converge. Penman (2000) expresses concern because there "were almost as many different usages of the word [dialogue] as [convention] sessions held." Yet, fundamental similarities are, we believe, more important. Dialogic approaches to communication influenced by these five philosophers are consistently holistic and tensional. When these paths intersect concrete cases, communicative events are described as multidimensional rather than as simply products of rationality, as dynamic rather than static, as emergent rather than defined in advance, as context-dependent, and as processual. Communication "moves" emphasize the whole that includes both reflection *and* analysis, listening *and* speaking. Authenticity is a central topic, ethical issues are foregrounded, collaboration is encouraged, facilitation and coaching are advocated as preferred leadership options, and provisionalism replaces certainty. Thus, along with the discipline of making distinctions, dialogue theorists and practitioners can acknowledge similarities and remember that "ultimately, dialogue means communication between simultaneous differences" (Clark & Holquist, 1984, p. 9).

Notes

1. The authorship of *Marxism and the Philosophy of Language* is disputed. V. N. Volosinov is credited in the 1973 Harvard University Press edition, but other scholars claim that Bakhtin

probably wrote the work. For a summary of this controversy, see Stewart (1995), pp. 165–167. In this chapter, we include this work in Bakhtin's corpus.

2. As Paul Ricoeur (1995) notes, Levinas's account of "the extreme passivity of the condition of being a hostage to the other" also breaks with the relational emphasis of dialogue theorists that we discuss in this chapter.

3. Heidegger's focal interest was the nature of being; his discussions of, for example, everyday Being-with (Heidegger, 1962) and language (Heidegger, 1971a) strongly influenced dialogue theorists, but dialogue was not Heidegger's primary interest. Habermas's language philosophy centers on universal pragmatics, not dialogue. As a critical theorist, power is crucial, and Habermas (1998) acknowledges that communicative action issues from an actor who is in part a product of the events surrounding her and her social and cultural milieu. Again, however, Habermas's main interest is not on what he, his followers, or his critics, call dialogue.

4. We are persuaded by arguments about the conceptual importance of these experiential bases in the growing body of works by philosophical biographers such as Ott (1993), Cook (1993), Safranski (1998), Matustik (2001), and Menand (2001). Like these authors, we believe that philosophies are biographical in important and substantive ways.

5. Rather than reinscribing the sexist language of these classic works or inserting "or she," we adopt this convention to emphasize the "humanity" meaning of the general male pronoun. We leave book and essay titles in their original form.

6. Buber notes that Kant's *Handbook* described the field of philosophy as the pursuit of four questions: "1. What can I know? 2. What ought I to do? 3. What may I hope? 4. What is [the hu]man? Metaphysics answers the first question, ethics the second, religion the third, and anthropology the fourth." Thus, philosophical anthropology "would be the fundamental philosophical science" (Buber, 1965a, p. 119).

7. Michael Theunissen's (1984) classic study of the social ontologies of Husserl, Heidegger, Sartre, and Buber highlights this feature.

8. The term *subject–subject* is misleading in that this mode of relating, Buber argues, occurs prior to any distinction in consciousness between subject and object. We use the term here because it contrasts conveniently with subject–object.

3

Taking a Communication Perspective on Dialogue

W. Barnett Pearce and Kimberly A. Pearce

The virtues of dialogue have been hailed in a variety of social contexts, including management, conflict resolution, community-building, interpersonal relations, and personal development (see, e.g., Chasin, Herzig, Roth, Chasin, Becker, & Stains, 1996; Dixon, 1996; Saunders, 1999; Yankelovich, 1991). Because most of these persons are not connected with our home academic discipline, we are glad that communication scholars have accepted the challenge of exploring the implications of society's new experience with dialogue for understanding and practicing communication. However, our interest also runs in what we might call the other direction. In addition to asking what dialogue has to offer communication, we wonder what communication theory and research might offer for understanding and practicing dialogue.

Until recently, the disciplinary study of communication has apparently had little impact on the development of thought and practice of dialogue. To the best of our knowledge, none of the seminal figures in dialogue formally studied communication and none based their thinking about dialogue on theories of communication. For example, although the first chapter of David Bohm's (1996) *On Dialogue* is titled "Communication," the short (four page) treatment shows no connection to the scholarly work done by the academic discipline of communication. Martin Buber's (1958) work was grounded in his philosophical investigations of the qualities of different forms of interpersonal relationships. Mikhail Bakhtin's concept of dialogue emerged from a preoccupation with language and literature from the perspective that "No word can be taken back, but the final word has not yet been spoken and never will be spoken" (Morson & Emerson, 1990, p. 52). In a similar manner, most practitioner organizations that focus on dialogue ground their work on sources other than communication theory and research. For example, the Public Conversations Project applies concepts from family therapy to the public discourse (Chasin et al., 1996); the National Issues Forum grounds their work on classical models of deliberation (Mathews, 1994, pp. 111–116); and Study Circles (2002) develop their practices on concepts of participatory democracy.

Although these thinkers and practitioners have somehow managed to overcome the handicap of not knowing communication theory and research (please read the preceding phrase as written with an ironic chuckle), we wonder how their thinking about dialogue might have differed if they had been acquainted with a robust theory or two of communication. Our curiosity is intensified because we realize that our own work as dialogic practitioners has distinctive elements that, for good or ill, result from our involvement with a particular theory of communication. In this chapter, we describe the ways this theory has informed our work, seeing this as a first step in exploring the potential for enriching dialogic practice from the basis of communication theory.

We are scholar-practitioners, deliberately working as "practical theorists" (Cronen, 2001) in whom theory and practice are fully integrated. As theorists, we have been involved in the development of the theory of the "coordinated management of meaning" or CMM (Pearce, 1999; Pearce & Pearce, 2000); as practitioners, we are founding members of the Public Dialogue Consortium (PDC; www.publicdialogue.org) and Pearce Associates (www.pearceassociates. com). The PDC is a nonprofit organization intending to improve the quality of public communication about public issues (Spano, 2001, pp. 29–36), and Pearce Associates is a consulting firm specializing in dialogic communication.

Dialogue From the Perspective of CMM

We use four key CMM concepts to explore dialogue: the communication perspective, coherence, coordination, and mystery. The most basic of these is the knack of looking *at* communication, not *through* it to things that are thought to be more real or substantial. We call this *the communication perspective*.

THE COMMUNICATION PERSPECTIVE

The communication perspective names an insight that Richard McKeon (1957) described in this way: "Communication does not signify a problem newly discovered in our time, but a fashion of thinking and a method of analyzing which we apply in the statement of all fundamental problems" (p. 89). Note that the "communication perspective" is a non-totalizing *perspective*. It proposes that we see events and objects as textures of communication; it does not make the "nothing-but" argument that events and objects are *only* patterns of communication.

Taking the communication perspective involves three steps. The first step consists of seeing organizations, families, persons, and nations as deeply textured clusters of persons-in-conversation. A family can be seen as constituted by the conversations that it permits and those that it does not, and by the people whom it allows to participate in certain conversations. The structure of the family is changed if, for example, the children are included in conversations that they have previously been excluded from, or if events or some outside person initiates a conversation unlike those that currently constitute the family (Cronen & Pearce, 1985; Stone, Patton & Heen, 1999). In a similar way, organizations can be seen as clusters of conversations and managers as orchestrating conversations rather than embodying information or power. Matters of efficiency, morale, productivity, and conflict can be handled by attention to what conversations occur, where, with what participants, in what type of language, and about what topics (Barrett, 1998; Cooperrider & Whitney, 2002; Kegan & Lahey, 2001). Much of the work of the Public Dialogue Consortium consists of starting conversations and shaping them. That is, we bring people into conversations who would ordinarily not talk to each other or, if they did, would talk *at* rather than *with* each other, and we facilitate the development of certain qualities of conversation in contexts where these qualities do not ordinarily occur. By focusing on the form of communication with principled disinterest in the topic and neutrality toward positions about those topics, we have been able to bring about significant change in the social worlds of participants (Spano, 2001).

The second step in the communication perspective is the realization that communication is substantial and that its properties have consequences. Tannen (1999) noted that public discourse in America is dominated by adversarial forms of communication. Although not denying the value and situational virtue of standing against that which one does not support, she calls into question the preference for

> using opposition to accomplish *every* goal, even those that do not require fighting but might also (or better) be accomplished by other means, such as exploring, expanding, discussing, investigating, and the exchanging of ideas suggested by the word "dialogue." I am questioning the assumption that *everything* is a matter of polarized opposites, the proverbial "two sides to every question" that we think embodies open-mindedness and expansive thinking. (p. 8)

Some consequences of this quality of public discourse include simplifying complex issues (into just two sides), eliminating possibilities for creative solutions not prefigured in the positions initially proposed, creating animosities and enemies who sometimes are more concerned with winning the contest with the other than with implementing the best policies, and driving from the public sphere those who do not relish no-holds-barred combat.

When comparing our ways of thinking about dialogue with others, it is perhaps significant that we usually work with groups who already see each other as enemies or opponents and have an established pattern of animosity and conflict. When we bring these persons and groups together, we note the importance of such "minor" matters as how a question is phrased, whether a statement is followed by a counterstatement or a question, nuances of timing and tones of voice, and the pattern of who responds to whom.

Communication is not a neutral vehicle by which an external reality is communicated about, and by which factors of psychology, social structure, cultural norms, and the like are transmitted or are influential. The communication process (a) exerts a role in the personal identities and self-concepts experienced by persons; (b) shapes the range of permissible and impermissible relationships between persons, and so produces a social structure; and (c) represents the process through which cultural values, beliefs, goals, and the like are formulated and lived (Sigman, 1995, p. 2).

Because communication is both material and consequential, rather than ask "what is it about?," we ought at least also to ask, "how is it possible for a turn of phrase (or other behavior) to emerge during interaction and to shape, in an unplanned-for manner, ensuing behavioral production?" (Sigman, 1995, p. 4).

The third step in the communication perspective consists of treating such things as beliefs, personalities, attitudes, power relationships, and social and economic structures as *made*, not *found*. From this perspective, they are seen as constituted in patterns of reciprocated communicative action (Pearce, 1989, pp. 3–31). The term *constituted* stands in the place of other verbs that connote different and, we believe, less useful concepts—forms of the verb *to be*, for instance, describe things as static and direct our attention to what they are made of and to their causes or effects. On the other hand, the term *constitute* directs our attention to *how* the events and objects of our social world are made.

For example, many people had asked what the carved stone heads on Easter Island meant, and suggested that they were evidence of Egyptian seafarers or monuments to aliens from space. At least as described in his own account of the events, Thor Heyerdahl (1960) employed a different method that generated very different results. He asked a native of the island if he could make one of the megalithic statues. When told that he could, Heyerdahl hired him to do so and filmed the process from beginning to end. Not only a clever way of outflanking interminable arguments among armchair pundits, what we like to call the *Heyerdahl solution* involves a major philosophical shift: describing the processes by which things are made rather than analyzing the final product.

In many ways, the communication perspective simply consists of applying the Heyerdahl Solution to such things as arguments, political policies, and interpersonal relationships. Like Heyerdahl, we shift from asking about what they *are* and begin to look at how they are *made* (Pearce, 1994, pp. 66–70).

The more traditional way of thinking about communication describes messages as expressing meanings or referring to events and objects. Taking the communication perspective, we speak rather of meanings, personalities, acts, institutions, and so forth as being constituted in communication, and of specific messages as responding to and eliciting other messages. Penman (2000) described her adoption of the communication perspective this way:

> I first began . . . with a seemingly innocent and obvious question: "What makes a good relationship?" It soon became apparent, at least to me, that this question needed to be reworded to "What makes a good communication process?" Communication is the observable practice of a relationship, and so it was to the actual process of communicating that I had to attend. (p. 1)

Although everyone acknowledges that dialogue has something to do with communication, many treatments look "through" communication to see something else that is considered more real or important. We are experimenting with the idea of radically foregrounding communication—what people actually say and do in specific contexts—to an extent that, we think, extends beyond others who are at the cutting edge of this field. When we read Isaacs (1999), we get the impression that "suspending assumptions" is the foregrounded aspect of dialogue, and that what people actually do and say is a means to that end. Gergen, McNamee, and Barrett (2001) and Cissna and Anderson (1998b) pay considerable attention to the give-and-take of communication, but, again, we get the impression that communication is understood in service to developing something else, such as "transcendent vocabularies" on which people may draw or the quality of interpersonal relationships. With deep respect to these theorists, we are still curious about what would happen if we were to follow more radically Penman's (2000, p. 1) lead and think of "the actual process of communicating" as constituting dialogue.

The practitioners whose work we have studied distinguish among dialogue, discussion, diatribe, and debate, noting that these forms of communication lead to substantially different outcomes (e.g., Chasin et al., 1996; Tannen, 1999). Like them, we believe that forms of communication are material, calling forth different ways of being in the participants and providing different affordances and constraints. Dixon (1996) described dialogue as talk—a special kind of talk—that affirms the person-to-person relationship between discussants and which acknowledges their collective right and intellectual capacity to make sense of the world. Therefore, it is not talk that is "one way," such as a sales pitch, a directive, or lecture; rather it involves mutuality and jointness. (p. 24)

Listening for understanding (rather than to find the flaw in the other's position) is easy when communicating dialogically but difficult in the reciprocated diatribe of a political campaign; expressing one's own commitments without eliciting an attack or being dismissed is possible when communicating dialogically but is virtually impossible when debating. Emotion, passion, confrontation, and challenge occur within dialogue, just as they do within other forms of communication (Pearce, 1995), but do so "within bounds that affirm the legitimacy of others' perspectives" (Dixon, 1996, p. 24), and these bounds enable very different things to be done with these emotions and in these relationships.

Taking a communication perspective, we want to go further than to differentiate dialogue from nondialogic forms of communication. Relevant questions include "how is dialogue made in communication?" and "what is made by dialogic communication?" (Kearney, 2002; Pearce, 1989, pp. 23–31). In the following paragraphs, we describe how these questions have directed our inquiry.

We noted that various practitioners use the term *dialogue* differently, both in terms of what they refer to as dialogue and in the grammars they use when talking about it. Here are two examples of grammar that fell heavily on our ears. A consultant coming to our area offered to "do a dialogue" for a client organization, pro bono. What is dialogue that one person can "do" it for another, even if pro bono? A participant in an online forum about the use of dialogue in organizational development, after acknowledging what had been said in the previous posting, described herself as "wondering why . . ." and then added, as a parenthetical comment, "Sorry if this inquiry sounds indirect but I was trying to ask the question dialogically rather than as a direct question." Is a direct question incompatible with dialogue? Is it impossible to ask direct questions dialogically? We think that there are clouds of philosophy in drops of grammar, and that these patterns of speech constitute different ideas about dialogue.

To explore these differences, we analyzed transcripts of conversations that the participants named as dialogues (Pearce & Pearce, 2000). We recognize that each transcript underrepresents the complexity, overrepresents the coherence, and misrepresents the fluidity of the grammar of practice of which it is a part. However, our study identified two traditions of practice with subtle but perhaps important differences in their concepts of dialogue.

One tradition uses dialogue as a noun naming a type of communication that is different from others. These practitioners work to create a stable "container" in which participants can engage in dialogue. They often describe dialogue as having no agenda or specific purpose other than "thinking together." In our observations, the form of communication within this container consists of the serial repetition of a single speech act with three parts. The speaker first acknowledges the preceding statement, perhaps by paraphrasing or expressing thanks for the contribution; performs a segue such as "that makes me think of;" and then states what she or he is currently thinking. The speech act is performed well when spoken "to the center of the room" and avoiding "interpersonal dynamics" (Isaacs, 1999, p. 380). Following these rules, it makes sense to offer "to do a dialogue for you," and asking a direct question is out-of-bounds because it risks "falling out of dialogue" and into interpersonal dynamics.

This tradition of practice has been widely used in corporate America and there are several professional consulting groups who offer training and facilitations (e.g., Dialogue Group, 2002). Those experienced in it claim that this kind of dialogue makes it possible for groups to think in a particularly useful way.

> Dialogue transforms the quality of tacit thinking that underlies all interactions. It thereby adds to these practices an in-the-moment insight and reflective quality that transcends the mechanical application of theories. In dialogue, people interact in a way that "suspends" habitual thought and action. They become free to engage in inquiry, about both the quality of interpersonal reasoning, and the nature of the underlying shared ground of meaning in which they interact. Even in high-stakes situations, percussive conflict is replaced with breakthroughs in collaborative inventiveness. (DIA•logos, 2001)

We identify with a different set of practitioners, who use *dialogic* as an adjective or adverb describing a distinctive quality of communication in which any speech act can be performed. Rather than naming some forms of communication as dialogue and contrasting it with other forms, such as *discussion, debate,* or *monologue,* these practitioners refer to a distinctive quality of "dialogic communication" or "communicating dialogically" that can be done in any form of communication. When communicating dialogically, one can listen, ask direct questions, present one's ideas, argue, debate, and so forth (Pearce, 1995). The defining characteristic of dialogic communication is that all of these speech acts are done in ways that hold one's own position but allow others the space to hold theirs, and are profoundly open to hearing others' positions without needing to oppose or assimilate them. When communicating dialogically, participants often have important agendas and purposes, but make them inseparable from their relationship in the moment with others who have equally strong but perhaps conflicting agendas and purposes.

The dialogic quality of speech acts is often achieved by verbal or nonverbal metacommunication (e.g., "my story about this . . . which might be different from yours . . . is that . . ."), the help of a facilitator, or the careful design of meetings. Dialogue happens in what Cissna and Anderson (1998b) call "moments of meeting" in which people respond to others as *Thou* rather than *it,* using Martin Buber's (1958, p. 4) terms, and find themselves transformed because the *I* of I-thou is not the same as the *I* of I-it. Such moments cannot be made to happen or delivered on schedule as a package.

> Dialogue thrives at the margins of human agency—those ill-defined situations in which we imagine we are somewhat in control but in which our plans surprisingly can blend into the unexpected. . . . Dialogue, which cannot be mandated, rarely happens accidentally either. (Anderson, Cissna, & Arnett, 1994, p. xxi)

However, if we attend to the quality of what people actually say and do in communicating with each other, then we think we have a better idea of how to invite and prepare the conditions for these moments to occur.

Practitioners in this second tradition tend to work in public or community contexts, often with people who are deeply committed to opposing political or social positions. Exemplary organizations include the Public Conversations Project (2002), Study Circles (2002), and the Public Dialogue Consortium (2002). Among these groups, the PDC's work is distinctive in that our work is explicitly based on communication theory and our practice includes members of the public discussing community issues in public meetings. Because we do not know who will attend until they arrive at the door, our ability to select and work with participants before the meetings is limited. This circumstance makes us stress careful design of these meetings and the use of trained facilitators. We spend a good bit of time training community members to facilitate conversations among their peers about issues they perceive as very important.

Hundreds of people, including middle school children, adult professionals, and seniors, have participated in training to learn to facilitate dialogic communication. The normal profile of participants in our training is a group of 20–30 volunteers representing a cross section of the community in which we are working. In our opinion, there is a turning point in the learning curve of most participants, occurring much sooner for some than for others, when they "get" what we are trying to teach. They begin to respond to novel situations in ways consistent with the grammar of dialogic communication and act with a high degree of self-confidence. We believe that this happens when they put together two concepts: the communication perspective, which focuses on communication itself, and the characteristics of dialogic communication, as the specific, desired quality of communication. In our workshops, we describe dialogic communication as remaining in the tension between standing your own ground and being profoundly open to the other.

The challenge in our work as practitioners is facilitating people not necessarily interested in dialogue to engage in this quality of communication in situations that are not conducive to it. Our attempts to achieve this objective are grounded in concepts from CMM: coherence, coordination, and mystery.

COHERENCE: MAKING MEANING TOGETHER

When CMM was introduced in the late 1970s, the claim that stories were integral to human life was far more controversial than it is now (see Bruner, 1990). Like many other theories, CMM assumes that these meanings take the form of stories. It sees persons as storytellers, attempting to ensconce both the extraordinary and quotidian aspects of our lives within stories that make them coherent. The stories we tell are fateful; they guide and direct the way we feel, think, and act. It is not too much to say that

> human beings [are] storytellers, at once immersed in linguistic webs that they did not spin and busily weaving webs in which to immerse [themselves and] others. Whether these "webs" are imprisoning snares or enabling scaffolds, is, of course, a matter of opinion. (Pearce, 1989, p. 68)

The term *coherence* is used to designate human activity as meaning-making, not as a judgment about the success of that process. As all researchers who have studied transcripts of actual conversations know, people seldom say all that they expect other people to hear them as having said, and sometimes say something quite different from what they expect to be heard as having said, but usually treat others as if they are responding to what they intended to be heard as having said. Our first clue for this insight came from analysis of ordinary conversation (Pearce & Conklin, 1979) and was supported by our studies of the desiccated discourse in intractable conflicts (Pearce & Littlejohn, 1997).

Based on these findings, what we call "enriching the conversation" (Pearce, 2002; Pearce & Pearce, 2001) is a key step in our work as dialogic practitioners. We teach facilitators to treat any statement as an anecdote rather than a complete story, and to ask questions inviting the speaker to describe the fuller story, to move among first- and third-person perspectives in telling the story, to probe for untold and unheard stories, to explore the differences between stories lived and stories told, and to bring in other voices to tell the story more systemically (for a description of these "ways of working," see Pearce, 2002; Spano, 2001, pp. 36–44). If we are able to create a situation in which participants feel respected and confident that their interests will be protected, they often welcome the opportunity to speak more fully than usual about the things that matter most to them, and in this process, both they and those listening to them discover new richness in their stories and find openings to move forward together.

CMM's "hierarchy model of actors' meanings" (Pearce, Cronen, & Conklin, 1979) is a useful tool for enriching conversations and for understanding the complex role of those who facilitate dialogue. Building on Bateson's (1972) use of the idea of logical types, Watzlawick, Beavin, and Jackson (1967) suggested that communication necessarily involves two levels, such that *relationship* is the context for and functions as a metacommunication about *content*. The idea of contextualization proved very useful. Among other things, it explained how saying the same thing can mean different things depending on the context, and that what is said as content sometimes functions just as a carrier for doing something at the relationship level.

CMM extended the idea of contextualization in several ways (Pearce, Harris, & Cronen, 1981). First, it suggested that we always tell multiple stories—an indefinite number, but always more than just two—about what is going on in any moment in communication. A way of parsing out these stories is that one deals with the relationships among the communicators (as Watzlawick et al. [1967] noted); another with concepts of self; another with the *episode* that the communicators are performing (this is the answer to "what are we doing together?"); and others with situational contexts (e.g., organizational culture, family stories, church, school, or play).

Second, CMM suggested that all of these stories stand in a contextualizing/ contextualized relationship with each other but one in which there is no fixed pattern. That is, "relationship" is sometimes the context for and sometimes contextualized by stories. One of the tasks for interpretive research is to explore not only what stories are being told to make a particular experience coherent, but also their ordinal relationship. The assumption is that some stories are, at any moment in time, at a "higher level" than others, exerting a nonreciprocal contextualizing function over them. The person to whom you are talking may be joking, of course, but it makes some difference if the "joke" is a momentary part of a higher context story about your relationship and what you are doing together, or if the joke is the highest level of context and your relationship and the episode are just part of it.

Third, CMM insisted that both the substance of these stories and the pattern of reciprocal contextualization are mutable. As Sigman noted (1995, p. 4), things that happen in a conversation can change a participant's story about the other participants and what is being done together. But even if the story is not changed, its position within the pattern of which stories are the context for, and which are in the context of, other stories can shift, and this may have important consequences. A story that was relatively unimportant can become the overarching context, and vice versa. For example, at the beginning of our public meetings, many participants are primarily concerned with expressing their position and refuting the position of those they perceive as opponents or enemies. As the meeting progresses, their story of the "other" changes;

now they are seen as partners or at least co-stakeholders. Rather than being perceived only as obstacles to achieving one's own goals, others are seen as persons with legitimate goals of their own. The story about the meeting changes from competition to collaboration. But perhaps the most important change is that their story of self (and their own agenda) moves from the highest position of contextualization to one much lower, while the story of episode moves from low to high.

In 1996, the PDC planned and facilitated a Town Hall meeting in Cupertino, California (for a more complete description, see Spano, 2001, pp. 102–115). This meeting followed a series of small group discussions during a 6 month period (for a description, see Spano, 2001, pp. 59–98), in which every group had named the implications of rapidly changing demographics in the community as their most significant concern; several used the phrase "a powder keg waiting to explode." We learned that residents of all racial groups spoke freely in homogeneous meetings, but that no one felt safe enough to talk about the issue publicly.

Although the small group sessions were valuable as a first step in enriching their stories about diversity in Cupertino, the objective of the Town Hall meeting was to help residents talk abut the issue publicly, in a racially heterogeneous meeting, in dialogic communication. We realized that it was important to shift participants' expectations from the Town Hall meeting as a place where they could get on their individual soap boxes to an expectation that they would listen as well as speak, and speak so that others would want to listen to them.

To create the conditions for dialogue, we did several things. During the 2 months before the Town Hall meeting, we trained 70 high school students to interview adults about positive experiences they have had with diversity in the city. Sixteen of these students talked about these interviews during the Town Hall meeting. During the meeting, we also provided an opportunity for residents to talk about their experiences in ways that would enrich the community's understanding of the issue. Among other things, representatives from the small group discussions reported what they had learned in their meetings, and trained facilitators guided small groups at the meeting in reflecting on what was heard.

Toward the end of the meeting, we invited participants to speak to the whole group in something resembling the usual open-microphone format of Town Hall meetings. One speaker was Cupertino resident and school board member Barry Chang. Mr. Chang forcefully articulated the Asian community's sense of living in a contradiction between being blamed for not participating in the community and shut out or accused of trying to "take over" when they tried. This was a hard thing for many in the audience to hear, because they correctly perceived it as an indictment. It could have been the divisive tirade that ignited the powder keg of smoldering resentments on all sides of the issue.

Instead, it was a breakthrough moment of dialogic communication. Both the circumstances and the manner in which he spoke enabled even those who were being accused of treating Asians with contradictory messages to hear what he said and acknowledge his passion. This is a transcript from the videotape of the community access television broadcast of the meeting:

Yes, my name is Barry Chang. I am not Michael Chang's [the first Asian elected to the city council] brother, ok. It just so happens to be the same last name.

I think there's a cultural gap in between, between when we're talking about the diversity here. For example, in my business, I went out door-to-door knocking a lot. I heard a lot of comments that Asian community or Asian owner doesn't participate. They are the takers. They are not the givers. And then, they don't take care of their yard. And when I went back and think about it, where I came from, Taipei, Taiwan, I mean barely you don't have a yard to take care of at all. So we have no custom, no tradition, no habit to take care of the yard. Now we end up here with a big yard and what are you going to do? If you don't do anything in summer, within 2 weeks, it die already. So a lot of those differences, a lot of people don't understand.

And then when I came out running for Cupertino School Board, last year, when Michael and I won, and the local newspaper want to have an article after they interviewed me and Michael, they say they would have an article wrote it in this way. Heading says, "Chang's Dynasty Taking Over Cupertino!" I mean when we're accused not coming to serve, to help, to participate, and then when we come out then they will say you are taking over Cupertino, which is not, you know, doesn't feel quite well from my feeling, so I have to protest.

And also when I started a couple of years ago when I was helping in the school with my wife. Then the other parents asked me "Why don't you help out in the PTA?" and I said, "What's the PTA?" and they say, "It's Parent Teacher Association is helping the school a lot." I went to the PTA meeting and as you men know, most PTA were attended by mother. So when I went over there, I was the few father in there. And added up with when every organization have their ongoing business going on, and when you cut in the middle, you really got lost. Then second, when I sit in there, I heard the mother said "I move this, I move that." I was very puzzled because I thought she was sitting there, she was not moving anywhere. Why is she keep saying "I move this, I move that?" And then someone follow would say "I second" and I was even more puzzled because I feel you don't have to be so humble, no one claim to be the first, why you have to be second. And that's the cultural difference.

Maybe I let you know back in the country where I came from, the government at the time wasn't purposely try to give you the democratic because they know if they give you the democratic, the people will ask for power. So we never been trained that way. So let alone coming here, you get all this different language barrier, and all this format, all this democratic process. So I thought it was someone inside the door waving to people outside "Why don't you come in and help?" and then the people outside couldn't find the door. So that's a situation we have to understand and I think the most important, we have to understand the cultural gap and also the tolerance between each other. And that's my comment. (Applause)

When Barry Chang told his story, the other participants at the meeting had an understanding and appreciation for the difficulties of recent immigrants that they hadn't had before. The ability to talk about diversity (or, as we had heard earlier, "a powder keg waiting to explode") using dialogic communication invites participants into a different kind of relationship with each other, enriching the stories of self, other, and community.

Coordination: Meshing Actions With Others

In addition to being storytellers, human beings are physical entities that occupy space and both respond to and elicit responses from others. From the communication perspective, these patterns of what Shotter (1993a) calls "joint-actions" are real, and their characteristics constitute our social worlds. Although we presented "coordination" after "coherence" in what we have written here, an immersion in language games comes prior to the development of individuals (Beebe & Lachmann, 2002, pp. 38–42; Stern, 2002). Even as adults, conversations are multimodal, with verbal interaction intertwined with intricate patterns of nonverbal cues-and-responses that are at least as important to the conversation although they are usually out of awareness and something about which the conversants have no story (Mehrabian, 1981).

The term *coordination* is used in CMM to direct attention to our efforts to align our actions with those of others. Among other things, the necessity to coordinate with others shows that communication is inherently and fundamentally social. No matter what speech act—whether threat, compliment, instruction, question, insult, or anything else—its successful performance requires not only your actions but the complementary actions of others (Pearce, 1994, pp. 109–125; Shotter, 1993a).

By recognizing the social nature of communication, dialogic communicators are alerted to recognize openings to invite others into dialogue. When others act in ways consistent with, for example, debate or diatribe, we can respond with planned incongruence in ways that have the potential to transform the conversation dialogically. These in-the-moment invitation and facilitation skills involve recognizing the "normal" response to what others say and do, and choosing instead to respond in ways that make a preferred form of communication. What can you say to make a passionate advocate of a position listen respectfully to the passionate advocacy of a different position? How can you act into a situation in such a way that it elicits from others a willingness to treat each other as co-stakeholders rather than enemies? If your goal is to invite people to speak in a manner that others want to listen, and to listen in such a way that others want to speak, what can you do to elicit that response? Much of the work that we do in our training consists of coached practice in these skills (Pearce, 2002, pp. 37–49).

MYSTERY: OPENNESS TO NOVELTY AND
ACKNOWLEDGMENT OF LIMITS

Although *mystery* is one of the least frequently cited concepts in CMM, it is perhaps the most relevant to an understanding of dialogic communication. An explication of this concept grounds a commitment to a life of dialogue, not just as a personal preference or because of its instrumental effects but as prefigured by the nature of communication itself.

Acting like a native in any group or culture involves using particular stories that, among other things, name persons, differentiate among foods that can be eaten raw and those that must be cooked, and evaluate acts by locating them in complex webs of responsibility and morality. A number of stories suffice for members of a group or culture to achieve *coherence* by taming the terrors of history and imposing meaning and order on the world. Further, they can *coordinate* if they make the same—or at least recognizable—nominations, differentiations, and evaluations. However, *mystery* is the reminder that these nominations, differentiations, and evaluations are ultimately arbitrary, and made rather than found. As Gergen (1999) put it, "the terms by which we understand our world and our self are neither required nor demanded by 'what there is.' . . . Every thing we have learned about the world and ourselves . . . could be otherwise" (p. 47).

One reading of mystery—a fairly shallow one, but still sufficient to imply that we should commit ourselves to a life of dialogue—is grounded on the observation that everything in human life can be, and probably has been, ensconced in multiple, contradictory stories, and that people with different life experiences and learning histories find different stories equally compelling.

This observation provokes very different responses, reflecting once again the wisdom of William James's (1975) observation that temperaments—or as he put it, "our more or less dumb sense of what life honestly and deeply means" (p. 9)—direct our theoretical commitments rather than vice versa. Those with a critical commitment can use the fact of multiple, contradictory stories as the basis for careers in which they expose patterns of exploitation and domination in particular stories, seeking to replace those stories with other stories, purportedly more benign or benevolent, and creating a world "in which mutuality predominates and satisfaction does not mean the triumph of one over the repressed needs of the other" (McCarthy, 1979, p. xxiv). On the other hand, the plurality of ways of being human can be seen as a warrant for a life of dialogue, in which those who are "natives" of different social worlds are enabled to achieve communication with each other, starting with an appreciative celebration of the richness of human experience rather than the immediate categorization into better and worse. This temperament resonates with Clifford Geertz's (1983) poetic pronouncement:

To see ourselves as others see us can be eye-opening. To see others as sharing a nature with ourselves is the merest decency. But the far more difficult achievement is that of seeing ourselves amongst others, as a local example of the forms human life has locally taken: a case among cases; a world among worlds. Without this largeness of mind, objectivity is self-congratulation and tolerance a sham. (p. 16)

A more radical and controversial concept of mystery focuses on the power of language and, in our judgment, unequivocally leads to a commitment to dialogic communication. The most common way of framing this discussion—but not the route that we follow—starts with the question of whether we are able to say what is "there" in nonlinguistic reality. Imagine a continuum in which those on one side say that nothing can be "said" as it is, and on the other side, that everything—or at least everything important—can be said and said well. The second side of this continuum is anchored by John Searle's (1969) "principle of effability," which declares that everything that can be thought can be said, and said clearly. Not far from this extreme position is the earlier Wittgenstein's (1921) dictum that "everything that can be said can be said clearly, but not everything can be said," and Steiner's (1967, p. 12) claim that "all truth and realness—with the exception of a small, queer margin at the very top—can be housed inside the walls of language." Kenneth Gergen's social constructionist position represents the extreme position on the other side. According to Gergen (1994), there is an inherent disconnect between what we say and what we are talking about. "The terms by which we account for the world and ourselves are not dictated by the stipulated objects of such accounts" (p. 49). Rather, he said, they "are social artifacts, products of historically and culturally situated interchanges among people" (p. 49) that have more to do with social processes than to the "objective validity of the account" (p. 51).

Our preferred way of framing the concept of mystery avoids this continuum of effability. Instead, it focuses on the work that language does rather than on that to which it refers. From this perspective, even Searle's principle of effability is seen as underrepresenting the power of language. Language does not just name the things of our experience, it creates them. The problem with words is not that they are too vague; it is that they are too precise. When something is named, language seduces us to forget all the other names that might have been used and all the other stories in which it might have been included. But moving beyond the linguistic function of naming, the communicative act of making speech acts requires not only a story, but the *telling* of a story—and this story is told by a specific person, in a specific language (dialect and all), and is told in a specific time and place (limited by acoustics, interrupted by other storytellers, etc.). Further, speech acts are not completed until they are responded to, and that response elicits another, and so on. As Shotter (1991) noted:

Everyday human activities do not just *appear* vague and indefinite because we are still as yet ignorant of their true underlying nature, but they are *really* vague . . . the fact is, there is no order, no already determined order, just . . . an order of possible orderings which it is up to us to make as we see fit. And this, of course . . . is exactly what we require of language as a means of communication: we require the words of our language to give rise to vague, but not wholly unspecified "tendencies" which permit a degree of further specification *according to the circumstances of their use,* thus to allow the "making" of precise and particular meanings appropriate to those circumstances. (p. 202)

The communication perspective focuses on the question of what is "made" by particular instances of communication. This creative aspect of communication is so powerful that it not only creates, but it also necessarily destroys. In any given moment of communication, the actor must act, but can only make real one of the many potential acts that he or she could potentially have performed. In this way, each momentary action destroys a myriad of potential social worlds. The stories we tell and the patterns of coordinated actions we engage in are, at last, understood simultaneously as scaffolds for comprehending and moving effectively in our world, and as snares that not only blind us to alternatives, but destroy other possible ways to be ourselves, to be in relationships, and to be in community.

Mystery is not so much an attempt to describe unnamable things in the world or to know the potential worlds displaced by the worlds we have created together, but is a persistent reminder that the worlds we know are only some of the many that exist, might have existed, or might yet exist, and that the lives we live are contingent on the interaction of our choices and circumstances. There is a kind of liberation that comes from being aware that there is always something more to every story and that every situation is unfinished (Gergen, 1999, pp. 47–48; Pearce, 1989, pp. 82–86).

As Shands (1971) expresses,

The problem is words. Only with words can man become conscious; only with words learned from another can man learn how to talk to himself. Only through getting the better of words does it become possible for some, a little of the time, to transcend the verbal contexts and to become, for brief instants, free. (pp. 19–20)

Dialogic communication is one way of achieving what Shands called "getting the better of words."

Concluding her review of approaches to dialogue in the business setting, Dixon (1996) defined the purpose of dialogue as

the intent to uncover that which is tacit—to become aware of the paradigm in which those individuals engaged in the dialogue are themselves embedded. By making manifest that which has been taken for granted, the participants in the dialogue are able to hold their assumptions up for examination and, when warranted, to construct new joint meaning that is tested against their reasoning. (p. 25)

That is a laudable goal, but it seems only a small part of what a rich appreciation of mystery would suggest. Both Dixon's approach to dialogue and the one that we have worked with over the years have in common the importance of reflecting on one's own assumptions. Our approach, we think, leads to two additional ideas: (a) understanding that one's own stories are partial, local, limited, or bounded, and (b) realizing the value of remaining in the tension between standing one's own ground and being profoundly open to the other. For this reason, we have usually thought of listening (rather than introspection or telling one's own story) as the most powerful opening for creating dialogic communication. Much of our work in designing and facilitating events focuses on modeling and creating the opportunity for participants to listen to others.

The key insight from mystery is that the world is far richer and subtler than any story we have of it, and that it changes because we perceive it, tell stories about it, and act into it. The good news is that the world contains Others who are not only not us but not like us, and that our relationships with them and even our own selves are transformed if we engage with them dialogically.

Reflections

We began this project with curiosity about a communication approach to dialogue. We posed a counterfactual conditional question: What would have happened if the seminal figures in dialogic thinking and practice had based their work on a formal study of communication? We addressed—rather than answered—this question by reflecting on our own work as dialogic practitioners, noting that our work has been explicitly based on a particular communication theory, the coordinated management of meaning (CMM). On the basis of these reflections, we propose that dialogue can be understood better by articulating the theories of communication on which various concepts and traditions of practice are based. Further, we suggest that new concepts of dialogue and ways of achieving dialogic communication might be found through the elaboration of various theories of communication that we can now access but that were not available to the seminal thinkers in this field.

Working out the implications of theory, or hermeneutically reading the implicit theory presupposed by concepts of dialogue is valuable but is limited in its impact. Any form of practice—not only dialogic practice—is affected by the sensibility, vision, and theory of the practitioner; the habits or models that the practitioner has developed; and the constraints and opportunities of the specific situation. Because these are multiple influences, articulating only the sensibilities, visions, and theories of the practitioner is likely to exaggerate the differences between actual ways of working in specific situations. That is, to the extent that practitioners from different schools of thought confront similar challenges and opportunities, their theoretical differences are likely to be eroded.

That having been said, traditions of practice in dialogic communication differ. Specifically, our work has characteristics that distinguish it from other practitioners, and these stem from our grounding in CMM. We make no assumption that the distinctive characteristics of our work make it better or worse than the work by those informed in other traditions. We do, however, know that our ability to act into difficult situations and to know how to go on as practitioners is greatly enhanced by the temperament that leads us to articulate formally the theory of communication upon which we draw.

4

The Ontological Workings of Dialogue and Acknowledgment

Michael J. Hyde

I write about two related phenomena: dialogue and acknowledgment. What I have to say about the relationship takes form from "the ground up," for I am especially interested in how the ontological nature and workings of the relationship inform our everyday ways of being-with-and-for-others. My discussion, which extends certain considerations of the phenomena that I have detailed in my work on conscience, rhetoric, and the euthanasia debate (Hyde, 1993, 1994, 2001a, 2001b, 2002a; Hyde & Rufo, 2000; Jost & Hyde, 1997; McMillan & Hyde, 2000), emphasizes a phenomenological appreciation of the matter at hand, for I agree with Heidegger (1962), "Only as phenomenology, is ontology possible" (p. 60).

As discussed by various communication and rhetorical scholars who have employed its theoretical orientation in their research, phenomenology defines a way of thinking devoted to disclosing with demonstrative precision the appearing or "presencing" of some phenomenon—how it reveals or manifests itself within the temporal horizon of human understanding. The discourse of phenomenology assumes the hermeneutical task of disclosing a phenomenon's own disclosure, its being and truth (see Deetz, 1973b; Hyde, 2001c; Hyde & Smith, 1979; Johnstone, 1978). Phenomenology thus offers itself as a truth-telling activity, for as Heidegger (1962) points out, truth happens first and foremost as a disclosing of the world, a revealing or uncovering of the "givenness" of something that presents itself to one's consciousness (pp. 256–273).

Heidegger's program of phenomenology, which will serve as a key directive here, lays out a path of thought devoted to developing a comprehensive understanding of the actual happening of this givenness; hence, the question that forever directs his investigations—What is the meaning, the truth, of Being?—and the distinction or "ontological difference" that he is constantly assessing—the difference between Being and beings (Heidegger, 1969). For example, an egg, to be sure, has being, but it certainly is not Being itself. The same can be said about all things (including human beings) that exist in the world. They have being but are not themselves Being. Heidegger is after the meaning of Being, not merely the meaning of some being. Yet, as a phenomenologist, the only way he can approach his particular topic is by seeing and observing how Being shows itself in that which it needs (i.e., beings) in order to be noticed at all. The existence of beings presupposes Being, but Being needs beings so that it can show itself and have its presence affirmed.

My discussion of the ontological relationship between dialogue and acknowledgment unfolds as I first offer some additional observations regarding the happening of such an event of affirmation. With these observations, I emphasize how existence has the structure of a dialogue or conversation and how this structure shows itself most clearly when attended to by way of a specific attunement of consciousness: acknowledgment. Acknowledgment is the modus operandi of phenomenological inquiry. However, it also can be employed as an ethical form of communication behavior that functions dialogically and that manifests itself as a life-giving gift. The dialogical workings of acknowledgment align us with an essential (truthful) aspect of existence: its dialogical structure. In developing this point I supplement Heidegger's teachings with those of Emmanuel Levinas, whose phenomenology of social relationships provides a richer account of the topic than one finds in Heidegger. I also offer a brief case study that illustrates how acknowledgment ought to play a fundamental role in our everyday ways of being-with-and-for-others. The case has come to be known as the "Columbine High School Massacre."

Phenomenology and the Affirmation of Being

The truth of Being is everywhere to be seen and observed. Being is wherever the existence of anything shows itself. The truth of Being is an empirical question, and for Heidegger this truth is most apparent in the existence of that being whose consciousness of the world is most advanced in its related capacities of reflection (critical thinking) and articulation (symbolic expression). Heidegger (1962) initially puts it this way: Human being "is an entity which does not just occur among other entities. Rather it is ontically distinguished by the fact that, in its very Being, that Being is an *issue* for it" (p. 32). In other words, what Heidegger designates as the "special distinctiveness" of human being that differentiates it from other entities is that this entity is concerned with its existence, its Being, its way of becoming what it is. This concern for

Being is constantly demonstrated in one's everyday involvements with things and with others. Reflecting on the meaningfulness of what is being demonstrated, one can, and often does (especially in times of personal crisis), raise the question of what it means to be. The question makes explicit a human being's concern for Being. Only human being is consciously concerned enough to do this. And because it is also capable of understanding to various degrees what it is doing out of concern for its Being, human being can provide an answer to the question. Heidegger (1959) thus tells us that "man should be understood, within the question of Being, as *the* site which Being requires in order to disclose itself. Man is the site of openness, the there," the place within all of existence where Being finds a "clearing" and whereby it can be seen and observed with rigor and care (p. 205).

This specific place, as Heidegger (1993) constantly reminds us, originates with the spatial and temporal structure of human being that—although typically measured by "man" with such inventions as clocks, calendars, maps, and computers—is not itself a human creation. The way in which what was (the past) and what is (the present) are constantly open to the objective uncertainty of what is not yet (the future) defines an event that is always already at work before we decide to notice and to calculate its presence. Human being, in other words, has something about its Being that is more and thus *other* than its own making—something whose objective uncertainty is forever at work in both a "deconstructive" way to call us and our claimed truths into question and in a "reconstructive" way to call on our ability to assume the ethical responsibility of affirming our freedom through resolute choice such that we can maintain some semblance of meaning in the face of uncertainty (Hyde, 2001a, pp. 40–78). Abraham Heschel (1951) has a wonderful way of making the point: "If man is not more than human, then he is less than human. Man is but a short, critical stage between the animal and the spiritual. His state is one of constant wavering, of soaring or descending. Undeviating humanity is nonexistent. The emancipated man is yet to emerge" (p. 211).

From a source of otherness comes a call for concerned thought and action. Heidegger (1972) thereby speaks of the importance of learning how to listen most carefully to the "call of Being," or what he also describes as that primordial "saying" that discloses itself in the "presencing" of all that lies before us and that waits for a genuine response (pp. 1–24; 1971a, pp. 111–156; 1971b, pp. 189–210). The specific "attunement of consciousness" that is required to offer such a response is designated by Heidegger (1977) as "acknowledgment": "Every affirmation [of Being] consists in acknowledgment. Acknowledgment lets that toward which it goes come toward it" (p. 237). Acknowledgment is consciousness "releasing" itself from the instrumental and calculative modes of thought that typically are at work in our habitual ways of being with things and with others, and that dictate, for example, how one might perceive a severely disabled person as someone whose "life is not worth living" (Hyde, 2001a, pp. 204–219). Acknowledgment is consciousness becoming as open-minded as possible to its intended object so as to allow for a "'letting be' of what is." Acknowledgment is consciousness being respectful of the fundamental relationship that holds between human being and the presencing of Being (Heidegger, 1966, 1977). Remember, human being is the "clearing," the site of openness that is needed by Being to disclose itself. Being calls. The phenomenologist, maintaining the receptive and caring outlook of acknowledgment, responds by entering into what Heidegger (1949) describes as a "conversation" with Being. "The foundation of human existence is conversation, in which being is established" (p. 284).

The call of Being; the openness of human being; acknowledgement; conversation: Heidegger would have us keep this process going in the name of a most "awesome" truth: how the existence of human being marks a place in space and time where Being can disclose itself and where we, after careful deliberation, might express (symbolize) this disclosure in language that perhaps can provide direction for the good thought and wise action of others. Heidegger (1949) has in mind such "authentic discourse" when he writes:

> Language is not a mere tool, one of the many which man possesses; on the contrary, it is only language that affords the very possibility of standing in the openness of the existent. Only where there is language, is there world, i.e., the perpetually altering circuit of decision and production, of action and responsibility, but also of commotion and arbitrariness, of decay and confusion. (p. 276)

As it shows itself in all the things and creatures of this earth, Being is in need of humankind's critical and symbolic competence if its call is to be responded to in a way that avoids such chaos as much as possible. Heidegger (1971b) points to the "great work of art" (p. 17) when discussing how acknowledgment and conversation facilitate this response. The talented and devoted artist is committed to remaining open to the presencing of what is so that he or she can maintain a conversation dedicated to having language become more attuned to the way things are disclosing themselves and thus to the truth of what and how they are. Such an evocative use of language is seen, for example, in Lincoln's Gettysburg Address (Hyde & Smith, 1979). Heidegger (1971a) maintains that the ability to express discourse in this manner is the most responsible way to acknowledge Being, for the dialogue going on here, given its subject matter, is obliged to remain open to that which is itself open (the temporality of Being). What is to come? Who can say for sure? The truth of existence announces itself as an objective uncertainty; Being is structured as a challenging call, a question, an ongoing process of deconstruction and reconstruction that, in its own way of disclosing the otherness that it is, tells of the importance of being open to and awed by the truth. In the midst "of commotion and arbitrariness, of decay and confusion," Lincoln's discourse at Gettysburg defined a monumental response to the call of Being (Hyde, 2001c, pp. 332–333).

By way of acknowledgment—which Heidegger (1968) also describes as an act of "devotion" (p. 141)—we enter into a conversation, a dialogue, with Being such that we can return "Being's favor" by giving "thankful" thought to what Being first gives us. The "highest and really most lasting gift given to us," writes Heidegger, "is always our essential nature [the distinctive relationship we hold with Being], with which we are gifted in such a way that we are what we are only through it. That is why we owe thanks for this endowment, first and unceasingly" (p. 142). Giving thanks to Being is, for Heidegger, a matter of the heart, of "taking to heart" what calls on us to think the truth of what is (p. 141).

Referring to the heart in this way is reminiscent of how the Old Testament speaks to us of *conscience,* of that wondrous gift that enables us to be awed by the happenings and mysteries of life and that thereby keeps us in touch with an Almighty call: "I will give them a heart to know me, that I am the Lord" (Jeremiah 23:7), the One whose saying—"Let there be . . ."—brought about the original letting-be of what is. For Heidegger, however, this saying and the gift that goes with it comes from Being—that which needs beings in order to show itself but also that which is more (other) than everything that is. Might it be the case that this otherness of Being is a sign of God's presence?

Heidegger leaves us to answer this question for ourselves. He is doing phenomenology, not theology. Maintaining the open-minded and devotional outlook of acknowledgment—which certainly is a "gift" of Being in that we are "gifted" with the capacity to engage in the act of acknowledging—Heidegger is caught up in a conversation that only human beings can maintain and whose primordial (dialogical) nature establishes the standard for conducting the dialogical interactions of everyday life. Hans-Georg Gadamer's (1989b) comments regarding the "genuine" nature of such interactions are worth noting:

> To conduct a conversation means to allow oneself to be conducted by the subject matter to which the partners in the dialogue are oriented. It requires that one does not try to argue the other person down but that one really considers the weight of the other's opinion. Hence, it is an art of testing. But the art of testing is the art of questioning. . . . [T]o question means to lay open, to place in the open. As against the fixity of opinions, questioning makes the object and all its possibilities fluid. . . . Thus a genuine conversation is never the one that we wanted to conduct. . . . [T]he partners conversing are far less the leaders of it than the led. No one knows in advance what will "come out" of a conversation. Understanding or its failure is like an event that happens to us. . . . All this shows that a conversation has a spirit of its own, and that the language in which it is conducted bears its own truth within it—i.e., that it allows something to "emerge" which henceforth exists. (pp. 367, 383)

The point I am making with Gadamer's help can be summarized as follows: The Being of dialogue is grounded in the dialogue with Being that the spatial and temporal openness of human existence forever presents as a possibility and as a challenge to question and to come to terms with what is understood to be the truth of any given concern. The specific attunement of consciousness of acknowledgment facilitates this event by keeping us open to the "dwelling place" (ethos) that we are—thanks to Being—and where we can return Being's favor by registering its showing/saying in language (Hyde, in press-b). For Heidegger (1977), this task defines the true *humanitas* of *homo humanus*. We need Being and it needs us to hear and respond to its call. Ethics (ethos), for Heidegger, originates in the "dwelling place" (ethos) where this primordial dialogue first happens (pp. 231–236).

Critics of Heidegger such as Richard Bernstein (1986) point out that there is a danger here because the ontological leanings of Heidegger's phenomenology virtually close "off the space for attending to the type of thinking and acting that can foster human solidarity and community" (p. 208). Hence, Bernstein would have us remember what he believes Heidegger seems to forget: "Our dialogue, and communicative transactions, are not only with Being itself, but with other human beings" (p. 219). Indeed, but as I have indicated elsewhere (Hyde, 2001a), Heidegger's forgetfulness does not preclude one from working out an application of his philosophy that addresses the problem raised by Bernstein.[1] In the remainder of this essay I provide such an application by considering how the ontological relationship between dialogue and acknowledgment manifests itself in our everyday ways of being-with-and-for-others. Certain phenomenological insights offered by Emmanuel Levinas will aid me in this endeavor, as will a case study wherein I appropriate both Heidegger's and Levinas's insights to analyze a tragedy (the Columbine High School Massacre) that might have been avoided if more concern had been directed toward the cultivation of interpersonal acknowledgment and its dialogical function. I begin with some general comments about acknowledgment and Levinas's appreciation of the phenomenon to help set the stage for the case study.

Acknowledgment as a Life-Giving Gift

What would life be like if no one acknowledged your existence? The question confronts one with the possibility of "social death," of being isolated, marginalized, ignored, and forgotten by others (the same fate that Heidegger feared for Being). The unacknowledged find themselves in an "out-of-the-way" place where it is hard for human beings, given their social instinct, to dwell in peace and to feel at home in their surroundings. The suffering that can accompany this way of being in the world is known to bring about fear, anxiety, anger, and sometimes even death in the form of suicide or retaliation against those who are rightly or wrongly accused of making one's life so lonely, miserable, and unbearable (Hyde, 2001a, pp. 204–219; Hyde, 2002b; in press-a).[2]

Acknowledgment provides an opening out of such a distressful situation, for the act of acknowledging is a communicative behavior that grants attention to others and thereby makes room for them in our lives. With this added living space comes the opportunity for a new beginning, a second chance, whereby one might improve his or her lot in life. There is hope to be found with this transformation of space and time as people of conscience opt to go out of their way to make us feel wanted and needed, to praise our presence and actions, and thus to acknowledge the worthiness of our existence. Offering positive acknowledgment is a moral thing to do. What is good for Being is good for people.

Granted, such acknowledgment may embarrass us, and it might even make us feel guilty if we know that our presence and actions have something deceitful about them or, at least in our humble opinion, are not really that great. But generally speaking, positive acknowledgement makes us feel good as it affirms something about our being that is felt by others to be worthy of praise and perhaps even remembrance after we are gone. Indeed, have you ever thought about your own death, your funeral, and who might show up to pay their respects? And when thinking about this last matter, have you ever become upset with those people who you believe should have attended the ceremony but did not? Even when we have passed to the most out-of-the-way place there is, we still crave the goodness of positive acknowledgment—the way it brings us to mind and thus, in a sense, keeps us alive. With Ernest Becker (1973), then, one might say that acknowledgment provides a way to satisfy a human being's "urge to immortality"—an urge that

> is not a simple reflex of the death anxiety but a reaching out by one's whole being toward life. . . . a reaching-out for a plenitude of meaning . . . . It seems that the life force reaches naturally even beyond the earth itself, which is one reason why man has always placed God in the heavens. (pp. 152–153)

Of course, not all acknowledgment that comes our way is positive. For example, in a certain situation hearing someone say to you "Looking good!" may be understood correctly as a compliment. In a different situation, however, these same words, coming from one with whom you have never gotten along, might also be legitimately heard as a sarcasm, a slight, an articulation whose tone of voice speaks ridicule, disrespect, and dislike. Such negative acknowledgment is also at work whenever we call people "stupid" or "worthless," thereby opening and exposing them to the further ridicule of others. Like its opposite, negative acknowledgement creates a place for being noticed. But the space provided here, even if it is given with the best of intentions—as when a parent, trying to provide careful guidance, scolds a child for being "naughty"—more often than not makes us feel bad. (This is not to suggest, of course, that all negative acknowledgment is harmful. For example, being shown by a student in a caring way that I have done something wrong in class can be beneficial to all concerned.)

Acknowledgment is a significant and powerful form of behavior, one that can bring joy to one's heart and also drive a stake through it. Acknowledgment functions as both a life-giving gift and a life-draining force. Moving from its positive to negative form and then to a state of no acknowledgement at all, we find ourselves in a place that is hard-pressed to support life because it is so barren of the nourishment provided by the caring concern of others. Institutionalized forms of negative acknowledgment such as racism, sexism, and ageism expose people to this fate of social death. Certain rituals of culture, on the other hand, are meant to protect us from it. Proper decorum dictates, for example, that we say "hello" and "goodbye" to people so that they feel noticed; that we make them feel important and respected by simply holding open a door and saying "after you"; or that we send them a birthday or condolence card to assure them that, at a moment of joy or distress, they are in our thoughts and perhaps our prayers. The presence of people in need of acknowledgement sounds a call of conscience, a call that Levinas (1985, pp. 85–122; 1991, pp. 144–165) would have us associate with the true basis of "religion" before its "language" becomes "institutionalized": "Where art thou?" Good manners encourage us to say, "Here I am!" (Hyde, 2001a, pp. 79–115). Knowing or at least believing that this response truly "comes from the heart," we are likely to feel better than if we know or believe that what we are receiving is mostly some ritualized behavior steeped in the shallows of unthinking habit rather than in the depths of genuine care.[3] With heart-felt acknowledgment there comes what Levinas (1969, pp. 265–66; 1987c, pp. 84–94) terms the life-giving gift of the "caress."

Levinas maintains that human existence is itself fundamentally structured as a caress: We exist in the caress of Being—a caress that promotes a "love of life" but that, as Levinas points out, can also become a "suffocating embrace" that breeds isolation, pain, and suffering. An example of one who is likely to experience the consequences of this embrace would be a person whose well-being has been interrupted by a serious and incapacitating illness that, among other things, undercuts the person's mastery of existence; breeds despair, helplessness, and a feeling of abandonment; and thereby directs the person to question life's meaning, purpose, and ultimate worth. In such a state of suffering, writes Levinas (1987c),

> there is an absence of all refuge. It is the fact of being directly exposed to being. It is made up of the impossibility of fleeing or retreating. The whole acuity of suffering lies in this impossibility of retreat. It is the fact of being backed up against life and being. (p. 69)

Existing in such a state, one's position in life is that of standing face-to-face with one's "own Being," with the openness and uncertainty of the temporal structure of existence that is other than a human creation but that still calls one into question while at the same time calling for action that might restore a sense of purpose and meaning to one's existence.

Heidegger (1962) writes about how the "uncanniness" (*unheimlich*) of such a state of isolation, pain, and suffering defines a major source of anxiety; for here we find ourselves in a position where, at least for the moment, our everyday habits and routines are interrupted such that we "no longer" (*un*) feel "at home" (*heimlich*) with our surroundings (pp. 232–235). The orderly workings of a culture's social domain, where "feeling at home" is an expected state, are designed to shield us from a direct encounter with Being. Heidegger, we have seen, favors this encounter; it comes with the vocation of phenomenology, which calls on its practitioners to realize how their work is grounded in the essential relationship between human being and Being. Remember, human being marks the clearing, the site, the dwelling place (ethos) where Being shows itself. Heidegger also commends the courage that it takes to meet the challenge of the encounter when it happens in and deconstructs the tranquility of everyday life and thereby calls for reconstructive action to restore some sense of "feeling at home" with things and with others. This activity of "home-making" also calls on one's rhetorical competence to the extent that it requires a person to make clear to others what he or she is feeling given the situation at hand and what might be done to resolve the anxiety of standing face-to-face with Being (Hyde, in press-a).

Levinas, too, speaks of the heroics that the encounter demands and of the importance of a person needing to reestablish a sense of feeling at home with one's environment. In doing so, however, he extends Heidegger's concern for the otherness of Being by discussing how the encounter calls into play another mode of otherness (or *alterity*) where the caress is present: that of other people. For Levinas (1984a), the importance of this mode of otherness cannot be overemphasized:

> I am defined as a subjectivity, as a particular person, as an "I," precisely because I am exposed to the other. It is my inescapable and incontrovertible answerability to the other that makes me an individual "I" . . . . I can never escape the fact that the other has demanded a response from me before I affirm my freedom not to respond to his demand. (pp. 62–63; also see 1996, pp. 72–74)

With this demand comes the ethical responsibility of answering the call of Being by thinking and acting with the welfare of others in mind. The other's mere presence is a "saying," a source of interruption, a calling into question of consciousness that raises the issue of accountability—"Are you being just in all that you say and do?"—and thereby summons to action the moral capacity of human being. "This is certainly not a philosopher's invention," writes Levinas (1987a), "but the first given of moral consciousness, which could be defined as the consciousness of the privilege the other has relative to me. Justice well ordered begins with the other" (p. 56).

Levinas's position presupposes the question of Being and its otherness. Without Being there would be no others to mention. Yet, in directing his attention away from the otherness of Being to the otherness of other people, Levinas provides a richer assessment of the caress characterizing the social relationship than one finds in Heidegger's (1962) discussion of the social relationship of "Being-with" others (pp. 149–224). This caress takes form with what was noted above as the self's exposure and inescapable answerability to others. Otherness calls into being the "individual 'I'"; it thereby "accomplishes human society" as it promotes "the miracle of moving out of oneself," out of one's preoccupations with his or her personal wants and priorities and toward what before anything else in this world really makes a difference (Levinas, 1987c, pp. 39–66). This difference (otherness) marks the relationship between human being and Being. It also marks the relationship between individual human beings whose "self-development" as social creatures is called into being by the presence of others.

The indelible communal character of human existence is made possible by a "movement," an altruistic and moral impulse, that lies at the heart of human being and that directs the self toward the other. Levinas (1978) thus claims that because of this impulse, "intersubjective space is initially asymmetrical" (p. 95). Human existence is so structured as to have the self move towards the other before the self can even raise the related issues of reciprocity and moral responsibility. Morality originates in a movement of "one to another," of "being-for" others (which is exactly what other selves are doing when they are responsible enough to acknowledge and assist other selves). The social event of "Being-with" others would be nothing more than an adventure in power, violence, and survival of the fittest if it were not for the fact that, at its most primordial level, human existence is not only a temporal happening, but something whose unfolding is directed toward the otherness of others. Thus, the happening of human existence displays a *rhetorical trajectory*: it is a "saying" that can be heard and must be responded to, to some degree, in order to continue living one's life. The saying says as much, especially in those moments of personal and interpersonal crises, when we are standing face-to-face with Being such that its call for action is right "in our face." This specific call for action is rhetoric in its most primal state of being (Hyde, 2001a, pp. 79–115). Søren Kierkegaard (1999) has a wonderful way of making the point: "The essential sermon is one's own existence. A person preaches with this every hour of the day and with power quite different from that of the most eloquent speaker in his most eloquent moment" (p. 263).

For Levinas, the saying going on here defines the primordial ground of ethics. He contends that ethics, not ontology, is "first philosophy." "When I speak of first philosophy," writes Levinas (1999), "I am referring to a philosophy of dialogue that cannot not be an ethics. Even the philosophy that questions the meaning of being [ontology] does so on the basis of the encounter with the other" (p. 97). What Levinas is saying here may generate confusion, given his earlier stated claim that "intersubjective space is initially asymmetrical." A genuine dialogue encourages the "two-wayness" of reciprocity, not the "one-wayness" of asymmetry. And as Levinas (1985) is fond of repeating, human existence is so structured that "I am responsible for the Other without waiting for his reciprocity, were I to die for it. Reciprocity is *his* affair" (p. 98). We *are* a being-for others, we *are* caught up in their caress; human existence *is* marked by an openness to and movement towards otherness. That defines its "goodness," its deconstructive way of being a constant interruption that raises a moral issue: Are you being just in all that you say and do? (Levinas, 1991, pp. 122–123, 138). The other calls: "Where art thou?" Goodness makes it possible to say "Here I am!" and thus to speak and to act on behalf of others. We can call all of this a dialogue once the response is made. And that, I believe, is Levinas's point. The response is already in the making, given that the self (ontologically and ethically speaking) is by nature open to the otherness of other selves and these selves are at the same time open to the otherness of the self.

As Heidegger says about the relationship between human being and Being, Levinas describes a dialogical relationship that holds the self in the caress of "the Other," lies at the heart of existence, and can be read as an ethical and moral directive: Open yourself to others and *welcome* their differences—what it is about them that calls into question your freedom. Only by doing this can one provide the necessary space, the requisite dwelling place (ethos), that is needed to create and maintain the moral ecology—the "knowing together" (*con-scientia*), of human fraternity, of feeling at home with others—and that rests on a relationship whose asymmetry is what it is only as it encourages the reciprocity of acknowledgment between the self and others.

A Case Study

The importance of heeding this ethical and moral directive is demonstrated, for example, in the case of the Columbine High School massacre. At approximately 11 a.m. on Tuesday, April 20, 1999, two students—17 year-old Dylan Harris and 18 year-old Eric Klebold—entered the school wearing black trench coats and armed with an assault rifle, two sawed-off shotguns, a semi-automatic pistol, and over 30 homemade pipe bombs and grenades. Once in the cafeteria, they shouted: "All jocks stand up! We're going to kill every one of you." One witness to the carnage reported that the two were laughing, "having the time of their life," as they fired their weapons and set off their bombs. After killing a student athlete, one of the boys was heard to say: "Oh, my God, look at this black kid's brain. Awesome, man!" Before they both committed suicide in the school library at approximately 12:30 p.m., Harris and Klebold had killed twelve students, one teacher, and wounded twenty-one others (Cloud, 2001; Gibbs & Roche, 1999).

For those who were there when it happened or who had some personal tie to it, this was a heart-breaking and psychologically damaging event, an unforgettable tragedy that, as its deconstructive nature unfolded, brought about a massive interruption in people's everyday lives. Loved ones were dead and their survivors now had to deal with the difficult task of coping with immeasurable loss, of living in a world void of a source of meaning that had once played a major role in maintaining this world's present and future well-being. The issue that is immediately raised by this situation is typically heard as a question of reconstruction and survival: "How am I to go on living without a certain love in my life?" The question expresses heart-felt concern for one's existence (Being) and its loss of meaning.

The issue of concern here lies at the heart of the everyday world of sociopolitical happenings, for this world is built upon the various pragmatic ways that we deal with the issue throughout our lives. An interruption that can shake this world to its very core and possibly even destroy it, defines, to say the least, a major existential setback—one that sets us back to the "beginning," to that primordial spatial/temporal dimension of existence that is not a human creation but whose "otherness" still supports all of our daily routines and whose presence is easily taken-for-granted as these routines condition us to *their* ways of being with things and with others.

With the Columbine High School massacre, people were set back to a place where experiencing the otherness of Being was unavoidable. The scene was filled with destruction and death. Anxiety prevailed. The spatial/temporal character of everyday existence was transformed. The moment was terrifying, disorienting, uncanny; people no longer felt at home. From this strange environment came a challenging call for thinking, action, meaning, and order—in short, for the rhetorical act of homemaking. Human beings helped to express and answer this call; its true source, however, was and is more primordial than their individual voices.

Ever since it first happened, the media have kept the public informed about how people involved in the situation have responded to this call with shock, grief, funerals, moving stories, lawsuits, and, of course, attempted explanations of why the massacre occurred. The explanation that seems most definitive now is this: Harris and Klebold were "outsiders"—two students who were not members of the "in crowd," with its population of popular and clean-cut kids and athletes who were known for teasing and bullying people like Harris and Klebold, who, in turn, were known for their alienation, their strange ways of coping with the situation (Hoerl, 2002; LeBlanc, 1999). Indeed, Harris was taking the medication Luvox, which is an antidepressant commonly prescribed for people suffering from obsessive–compulsive disorder. Both boys hung out with each other; played violent video games; listened to German punk rock bands whose message was despair, hate, violence, and cruelty; and sometimes greeted each other with a Nazi stiff-armed salute. Harris kept a diary that was filled with "Nazi rhetoric" and that detailed how he and Klebold had been planning the massacre for the past year. On April 20, Adolph Hitler's birthday, blood would be spilled. The diary also made clear that Harris and his friends were tired of having jocks "putting them down" (Gibbs & Roche, 1999; also see "Teens," 2002).

Yes, these two boys were strange. How could their parents and teachers not have known that something terribly wrong was going on in these children's lives? Accusations of parental and teacher neglect were announced in the media. Moreover, reported the media, being bullied and shamed by one's high school peers was nothing new. The practice could be recalled by many adults who went through the same thing but who, for one reason or another, never went so far as to "crack" under the pressure and kill as a result of some childish setbacks in their lives (Belkin, 1999). The so-called "*real* bottom line" of the massacre was that Harris and Klebold were weak, misguided, and disturbed souls who could no longer stand their lives (Hoerl, 2002; LeBlanc, 1999). Phrased in terms of the rhetoric of acknowledgment, one might say that Harris and Klebold were incapable of responding to the call of Being in a positive and healthy manner; they were beyond the point of being saved from the suffocating embrace of their tormented existence. One solution remained, however: bombs could be ignited and triggers could be pulled. It was time for revenge; it was time to die. A totally deconstructive act was deemed appropriate. Trying to reconstruct a dwelling place where these teenage boys could feel at home with their peers was no longer an option.

Harris and Klebold perpetrated the most finalizing act of negative acknowledgement that there is. They were murderers, to be sure; and given their suicides, one might also brand them as cowards. But if one accepts the above explanation as a fair account of why these boys committed their heinous act, then I believe that one also has an obligation to ask a specific question: Would Harris and Klebold have committed their crime if they had received more positive acknowledgment from their peers and others during, say, the last year of their lives, such that their ongoing state of social death may have subsided as they were welcomed into a dwelling place where they could feel more at home with others? I suspect that this question may make some people feel a bit uneasy and, perhaps, may even stimulate outrage, for the question allows for the possibility of spreading the blame beyond the killers and to those "innocent" folk whose only "crime" was that they just happened to be people who had some role to play in maintaining the outsider status of Harris and Klebold. Holding on to that bit of cultural commonsense that tells of how insiders and outsiders have always been with us and that such a class distinction should thus be accepted as a fact of life, one could certainly argue that my raising of the question, at best, is making a mountain out of a mole hill. Moreover, it must be admitted that although positive acknowledgment can be a life-giving gift, no "official" law exists that requires us to give it.

Since the Columbine massacre took place, I have wondered what a world would be like that enacted such a law. I suspect that the force of this law would become unbearable. Human beings are not known as creatures having the unbridled energy it would take to be compassionate every second of the day and to save all those souls suffering from the suffocating embrace of their own existence. We have not yet evolved biologically and spiritually to this level of perfection. Social death is still a common way of being. We are capable, however, of asking a relevant question, one that encourages the raising of consciousness: What would life be like if no one cared enough to acknowledge our existence in a genuine and positive way? The question calls for a consideration of what it would take to live in a world where positive acknowledgment is the rule of the day. Human beings, of course, would have to be in much better shape given the stamina that would be needed here. And we also would have to sharpen our ability to be keen observers, acknowledgers, of all that stands before us. Indeed, in the case of Columbine, the problem was not that Harris and Klebold were not *seen* by others, but that not enough (or the right) people took the time to *acknowledge* their situation and the evil that permeated it. An ethical and moral directive that lies at the heart of existence was ignored by killers, their victims, and other innocent people. The murder scene, to be sure, was not a dwelling place where a knowing-together and a feeling at home with others was operating in good order and where a loving caress barred the door to evil.

I think it is absurd to excuse the sickness here as something that is "normal" because of its long history. Human beings have the potential to say and to do greater and nobler things than this. We belong to a species that exalts its own status in the animal kingdom by offering itself as a showcase of biological and spiritual evolution (Wright, 1994): We are creatures who can hear and who have the responsibility to respond to the related calls of Being and conscience. We are gifted with the capacity to remain open to the good and the bad going on in the world. We are capable of inventing, using, and correcting symbolic expressions to disclose and share with others our understanding of the situation. We are fated to be challenged as homemakers—rhetorical architects who must construct dwelling places where ethics and moral character can be cultivated and, hence, where people can learn to take those things to heart that warrant such care. And in *being* all of this, we owe it to ourselves and others not to bolster the effects of the sickness that was the Columbine High School massacre by accepting and facilitating its presence with a lame excuse made possible by a history of simple-minded behavior. Students and parents expressed this excuse with the help of the media. Hoerl (2002), I believe, is correct to criticize the media for its lack of critical reflection in airing the excuse. My agreement with Hoerl, however, arises from an appreciation of ontology that escapes her attention: A genuine response to the call of Being requires a greater degree of rhetorical competence than today's popular media is known to exhibit with its "evocative" use of language.

Conclusion

Human existence calls: Where art thou? We have an obligation to respond: Here I am! It is a matter of acknowledgment, of keeping a conversation going with the things of this world and with others, and thus of trying to be true to something essential about the human condition, something that we, in fact, did not create but that we nevertheless must take charge of in our everyday lives: the ontological structure of openness that holds us in its caress and that defines the dialogical nature of our Being. My earlier examination (Hyde, 2001a) of how this nature of ours is managed and manipulated in such related health-policy issues as the ethics of doctor-patient-family communication and the euthanasia debate helped me to appreciate more fully how acknowledgment is a life-giving gift. Situations like the Columbine High School Massacre also bring to mind this fact of life that is all too easily taken for granted and forgotten because of the anxiety it is known to produce in people when, for whatever reason, they have to deal with a fundamental question of existence: What would life be like if nobody acknowledged one's presence? The question gives expression to the call of Being that, whether heard or not, is always at work in the spatial and temporal unfolding of our lives.

With the present examination of the matter, I continued to maintain that there is something fundamentally rhetorical about this phenomenon. The call of Being calls for concerned thought and responsible action—the very things that the art of rhetoric is dedicated to producing. We owe it to ourselves and others to become rhetorically competent beings. Such competence aids in the sharing of the life-giving gift of acknowledgment. As indicated with the brief case study offered here, my ongoing research of this matter is directed toward an expanded treatment of acknowledgment and its relationship to such phenomena as the call of Being, conscience, recognition and the attunement of consciousness, the discursive transformation of space and time, the deconstructive and reconstructive nature of existence, and the persuasive use of language to create dwelling places for responsible thought and action. I hope to show with my research that there are lessons to be learned about all of these related matters from topics ranging from cosmology to religion, poetry, politics, and the media. These lessons make up a narrative whose moral is this: For the benefit of all concerned we need to become more observant of all that stands before us—which is to say that we need to learn how to open ourselves to a call that informs the dialogical workings of human existence and that thereby warrants the affirmation of heart-felt acknowledgment. We must take seriously the ethical and rhetorical task of being good homemakers.

Notes

1.   Heidegger's critics also associate this problem with his unfortunate political engagements beginning in 1933. Motivated by an ultraconservative sociopolitical outlook and a sense of his own intellectual genius and importance, Heidegger lent his voice to the movement of National Socialism, naïvely believing that his intellectual endeavors could provide philosophical direction for the movement and thereby free it from the hands of Nazi ideologues who erroneously justified the revolution on biological and racist grounds. For an expanded discussion and treatment of this issue, see Hyde (2001a, pp. 7–10, 76–78, 90).

2.   What I continue to say about acknowledgment in this section of the chapter may bring to mind Martin Buber's (1998) theory of *confirmation,* which, stated briefly, maintains "The basis of man's life with man is twofold, and it is one—the wish of every man to be confirmed as what he is, even as what he can become, by men; and the innate capacity in man to confirm his fellow man in this way. That this capacity lies so immeasurably fallow constitutes the real weakness and questionableness of the human race: actual humanity exists only where this capacity unfolds" (pp. 57–58). The influence of this theory is seen, for example, in the work of Watzlawick, Beavin, and Jackson (1967, pp. 82–90), Laing (1969, pp. 98–107), Sieburg (1985, pp. 183–189), Cissna and Sieburg (1981), and Cissna and Anderson (1994b). In their appropriation and various ways of utilizing the theory, these authors help to address the problem referred to above by Buber regarding how the capacity for confirmation "lies so immeasurably fallow." I agree with Buber's point here; I am thus supportive of the theory and research offered by these authors. I believe, however, that neither Buber's theory nor its utilization by others so far fully discloses and assesses with the necessary analytic (phenomenological) rigor the matter in question. The capacity of confirmation retains something of a "fallow" character as long as its essential (ontological) nature remains unclarified.

3.   The difference in "feeling" being noted here corresponds to what I take to be the essential difference that exists between the phenomenon of acknowledgment and simple "recognition." People speak of these two phenomena as if they were the same. For the purposes of the current project, however, their difference must be kept in mind: The ethos of acknowledgment establishes an environment wherein people can take the time to "know together" (*con-scientia*) some topic of interest and, in the process, to gain perhaps a more authentic understanding of those who are willing to contribute to its development. Recognition is only a preliminary step in this process of attuning one's consciousness toward another and his or her expression of a topic in order to facilitate the development of such existential knowledge and personal understanding. Acknowledgment requires a sustained openness to others even if, at times, things become boring or troublesome. Considering the definition of *recognition* found in the *Oxford English Dictionary*— "The action or fact of perceiving that some thing, person, etc., is the same as one previously known; the mental process of identifying what has been known before; the fact of being thus

known or identified"—can also help to distinguish this phenomenon from acknowledgment as I am defining it here. The phenomenon of acknowledgment entails more than the mental process of identifying what has been known before. I wish to thank Lisbeth Lipari for personal conversations regarding this insight. Honneth (1996) analyzes the role of recognition in the philosophies and social theories of G. W. F. Hegel and George Herbert Mead, and mentions its occurrence in the work of Immanuel Kant, Karl Marx, Georges Sorel, and Jean-Paul Sartre. From my phenomenological perspective, what Honneth says about these individuals' respective assessments of recognition (*Anerkennung:* to ascribe to individuals "some positive status") would be more accurately expressed with the term "acknowledgment," at least as I am developing it here. Also see Fraser (2000) and Hanssen (2000) who, in extending Honneth's work, still fail to clarify the difference between the workings of acknowledgment and recognition.

5

A Dialogic Ethic "Between" Buber and Levinas

A Responsive Ethical "I"

Ronald C. Arnett

A Continuing Conversation

MacIntyre (1998) outlines ethics theory since the pre-Socratics, revealing the evolution of new ethics theories in response to traditional approaches and providing increasing texture and insight. We now live in a world of multiple ethical frameworks, from situational ethics (Fletcher, 1962), to ethics driven by unreflective, unresponsive standpoints (Wood, 1997, pp. 8–22), to ethics framed in religious dogma, to ethics shaped by the marketplace. Just as a postmodern culture grapples with a world that includes hunting and gathering, farming, industry, and an information age, we must also understand that multiple approaches to ethics are copresent in daily life.

Postmodern scholarship questions our fascination or obsession with metanarrative assurance, the self, and agency. Questioning unreflective reliance upon the self prompted much of my previous scholarship—from early critiques of self-actualization (Arnett, 1978), through rejection of therapeutic communication (Arnett, 1997) and efforts to reclaim temporal narrative agreement as a public standard for interpersonal interaction (Arnett, 2001), to a

Author's Note: This essay, offered in celebration of Richard L. Johannesen's career as mentor, teacher, and dialogic scholar, acknowledges my debt and the responsibility of continuing the conversation.

current unpublished manuscript on public confession of standpoint in postmodern relations and this chapter on the importance of an "ethical I." All of this work was begun in response to the Other and the historical situation, not out of willed agency on my part. Throughout this scholarly journey, dialogue has guided the inquiry—dialogue defined as a humble or particular narrative standpoint engaging the Other and the historical situation, inviting learning from clarity of position, attentiveness to the Other, and responsiveness to the historical situation, ever propelled by a commitment to learn, shift, and adjust. The absolute of dialogue is a "unity of contraries" (Buber, 1965b, p. 111)—the courage to state and maintain a position and the courage to change when responsively appropriate. In this chapter, I continue this scholarly conversation, placing Buber and Levinas in dialogue for the first time in my published work, listening for ethical insight into a postmodern world, and then responding to their work with the construct of a "responsive ethical I."

Buber and Levinas interpret otherwise than modern psychological assumptions, providing a paradigmatic alternative that enriches the conversation that questions the ongoing historical trends toward increasing focus upon the self:

> The only authority which moral views possess is that which we as individual agents give to them. This view is the final conceptualization of the individualism which has had recurrent mention in this history: the individual becomes his own final authority in the most extreme possible sense. (MacIntyre, 1998, p. 264)

In addition, Buber and Levinas frame a powerful sense of "I" shaped in response, not in agency. Neither rejects the notion of I; each attends to a responsive construction that moves from individualism to responsible attentiveness to the Other and to the historical situation.

Their work rests within a conversation of persons, such as Harding (1991) and Cortese (1990), who move us beyond the individual into socioculturally and ethnically situated standpoints and assumptions about ethics. Postmodern scholarship questions the validity of a metanarrative and, in addition, questions modern confidence in individual agency. Buber and Levinas do not offer *the* answer to the dilemma of increasing individual focus, but they contribute significantly to the conversation. This chapter engages their work, extending my own scholarly journey, pointing to an alternative understanding of agency—a "responsive ethical 'I.'"

Before discussing Buber and Levinas, I want to comment on scholarship situated in philosophical hermeneutics (Gadamer, 1976), one of the approaches to dialogue outlined by Cissna and Anderson (1994b). The key to such work is the question one brings to a text (standpoint) and willingness to listen to a given text for a temporal and partial answer (respect for the Other). Such is one form of dialogic research. My question is, "What might a communication ethic look like that does not begin with a sense of will?" From such a position, this work listens to Buber's and Levinas's responses, then frames a concept, a "responsive ethical 'I'"—a result not owned by Buber, Levinas, or me. The fruit of dialogical research is both participation in and temporal contribution to an ongoing conversation.

BUBER'S PHILOSOPHICAL ANTHROPOLOGY

In the field of communication, numerous works examine the ideas of Martin Buber, with the lineage of this scholarship reflected in Jeanine Czubaroff's (2000) essay. Her work frames dialogic characteristics of Buber and his commitment to "philosophical anthropology" in which philosophy and human interaction co-inform one another. Emphasizing philosophical anthropology situates Buber's dialogic project and privileges a space for the discipline of communication.

Communication, understood as a verb, connects the two nouns, *philosophy,* which is concerned with presuppositions, and *anthropology,* which examines the social practices of people. Communication brings philosophy into human action. Understanding communication as a verb relegates communication not to secondary status but to hermeneutic significance. Communication is akin to Hermes, the Greek messenger god. Hermes linked the wishes of the gods (philosophy) with the people (anthropology). The role of Hermes was to accomplish a creative "doing" task; he was a messenger who made a difference. In the *Odyssey* (Homer, trans. 1996), Hermes has three major roles: messenger god, the guide for souls to Hades, and giant killer. In addition, Hermes functions as the patron saint of herdsman. Hermes, the messenger between the gods and the people, between philosophy and anthropology, makes a fundamental difference in lives, bringing divergent results, from death to security and protection.

Buber addresses the importance of making a difference in a historical moment in his essay, "The Crisis and Its Expression" (1965a, pp. 157–163), outlining philosophical anthropology and the importance of communication in negotiating differing discourses, contrary forms of ethics propelled by differing philosophical anthropologies. Buber stressed the importance of phenomenology in philosophical anthropology, noting differing philosophies that shape competing anthropologies about the human being. Buber questions the individualistic work of Heidegger and the insight of Kierkegaard, who placed human connections secondary to the solitary connection with God. Interestingly, Buber's hope rested in the last work of Edmund Husserl, the creator of the phenomenological method:

> in his last, unfinished work, a treatise on the crisis of the European sciences, he made, in three separate sentences, a contribution to this problem. . . . The

first . . . asserts that the greatest historical phenomenon is mankind wrestling for self-understanding. . . . The second sentence runs: "If man becomes a 'metaphysical,' a specifically philosophical problem, then he is called in question as a reasoning thing." . . . The third sentence runs: "Humanity in general is essentially the existence of man in entities of mankind which are bound together in generations and in society." (Buber, 1965a, pp. 159–160)

Buber turned to Husserl's last work to discern the importance of generational thinking and the danger of reifying the person into a metaphysical concept.

Buber questioned Heidegger's "call of conscience," which rested with Being, too far removed from the person. Instead, Buber opted for real people, real problems, the calling of conscience in the existential moment. Buber placed Heidegger within a lineage that recognized the solitary person reaching out to something beyond the world, whether to God or Being. For Buber, the cry that God is dead leads back to an emphasis on Being more akin to one's own mirror image.

The point of the above is not to determine whether Buber is correct in his interpretation of Heidegger, but to stress two basic issues: (a) Buber reacts to Heidegger in a manner parallel to Levinas, contending with Heidegger's idea of being-in-the-world as unduly individualistic; and (b) Buber situates phenomenology within anthropology of persons meeting persons, not in metaphysics: "Man can become whole not in virtue of a relation to himself but only in virtue of a relation to another self" (Buber, 1965a, p. 168).

For Buber, Heidegger's "being-in-the-world" misses human meeting. Buber, in pejorative form, contends that Heidegger does not meet the Other, but engages in a caring solicitude that is an "extreme pity," without bridging "the barriers of his own being" (1965a, p. 170). Buber does not discuss a being-in-the world, but persons-in-the-world. Buber calls for a Thou that addresses the I, but not a monologic I reaching in pity toward the Thou. For Buber, Heidegger offers a secular version of Kierkegaard's religious "single one" (1965a, pp. 40–82). Buber differentiates the Thou from Heidegger's faceless crowd. "The connexion with the faceless, formless, nameless many, with the 'crowd,' with the 'one,' appears in Kierkegaard, and following him in Heidegger, as the preliminary situation which must be overcome for self-being to be attained" (Buber, 1965a, p. 178). Buber considered Kierkegaard's person on the edge and Heidegger's version further on an edge "where *nothing* happens" (1965a, p. 181).

Buber's phenomenological focus of attention includes real life as meeting, as relational connection. In *I and Thou* (1970), Buber frames all of life as relational—whether I-It or I-Thou. However, life is lived in the existential world, not a phenomenological world—a world of monologue, technical dialogue and dialogue (Buber, 1965a). Buber considers all three modes of discourse necessary: (a) monologue as self-talk; (b) technical dialogue open to feedback and informational correction; and (c) dialogue responsive to I and Thou, responsive to nonownership, to the "between." What distinguishes the above three elements of communication is the shift in the locus of communicative meaning from self to information accuracy to the notion of the "between."

Buber's (1996) contention with utopian thinking illuminates the danger of looking for a utopian answer, placing faith instead in the "meeting of ideas and fate in the creative hour" (p. 138). Buber's emphasis on community as emergent between persons, fueled by ideas responsive to the historical moment, lives within the "between"—a sphere unresponsive to rigid principle and "sentimentality or emotionalism" (1996, p. 134). Buber, in one work after another, returns to the metaphor of the "between" and the possibility of emergent reciprocity. He wages battle in the existential moment against individualism *and* collectivism—looking for emergent answers between extremes that invite reciprocal concern.

From Hasidic tales to a philosophy of dialogue, Buber points to a life without ownership within the self or ownership by an outside agent or principle, emphasizing the pragmatic necessity of the "between." In "Hope for This Hour" (1967a, pp. 306–312), Buber offers words as relevant to the beginning of the 21st century as they were to the middle of the 20th century:

> The human world is today, as never before, split into two camps, each of which understands the other as the embodiment of falsehood and itself as the embodiment of truth. . . . Each side has assumed monopoly of the sunlight and has plunged its antagonist into night, and each side demands that you decide between day and night. . . . Expressed in modern terminology, he believes that he has ideas, his opponent only ideologies. This obsession feeds the mistrust that incites the two camps. (p. 307)

The "between" is Buber's alternative to ideological camps, guiding Buber's existential message about dialogue. He might suggest that, today, technology has enhanced our capacity for "technical dialogue," and what Lasch (1979) terms a "culture of narcissism" continues to fuel "monologue." Buber would not eliminate either technical dialogue or monologue; they are needed spheres of life. He would counter them with dialogic invitations—invitations into a sphere of coconstruction, the "between," the discovery of emergent reciprocity appropriate for yet another world hour.

The connecting point with Levinas examined in the next major section is the calling out of the "I." Out of lack of ownership, the "I" finds the power of responsibility. "Through the *Thou* a man becomes *I*" (Buber, 1970, p. 28). The Thou calls the "I," with engagement beginning in distance. Without distance, with self-imposed relation upon the other (demand), the "I" of the Thou remains the "I" of the world of "It," seeking to impose one's own will. The Thou begins with the invitation of distance, "acceptance of otherness" (Buber, 1965b, p. 69).

Buber begins with distance, inviting the "between," a place of unilateral importance not owned by self or outside force. In the "between," the Thou calls forth an "I" attentive to the Other, knowing that only the Thou can call forth the "I." A called out, or responsively shaped, "I" then works to assist the Other—out of "guilt" cognizant of the primacy of the Thou over the "I." As Buber (1965b) stated, "I have met many men in the course of my life who have told me how, acting from the high conscience of men who had become guilty, they experienced themselves as seized by a higher power" (p. 138).

The higher power of responsibility to the Other forges a sphere without ownership, a place where the Thou meets the Other in distance, calling forth an "I" in the act of responsibility to the Other. Levinas frames an equally powerful picture of a unique understanding of the "I."

LEVINAS'S PHENOMENOLOGICAL REMINDER

Levinas attends to the face of the Other, pointing to an a priori obligation: "I am my brother's keeper" (Cohen, 1998, p. xii), a statement that is the key to Levinas's ethics. Levinas (1981) states, "Humanism has to be denounced only because it is not sufficiently human" (p. 128). The "face," read as a humanist concept, misses a phenomenological reality that the Other calls forth as a sense of "I." Phenomenologically, the Other makes an "I" possible. Ethics as responsibility for the Other is an act that makes possible human life—without the "Other," there is no "I." Ethics, for Levinas, is a phenomenological first principle: attending to the Other, calling forth an "I" into ethical responsibility. The face of the Other is a "trace" (Levinas, 1983, p. 115) reminding the "I," "Thou shalt not kill" and that "I am my brother's keeper" (Cohen, 1998, p. xii). Levinas assumes, phenomenologically, that to kill the Other is to kill the "I." Levinas does not offer us a "Sunday school" version of ethics, but rather a phenomenological reminder that the "I" finds identity in response to the Other. The "I" is not the parent, but the child. Metaphorically, the Other is the parent with the "I" constructed as the son or daughter. The "I" is derivative of the Other.

Levinas "interprets otherwise" (Manning, 1993, pp. 15–135). The notion of interpreting otherwise is much more than Schutz's (1966) notion of examining taken-for-granted assumptions (pp. 120–121). Interpreting otherwise suggests interpreting otherwise than Being. Levinas offers a counter to Being and willfulness—he interprets otherwise than Being, making his work on Heidegger central to his philosophy. Levinas suggests a pragmatic and natural concern for the Other—without the Other there is no "I." Levinas posits ethics, not Being, as first philosophy. Ethics is primordial, a priori to Being. Levinas was described as "the "greatest moral philosopher of the twentieth century," and "his philosophy [was] hailed as a way to uncover 'an ethical demand in the postmodern'" because of Levinas's ability to interpret otherwise (Eaglestone, 1997, p. 5). More specifically, Levinas is a central figure in the work of Jacques Derrida (Eaglestone, 1997, p. 5).

Levinas rejects beginning agency with the "I" for only in response to the Other does the "I" find a sense of formation. Each time one thinks one "has" Levinas, he moves to interpret otherwise than conventional wisdom, inviting a corrective conversation to the modern project of metanarrative and self-assurance, questioning metanarrative agreement that makes agent autonomy seemingly possible. Reliance upon the self made sense within assumed narrative agreement that no longer required questioning. Modernity constructed a metanarrative background that propelled the appearance of autonomous individual action. Levinas's postmodern understanding led him to reject both.

Reading Levinas for answers (a sense of totality) misses the courage and insight of his suggestive "corrective conversation" about the modern foundation of reliance upon the self or agency. Levinas offers an alternative to the self as the guiding metaphor, in addition questioning the ontological assumption of Being. Levinas rejects the psychological (Rieff, 1990) foundation of modern life. He reemphasizes the importance of the transcendental, emphasizing the construction of the "I" from encounter with the concrete face of the Other.

Levinas's scholarship, written in the shadow of darkness emanating from the evil of the Third Reich, offers light and hope in the midst of dark times. Just as Buber's insights once again offer hope for this hour, Levinas offers hope for dark times, times of violence, times of competing camps of ideological insistence. Arendt (1968) reminds us of the power of light in dark times: "Eyes so used to darkness as ours will hardly be able to tell whether their light was the light of a candle or that of a blazing sun" (pp. ix-x). Dark times require us to reexamine presuppositions and social practices, reconnecting differently, "interpreting otherwise," in order to connect theory to the practice of everyday life. In darkness, Levinas penned a call for responsibility, not out of humanism, but out of phenomenological recognition of an ethical call witnessed in the face of the Other. "The responsibility to respond to the other is, for Levinas, precisely the inordinate responsibility, the infinite responsibility of being-for-the-other *before* oneself—the ethical relation" (Cohen, 1985, p. 12).

Ethics as first philosophy (Levinas, 1969, p. 304) is a competing metaphor to Heidegger's *Being and Time* (1962). Levinas considered Heidegger's work "one of the finest books in the history of philosophy" (1985, p. 37). Yet, Levinas offered an alternative to Being as the foundation for philosophy.

As brilliant as Levinas thought Heidegger's work was, he viewed it as a "moral cul-de-sac" (Arnett, 1997, pp. 149–160) too representative of a Western error pointing to individual development. Levinas's concern registers with the work of Buber and Arendt. Arendt, in correspondence with Karl Jaspers (August 16, 1947), frames a picture of supreme individualism at the service of social order:

> The Nazi division between German superhumans and Jewish less-than-humans has made inhuman monsters. . . . That is, this guilt, in contrast to all criminal guilt, oversteps and shatters any and all legal systems. That is the reason why the Nazis in Nuremberg are so smug. . . . We are simply not equipped to deal, on a human, political level, with a guilt that is beyond crime and an innocence that is beyond goodness or virtue. (Arendt & Jaspers, 1992, pp. 53–54)

The notion of the superhuman, the individual worshipped within a corrupt narrative or at the beckon of Being, was counter to the alternative perspective framed by Levinas.

Levinas questioned Heidegger's unwillingness to recant his support of the National Socialist Party, continuing his suspicion of Heidegger's notion of Being. One's being-in-the-world makes a difference, what one does not recant speaks. Levinas and Heidegger part ways around the issue of Being. The key difference between Heidegger and Levinas rests in their accounts of why Being or *Dasein* is in flight, pursued. For Heidegger, the flight unto death is radically different from Levinas's responsibility for the Other:

> This fleeing of *Dasein* from itself is explicitly not what Levinas means by the escape from Being. He insists that the escape has absolutely nothing to do with death, because the escape Levinas describes is not the escape of the self from itself, from its own potentiality for being, but rather is the self's escape from Being itself, from Being in general. (Manning, 1993, p. 31)

Manning (1993) suggests that Levinas follows Heidegger, taking important twists from Heidegger's interpretive frame. Instead of flight, Levinas calls attention to weight, to burden, to the phenomenological fact—"I am my brother's keeper."

Levinas rejects "being unto death," interpreting otherwise with burden lived out in the call of responsibility. Like Frankl's (1974) logotherapy, meaning-centered philosophy, Levinas does not eliminate burden. Levinas does not look to death, but to ethics or responsibility for the Other, as the manner of lessening the weight of one's burden. It is responsibility to the Other that makes possible escape from Being in a twofold fashion: first, ethics is primordial to ontology, and second, responsibility for the Other lessens the burden of Being. Levinas's sense of responsibility called forth from the face of the Other registers a trace, a reminder of a primordial message or call that ethics as first philosophy, "I am my brother's keeper," trumps the weight of Being. The responsive ethical "I" is called forth by the face of the Other from a primordial world of responsibility.

Central to Levinas's position is the assumption that the primordial call of ethics as first philosophy lives in unilateral responsibility, unresponsive to the question of reciprocity. Levinas's ethics assumes asymmetry, not reciprocity:

> I am responsible for the Other without waiting for reciprocity, were I to die for it. Reciprocity is *his* affair. It is precisely insofar as the relationship between the Other and me is not reciprocal that I am subject to the Other; and I am "subject" essentially in this sense. It is I who support all. You know that sentence in Dostoyevsky: "We are all guilty of all and for all men before all, and I more than the others." (1985, p. 98)

Ethics as first philosophy leads us to the importance of responsibility for the Other, not the self. *Ethics/the call of responsibility* interprets otherwise than *Dasein's* use of the human as the "Shepherd of Being," the human charged with the unfolding of Being. Levinas's critique of the human as the "Shepherd of Being" rejects the human as the Shepherd pursuing opportunities that permit Being to unfold. Pursuing is at the heart of the Western model that naturally leads to acquisition. Understanding philosophy that places the human as the agent or Shepherd pursuing the unfolding of Being is counter to Levinas's disinterested attentiveness to the Other; Levinas does not pursue or acquire, but responds to a phenomenological ethical reality.

The difference between pursuit and response is that pursuit suggests a Western story of accumulation, and response suggests a call of responsibility that embraces burdens in responsible action in an unfinished world of infinity, not a world of totality and accumulation:

> We think that the idea-of-the-Infinite-in-me . . . comes to me in the concreteness of my relation to the other person, in the sociality which is my responsibility for the neighbor. This is a responsibility where, not in any "experience" I have contracted, the face of the Other, through its alterity, though its very strangeness, speaks the commandment which came *from one knows not where.* (Levinas, 1987c, p. 136)

The Other begins a cycle of responsibility, from the trace in the face to a primordial call of responsibility to attend to the Other.

In "the face of the Other," Levinas sees the image of God. For Levinas, phenomenology points to a theological set of coordinates—the Other is not just a person, but also the face of God. "Monotheism signifies this human kinship, this idea of a human race that refers back to the approach of the Other in the face, in the dimension of height, in responsibility for oneself and for the Other" (Levinas, 1969, p. 214). The Other, as the face of God, reminds us of our responsibilities to one another. The Other permits us to see what our own embeddedness would naturally miss. In phenomenological terms, instead of God, the Other is a form of "radical alterity" (Levinas, 1969, p. 192). "In positing the

Other's alterity as mystery, the other bears alterity as an essence" (Levinas, 1987c, pp. 87–88). It is the face of the Other that demands transcendence of ourselves; responding to the call of Other shapes an "I" in responsible action.

Radical alterity in the face of the Other calls us to responsibility, questioning reliance on technology that obscures the face and self-attention that obscures attentiveness to the Other:

> Through the face of the Other, through his mortality, everything that in the Other does not regard me, "regards me." Responsibility for the Other—the face signifying to me "thou shalt not kill," and consequently also "you are responsible for the life of this absolutely other other"—is responsibility for the unique one. The "unique one" means the *loved one*, love being the condition of the very possibility of uniqueness. (Levinas, 1987c, p. 108)

Levinas points to communication as "face education" in a postmodern age— not face in a psychological sense, but in a responsive ethical sense. Radical alterity reminds us to live life beyond self-occupation.

Like Buber, this interpreting otherwise ends in an "I" responsive to something other than the self and outside agents and ideas, in this case to radical alterity of the Other. Distance in Levinas's (1969) radical alterity of the face of the Other "welcomes" (p. 84) into "*Recollection* and *representation* . . . concretely as *habitation in a dwelling* or a Home" (p. 150). One is welcomed back to a dwelling, a home of primordial meaning, ethics, and responsibility. Like Buber, the "I" finds life in response:

> In the face to face the I has neither the privileged position of the subject nor the position of the thing defined by its place in the system; it is apology, discourse *pro domo*, but discourse of justification before the Other. The Other is the intelligible, since he is capable of justifying my freedom. (Levinas, 1969, p. 293)

The face of the Other is not a psychological gesture; it is a trace directing us back to a home of primordial responsibility (Levinas, 1985, pp. 85–86).

In this chapter, I underscore and accept the biases of both Levinas and Buber; their disagreements offer texture and insight about engagement with the Other and responsibility, contributing to our understanding of communication ethics and human dialogue.

Interpreting otherwise acknowledges *la différance* (Derrida, 1997), opening conversation between Levinas and postmodern scholars. I do not accept Levinas's pure phenomenological perspective. However, engaging phenomenological bracketing of such disbelief places attention upon the unique contribution of Levinas, holding in abeyance the question of agreement or disagreement with Levinas's phenomenology. Such bracketing permits one to do what is central to Levinas's project: respond to difference.

Recognition of difference, of uniqueness, guided Levinas's phenomenological reading. A phenomenological attentiveness to difference permits understanding of a phenomenon in its own right. Levinas's commitment to "the things themselves" (Husserl, 1962) necessitated his repudiation of Derrida's (1999) suggestion that Levinas's project extends only from the Old Testament directive, "I am my brother's keeper." Levinas understood that religion and phenomenology could agree on a given issue while addressing differing phenomena. Religion offers a story-laden *why* for action. Phenomenology describes the phenomenon at hand, the *is* of a given phenomenon. In the case of attending to and protecting the Other, religion and phenomenology coincide, the former guided by a story of compassion and the latter by the construction of phenomenological perception.

Levinas's commitment to difference illuminated the *why* of his insistence to distinguish his work from that of Buber. Levinas questioned Buber's ontology— Buber's emphasis upon reciprocity. In contrast, Levinas privileged ethics and responsibility, irrespective of reciprocity (1998, p. 150). Levinas stressed terms such as "hostage" (1987c, p. 108), emphasizing the Other's demand for responsible action from me, belying emphasis on reciprocity.

Levinas contended with Buber's attention to the reciprocity and ontology inherent in Buber's notion of the *between*. For Levinas, "the 'Between' is a *mode of being*" (1984b, p. 307). Levinas rejected Buber on the ontology issue, as he did Heidegger. Levinas placed ethics as primordial before Being, primordial to ontology (1969, p. 304). Levinas "interprets otherwise" than Being, suggesting "disinterestedness which does not mean indifference, but allegiance to the Other" (Levinas, 1984b, p. 318). To deny the importance of Levinas's argument misses the horizon of his project. On the other hand, this chapter simultaneously accepts Buber's disagreement with Levinas's critique of reciprocity.

Buber contended with Levinas's assessment, reminding that as the "I" demands or even reflects the question of reciprocity, the possibility of dialogue ceases. Buber rejected dialogue upon demand, affirming the necessity and importance of monologue and technical dialogue as fundamental companions in the engagement of the Other. Buber recounted his action as a young boy grooming a horse. While grooming the horse, Buber thought of the uniqueness of the moment (the act of grooming), which destroyed the moment, banishing the "dialogue between" them. Any teacher can relate to moments in the classroom interrupted by the thought: "I am good today; the students are really responsive," only to feel misdirected during the remainder of the class, unable to reclaim the previous connection with the students. Monologic reflection upon the event of reciprocity destroys; it "bursts asunder" (Bonhoeffer, 1955) the possibility of dialogue. The possibility of dialogue lives only in the unreflective action of reciprocity. Buber rejected the "demand" of reciprocity, without rejecting the existential reality of emergent reciprocity that appears organically between persons, without insistence or demand.

Buber does interpret differently than Levinas. Buber accepts reciprocity when it emerges organically, acknowledging reciprocity as an existential reality. Buber rejects reciprocity upon demand and recognizes the emergent, invitational existential reality of reciprocal concern. Buber contends that the demand for reciprocity moves reciprocal life from dialogue to monologue, whereas emergent reciprocity offers interpersonal meaning between persons. Buber states, "All real living is meeting" (1958, p. 11). Reciprocity makes existential life meaningful. Reciprocity is not a form of social exchange or some form of caring upon demand; Buber's emergent reciprocity is a natural dialogic response that offers interpersonal meaning between persons.

Just as Buber's recognition of dialogic reciprocity and its destruction through monologic reflection make sense in everyday life, Levinas's attention to unilateral responsibility irrespective of reciprocity is more than wishful theorizing. Such unilateral responsibility manifests itself when a person risks one's life to save another without asking, "Who is this person? What is the risk to me? What is my obligation in this situation?" One simply acts from a phenomenological call from the Other. In addition, in the daily act of parenting, one attends to the scream of a child in the middle of the night without asking, "Should I get up? I wonder if all is okay?" Levinas describes a phenomenological ethical reality that evokes a call of responsibility and unreflective action, attending to a phenomenological description or assertion, "I am my brother's keeper."

The unilateral ethical demand to which Levinas points and the possibility of emergent dialogic reciprocity from Buber define differing spheres of human life, the phenomenological present and the existentially emergent. Levinas's world of phenomenological description suggests a one-sided ethical demand. Buber's existential world understands that particular acts are essential for the good of the community, but can only add character to the life of a people when invited, emergent, and without demand. Buber's world of the existentially emergent explains meaningfulness between persons without demand. Buber's understanding of reciprocity is akin to Aristotle's understanding of genuine friendship (1991, pp. 506–507), an act of mutual, invited reciprocity of concern. Buber understood the social significance of reciprocity for dialogue between persons in the existential world of work, family, and friendship, while rejecting reciprocity upon demand.

Numerous authors have explored the disagreement between Levinas and Buber regarding reciprocity (e.g., Bernasconi, 1988; Casey, 1999; Gordon, 1999; Kelly, 1995; Lawton, 1976; Levinas, 1984b; Lumsden, 2000; Tallon, 1978; Warner, 1996). Levinas and Buber debated whether reciprocity or ontology should guide the human discourse. Accepting *la différance* as key to negotiating a postmodern world encourages attending to multiple voices, in this case both Levinas and Buber. As Suurmond suggested (1999, pp. 65–68), Emmanuel Levinas and Martin Buber are two of the foremost authors on ethics and dialogue, respectively. Attending to each voice makes pragmatic sense as one seeks to learn from each project. Permitting voices of difference to inform the discipline about Levinas and Buber guided Lipari's (2001) presentation in which she called for recognition of their differences, permitting each scholar to be correct in order to hear the nuances of each respective project.

Accepting the voices of Levinas and Buber embraces a "unity of contraries" (Buber, 1965b, p. 111), rejecting *and* accepting reciprocity. Levinas contended with reciprocity; Buber claimed that demand eliminates dialogic reciprocity but that emergent reciprocity connects persons in existential life together. Accepting both positions on reciprocity permits a pragmatic appreciation of two connected, but differing, perspectives: the phenomenological world of the descriptive (Levinas) and the existential world of emergent reciprocity between persons (Buber).

Levinas, the phenomenological scholar of ethics, and Buber, the existential-phenomenological scholar of dialogue, offer different but equally important insights. Levinas's phenomenology attends to "the things themselves." Buber's existential philosophical anthropology attends to human connection in the mud and confusion of everyday life. Levinas offers a phenomenology of an ethical *is;* Buber attends to the relationally emergent existential *between* persons. Uniting Levinas and Buber embraces a phenomenological ethical *is* of unilateral demand and an existentially emergent recognition of reciprocity *between* persons.

A Dialogic Ethic: Engaging a Responsive Ethical "I"

Buber's reciprocity of dialogue and Levinas's unilateral call to responsibility both depend upon an "I" interpreted otherwise. The following section frames this "I" as a "responsive ethical 'I,'" the heart of a dialogic ethic.

Both Levinas and Buber offer an alternative to the focus upon the self. These two Jewish philosophers, one known for ethics and the other for dialogue and each responsive to the "oppressive narrative" of Nazi Germany, point to a dialogic ethic within a phenomenological focus of attention upon ethics and responsibility and the dialogic importance of existential invitational reciprocity. They point to a dialogic ethic steeped in responsibility, not dependent upon one's own personal preferences or the dictates of outside principles and agents.

Neither Levinas nor Buber begins with the notion of the "I"; they understand the "I" emerging as a by-product, responding to a call of responsibility.

The "I" enacts responsibility; the "I" finds identity in response to a call from the Other (Levinas) and the "between" (Buber). Emphasis upon the "I" is not unique in communication literature or in the West; *how* Levinas and Buber understand the identity formation and construction of the "I" in response is key to their "interpreting otherwise." For instance, Levinas tells us to *forego* focus upon the color of the Other's eyes, or we risk missing the face of the Other (1985, pp. 85–86). Levinas, as a nonhumanist, points to the phenomenological importance of the notion "to the things themselves." Levinas desires a phenomenological knowing—"to the things themselves"—to which one responds; focusing upon perception of the Other misses the phenomenon of the Other. Levinas's *what* or phenomenon (the Other) carries a "trace" (1981, pp. 12–13) of a primordial call to ethics or responsibility for the Other. In the face of the Other, one finds a primordial trace pointing to an ethical primordial responsibility (Levinas, 1969, p. 304), which, as a by-product and in response, forms identity for the "I" in responsible action on behalf of the Other. The Other is the "penultimate" (Bonhoeffer, 1955, pp. 120–187). The Other points to an ethical primordial call of ethics as "first philosophy" (Levinas, 1969, p. 304).

Responsibility for the Other is the ultimate (Bonhoeffer, 1955, pp. 120–187) in Levinas's description of ethics. Missing Levinas's reading of the "I" misses the conversation he brings to communication ethics. Understanding the Other as a nonhumanistic sign pointing to a primordial trace of an ethical call of responsibility enters the horizon of Levinas's phenomenological description.

Buber, also "interpreting otherwise," points to a twofold form of inquiry: knowledge of moral stories and responsiveness to the concrete situation of the "between," from which the "I" finds identity. Buber understands dialogue as beginning with ground under one's feet—story-informed ground, not self-concept. A story-formed person meets the historical situation and the Other, permitting a unique "I" to emerge. Buber's love of Hasidic tales reveals the union of story and concrete response (1991). Whereas Levinas understands the "I" as responsive to a primordial ethical call, Buber sees the "I" as a responsive resultant encounter "between" story, historical situation, and the Other. For Buber, the "between" informs the "I" in meeting, in responsiveness.

The monologic "I" guides much of existential life, but at moments a dialogic "I" formed in response offers insight about responsibility. Buber, responsive to the existential moment, and Levinas, responsive to the phenomenological face of the Other, point to ethical responsibility that in action forms the identity of the "I." The formation of the "I" as a by-product of responsiveness to Otherness shapes what in this chapter I call a "responsive ethical 'I.'" The "responsive ethical 'I'" within the horizons of both Emmanuel Levinas and Martin Buber finds life in responsiveness and responsibility to the Other and the historical situation. Levinas and Buber point to a "responsive ethical 'I'" capable of meeting and contending with narrative oppression, capable of anchoring a dialogic ethic. Meeting Nazi tyranny required an immediate alternative to destructive narrative life.

Levinas reminds us of the primordial importance of ethics, which frames the "I" of responsibility. However, Buber gives us insight into what to do when the way is unclear. The region of the "between" is a place of "fuzzy clarity" (Arnett, 2001, p. 316), suggesting that a "responsive ethical 'I'" engage the historical situation and the Other, discerning answers that are temporal, guiding within the existential moment of decision. A dialogic ethic begins with Levinas's phenomenological reading and then seeks how to do implementation in the confusion of a postmodern world, falling back upon the existential insight of Buber.

Buber's "between" is concrete. It suggests a place of "real living" (Buber, 1965a, p. 168). Buber interpreted otherwise in his construction of *concrete* and *abstract* (see Arnett & Arneson, 1999, p. 140), contrasting the "everyday" view of the concrete—the ordered, the logical, the unresponsive to interruption and discordant, with a *dialogic concrete* that, on the other hand, responds to unexpected intrusions, to invasion upon our predetermined plans. The dialogic concrete is akin to holding sand, consistently discovering seepage through one's fingers, beyond one's grip, beyond one's control. "Interpreting otherwise" engages the concrete as evasive, beyond our grasp. In contrast, Buber viewed the abstract as grasping, holding onto, making sure nothing escapes—missing real living, as Buber understood dialogic engagement. For Buber, poetry is more concrete than a logical description of issues such as friendship, love, hope, or loyalty.

Buber's communicative poetry guides without dictating a linear series of expectations (Arnett & Arneson, 1999, pp. 140–142). Following the horizon of Buber's perspective, this essay suggests that a dialogic ethic "interprets otherwise," unable to provide a graspable answer, pointing to "concrete" life in which real meeting lives in fuzzy clarity, in a guided temporal response. The "between" is the concrete existential signpost for implementation, fueled by a phenomenological conviction that the "I" finds identity in the trace within the face of the Other that calls one into responsible action. A dialogic ethic offers phenomenological conviction, the necessity to learn, and the importance of attentiveness to the "between," finding answers among the "responsive ethical 'I,'" the historical situation, and the Other.

Guidance without authoritative promise situates the horizon of a dialogic ethic not with universal confidence, but as responsive to ethical decision making in the existential world of fuzzy clarity and "maybe." Dialogic ethics unites Levinas's phenomenological "is," a primordial call to responsibility, with Buber's existential "emergent," contingent discernment in the sphere of the "between" (Buber, 1965a, pp. 202–203). Together the "is" and the "emergent" offer a communication ethic with phenomenological support and existential invitation, a communication ethic with content—"I am my brother's keeper"—and openness to the complexity of dialogic implementation. A dialogic ethic accepts Levinas's phenomenological view of ethics, tempered by Buber's invitational and existential spirit.

A "responsive ethical 'I'" provides one postmodern dialogic ethic. Ethics are not located in place, in the self, or in a metanarrative sense of assurance (Arnett & Arneson, 1999, p. 52), but in a response that calls forth a responsible "I" that attends to the Other and the historical situation, not out of technique, but from a creative pragmatism that ever recalls "I am my brother's keeper." Without the Other, there is no "I."

As I sit here one day from the first year anniversary of September 11, 2001, a "responsive ethical 'I'" offers no answer, but does offer caution. We cannot live in a world without others; how we address the Other shapes the "I" of a people. Levinas and Buber witnessed a narrative of utter horror authored by Nazi evil; yet they offer a call to remember our responsibility to the Other: it is a phenomenological fact. Do your best to attend to what is called for in action "between" you and the Other. Be thankful when mutual concern bonds relationships—such moments make life worth living under the most dire of circumstances. Such was the response of Buber and Levinas to collective evil, reminding that it is possible to "interpret otherwise," pointing to a dialogic ethic, pointing to a "responsive ethical 'I,'" reaching out *in return* to the Other, even in dark times.

6

Dialogue, Creativity, and Change

Sheila McNamee and John Shotter

I t seems odd to us to write about dialogue, creativity, and change without attempting to integrate explicitly the conversational partners with whom we are engaged. This means not only incorporating others' ways of describing dialogue processes, but also embodying in our text *our* voices as respondents to each other. Thus, we begin this chapter with a transcript of a conversation we had about dialogue, creativity, and change. After our initial comments, we each take some time to elaborate our specific points. In this way, our hope is to present a chapter that is emblematic of open dialogue (Seikkula, Aaltonen, Alakara, Haarakangas, Keranen, & Sutela, 1995).

Our Conversation

John: Sheila, a central reason for my interest in dialogue is that I think it makes possible a special kind of first-time creativity, the creation "out of the blue" of a way of acting in response to, or in relation to, the unique character of one's current surroundings. In a moment, I would like to say something about how this might come about. But let me first invite you to say something about the reasons for your interest in dialogue.

Sheila: Well, where I would like to begin is really only arbitrarily a beginning because it is actually a *response* to you. I was caught by your comment about creativity and coming "out of the blue." This is where I want to focus: on the construction of possibilities. But I am also interested in another dimension of dialogue. I'm interested in how we position ourselves in conversation as if we already know what the other person is going to say. It is as if we can be certain about how things will unfold. We come from a tradition where we often rehearse a scenario, whether it be the first time to declare love for somebody or trying out different possibilities for disciplining your child. I believe that our presumption is that we think we know how things will go. And having this presumption affords us the opportunity to rehearse. I see this as adding a significant second dimension to dialogue that appears to be just the opposite of what you were just describing. There is the unimaginable *newness* of dialogue along with what seems to be the predictable. My own curiosity is with the former feature; how do we capture the unknown, the sense of creating something anew? I think we are both interested in putting more emphasis on that domain. Yet, I think it must be discussed against the backdrop of how we assume we can predict dialogue.

John: Yeah, so precisely, on the one hand, a clear set of expectations before the other person responds, and on the other, the possibility of being truly surprised and being "arrested" or "struck"–of having something quite other than what you expected influence you in some way. As I see it, it's in this way that dialogue can bring about change in us that nothing else can.

Sheila: Yes, I agree. An impetus for my work is to try to find ways of talking and writing that alert people to this possibility of the unknown, of the surprises, of the newness. This goes back to the pioneering work of the group associated with the Mental Research Institute (e.g., Watzlawick, Weakland, & Fisch, 1974). They talked about first and second order change. Often, something in a conversation with another could really be an opening to something entirely different, but it's read as, or interpreted as, a variation on the theme, the same old thing. I think what I see as an important step is the opening of possibilities for people to pause and consider various other voices that they could use. We all know how communication quickly can become ritualized within given relationships or situations. What I find useful is to find a way to draw on the other voices that we have within our repertoire of actions. We should become curious about how we might use other voices, other responses, actions, or moves that are simultaneously quite familiar to us but very strange within the situation with which we are currently engaged. It is only in that moment that I think we really can appreciate this creativity, this newness. Otherwise, we do feel like we're doing the same old thing day in and day out in our conversations.

John: Something Arlene Katz (Katz, Conant, Inui, Baron, & Bor, 2000) has emphasized is that one cannot just say: "Let's have a dialogue.

Let's set up, between people who haven't properly met before, the opportunity for them to meet." We have found that one needs quite a degree of preparation—where preparation is quite different from planning. Preparation has to do with one's orientation, with one's background expectations, the kind of overall language-game one thinks of oneself as involved in; planning has to do with ground rules and suchlike.

Sheila: Absolutely. I've come to think of this feature—the preparation for dialogue—in very specific terms. I have found it useful to focus on two notions that seem to "tell it all" for me. One is, as of course you know, that I like to draw on Wittgenstein's notion of "How do we go on together?" (Wittgenstein, 1963). To me, he raises *the* central question. Social interaction, human engagement, is not concerned with explaining something or with figuring out why relationships or people work this way or that. Rather, our focus should be on how we craft livable futures together. This is a very important issue. In the simplest, and probably also vaguest, terms, this question suggests the need to create the conversational space, where *different* kinds of conversations can transpire. For me, this implies that planning is not really the central feature but, rather, that the preparation for generative dialogue should be central. What I mean by this is that we must engage in reflexive inquiry where we consider how to invite participants to engage in the dialogue with *different* voices. This is where my second focus—creating a context where participants avoid speaking from abstract positions—becomes significant. Often in conversations, we find ourselves speaking from abstract positions. This frequently takes the form of statements like, "This is what I believe," "This is true," "This is right," "This is wrong," and those are abstractions. Instead, I like to invite people to root those abstractions in a life story of their own. It doesn't need to be extremely self-disclosive, but it's rooted in a story. And while I may disagree with your position on something, I can't tell you that your story is wrong. And that opens a possibility for us to be in a different kind of conversation than we would otherwise have.

John: Your first thing, emphasizing going on together, and then the second, rooting what you say in some personal experience, connects for me with what seems to be the major theme in what makes a dialogue a dialogue: that everything is connected to everything else in terms of what can simply be called "spontaneous living responsivity." It matters that people genuinely talk in response to what either the immediate situation requires or what somebody else has just said.

Sheila: Or what they imagine, and this goes back to my opening comment. Often, people are responsive to what they imagine the other person will say based on a history of a relationship. But, that is not what *has* to happen and that's where conversations go awry quite often, I think. And so, what you called responsivity I would call "relational responsibility"—being attentive to the process of relating. If I'm truly being attentive to the process of relating, no matter how many times you and I may have gotten into an argument about something, when I'm talking with you now I won't necessarily—I won't be too fast to—listen to what you're saying *in that frame.* Rather, I will be attentive to what we are doing *right now.* And the history of that becomes a part of it, but doesn't dominate it. And that leaves, again, that open space for the creativity.

John: Yes, and it's in that space where Bateson's (1972) notion of "information being the difference that makes the difference" can operate. The difference arises at that moment when, on the one hand, you have an expectation, and on the other hand, it isn't exactly fulfilled as you expect. Thus, there is a difference between that expectation and its fulfillment. And in a dialogical context, that's where the otherness of the other comes in. In a marvelous phrase of George Steiner's (1989), "The 'otherness' which enters into us makes us other" (p. 188).

Sheila: Yes, yes.

John: And that is how it is, at least for me. Not only is dialogue creative, but it can make for a genuine change. Not a mere change, one more bit of information, or a change in opinion. It's actually changing you and your active, living relations to your surroundings.

Sheila: Right, I love that Bateson phrase too, "the difference that makes a difference." And the question is how can we build that in, that kind of sensibility of pausing and waiting to hear the potential difference. And another thing that quote always draws me to thinking about is how we talk about dialogue as a natural activity. We engage in dialogue every day. And in contrast, we think of debate as something in which we must be trained. In debate, we have all these rules and procedures to follow. You know, my opening statement, then, in so many minutes, you respond, I respond, so on and so forth. There is an order to it. So, I have started playing around, ironically, with the need for rules about this seemingly ordinary activity. That is, in order to make the difference, for these different kind of dialogues, for the newness to emerge, we must make the ordinary unusual. To make the familiar unfamiliar by providing ground rules when we can. One can do that whether setting up a formal dialogue session, as I frequently do in various communities, or in an interpersonal relationship. It is not so difficult to say, "Let's make a rule before we have a conversation that we won't talk in this way or we won't be too quick to judge each other." Personally and intellectually I find that those operations remind us that dialogue is full of potential. But we need to be reminded by making it into something that's foreign. This speaks directly to the point we both have been making concerning the need for *preparation* for dialogue.

John: I've got two responses to that which may, at first, seem contradictory, both with each other, and in disagreement with your need to make dialogue into something "foreign."

Sheila: That's okay. We can contradict each other.

John: One, concerns how conversation connects with our "natural" reactions to things, with what we might call our animal natures. As perhaps you know, recently I have become more and more intrigued—particularly by that program "Why Dogs Laugh And Chimpanzees Cry"—with just looking at animals' very, very natural reactions to each other, their social reactions, and their understandings of each other's (what psychologists might call) "states of mind," or whatever (Shotter, 2003). They care for each other much as we do. As I see it, conversation is a very natural extension of our animal responses to each other. We cannot *not* care when the others around us suffer. We find it very difficult to turn off these very basic, spontaneous responses. On the other hand, your comment about making our ordinary ways of going on strange is like the lights going down on the theater auditorium and coming up on the stage. We create a little magical setting as if something very special is going to happen. I think this is very important, too. And I think both these comments are connected. What we could call our everyday Western ways of going on have become so infused with so many routines, so many taken for granted assumptions. These taken for granted routines and assumptions have got to, in some way, be broken up, deconstructed, and our practices opened up to see in them the new but unnoticed possibilities they still offer.

Sheila: Right. This reminds me of my intermediate-level family communication class. We're talking about all these ideas in terms of the family, and so I want them to be able to know the difference this way of talking offers. So, what I do is I ask them to create a simulated family. And of course, at first, what happens is they call this a "role play." I never use that term so it is always very interesting to me that they immediately term it such. It seems to me that, once identified as a "role play" activity, they feel compelled to wait. They look at me as if to say, "Well, am I the mother? Am I the father? And what's our story?" I say, "No, no—you're a family, go ahead, just start." And so they start by drawing on extremely stereotypical images. Yet, slowly they create an identity that is beyond any one of them—a beautiful illustration of the performative notion of developing into who you will become. They engage in precisely the sort of creative, unusual, and spontaneous reality that we have been describing. They create identities, relationships, and even *histories* that are part of all of them but not identifiable with any single one of them. They engage in a conversation and questions are asked and accusations made and things happen. And then, if those of us observing ask them questions, we find that our questions can change the direction or nature of what is being created and so forth. And it becomes so powerful that in every single instance of doing this, there has been at least one person in the simulated family who has felt it necessary to declare openly to the class, when it's all said and done, "I am not like that! That is not who I am. I don't act that way. I don't believe in those things." Anyway, I think of this activity as an opportunity for students to see the power of being in dialogue and how they never question *how* we accomplish the creation of beliefs, values, and identities in this ordinary practice called dialogue. They might believe that it's ordinary to be a mother this way or be a father that way, but very quickly it becomes unusual, not ordinary. It becomes an incredibly unique and unpredictable dynamic. The interactive moment constructs the identity of the family, of each individual and so forth. And so as you were talking, I was thinking of that as an illustration of the tension in dialogue to recognize the routine, to take for granted the assumptions and routines with which we engage while also recognizing the open potential for transformation, something beyond the usual.

John: It does seem to me that in our last 40 or 50 years of intellectual talk in the West, we've created some extremely empty and neutral circumstances for ourselves, as if our surroundings are purely physical, and the only subjective things in the world are in our heads. But the idea that we can be in an environment, a conversational or dialogical environment that, itself, takes on an anthropomorphic quality, is a tremendously powerful idea. When we say things like, "Society tells us" or "This is the way it has to be done" without ever identifying the dialogues that construct these abstract beliefs, we are operating within this idea. And, as perhaps you know, I have begun to think back to people like Lucien Levy-Bruhl (1926), and what he calls "the mental functions of inferior peoples," and his claims of how this "participatory" or "anthropomorphic" thinking was an enormous mistake, and how we have now grown beyond it. Whereas, in fact, rather than growing beyond it, I think we've simply failed to recognize the enormous importance and power that such forms of thought—in which we feel the presence of a personified agency "calling" on us to act—still have for us.

Sheila: Enormous, enormous. Think of how many times in a day someone says, "Society says," "Society tells us." My question always is, "Who is society?" It's us. I see this all the time in the classroom. I often ask people what they would consider the features of an outstanding, learning environment/classroom in a university setting or in their lifetime. People can list off all sorts of features. For example, they tell me that in a formal educational context clear lectures, good note-taking abilities, raised hands when questions occur are typical. It is as if the best learning situation is already scripted. And then I say, "Now tell me what *your* best learning experience was like." They have no problem describing their experiences but these stories have *none* of the features they have already listed in response to my first question. There's nothing like those activities. Instead, they say things like, "Oh, we would go outside and we'd talk about things, and we'd gather around coffee and talk ideas and do this and that." For me, this illustrates how these abstractions become a dominating discourse, as when people say, "society says." We often forget how we create possibilities moment by moment in dialogue with others. I don't know if we've gotten off track.

John: I think we've provided a good beginning from which each of us individually can now expand in our own directions.

Sheila: All right.

John: Thanks very much, Sheila.

Sheila: Thank you.

Joint Action and the Chiasmic Inter-Relating of Spontaneously Responsive, Bodily Activities

—John Shotter

I mentioned that I would like to say something about how dialogue makes possible a special kind of *first-time creativity,* the creation "out of the blue" of a way of acting in response to, or in relation to, the unique character of one's current surroundings. In referring to a "first-time" creativity, I have in mind a phrase of Garfinkel's (1967). In his discussion of a community's shared "accounting practices," he remarks that, by their use, a member of a community "makes familiar, commonplace activities of everyday life recognizable *as* familiar," and that, on each new occasion, it is done for yet "another first time" (p. 9).

As is well known, early work by Mills (1940), followed by Scott and Lyman (1968), directed attention toward the importance of all members of a speech community being trained into an extensive network of normative "background expectations." It is these anticipations that work to hold all the different actions within that community together as an intelligible whole. Members failing to satisfy such background expectations in their actions will puzzle, bewilder, or disorient other members who will then question their conduct.

But it is precisely these background expectations that make it possible for us to use our utterances in new ways. As Bakhtin (1986) notes, "An utterance is never just a reflection or an expression of something already existing and outside it that is given and final. It always creates something that never existed before, something absolutely new and unrepeatable" (p. 119). This kind of continuously occurring, first-time, unpredictable, and unanticipated but nonetheless (once it has occurred) intelligible creativity, has not yet, I want to claim, been adequately appreciated and characterized in our social thought, although relatively recently, Wittgenstein-inspired accounts of this problem have begun to appear (Johnston, 1993; Mulhall, 1990). Indeed, the pervasive Cartesianism (Taylor, 1995) at work in our everyday accounting practices has led us both to locate the sources for all our social activities inside the heads of individuals and to characterize these sources in terms of rules, or laws, that is, in terms of regularities and repetitions. It has led us, also, to ignore precisely those events which occur only *between* people and which occur *only* once.

Thus, to understand what is possible for us within such dialogically structured events, and only within such events, we must think of such relations in some radically new ways. Indeed, as we shall see, we must think of them in *extra* ordinary terms, in terms that can perhaps shock us into spontaneously responding to the events occurring around us in uniquely new, first-time ways.

As an initial step in this exploration, let me first turn to the importance of our living, bodily responsiveness. This is basic, because we cannot *not* be responsive both to the others and the othernesses around us in our surroundings. Thus, in such a spontaneously responsive sphere of activity as this, instead of one person first acting individually and independently of an other and then the second replying, by acting individually and independently of the first, we act jointly, as a *collective we.* And we do this bodily, in a "living" way, spontaneously, without us having first "to work out" how to respond to each other. This means that when someone acts, their activity cannot be accounted as wholly their own activity—for a person's acts are always partly shaped by the acts of the others around them—and this is where all the strangeness of the dialogical begins (see Shotter, 1980, 1984, 1993a, 1993b).

Our dialogical actions are neither yours nor mine; they are truly *ours*. Indeed, what is produced in such dialogical exchanges is a very complex mixture of not wholly reconcilable influences, which Bakhtin (1981) refers to as both "centripetal" tendencies inward toward order and unity at the center, as well as "centrifugal" tendencies outward toward diversity and difference on the borders or margins. Further, because the overall outcome of any exchange cannot be traced back to the intentions of any of the individuals involved, the "dialogical reality or space" constructed between them is experienced as an external reality or a "third agency" (an *it*) with its own (ethical) demands and requirements. Thus, as Taylor (1991a) points out, more is involved here than individuals merely coordinating their actions. From their embedding within the common "rhythming" of their activities—be it moving a piano, sawing with a two-person crosscut saw, dancing, or participating in a conversation—the individuals involved become participant parts of "an integrated, nonindividual *agent*" (p. 311, emphasis added). As such, they answer to the "demands" they all feel coming to them, not from other individuals, but from the jointly shared activity within which they are all involved. "The word [in an utterance] is a drama in which three characters participate (it is not a duet, but a trio)" (Bakhtin, 1986, p. 122).

But from whence does this strange dialogically structured, dispersed agency emerge? How are all the influences that go into its formation interlinked with each other to form such an integrated unity? We can take *binocular vision* as a major analogue in bringing out this aspect of the peculiar nature of dialogically structured activities into the light of day. Why? Well, Bakhtin (1984) remarks that "a *plurality of independent and unmerged voices and consciousnesses* . . . combine but are not merged in the unity of the event" (p. 6). In other words, just as the two different, moment-by-moment changing views of a landscape before us, given us by our two different eyes as we scan over it, are not merged into a blurred, average, two-dimensional image, but work together to create for us a sense of *depth*, a third dimension, so the different voices speaking from different momentary positions in a shared "space" can also give us a sense of that space as having some "depth" to it, can constitute it as a "landscape" of possible places to "go on" to, of "mental movements" that one might make.

In Bateson's (1979) discussion of the question of "What bonus or increment of knowing follows from *combining* information from two or more sources," he picks up on two of our themes: the importance of the "difference that makes a difference," of "news," that is, of first-time events, and of the unmerged combining of "at least two somethings to create a difference" (p. 78). In particular, something special happens, he notes, in the optic chiasma (the crossing of the optic nerves from the two eyes in the hypothalamus of the brain), "the *difference* between the information provided by the one retina and that provided by the other" works to help the seer add "an extra *dimension* to seeing" (p. 79), the dimension of depth. Instead of seeing things as just large or small, we see them as near or far.

But in considering seeing with two eyes, are we, perhaps, getting just a little ahead of ourselves and moving to a higher level of complexity before considering seeing "something" with just one eye? Perhaps we should consider, first, what is involved, even with one eye, in scanning over a face and seeing it— with all its changing expressions—as the *same* face, only now as a smiling face, now as frowning, now as sad, as welcoming, as threatening, and so on? How do we join together all the different fragments collected at different moments into a coherent, unitary whole, into the "seeing" of a person's face? That seeing a person's face *as a face* is an achievement in which it is possible to fail, is shown by Sacks's (1985) Dr. P. Although he knew perfectly well what eyes, noses, chins, and so forth, were, he could not spontaneously recognize people's faces as such, and thus it was that he mistook his wife's face for his hat.

In other words, what is at work here is a kind of understanding which, in Wittgenstein's (1963) terms, "consists in 'seeing connections'" (no. 122), a kind of understanding we might call a *relationally responsive* form of understanding, to contrast it with the *representational–referential* forms of understandings more familiar to us in our intellectual dealings with our surroundings.

But these relationally responsive forms of understanding all entail our seeing connections and relations within a living whole, a whole constructed or created from many different fragmentary parts, all picked up in the course of one's *continuous, living, responsive contact* with a particular circumstance in question, whether it is a text, a person, a landscape, or whatever. So, perhaps we were not so ahead of ourselves in seeing the kind of chiasmatic interweaving that occurs in binocular vision, as paradigmatic of the creation of many further "relational dimensions" in other spheres of understanding. As Merleau-Ponty (1968) points out, chiasmatic interweaving seems to be involved in all our bodily understandings of our relations to our surroundings: "There is a double and a crossed situating of the visible in the tangible and of the tangible in the visible; the two maps are complete, and yet they do not merge into one" (p. 134). Indeed,

> my two hands touch the same things because they are the hands of one same body . . . [and] because there exists a very peculiar relation from one to the other, across corporeal space—like that holding between my two eyes—making my hands one sole organ of experience. (p. 141)

These understandings—the creation of these relational dimensions— might range all the way from simply "seeing" a person's facial expression as a smile or utterance as a question, to "seeing" quite complex connections between people's behaviors in their lives—as, for instance, Margaret Schegel in E. M. Forster's (1989) *Howard's End* "saw" connections between her forgiveness of Herbert Wilcox's sexual peccadilloes and his lack of forgiveness of those of her sister. But all such understandings have their beginnings in those moments when something occurs that "moves" or "strikes" us, when an event makes a noticeable difference to us because it matters to us.

> There is, it seems to us, at best, only a limited value in the knowledge derived from experience. The knowledge imposes a pattern, and falsifies, for the pattern is new in every moment and every moment is a new and shocking valuation of all we have been. (Eliot, 1944, p. 23)

In other words, for something to make a difference that matters to us, something must surprise us, be unanticipated, unexpected, fill us with wonder. But, as Fisher (1998) notes,

> the experiential world within which wonder takes place cannot be made of unordered, singular patches of experience. We wonder at that which is a momentary surprise within a pattern that we feel confident we know. It is *extra* ordinary, the unexpected. For there to be anything that can be called "unexpected" there must first be the expected. In other words, years or even centuries of intellectual work must already have taken place in a certain direction before there can be a reality that is viewed as ordinary and expected. (p. 57)

And it is against this background, the background of our ordinary, everyday, shared accounting practices, that such events can occur and strike us with wonder. And it is our passion for wonder—the gift made to us by our shared dialogically structured accounting practices—that distinguishes us from all other living animals.

Shifting Our Orientation to Everyday Practices

—Sheila McNamee

John's comments serve as an invitation to me to offer some specific, yet fluid, resources we might use to promote dialogue in our everyday interactions (see McNamee, 2002a, 2002b). I can now fill in the pragmatics (so to speak) of constructing something "out of the blue," unknown, new. Basically, my interest is with how to orient ourselves to the mundane activities in which we participate such that—when so desired—the predictable or expected does not reemerge. It is important to note that I am not suggesting that this is how we would prefer to engage in every interactive moment. Yet, those that appear so ritualized and unwanted, old routines that have become cumbersome, can be transformed only if we orient ourselves differently. In a similar vein, those relationships that are haunted by conflict, discord, and animosity might well shift toward generative patterns of engagement if only we orient ourselves within a relational frame.

John references Bakhtin (1986) in his proposal that language/activity is never a representation of the world as it is but is, rather, a creation of the world as we construct it. The former, modernist orientation, with its focus on both individuals as independent units with certain capabilities and deficiencies *and* its focus on language/action as a vehicle for representing the world as it is, has given birth to our unquestioned orientation to everyday activities. Specifically, if we believe that we are autonomous beings, each equipped with our own, private abilities to represent reality accurately, then, obviously, we approach our everyday engagements as if each participant either knows or does not know, can do or cannot do, will excel or not excel—precisely the sort of routinized, predictable orientations we were discussing earlier. On the other hand, if we take seriously the relational sensibility required of dialogue, we would probably enter into the mundane activities of our lives in very different ways. We might, for example, enter into a conflict with curiosity about *how* it emerged and what purpose it was serving, rather than from the perspective of *why* it was occurring and *who* was at fault. We might just as well enter into a smoothly flowing relational moment with a fresh curiosity for how, among all the complexity of human affairs, we manage to engage ourselves and others in such a coordinated performance. The distinctions between the individualist and the relational sensibilities are miles apart in terms of the possibilities they invite.

John has suggested that "for something to make a difference that matters to us, something must surprise us, be unanticipated, unexpected, fill us with wonder." So, for me, the issue becomes one of reorienting ourselves to daily activities. How might we enter into dialogue *expecting* to be surprised or filled with wonder rather than enter into dialogue *hoping* we will somehow magically encounter the unanticipated?

I would like to propose some general notions that, I believe, orient us toward the creative possibilities of dialogue. These resources are by no means exhaustive. I offer these as only an entrée into the imaginative construction of further dialogic potential.

First, and probably most contrary to our traditional, individualist orientation to the world, is the constant use of reflexive critique. Reflexive critique can take many forms in any interactive moment. We might, for example, pause at the moment we *know* we are correct, we *know* we have the best method or plan, we *know* how something should be. If we pause and ask ourselves, "how else might this be," "what else could I do at this moment," "is there a different way to make sense out of the other person's comments or actions," we open ourselves to the sort of inquiry that invites alternative meanings (McNamee & Gergen, 1999). This is just the sort of inquiry Jaakko Seikkula and his colleagues (1995) engage when they respond to a psychiatric crisis. Rather than assume they, as the professionals, should provide a diagnosis and treatment plan, Seikkula and his team gather all interested parties together (the person in crisis, family members, friends, neighbors, medical professionals—anyone who might have something to contribute). Collaboratively they develop a plan of action that is responsive to the multiple ways of approaching and understanding the situation. The person in crisis is an active participant in this process. Seikkula calls this process *open dialogue*. It requires a suspension of the professionals' certainty that they can provide an accurate diagnosis from which they can develop a successful treatment plan.

When we engage in self-reflexive critique like this, we avoid certainty. And, although certainty (as one hallmark of the competent individual) logically sounds appealing to us, it is precisely the stance that closes us to alternative views. Certainty also separates participants by establishing levels of expertise. Ironically, one of the very qualities we are trained to develop—certainty—inhibits our ability to move beyond conflict and discord toward transforming dialogic possibilities.

Another resource I find useful, as I mentioned earlier, is to avoid speaking from abstract positions. As with the stance of certainty, abstractions invite hierarchy and thus, separation—features not found in dialogue. Principles, values, and beliefs are crafted out of our day-to-day engagement with others. Understanding the principles from which you speak, the values that so strongly shape your position, or the beliefs that you hold dear, requires some sense of the relationships, the communities, the situated activities that have given these abstractions meaning for you. If you tell me a story about your family's rituals, I am more likely to appreciate how you raise your own children. Such appreciation does not require agreement. Yet, the difference between acknowledging the coherence of your beliefs or values and simply declaring them wrong, evil, or bad (because they do not fit with my beliefs or values) is tremendous.

This is aptly illustrated in the work of the Public Conversations Project (e.g., Chasin, Herzig, Roth, Chasin, Becker, & Stains, 1996). They show us how dialogue among people with incommensurate views is facilitated by inviting them to talk about the relational communities within which their beliefs (i.e., abstract positions) have been constructed. We can remain in dialogue if we appreciate the *situated* coherence of each other's position. And, to craft a reality together, remaining in dialogue is necessary. Thus, we can see that speaking from abstract positions closes our opportunities to *go on together* and locks us in endless attempts to achieve agreement (which we may never achieve). Avoiding abstraction helps us focus on recognizing the *local* significance of opposing views and in that recognition lies the potential to remain in dialogue.

An additional resource that orients us toward dialogic potentials can be called the imaginative. Here, I find it useful to engage in conversations in which we allow ourselves and invite our conversational partners to talk "as if" (Anderson, 1997). Can we talk *as if* we are the other in this situation? Can we talk *as if* we were a spouse, rather than a colleague? How might we invite the other in a situation to speak as if he or she were curious about alternative views? These questions open dialogic possibilities by encouraging participants to move beyond sedimented images of self and other.

Along with *as if* conversations, we might engage in *what if* talk. As with *as if* conversations, when we play with potential scenarios beyond the expected, we have a stronger chance of inviting our relational partners into the crafting of new scenarios. Often, both *as if* and *what if* conversations can be usefully positioned within a broader dialogue about the future. When we speak from certainty and abstract positions, we tend to focus our attention on the past and why things are a particular way. However, when we engage in talk about the future, our idealized hopes for how it might be crafted jointly, our focus shifts from why to how our views and practices are in conflict. This shift to how from why suggests a final resource we might use to encourage dialogue.

When we focus on how we differ (or even how we manage to coordinate our activities together so well), we attend to our joint activities. How do *we* do this *together?* My actions alone are not wholly mine. They are *ours.* They are responsive to the situated moment, to our traditions of discourse, and to our imagined futures. We should not be concerned with asking, "How did we get here?" but rather be interested in asking, "How can *we* get *there?*" These pragmatic resources can enhance our potential for inviting ourselves and others into the openness of dialogue.

Some Concluding Remarks

Clearly, there is more to be said about dialogue, creativity, and change. We hope that our reflections here open further possibilities for the future of dialogue as a means for social transformation. We have tried to articulate the tension created by our typical focus within dialogue on the ordinary, routinized, taken-for-granted aspects of interaction while largely ignoring the open potential within dialogue for transformation. Our own emphases, as we offer them here, remind us that dialogue is a joint performance wherein participants are responsive to each other and to their environment. Such responsivity renders dialogue unusual and unexpected. Yet, as we have tried to point out, entering into dialogue so as to invite the unexpected requires preparation. It requires us to give up our desire to explain the present by pointing to the past. It requires us to replace our abstract positions with our lived stories—the richly textured, relational scenarios we engage in with others. It requires us to listen for, to provide the space for, and to invite difference—for ourselves and for our dialogic partners. This unusual aspect of dialogue, we believe, opens possibilities for creativity and change.

Part II

Personal Voices in Dialogue

7

Dialogues of Relating

Leslie A. Baxter

The single adequate form for verbally expressing authentic human life is the open-ended dialogue. Life by its very nature is dialogic. To live means to participate in dialogue.

—Mikhail Bakhtin (1984, p. 293)

In writing this chapter, I invite you to join me in an intellectual conversation on the matter of how to think about interpersonal communication, relating, and personal relationships. About 15 years ago, I began rethinking my conception of, and approach to, interpersonal communication in the context of personal relationships—friendships, romantic relationships, marital relationships, and family relationships. I, like most interpersonal communication scholars of my generation, was trained in a tradition heavily influenced by social psychological assumptions, theories, and methods. Central to my rethinking process was my encounter with dialogism theory as articulated in selected works by the Russian theorist Mikhail Bakhtin. The primary goal of this chapter is to summarize five ways in which the concept of *dialogue* can be read in Bakhtin's work and to discuss how Bakhtin's notions of dialogue are featured centrally in my theoretical orientation to communication in personal relationships—relational dialectics (Baxter & Montgomery, 1996).

Mikhail Bakhtin (1895–1975) was a Russian scholar of literature, culture, language, and philosophy who spent much of his career working in relative obscurity, largely because he was at political odds with Leninist and Stalinist regimes in the Soviet Union. Because of his marginalized status, his scholarly work was slow to reach publication and even slower to receive English translation. However, he was a prolific scholar whose writings span the period from

1919 to 1973, with the bulk of his work produced in the 1920s through the 1940s. Discovered by Western scholars in the 1970s and 1980s, Bakhtin has now been hailed by some as one of the foremost intellectual forces of the 20th century (e.g., Holquist, 1990; Morson & Emerson, 1990; Todorov, 1984).

Given the wide range of topics addressed by Bakhtin, it comes as little surprise that his work means different things to different people (Gardiner, 1992; Holquist, 1986). Despite variability in how Bakhtin's work is understood and used, the concept of "dialogue" is central in that work (Clark & Holquist, 1984; Holquist, 1990; Morson & Emerson, 1990; Todorov, 1984). In fact, Holquist (1990) invoked the term "dialogism" to label Bakhtin's body of work based on his view that "dialogue" is the concept that brings coherence to the whole. Throughout his intellectual career, Bakhtin was critical of the "monologization" of the human experience that he perceived as rampant in the dominant linguistic, literary, philosophical, and political theories of his time. His lifelong intellectual project was a critique of theories and practices that reduced the unfinalizable, open, and varied nature of social life in determinate, closed, and totalizing ways. To Bakhtin, social life was not a closed, univocal monologue in which only a single voice (perspective, theme, ideology, person) could be heard; social life was an open dialogue characterized by multivocality and the indeterminacy inherent when those multiple voices interpenetrate.

However, a careful reading of Bakhtin reveals that the concept of "dialogue" is itself multivocal, with multiple radiants of meaning. In particular, five related conceptions of dialogue, which hold particular relevance to relational dialectics, are evident in the corpus of Bakhtin's work. I will discuss all of these conceptions in the remainder of the chapter, devoting more attention to some conceptions than to others not because they vary in their salience in Bakhtin's work but rather because my research program has emphasized some conceptions of dialogue over others.

Dialogue as Epistemology: The Constitutive Turn

The Enlightenment gave birth to many modernist conceptions, perhaps the most important of which is a monadic view of self, what Geertz (1979) describes as "a bounded, unique, more or less integrated motivational and cognitive universe, a dynamic center of awareness, emotion, judgment, and action organized into a distinctive whole and set contrastively both against other such wholes and against a social and natural background" (p. 229). According to this conception, the individual self is an autonomous knower of the world and actor upon that world. By contrast, as Holquist (1990) summarizes dialogism, "the very capacity to have consciousness is based on otherness" (p. 18). The self of dialogism is a *relation* between self and other, a simultaneity of sameness and difference out of which knowing becomes possible. In Bakhtin's words,

> I achieve self-consciousness, I become myself only by revealing myself to another, through another and with another's help. . . . Cutting myself off, isolating oneself, closing oneself off, those are the basic reasons for loss of self. (Bakhtin, as quoted in Todorov, 1984, p. 96)

At once, self and other are similar yet different. During interaction, they occupy approximately the same time and space, what Bakhtin (1981) referred to as a *chronotope* (literally time-space). Yet they occupy this shared chronotope differently. Each individual has a unique "excess of seeing" that Bakhtin (1990) described this way:

> When I contemplate a whole human being who is situated outside and over against me, our concrete, actually experienced horizons do not coincide. For at each given moment, regardless of the position and the proximity to me of this other human being whom I am contemplating, I shall always see and know something that he, from his place outside and over against me, cannot see himself: parts of his body that are inaccessible to his own gaze (his head, his face and its expression), the world behind his back, and a whole series of objects and relations, which in any of our mutual relations are accessible to me but not to him. (p. 23)

Other's unique excess of seeing provides self with a more complete and whole view, and in this sense is central to one's capacity to know. An individual knows self only from the outside, as he or she conceives others see him or her. The self, then, is invisible to itself and dependent for its existence on the other. Self cannot be a unitary, autonomous phenomenon, according to dialogism; rather, it is a fluid and dynamic relation between self and other. Bakhtin's metaphor for this relation is a dialogue—a simultaneous unity of differences in the interpenetration of utterances.

Dialogue-as-epistemology is a core concept in the theory of relational dialectics that Barbara Montgomery and I have formally articulated (Baxter & Montgomery, 1996). We argue that selves and relationships are constituted in communication. Put simply, a constitutive approach to communication asks how communication defines, or constructs, the social world, including our selves and our personal relationships. Bakhtin (1990) referred to this constructing process as authoring.

For the most part, nonconstitutive approaches still dominate the study of communication in personal relationships (for exceptions, see Shotter, 1993a, 1993b). The prototypical view of relationship development, a legacy from social penetration and other resource exchange theories (e.g., Altman & Taylor, 1973), frames the formation, maintenance, and disengagement of relationships as the coordination of individual cost/benefit decision-making between the two parties. As acquaintances project a social profit in which the benefits of being in a relationship exceed costs, they increasingly engage in self-disclosure that propels the relationship forward to even greater closeness. In this conception, the parties' selves are preformed and the business of establishing a relationship is the process of revealing those preformed selves to one another. Self-disclosure thus is positioned as the most important communicative activity for the development and maintenance of relational closeness and intimacy; it is the communicative currency that ratchets parties to greater closeness (or to lesser closeness as parties withdraw from disclosure during disengagement).

From the constitutive perspective of relational dialectics, relationships are close not because preformed selves get revealed but because selves are defined, or authored, in the interaction between the relationship parties. Relationships are close to the extent that they enable selves to become (Baxter & Montgomery, 1996).

According to nonconstitutive approaches, self-disclosive communication functions as a carrier of information about potential rewards to Other, the most important of which has been similarity between the parties' preformed selves—similar styles of communication, attitudes and values, personality dispositions, habits and interests, and background experiences.

Relationships necessitate similarity between the parties to sustain coordinated interaction. To complement the list of bases of similarity just mentioned—bases that preformed selves bring to the relationship—relational dialectics adds an important form of dialogic similarity that I shall refer to as *chronotopic similarity*. Chronotopic similarity is the stockpile of shared time–space experiences that a pair constructs through their joint interaction events over time. Chronotopic similarity is accomplished in both the mundane communication events that a pair engages in while conducting everyday relating and those major events that function as turning points in transforming a relationship. Daena Goldsmith and I (1996) found that everyday events of "small talk," "gossip," "joking around," "catching up," and "making plans" are particularly frequent kinds of mundane events in the doing of relationships. These informal events enable parties to build jointly a shared history—an emergent chronotopic similarity rather than predetermined similarity based on the qualities brought into the relationship by the parties.

In several studies, colleagues and I have examined the major turning-point events that parties perceive retrospectively to have altered their relationships in profound ways (Baxter, Braithwaite, & Nicholson, 1999; Baxter & Bullis, 1986; Baxter & Erbert, 1999; Baxter & Pittman, 2001). Through such events as *Quality Time* in which relationship parties escape mundane routines to have special time together, *Passion* events such as first sex, and *Relationship Talk* events in which the parties talk explicitly about the state of their relationship, relationships are constructed in transforming ways. These turning-point events hold a double significance. First, the parties experience them jointly at the time of their occurrence. Second, the parties communicatively remember these events through the subsequent enactment of a variety of dyadic traditions, including reminiscing, storytelling, commemorations or celebrations, rituals, and use of idiomatic expressions whose meanings are rooted in these turning-point events (Baxter, 1987; Baxter & Braithwaite, 2002; Baxter & Pittman, 2001; Braithwaite & Baxter, 1995; Braithwaite, Baxter, & Harper, 1998). Turning-point events, and their subsequent joint remembering, complement parties' mundane communicative events, building an emergent scaffold of chronotopic similarity from which parties' selves and their relationship are crafted.

In addition, however, relational dialectics presupposes that the business of relating is as much about differences as similarities. Apart from some early psychological work on need complementarity (e.g., Schutz, 1960; Winch, 1958), scholars of communication and relationships have tended to ignore the positive functions of difference or to frame difference exclusively as conflict. To relational dialectics, and dialogism more generally, difference between parties is the basis of the excess of seeing and essential to the construction of selves and relationships. A former student and I (Baxter & West, in press) recently examined the interplay of similarity and difference by asking platonic friends and romantic couples to reflect jointly on their respective similarities and differences. Over and over, participants discussed how their differences were the foundation for individual growth in each partner. Partners exposed each other to different perspectives, interests, and approaches, thereby helping one another's selves to become. As one participant expressed it,

> we accent each other in a way that we have a lot to learn from each other. . . . I'm learning a lot about how somebody else views the world. . . . It keeps me with an open mind and makes me more understanding of other people. (p. 31)

This person nicely captures what Barbara Montgomery and I (Baxter & Montgomery, 1996) meant by self becoming as a result of relating with another. The process of self-becoming provides us with a way to conceive of openness differently from that found in nonconstitutive approaches to communication in relationships. Nonconstitutive approaches conceive of openness as self-disclosure, what we referred to as the openness-*with* conception; by contrast, self-becoming realizes what we referred to as the openness-*to* conception (Baxter & Montgomery, 1996). In being open *to* another person, one is willing to listen to him or her from that person's perspective, to display receptivity to what that person has to say, to be open to change in one's own beliefs and attitudes.

Similarity and difference do not exist in isolation from one another but in complex interplay with and against each other. Relationship pairs appear to identify at least one phenomenon that is simultaneously a basis of both similarity and difference, a condition labeled *tight dialectical unity* (Baxter & West, in press). Two kinds of dialectical unity are evident, capturing different interweavings of similarity with difference. First, relationship parties recognize that a given similarity does not mean absolute equivalence. Rather, partners recognize that they are in a zone or latitude of approximate similarity. If one or both parties act in a way outside of this latitude of approximate similarity, a qualitative change in judgment occurs and the partners experience a contrast effect in which the similarity is transformed into difference. Thus, a pair can move in and out of similarity and difference, depending on whether action at that time is within, or outside, the latitude of approximate similarity—itself a dynamic construction.

Second, relationship parties can perceive themselves similar with respect to the core, or essence, of a given phenomenon. However, they recognize simultaneously differences in any number of dimensions, or radiants, of the phenomenon. Usually, joint awareness of the similarity enables the pair to become aware of differences. For example, a pair could recognize that their joint love of music led to hours and hours of pleasurable conversation, during which they realized subtle differences with respect to particular musicians or musical groups.

To this point, I have discussed how selves and relationships are constructed from the inside, that is, through interaction between the relating partners. However, relationships, like selves, are not autonomous, monadic entities. A given relationship gains its meaning through interaction with others located outside of the boundary of the relationship in addition to the interaction between the relationship's parties. As Volosinov[1] (1973) stated, "The organizing center . . . of any experience is not within but outside—in the social milieu surrounding the individual being" (p. 93). Traditional approaches to relationship development and maintenance focus almost exclusively on interaction between partners in studying relationships. In de-centering such an interior focus, relational dialectics argues that researchers also need to pay as much attention to the ways relationships connect with the social order that exists outside the immediate boundary of the dyadic or familial unit.

The term *social order* is meant to place less emphasis on the physical groupings of humans (e.g., social networks, groups, society, culture) and more on their communication patterns and the systems of values and beliefs that give meanings to those patterns (Baxter & Montgomery, 1996). Social collectives are not the sum of their individual members so much as what people say and do communicatively with each other. These communicative enactments are far from unitary, functioning to repeat, reformulate, and rebut one another (Streeck, 1994).

Relationship parties are immersed in ongoing communication with outsiders to the relationship as they go about the business of crafting an identity for that relationship. At all developmental points of a relationship—entry, development, maintenance, and break-up—relationship parties are actively engaged in conversations with others about how that relationship should be conducted (Baxter, Dun, & Sahlstein, 2001). Solicited and unsolicited advice-giving, gossip about others' relationship experiences, and direct sanctioning in the form of approval and disapproval are frequent ways that relationship parties hear about others' rules for relating (Baxter, Dun, & Sahlstein, 2001). Through storytelling and jointly-enacted couple performances (e.g., holding hands in public), relationship parties carefully seek to regulate how much, and what kind, of knowledge outsiders have about the relationship (Baxter & Pittman, 2001; Baxter & Widenmann, 1993; Braithwaite & Baxter, 1995).

Interaction with third parties often carries contradictory assertions about how relationships should be conducted. Relationships are at once public and private. Relationship parties are involved in ongoing negotiation with outsiders on what is public knowledge and what is private knowledge between the parties themselves (e.g., Bridge & Baxter, 1992). Relationship identities necessitate social recognition, yet at the same time, relationships are built on a presumption of privacy from others (Baxter et al., 1997; Baxter & Widenmann, 1993; Braithwaite & Baxter, 1995). Relationship parties are also involved in ongoing negotiation with outsiders on the ways in which the relationship's identity is conventionalized and the ways in which it is constructed as unique. Others' support for, and legitimation of, a relationship requires that the relationship be compatible with social conventions for relating; at the same time, however, at least in the U.S., relationships are defined as close to the extent that they are non-replaceable or unique (Braithwaite & Baxter, 1995). Thus, the social conventions of relating often hold contradictory strands. For example, a colleague and I (Baxter & Braithwaite, 2002) examined how couples use the marriage renewal ritual as a way of communicatively navigating two contradictory ideologies of marriage in the U.S.: utilitarian/expressive individualism and moral/social community (Bellah, Madsen, Sullivan, Swidler, & Tipton, 1985). As a second example, a group of students and I (Baxter et al., 1997) examined how the construct of *loyalty* in relationships often implicates disloyalty at one and the same time: Loyalty to one relationship is often constructed out of disloyalty to another.

As it has unfolded, this section has moved from the contradiction of similarity-difference to examine other dynamic tensions involved in the construction of selves and relationships. The second sense of *dialogue* recognizes explicitly this wider knot of contradictions.

Dialogue as Centrifugal–Centripetal Flux: The Dialectical Turn

To Bakhtin (1984), the essence of dialogue is its simultaneous fusion with, yet differentiation from, another. To engage in dialogue, participants must fuse their perspectives to some extent while sustaining the uniqueness of their individual perspectives. Participants thus form a unity in conversation but only through two clearly differentiated voices, or perspectives. Just as dialogue is simultaneously unity and difference, Bakhtin (1981, p. 272) regarded language and culture as the product of "a contradiction-ridden, tension-filled unity of two embattled tendencies," the centripetal (i.e., forces of unity, homogeneity, centrality) and the centrifugal (i.e., forces of difference, dispersion, decentering). The dialogues of language and culture are constituted in the dialectical, or contradictory, interplay of centripetal and centrifugal forces. These forces are "verbal–ideological" (Bakhtin, 1981, p. 272) in nature. Bakhtin used the term *ideological* in its broadest sense to mean any idea system (Holquist, 1981, p. 429). The centripetal–centrifugal tension of verbal–ideological forces simply means that communication involves tracings of unified-yet-competing values, orientations, perspectives, functions, or ideas. As Bakhtin (1981) expressed it, "Every concrete utterance of a speaking subject serves as a point where centrifugal as well as centripetal forces are brought to bear. The processes of centralization and decentralization, of unification and disunification, intersect in the utterance" (p. 272).

It is important to note that Bakhtin's centripetal–centrifugal tension is dialectical but not in the Hegelian sense of a thesis, which produces its opposite in an antithesis, which then culminates in a synthesis. In fact, Bakhtin was highly critical of Hegelian–Marxist dialectics on two counts: first, its highly abstracted treatment of contradiction that was far removed from lived experience; and second, its fundamental monologic privileging of synthesis that evolves from the struggle of thesis against antithesis (Bakhtin, 1986). To Bakhtin, the centripetal–centrifugal dialectic is a dynamic, fluid, and ongoing process whose particular shape varies chronotopically, or contextually.

Grounded in Bakhtin's view of the social world as centripetal–centrifugal flux, relational dialectics views communication in relationships as the dialectical tension of contradictory verbal–ideological forces. This view stands in sharp contrast to dominant approaches to relational communication. Traditional approaches to communication in relationships have articulated the grand narratives of connection, certainty, and openness. The prototypical conception of a close relationship is one in which partner autonomy or separation has been supplanted by interdependence (e.g., interdependence theory, Kelley et al., 1983). In this conception, partner autonomy is read as evidence of noncloseness between partners. Traditional approaches also view the process of relationship development and maintenance as one of reducing uncertainty about the partner and the relationship (e.g., uncertainty reduction theory, Berger & Calabrese, 1975). Finally, as discussed above, self-disclosure is viewed by traditional approaches as the means by which openness is accomplished; according to these approaches, closedness is viewed as a problematic barrier to relationship development and maintenance.

According to relational dialectics, however, these approaches are mono-logic and ignore the dynamic interplay of these centripetal forces with their centrifugal counterparts. From the perspective of relational dialectics, relating is a complex knot of contradictory interplays, including but not necessarily limited to integration–separation, certainty–uncertainty, and expression–nonexpression. Relationships are built as much on the separation of the parties as their integration; uncertainty, novelty, and change are as important to rela-tionships as certainty and stability; nonexpression is as necessary as expression (for an extensive discussion, see Baxter & Montgomery, 1996). These bipolar forces do not exist in parallel to one another but interweave in ongoing dialec-tical interplay.

Bakhtin (1981) positioned the chronotope as central to dialogue, asserting that "every entry into the sphere of meaning is accomplished only through the gates of the chronotope" (p. 258). Similarly, relational dialectics asserts that dialectical interplay is an in situ process. The implication of this assertion is that the abstract contradictions I just mentioned (integration–separation, certainty–uncertainty, expression–nonexpression) must be examined in the concrete particulars of specific contexts. In doing so, the multivocality of each of these contradictions becomes evident.

The negotiation of integration and separation has been given a variety of labels in my program of research, and in the research of others (see Werner & Baxter, 1994). Although some of these labels are mere synonyms, others reflect subtle, situation-specific enactments of the interplay of integration and sepa-ration (for an elaboration of this point, see Baxter & Montgomery, 1996). Earlier, I discussed one possible radiant of integration–separation interplay—similarity and difference between partners. I also discussed how this contra-diction can also be enacted as a dilemma of identity construction for the parties; that is, constructing and sustaining an identity as an individual beyond the *we* of the relationship, while relying on the partner to construct and sustain that *I*.

At a more mundane level, integration–separation can be enacted by relationship parties in terms of how much time they spend with one another versus apart in meeting other obligations. This radiant of the integration–separation contradiction appears to be particularly salient in romantic and friendship relationships (Baxter et al., 1997).

This contradictory interplay can also be enacted as a dilemma of rights versus obligations—for example, the individual right to have his or her own needs fulfilled versus the obligation to fulfill the partner's needs. This radiant of the integration–separation dialectic has been identified for both friendships and romantic relationships (Baxter et al., 1997). Colleagues and I have also recently identified this form of the contradiction in the relationships between stepchildren and their nonresidential parents (Braithwaite & Baxter, 2002). In this context, children report that they are trapped in a problematic relationship with a person who is a parent but who does not act like one.

Yet a different manifestation of this dialectical interplay is in emotional communication: The communication of emotional closeness, liking, and love are integrally bound up with expressions of opposing emotions (Baxter & Montgomery, 1996). For example, colleagues and I have identified an agonizing love that characterizes the presence–absence dialectic in the relationships of wives whose husbands have Alzheimer's disease. These men were still physically present yet emotionally and cognitively absent; wives continued to love their husbands yet were in emotional agony about the "married widowhood" nature of the relationship (Baxter, Braithwaite, Golish, & Olson, 2002). A second example of how emotional closeness and distance are enacted simultaneously was found in one of our recently completed studies of stepfamilies (Baxter, Braithwaite, Bryant, & Wagner, in press). Stepchildren reported to us that communication with the stepparent was a complex weaving of closeness and distance, a dialectical dance that they described as "constantly walking on eggs."

The dialectic of certainty and uncertainty is similarly enacted in multivocal ways in relating. For example, it might be experienced as the interplay of the past with the present. In our study of long-term married couples who elected to renew their marriage vows, Dawn Braithwaite and I (1995) found this theme featured prominently in the renewal event. Couples used the ceremony to demonstrate how their relationship had changed over the years at the same time that they demonstrated the underlying stability of the marriage. Colleagues and I identified a similar interplay of past with present in our study of rituals in stepfamilies (Braithwaite, Baxter, & Harper, 1998). Rituals that family members regarded as successful were those in which the past, in the form of the family of origin, was honored at the same time that the present, in the form of the stepfamily, was equally honored.

Another variant of this contradiction is conventionality versus uniqueness. The long-term married couples who renewed their marriage vows constructed certainty, in part, by conforming to an ideology of marriage as a stable institution with traditional roles, expectations, and obligations; at the same time, they embraced uncertainty by enacting an ideology of marriage as a unique pairing of selves (Baxter & Braithwaite, 2002; Braithwaite & Baxter,

1995). Relationships, like jazz, are constructed in the complex interplay of the "given" with the "new" in relationships (Baxter & Montgomery, 1996). Just as this interplay varies from one jazz ensemble to another and from one performance to another, so the dialogue of certainty and uncertainty varies chronotopically.

The interplay of expression and nonexpression also is chronotopically multivocal. I will illustrate this assertion with one of our stepfamily studies (Baxter, Braithwaite, Bryant, & Wagner, in press). Stepchildren reported several strands of complexity in this contradiction. For example, in important ways, open expression was opposed to the protection of self afforded by closedness—because the stepfamily was high in uncertainty, family members feared that they could be embarrassed or hurt yet they wanted to speak their minds openly. At the same time, open expression was opposed to the protection of others afforded by closedness—family members wanted openness but felt that closedness protected the feelings of fellow family members (particularly members from the family of origin). A third strand of this contradiction was framed in terms of loyalty issues, with both openness and closedness regarded as loyal and disloyal to various family members. A fourth strand of this contradiction was idealization versus reality; family members felt that open expression was characteristic of their idealization of "real families" against which the reality of their stepfamily was lacking. In sum, then, expression and nonexpression are in dialectical tension at multiple levels. Doubtless, similar complexity characterizes this contradiction in other relational contexts, as well.

Dialogue, to Bakhtin, is an indeterminate and emergent process. The interplay of utterances takes the interactants to places unforeseeable at the beginning of the conversation and in unscripted ways. Extending this notion of indeterminacy, relational dialectics is premised on the assumption that the ongoing flux of centripetal and centrifugal forces requires a more complex approach to relationship development than the traditional approaches provide (Baxter & Montgomery, 1996). A model of linear progression characterizes traditional approaches to relationship development. Relationship parties march to the drummer of "More," either incrementally or through a series of successive stages: more disclosure, more integration, and more certainty. By contrast, relational dialectics regards change as a much less tidy process, one in which the ongoing interplay of contradictory forces simply moves a relationship to a place different from the places it has been before. The major transformation points of a relationship's history—what I described above as turning points— appear to be moments of heightened dialogic struggle for relationship partners (Baxter & Erbert, 1999; Baxter & Simon, 1993). These moments appear to propel a relationship by fits and starts, in what can be an erratic process of backward-forward, up-and-down motion (Baxter, Braithwaite, & Nicholson, 1999; Baxter & Bullis, 1986; Baxter & Erbert, 1999).

Central to the relational dialectics conception of change is its non-Hegelian nature. Relationship parties do not move from thesis (e.g., separation) to antithesis (e.g., integration) to a resolution of the opposition in some form of synthesis. Instead, the interplay of contradictory forces is a process of ongoing flux. However, dialogism and relational dialectics celebrate fleeting moments of wholeness or unity, which brings me to Bakhtin's third sense of dialogue.

Dialogue as a Momentary Completion: The Aesthetic Turn

Bakhtin (1981) viewed social life as a fragmented, disorderly, and messy inter-weave of opposing forces. In such a social world, order is not given; it is a task to be accomplished (Bakhtin, 1990). Through dialogue in the third sense, parties can occasionally create a fleeting moment of wholeness in which fragments and disorder are temporarily united. These aesthetic moments (Bakhtin, 1990, p. 67) create momentary consummation, completion, or wholeness in what is otherwise a messy and fragmented life experience.

Not all forms of wholeness are aesthetic, according to Bakhtin. He distinguished aesthetic wholeness from monologic wholeness, and his lifelong intellectual project was to challenge the latter (Morson & Emerson, 1990). Monologic wholeness, a oneness or unity achieved through the hegemony of a single voice dominant over other voices, is the wholeness of totalitarianism, and I will discuss this further as I develop the fifth meaning of dialogue. By contrast, aesthetic wholeness accomplishes a momentary sense of unity through a profound respect for the disparate voices of dialogue.

Aesthetic wholeness, to Bakhtin, comes from dialogue characterized by answerability, response-worthy participation, and aesthetic love (Emerson, 1997). Answerability refers to the moral and ethical responsibility that individuals bear toward others in order to "author" or complete them (Bakhtin, 1990). Parties owe each other the opportunity for their selves to become. Authorship, in turn, comes through response-worthy participation, that is, an empathic response coupled with the gift of one's surplus of seeing (Bakhtin, 1990). When engaged in aesthetic dialogue, parties strive to identify with and understand the other as completely as they can, but they do not stop there; in addition to empathy, parties complete one another by contributing their unique surplus of seeing. Bakhtin (1990) expressed this two-step process in this way:

> The first step in aesthetic activity is my projecting myself into him and experiencing his life from within him. I must experience—come to see and to know—what he experiences. . . . But in any event my projection of myself into him must be followed by a return into myself, a return to my own place outside the suffering

person, for only from this place can the material derived from my projecting myself into the other be rendered meaningful ethically, cognitively, or aesthetically. If this return into myself did not actually take place, the pathological phenomenon of experiencing another's suffering as one's own would result—an infection with another's suffering, and nothing more. (pp. 25–26)

Bakhtin was mindful that these two steps—projecting into the other and consummating the other—are "intimately intertwined and fuse with one another" (1990, p. 27).

Aesthetic love is the third element of dialogue as an aesthetic moment. In aesthetic love, parties respond to one another as whole beings, not fragments of being. When I go to the bank and engage my bank clerk in conversation, I am engaging only one facet of her—her role as bank clerk—not the coherence of her many facets. I am not engaging her from a stance of aesthetic love, because of my partial and limited engagement with her. When I interact with a close friend, I might or might not be engaging his whole being; maybe I am asking him for advice on buying a new car and thus responding only to one facet of his being—his experience as a car buff.

Bakhtin's conception of dialogue as an aesthetic moment in the consummation of selves obviously bears close correspondence to the concept of the dialogic moment conceived both separately and jointly by Martin Buber and by Carl Rogers (Cissna & Anderson, 1998b). To these theorists, a dialogic moment is a fleeting experience of mutuality in which parties perceive some transcendent sense of invented or created wholeness from the complete attention that each gives to the other's whole being.

Relationship parties appear to experience aesthetic moments in their friendship, romantic, and familial relationships (Baxter & DeGooyer, 2001). However, the aesthetic pleasure that is evoked in communication encounters is the result of several kinds of consummation. The first of these kinds of realized wholeness bears close resemblance to Bakhtin's conception of the completion of self through other. However, additional kinds of completion can be identified, as well (Baxter & DeGooyer, 2001). Relationship parties report a sense of relationship wholeness achieved by seamless temporal continuities between the past and the present or from the present to the projected future. Parties also report a sense of relationship wholeness in the present, achieved through the seamless merging of the two parties into one relational entity. Conversational flow is another form of aesthetic moment, in which parties feel that discrete utterances flow into one another effortlessly and the conversation seems to take on a life of its own. Parties also report a sense of cosmic oneness, a feeling that they are one with their environment, the universe, or God. In short, Dan DeGooyer and I noted that aesthetic moments could take several different forms in relationships. What these recalled instances share in common across participants is a sense of deep pleasure, stimulation, and joy evoked in what were perceived as non-reproducible fleeting moments of consummation.

Encouraged by these findings, I am conceptualizing the aesthetic moment more broadly than Bakhtin to include any occasion in which the flux of centripetal–centrifugal interplay is momentarily constructed as a seamless whole. It is important not to confuse an aesthetic moment with the Hegelian notion of synthesis. Synthesis is a permanent resolution of thesis–antithesis tension; by contrast, an aesthetic moment is an ephemeral experience that momentarily punctuates ongoing centripetal–centrifugal flux.

I think rituals are likely candidates for aesthetic moments. I define *ritual* not in the pedestrian sense of any routinized pattern, but rather in reference to a structured sequence of symbolic acts in which homage is paid to some sacred object such as the relationship (Goffman, 1967). Several scholars have argued that a ritual is successful because it is responsive simultaneously to contradictory forces. As Turner (1969) argued, "It represents many things at the same time; it is multivocal, not univocal. . . . Its referents tend to cluster around opposite semantic poles" (p. 52). A ritual, then, is a joint performance in which competing, contradictory voices in everyday social life are brought together simultaneously. If it is performed in a meaningful way, it can function as an aesthetic moment: opposing voices are united in a seamless whole through which homage is paid in some way. For example, the marriage renewal ceremony weaves together public–private, conventionalized–unique, stability–change, and institutional–personal dialectics (Baxter & Braithwaite, 2002; Braithwaite & Baxter, 1995). Similarly, rituals regarded as successful by stepfamily members are those in which the contradiction between the "old family" (of origin) and the "new family" (the stepfamily) are seamlessly integrated at a symbolic level (Braithwaite, Baxter, & Harper, 1998).

Aesthetic moments, including rituals, are not individual communicative acts. Rather, they are communication events jointly enacted by the relationship parties. This observation moves us to the fourth sense of dialogue.

Dialogue as Language in Use: The Discursive Turn

To this point, *dialogue* has been used more or less metaphorically to reference qualities of social experience. However, in this fourth sense of the term, Bakhtin engaged the study of language in use, or the utterance. He critiqued Saussure's overemphasis on language as an abstract system (*la langue*) to the relative neglect of enacted language in use (*la parole*) (Volosinov, 1973). However, Bakhtin's concept of the utterance does not refer to the individualized act of an autonomous speaker. Instead, as Bakhtin (1986) conceived it, an utterance exists only at the boundary between consciousnesses. An utterance can be viewed as a link in a chain, a link bounded by both preceding links and the links that follow (Bakhtin, 1986, p. 94). Bakhtin's conception of communication is notably social, not individual. Utterances are not the product of individual cognitive work in which speakers assemble messages responsive to preformed goals, needs, and motivations. Instead, utterances are jointly constructed by interacting parties. As Volosinov (1973) expressed it, "Word is a two-sided act. It is determined equally by whose word it is and for whom it is meant. As word, it is precisely the product of the reciprocal relationship between speaker and listener" (p. 86).

Relational dialectics, like Bakhtin's fourth sense of dialogue, emphasizes communication as a social, or joint, enterprise between interlocutors (Baxter & Montgomery, 1996). Contradictions are not internal cognitive dilemmas located in the individual mind that, in turn, serve as the basis of the individual's goal-directed communication. Instead, contradictions are located in the relationship between parties, produced and reproduced through the parties' joint communicative activity.

Barbara Montgomery and I (Baxter & Montgomery, 1996) have articulated seven kinds of joint communicative activity through which the contradictions of relating are constituted. Considered as a whole, these activities take either synchronic or diachronic form. Synchronic communicative activities are characterized by the simultaneous equality of opposing voices, with neither opposition in a position of centripetal dominance in the communicative moment. Foremost among these synchronic communicative activities are aesthetic moments, which I discussed above.

More common than synchronic communication activities are diachronic ones. Diachronic communication activities are those in which a given voice is privileged as the centripetal center at a given time–space, while opposing voices are relatively muted at the centrifugal margins of discourse; at another time–space, what was once a muted and marginalized voice occupies the center while the formerly centripetal voice is relegated to the discursive margins. Over time and space, the process of contradiction takes on a cyclical quality as opposing voices move in and out of the centripetal center. We have identified two key diachronic activities: *spiraling inversion* and *segmentation* (Baxter & Montgomery, 1996). When parties enact *spiraling inversion,* they tack back and forth through time, alternating an emphasis on one dialectical voice with an emphasis on another dialectical voice. For example, a long-distance couple will tack back and forth between spending time together and time apart in constructing their integration–separation dialectic. In enacting *segmentation,* relationship parties negotiate by topic domain. On topic A, for example, a couple might privilege openness and candor, yet topic B would be defined as a "taboo topic" in which openness was disallowed. The diachronic activities of spiraling inversion and segmentation appear to be the most frequent ways that relationship parties constitute their contradictions of relating (Baxter, 1990; Baxter, Braithwaite, Golish, & Olson, 2002; Baxter & Simon, 1993; Baxter & Widenmann, 1993).

To date, my work on communication activities has been conducted at the macrolevel of analysis, glossing over the microlevel details of talk. Researchers need to examine the microlevels of enacted conversation to illuminate further how contradictions are enacted. Bakhtin's (1984) conception of double-voicedness will be important to that enterprise. Utterances, argued Bakhtin, can be placed along a continuum of monologic single-voicedness to dialogic double-voicedness. Single-voiced utterances are utterances that recognize only one voice, whereas double-voiced utterances are multivocal in nature. Because *voice* means not only the uttered talk of an embodied person but rather any perspective, value, function, or ideology, the intellectual task becomes that of interrogating utterances to discern their univocal or multivocal quality. Discourse markers such as "but" or "however" (Schiffrin, 1987) are obvious discursive clues to multivocality. For example, the utterance "I look forward to our time spent together, but it means I often fall behind in my work obligations," discursively constructs a tension between integration with separation. However, I suspect that multivocality is often marked less directly, what Haspel (2001) refers to as "the but in the air." For example, the same integration–separation tension is constructed implicitly in the following utterance, despite the absence of an explicit "but" marker: "I work overtime during the week so that we can spend our time together on the weekends."

The enterprise of locating multivocality in interaction will also benefit from Bakhtin's (1986) conception of the speech genre. A speech genre refers to a culture's normative forms of talk—for example, "small talk," "having a fight," "having a serious talk," and so on (Goldsmith & Baxter, 1996). Bakhtin (1981) viewed the novel as the most dialogic or multivocal of literary genres, particularly in the hands of such writers as Dostoevsky (Bakhtin, 1984). Among the several forms of everyday spoken talk, we have little sense of which enable or constrain double-voicedness. The possibility of single-voiced talk opens the door to totalitarian wholeness: the dominance of one hegemonic voice over muted opposing voices. This brings us to the fifth, and final, meaning of dialogue.

Dialogue as Critique: The Critical Turn

The possibility of totalitarian wholeness may appear strange in light of the dialogic imperative (Holquist, 1981, p. 426) captured in Bakhtin's first two senses of "dialogue." As with dialogue-as-aesthetic-moment, however, it is important to recognize that wholeness (whether aesthetic or totalitarian) is never absolute and always indeterminate. Wholeness accomplished through single-voiced discourse obligates response-worthy participation and the articulation of an opposing response. In this fifth sense, then, dialogue is the obligation to critique dominant voices. This sense of dialogue is probably best captured in Bakhtin's work on the medieval carnival (Bakhtin, 1965). Bakhtin's carnivalesque—the carnival sense of the world—is characterized by "mockery of all serious, 'closed' attitudes about the world, and it also celebrates 'discrowning,' that is, inverting top and bottom in any given structure" (Morson & Emerson, 1990, p. 443).

In writing *Relating: Dialogues and Dialectics*, Barbara Montgomery and I (1996) attempted to perform "discrowning" in our critique of the monologues of closeness, certainty, and openness that pervade traditional approaches to communication and relationships. I continue to use the carnivalesque as a heuristic in identifying apparent absences in scholarly conversations, for example, rethinking relational commitment (Sahlstein & Baxter, 2001) and persuasion (Baxter & Bylund, in press) along dialogic lines. For example, the traditional conception of persuasion frames the change process as single-voiced. It assumes that the persuader has a preformed goal of changing the target person's attitudes and beliefs so that they align with those of the persuader; this goal is manifested in a persuasive message transmitted to the target. By contrast, a dialogic approach to persuasion recognizes that a powerful kind of social influence takes place in aesthetic moments of reciprocal authoring. The parties do not act in these moments because of preformulated intentions to persuade one another; rather, change emerges out of the communicative moment. Further, social influence is not a one-way experience with clearly designated roles of persuader and target; instead, both parties are engaged in mutuality out of which both parties have changed.

The carnivalesque eye can be brought to bear, as well, in identifying single-voicedness in relationship conversations. For example, Dawn Braithwaite and I, joined by others, are currently working on several studies on reported speech in stepfamilies. Reported speech is talk in which another's words are referenced directly (e.g., by quoting them) or indirectly (e.g., by implication) in a speaker's own utterance (Bakhtin, 1981). Reported speech can function as a powerful control mechanism in which speakers can co-opt another's voice for their own purposes. We are studying how stepchildren co-opt the stepparent's voice in expressing complaints to the parent, how stepparents co-opt the stepchild's voice in expressing complaints to the spouse, and how the residential and non-residential parents-of-origin co-opt one another's voices when they communicate with their children. We are viewing these discursive practices as processes of control as parties negotiate the social reality of their stepfamily life.

Conclusion

In this chapter I have attempted to present five interrelated conceptions of dialogue in Bakhtin's works that hold particular importance in my work on communication in friendships, romantic relationships, and families. My research interests have undoubtedly affected my understandings of Bakhtin, and the weights I have given to each of his conceptions of dialogue. Nonetheless, I hope that the chapter leaves you with two lingering thoughts. First, Bakhtin's body of work on dialogism provides us with a richly layered and complex view of dialogue. Second, relating is a complex process of dialogue.

Note

1.   Many scholars think that Bakhtin authored at least some of the works published under Volosinov's name, including *Marxism and the Philosophy of Language.*

8

Dialogue as the Search for Sustainable Organizational Co-Orientation

James R. Taylor

In reality, the relations between A and B are in a state of permanent formation and transformation; they continue to alter in the very process of communication. Nor is there a ready-made message X. It takes form in the process of communication between A and B. Nor is it transmitted from the first to the second, but constructed between them, like an ideological bridge; it is constructed in the process of their interaction.

—Todorov (1984, p. 55)

M any of the ideas I have defended over the years—the importance of text and authoring, the tension between the situatedness of conversation and the objectifications of text, the forever-still-to-be-achieved finality of organization—have a resonance with dialogic thinking. Nevertheless, I have not previously thought of my work as following in the tradition of Bakhtin, Buber, and others who have inspired the current revival of dialogism. In this chapter, however, I try to align my own reflections on organization with those of one of the great innovative theorists of dialogue, Mikhail Bakhtin. Although Bakhtin lived and worked in an obscure corner of Stalin's brutal reign over the vast Russian empire of the USSR, he speaks to us in a remarkably contemporary voice about the bases of communication in discourse. I begin by reviewing the notions about organization that I have developed in my own work, and then I consider what I understand to be their compatibility with the principles of dialogism, as developed by Bakhtin. Theories, like people, have what Bakhtin calls an *outsideness* (Holquist, 1990; Todorov, 1984). As my own theorizing about organization also reflects a variety of influences, this chapter is perhaps best thought of as a four-way conversation (authored by me, to be sure) between Bakhtin's dialogism, Theodore Newcomb's concept of co-orientation (that I have appropriated as a basis for my own work), the ideas on "languaging" and its organizational implications of Humberto Maturana, and my current thinking on communication as the basis for organization.

Organization as It Emerges
Out of Processes of Co-Orientation

In 1953, Theodore Newcomb published an article, "An Approach to the Study of Communicative Acts," in which he argues that "phenomena of social behavior which have been somewhat loosely studied under the label of 'interaction' can be more adequately studied as communicative acts" and that "observable group properties are predetermined by the conditions and consequences of communicative acts" (p. 393). Newcomb builds his theory on three assumptions: (a) human interaction is "communicative" (it remains to see what might be meant by communication); (b) communication may be decomposed into units (again it remains to be seen what might be meant by units); and (c) organization (an "observable group property") emerges *out of*—and is therefore always at least virtually present *in*—communication, another idea that cries out to be unpacked.

Newcomb is thus taking an ontological stand on the nature of organization. Like Dewey (1916/1944) before him, he sees social forms such as organization emerging *in* and *through* communication, like a novel in the reading of it (I will come back to the image of organization as a novel later). Newcomb invites us, in other words, to invert the usual communication-in-organization image, turning figure into ground, and ground into figure. We arrive at organization-in-communication—a metaphor, however, that also needs to be justified.

COMMUNICATION AS CO-ORIENTATION

Communication serves, Newcomb (1953) argues, to maintain what he calls *co-orientation* in two respects: (a) subject-to-subject and (b) subject-to-object. His unit of co-orientation (two subjects, A and B, linked to each other by their focus on a common object, X) he calls an "*A-B-X* system" (I prefer the term *relationship* to *system*). The triadic character of that relationship is essential. There are not two distinct phenomena of co-orientation, one subject-to-subject, the other subject-to-object. We are caught up, implicated, in a world of action that is simultaneously material and social. We are a becoming: a still-to-be-resolved working through of a triadic puzzle—how to reconcile two orders of orientation, to other people and to objects, simultaneously *I-you*, *you-it*, and *I-it*. Interpersonal relations necessarily imply a common orientation to some object, an "*A/B-X*-ness." Vice versa, subject–object relations (*A-X*, *B-X*) necessarily occur within a framing of sociality, an "*A-B*-ness." The maintenance of such a two-faceted state of co-orientation is, of course, inherently contingent: something to be more-or-less realized. Thus, Newcomb (1953) says, "Communication among humans performs the essential function of enabling two or more individuals to maintain simultaneous orientation toward one another as communicators *and* toward objects of communication" (p. 393).

Nothing in Newcomb's formulation should be taken to exclude the possibility that the relationship people establish in communication is less than perfectly consensual. On the contrary, people frequently find themselves in conflict with others, precisely because their respective *X*-orientations are incompatible: the valence of the *A-X* and *B-X* links may be negative as well as positive. Organization is not made up of only harmonious relationships; it is also an arena for the playing out of aggression, personal ambition, and competing agendas. Nor are we entitled to assume that co-orientation is solely about maintenance; it is also a site where the evolution— change over time— of human relations is taking place, sometimes impelled by evolution of the object, sometimes not.

Newcomb (1953) sees his theory as offering three important insights: (a) the situatedness of communication ("it is not certain that even their most person-oriented communications are devoid of environmental reference," p. 394); (b) the sociability of purposive activity (orientations to objects are "rarely, if ever, made in a social vacuum," p. 394); and (c) the language-dependency of communication ("a good deal of social reality is built into the very language with which we communicate about things," p. 394).

CONDITIONS OF CO-ORIENTING

For Newcomb, co-orientation is about arriving at, and maintaining, compatible *A-B* attitudes to *X*, but he is not entirely clear about how this occurs. I think he is right in emphasizing the attitudinal dimension, but I also think that the communication of attitude is more complicated than he would lead us to believe. For there to be co-orientational compatibility, attitudes must be communicated from one person to another. At the same time, we must not forget the triadic principle: These communicated attitudes are with respect to an object that engages the attention of the communicators, and may indeed impose itself on them, whether they like it or not. Nothing, as he says, happens in a vacuum. These are not "attitudes" in the abstract (i.e., opinions), but something closer to involvements in a practical, situated, ongoing world of activity.

Because the communication of attitude occurs as a discursive phenomenon, we need to look into the properties of language that are brought into play for such communication to take place. I suggest we need to take account of three factors: context, interaction, and translation.

Context. For communication to occur in the ordinary face-to-face world of conversation, the interlocutors need to establish an appropriate communicational context. Beyond the purely physical positioning of bodies, the interlocutors need to establish, and share, a common preoccupation with a similar object of attention. In the circumstances of group work, such an alignment of focus mostly comes with the territory. But even people in more casual conversational contexts need to establish a theme with which they are jointly concerned. Only when both participants in the interaction can bring to bear background knowledge can they make sense out of the inevitably equivocal verbal formulations they are confronted with. Listening is an active accomplishment.

Interaction. Conversational interaction cannot occur unless people respect basic rules for the rotation of speaking roles among participants. For people to make sense of what is going on, there has to be alternation of contributions to the conversation. As Maturana (1990, p. 20) puts it, "We say that two people are having a conversation when we see that the stream of their interaction has the character of a sequence of coordinated actions."

Translation. The ability of people to perform work requiring the coordination of individual activities normally depends on verbal interaction. The issue then becomes one of translation: How are one person's attitudes translated into those of another, through the medium of language, to constitute an A-B-ness?

Reality, therefore, unfolds on two levels. A and B are simultaneously X-involved. They share a tacitly understood context and interactional framework. However, if they need to "consensually coordinate their actions," as Maturana (1990, pp. 20, 28) puts it, it is because they aim to work together harmoniously. "Consensual," at this level, means that the A-X and B-X orientations to the practical world of personal involvements are in sync. What is to be coordinated—brought into a satisfactory alignment—are the respective attitudes of A and B: their orientations to X. Explicit, verbalized communication becomes a necessity. What we then need to consider is the property of language that might explain the transmission of attitude from one actor to another: how one's orientation to X is translated into another's.

MODALITY

The basis of all language, Maturana (1997) argues, is interaction. By interacting through "languaging," the transmission of attitude from A to B is accomplished through a unique feature of language: modality. *Mood*, as Bybee and Fleischman (1995) observe, "refers to a formally grammatical category of the verb which has a *modal* function" (p. 2). *Modality*, on the other hand, "is the semantic domain pertaining to elements of meaning that languages express. It covers a broad range of semantic nuances . . . whose common denominator is the addition of a supplement or overlay of meaning to the most neutral semantic value of the proposition of an utterance, namely factual and declarative" (Bybee & Fleischman, 1995, p. 2).

Modality may be expressed directly by the choice the speaker makes of the mood of the verb he or she uses: interrogative, for example, or imperative. But modality can be expressed in many other ways, including sentence order, choice of word, and intonation of the voice. Modality is a property, not so much of the utterance, as of the interaction: "Many of the functions of modality are inextricably embedded in contexts of social interaction and, consequently, cannot be described adequately apart from their contextual moorings in interactive discourse" (Bybee & Fleischman, 1995, p. 3). "Many modal functions," they go on, "surface only in face-to-face interactive discourse. That is, they depend not just on a monologic speaker (the narrator in narrative discourse), but on a dialogic (explicitly or by implication) speaker-addressee interaction" (p. 8). The meanings of modals are rooted in the social, interactional functions of language, transcending the transmission of information.

The business of modality is to express "a speaker's attitude toward the proposition of an utterance produced in a dialogic exchange" (Bybee & Fleischman, 1995, p. 9; note their use of the word *attitude*). Modal theory (a branch of logic) has systematically distinguished between two kinds of modality: *epistemic* and *deontic*. The markers of epistemic modality serve to express the speaker's commitment to the truth of the proposition his or her utterance conveys; it is thus concerned with knowledge and belief. A sentence such as "I don't agree with you; I think the movie was just great" is a sentence that conveys an epistemic effect (in this case evaluative, as well as factual). Deontic modality, by contrast, focuses on notions of obligation and permission, and thus expresses the speaker's sense of the necessity or possibility of acts to be performed by "morally responsible agents" (Lyons, 1977, p. 823, cited in Bybee & Fleischman, 1995, p. 4). "Let's take in a movie" has a deontic force. Epistemic modality is thus concerned with what the situation is and deontic modality with what needs to be done about it.

A-B-X, then, is about how people manage to coordinate and resolve (or fail to resolve) differences about their attitudes. Both dimensions of modality, epistemic and deontic, are always in play, although perhaps indirectly, by implication.

CONVERSATION IS ALSO TEXT

The complexity of language arises from its contrasting functionalities: On the one hand, as I have just been describing, it is an instrument of co-orientation and the basis of conversation. Language in its social extensions as the instrumentality of co-orientation is an intersubjective phenomenon. It indexes the more or less successful joint positioning of two or more partners in the construction of a collective unit of action. This is the essence of group work: an ongoing mutually adaptive adjusting and readjusting of behaviors and attitudes to produce a team.

On the other hand, language is text: People who speak are always generating text (Halliday & Hasan, 1989), "speaking prose without knowing it," to use Molière's expression. Language becomes text, in its usual connotation, when it is abstracted from context (Ricoeur, 1991): when its modal role in transmitting attitude is stripped away (and it thus sheds its direct role in mediating social relationships through interaction). In its guise as text, language may take on whatever elaboration the speaker is capable of—including compositions as complex and extended as the novel, or the essay, or the scientific report, or a body of laws.

Language in its individual extensions, therefore, is an instrument of objectification: a transposition of participant into observer role (Maturana, 1990, 1997). It is how the subjectivity of experience is transformed into an objectified account. As text, it accomplishes what Bakhtin calls "outsideness" (Holquist, 1990; Todorov, 1984). It is no longer intersubjective, but *intertextual*. It is a way of marshalling the available resources of established linguistic forms and expressions to step outside the subjectivity of conversation and to hold a mirror up to it by its translation into text.

Some of the ways language-as-text objectifies subjective experience are obvious enough: The dictionary is a compendium of names of nouns, verbs, and their modifiers, each defined in general terms that reflect the culture and society in which the language is current. An even more subtle effect of language is narrative. Stories serve to objectify not just individuals, or their acts and relationships, but the *dynamics* of A-B-X transactions. For example, A, impelled by the need to act as a result of some event, enlists the aid of B in the performance of X, leading to first, a relationship of agency where B acts for A, and second, a relationship of indebtedness by A to B. In such sequences, the modalities become articulated over time: from perception of situation (epistemic modality) to perception of what is to be done about it (deontic modality), to a transfer of attitude from A to B, to actual performance, to perception of the new situation (epistemic modality). Stories are about the complex ways people find to co-orient to each other. They cover the entire gamut of unfolding relationships, from conflict to cooperation.

Language, then, is an instrument of socialization in two distinct senses. On the one hand, as medium of conversation, it furnishes the basic resource necessary for individuals to create bonds of sociability with others, in the to-and-fro of interaction. On the other hand, as text, it imposes the objective categories that are typical of, and recognized by, a certain culture and society. It defines the identities that are recognizable, not just of individuals and objects, but of activities as well. It is essentially normative. In this role, it is an agent of outsideness. Language, then, is how people enter into collaborative relationships with others, even as they constitute themselves as each other's observers.

Co-orientation is a double-edged sword: It both brings people into an intersubjective mutuality of perspective and action, but it also separates them from each other by making each the observer and potential judge of the other.

Co-Orientation Theory and Dialogism

I now examine a co-orientation theory of organization as it is revealed by the dialogic philosophy of Bakhtin, consider where I perceive there to be convergence, and reflect on some of what I see to be differences.

DIALOGICS AS EPISTEMOLOGY

More than one commentator has observed that Bakhtin's corpus constitutes an epistemology: an essentially pragmatic theory of knowledge (Holquist, 1990; Todorov, 1984). Our very consciousness of experience, Bakhtin argues, is an effect of our relations with others. In and of ourselves, we are no more than a flow of sensations. Meaning is not to be found in the sensations as such, but in the relationship our experience has with the world of the other. Without relationship, we are a figure without a ground, for nothing is even minimally perceptible in the absence of a figure-ground contrast.

Our experience as self-conscious beings is not a fixed and stable point in time–space, however, but is defined by shifting coordinates that delineate our relative position with respect to others. The self is a relation to others, a point of view that has no perspective in the absence of a landscape on which it serves as a vantage point of observation, thus allowing the observer to grasp his or her own location. Remove the other, and the self vanishes with it. And because relations are continually in flux, existence is forever open-ended, unfinalized. Our identity emerges, it follows, only in the events that make up the endless kaleidoscope of our experience. We understand the meaning of our own existence—incomplete in and of itself—only by its reflection back to us in the interpretation of others, and that we in turn re-interpret, in a sequence that has no intrinsic point of rest.

To be "oneself" means to have been recreated as an actor in a drama that is constituted in our evolving relationship to others. Meaning, for Bakhtin (Holquist, 1990, pp. 29, 38), is found in a triad of center, not-center, and the relationship that links them: utterance, reply, and a relation between the two (an A–B, in other words). In the absence of the A–B, neither the A nor the B yet exists, socially and cognitively. No event can be seen entirely from the inside; otherwise it is just a happening without a meaning. It is only by stepping out of the raw flow of sensation to take the role of an observer that experience can be understood (Maturana, 1997). There must be what Bakhtin calls *authorship* (Holquist, 1990). This is an epistemology that not only supports, but illuminates, co-orientation theory.

THE ROLE OF TEXT

Text is central to the theory of knowledge that Bakhtin espouses. For him, making a text is equivalent to expressing oneself in speech, because only by expression in speech is the self–other relation forged. Todorov (1984) cites Volosinov (in *Marxism and the Philosophy of Language*) as saying,

> The spirit, mine as well as the other's, is not a given, like a thing (like the immediate object of the natural sciences); rather, it comes through expression in signs, a realization through "texts," which is of equal value to the self and to the other.[1] (p. 18)

As Todorov observes elsewhere, "Language is constitutive of human existence" (p. 29). Text, then, is the clue to how the inchoate organic response of the individual is transformed into understanding, in which the person emerges in its selfhood, in relation to others.

Bakhtin draws a very explicit distinction between the moment of Being, in its "transitiveness and open event-ness" (Bakhtin, 1993, p. 1) and its objectification in one kind of text or another, in which the experience takes on a content or sense. "Two worlds," he writes, "confront each other": a world of culture and a world of life, one where "the acts of our activity are objectified" and the other where "these acts actually proceed and are actually accomplished once and only once" (1993, p. 2). On the one hand, it is text in its manifold variety that projects us into the domain of culture; on the other hand, that same text is no more than a shadow of the actual lived and experienced life.

Text is saturated through and through with sociability. It is a resource shared by all members of the community. Language is like a do-it-yourself toolkit, complete with all the parts (and an instruction manual to accompany them), with which you can build some kinds of texts, and not others—*genres*, in Bakhtin's (1984) terminology. Holquist (1990) explains:

> For, as denizens of the logosphere, we are surrounded by forms that in themselves seek the condition of mere being-there, the sheer givenness of brute nature. In order to invest those forms with life and meaning, so that we may be understood and so that the work of the social world may continue, *we must all perforce become authors.* (p. 66)

Language is profoundly *inter*textual. The elements you have at your disposal have already been honed through repeated usage and carry with them the "smell" of their previous contexts of employment. In interacting with others using language, you purchase more than a convenient device to express yourself; you buy a customized package that comes ready-made with the very categories of relationship and identity with which the other is enabled to respond: to represent—*re*-present—you to yourself, them to themselves, and both to the other. Even though, as Holquist (1990) puts it, "In order to see ourselves, we must appropriate the vision of others . . . it is only the other's categories that will let me be an object for my own perception" (p. 28), nevertheless, the "categories" are already social.

Do Bakhtin's writings support a co-orientation, or *A-B-X*, view of relationship? On the whole, I think so, as I now turn to show, but there are significant differences.

Bakhtin's Perspective on Co-orientation

Perhaps language is not quite the tyrant I may have made it seem. As Bakhtin (1986) observes, "After all, language enters life through concrete utterances (which manifest language) and life enters language through concrete languages as well" (p. 63). We dance—you and I—in borrowed clothes, but it is *we* who dance, and each time we dance is a unique event. How life enters language, and vice versa, is the topic of one of Bakhtin's (1986) late essays, the one in which he addresses speech genres. What I concentrate on is the process of communication he describes there, because it bears directly on co-orientation.

He begins by taking his distance from conventional views of communication, which assume that thought exists independently of communication. The conventional view is founded on the Cartesian image of people engaged in a silent conversation with themselves, called *thinking*. Communication, in this perspective, is simply a speaker who verbalizes his or her thoughts in the presence of a listener.

As against this impoverished image of communication and language, Bakhtin counterposes an explanation that is remarkably similar to that of conversation analysis, even though Bakhtin's article was penned fully two decades before the publication of Sacks, Schegloff, and Jefferson's (1974) landmark article, which is often taken to have established the basis for a new discipline.

THE ROLE OF UTTERANCE

The unit of language, Bakhtin asserts, is not the sentence, but the utterance. And an utterance is defined situationally, because its boundaries are "determined by a *change of speaking subjects*" (Bakhtin, 1986, p. 71). An utterance, for Bakhtin, may range from a single epithet to a full speech. It is not a conventional, but a real unit, "delimited by the change of speaking subjects" (p. 71). Rejoinders, he says, "are all linked to one another" (p. 72). The relations that exist among rejoinders "are impossible among units of language (words and sentences)": such supra-sentential sequences as question and answer, assertion and objection, assertion and agreement, suggestion and acceptance, order and execution, and so on, which in conversation analysis would be called "adjacency pairs." Bakhtin (1986, p. 84) writes: "Any utterance is a link in the chain of speech communion."

The "listeners," furthermore, are far from passive. The listener is active, participative, "imbued with response" (p. 68):

> And the speaker himself is oriented precisely toward such an actively responsive understanding. He does not expect passive understanding that, so to speak, only duplicates his own idea in someone else's mind. Rather, he expects response, agreement, sympathy, objection, execution, and so on. (Bakhtin, 1986, p. 69)

This is how I also conceive the *A–B* dimension of co-orientation to unfold (Taylor & Van Every, 2000). But Bakhtin goes further, arguing that "our *thought* and our *practice* . . . take place between two boundaries: the relation to the *thing*, and the relation to the *person* (*thingification* and *personification*, translated and cited by Todorov, 1984, p. 18). As Bakhtin, 1986) also writes: "The relationship to others' utterances cannot be separated from the relationship to the object (for it is argued about, agreed about, views converge within it), nor can it be separated from the relationship to the speaker himself. This is a living tripartite unity" (p. 122).

THE ROLE OF CONTEXT

There is another perspective on utterance that Bakhtin offers us: the importance of its contextual grounding. Linguistic expressions (i.e., text), important though they may be to understanding, are only part of what constitutes an utterance. For an utterance to take on meaning, there must be a synthesis of two parts, one of which is explicitly verbal, and another that is implicit in the situation itself. The tacit part is a shared spatial–temporal context or *chronotope* (Bakhtin, 1981, p. 84): a simultaneity of co-presence (or at least virtual co-presence). It is also an already shared common experience, so that both parties to the exchange have a joint sense, and evaluation, of the situation they are in, in which I understand situation to mean a moment in an unfolding stream of events (Taylor, Groleau, Heaton, & Van Every, 2001).

This context-dependence of all interpretation is what is known in ethnomethodology, following Garfinkel (1967), as *indexicality:* It refers to the supplement of background knowledge that has to be exploited to make sense of the necessarily incomplete fragments of language with which one is confronted in speech. In Bakhtin's words, "Verbal communication will never be understood or explained outside of this link to the concrete situation" (cited in Todorov, 1984, p. 41), and "the expression of an utterance can never be fully understood or explained if its thematic content is all that is taken into account" (Bakhtin, 1986, p. 92). Language, after all, is a system of *general* categories; for it to be employed in *specific* circumstances, there must intervene what logicians call *instantiation:* transforming multipurpose variables into circumstantially delimited and relevant constants.

Both speaker and listener perceive what they say and hear as intending to address the situation as a whole. Context, then, is crucial. If there is no X, then A-B exchanges are no more than empty symbolic posturing.

BAKHTIN AND MODALITY

The third aspect of interactive communication that Bakhtin emphasizes is its *expressivity,* "the speaker's subjective emotional evaluation of the referentially semantic content of his utterance" (Bakhtin, 1986, p. 84). It is worth citing him at some length, as what he is saying is fundamental:

> The expressive aspect has varying significance and varying degrees of force in various spheres of speech communication, but it exists everywhere. There can be no such thing as an absolutely neutral utterance. The speaker's evaluative attitude toward the subject of his speech (regardless of what his subject may be) also determines the choice of lexical, grammatical, and compositional means of the utterance. The individual style of the utterance is determined primarily by its expressive aspect. . . . Language as a system has, of course, a rich arsenal of language tools—lexical, morphological, and syntactic—for expressing the speaker's emotionally evaluative position, but all these tools as language tools are absolutely neutral with respect to any particular real evaluation. . . . Words belong to nobody, and in themselves they evaluate nothing. But they can serve any speaker and be used for the most varied and directly contradictory evaluations on the part of speakers. (pp. 84–85)

Bakhtin is outlining, in remarkably similar terms, what I earlier described as a linguistic theory of modality (note that his translator too uses the term "attitude," as indeed Newcomb does in his article). Like Bybee and Fleischman (1995), Bakhtin sees modality as a feature of the interaction, and not simply a linguistic category (although there *is* such a linguistic category, i.e., the mood of the verb). And like these later writers, he too observes that one of the most effective means of expressing "the speaker's emotionally evaluative attitude toward the subject of his expression" (1986, p. 85) is intonation: Tone of voice conveys reactions such as surprise, incomprehension, inquiry, doubt, affirmation, refutation, indignation, admiration, and so forth (1986, p. 110). As he observes, although the mood of the verb is a direct index of modality (e.g., interrogative, exclamatory, imperative), such explicit expressions of attitude are relatively infrequent in actual speech (Labov & Fanshel, 1977). Intonation is the most effective way to express attitude, but intonation is a property of the utterance, not of the sentence. It is part of how the speaker orients, not just to an object identified by the sentence, but to another's utterances. It is a way, in other words, for people in interaction to negotiate, through subtle signs of their attitude, a commonality of perspective on the situation they are in. The utterance, as Bakhtin puts it, "is filled with *dialogic overtones*" (1986, p. 92). "After all," he goes on, "our thought itself—philosophical, scientific and artistic— is born and shaped in the process of interaction and struggle with others' thought, and this cannot but be reflected in the forms that verbally express our thought as well" (1986, p. 92).

Again, I find expressed here what I mean by the dynamics of co-orientation. However, it is here also that there emerges a difference of emphasis between Bakhtin's and my interpretation of co-orientation.

THE MATERIAL WORLD AS OTHER-NESS

Part of what preoccupies Bakhtin, in the tradition of Dilthey and Weber, is clarifying the distinction between the human and the natural sciences. It leads him to draw a cut-and-dried line between "Nature" and "Society." In his essay "The Problem of the Text," for example, Bakhtin says flatly that "the relation to the thing (in its pure thingness) cannot be dialogic (i.e., there can be no conversation, argument, agreement, and so forth)" (Bakhtin, 1986, p. 121). And again: "No natural phenomenon has 'meaning,' only signs (including words) have meaning" (p. 113). Similarly, he sees the life of the text as always developing "*on the boundary between two consciousnesses, two subjects*" (p. 106).

I think Bakhtin overstates his case. Since he penned these essays, the sociology of science has blossomed into a full-blown discipline and its findings reveal a very different picture of the actual conduct of science from that which presumably motivated the view of Bakhtin. To cite but one example, Pickering (1995) describes what happens in the experimental laboratory as "a dance of agency." There is, he observes, "if not a perfect interchangeability, a very important degree of symmetry and interconnection between human agency and material agency" (1995, p. 16; by "material agency," he means the kind of behaviors of subatomic particles that a physicist observes in an experiment). To account for the symmetry, Pickering (1995) employs the term *tuning*. Tuning, he says, "*works both ways,* on human as well as nonhuman agency. Just as the material contours and performativity of new machines have to be found out in the real time of practice, so too do the human skills, gestures, and practices that will envelop them" (p. 16). Not only do we learn about what other people are up to by interacting with them and observing the information they give off (Goffman, 1959), we figure out what Nature is about in the same way. Karl Weick (1979) draws an organizational meaning from this act–observe sequence; he refers to it as *enactment*. Perhaps, Pickering speculates, "the vectors of human practice are just as temporally emergent from moment to moment and situation to situation as is material agency" (p. 18).

Pickering's "dance of agency" sounds remarkably like dialogue to me. The difference between Bakhtin's writing and that of the newer analysts is that whereas the former's was in the tradition of sociologists who resisted the colonization of the human sciences by the natural sciences (Dilthey, Weber, etc.), the current sociologists are showing that the natural sciences are themselves a branch of the interpretive sciences. They are no more "objective" or "rational" than other ways of knowing (Maturana, 1997).

A critical enabler of Pickering's dance of agency is the role of text. As Latour and Woolgar (1986) and Latour (1987) report, the communication between the scientist and the material world is endlessly mediated by text: inscriptions of one kind or another. Scientists do not observe directly the system that interests them; they observe, record, and analyze *signs*. The laboratory technicians are "compulsive and almost manic writers" (Latour & Woolgar, 1986, p. 48). Scientists, too, we are reminded, are authors like everyone else: "When not writing, [they] scribble on blackboards or dictate letters, or prepare slides for their next talk" (p. 49). Scientific practice, moreover, is imbued with intertextuality. It is an ongoing two-sided dialogue: partly a conversation with the natural world, via the intermediary of machines, and partly with colleagues and other audiences.

When you read the sociologists describing the lives of scientists, you hear echoes of Bakhtin's reflections on the role of the author. As is the case of the novelist, "The object is created in the process of creativity, as are the poet himself, his world view, and his means of expression" (Bakhtin, 1986, p. 120). Dialogism, whatever its manifestation, is, he writes, a "layering of meaning upon meaning, voice upon voice, strengthening through merging (but not identification), the combination of many voices (a corridor of voices) that augments understanding, departure beyond the limits of the understood, and so forth" (p. 121). The notion of layering of meaning on meaning, and voice on voice, could as well be construed as an insightful description of what sociologists find when they observe scientists at work. Dialogue, it would seem, is not just a description of interpersonal relationship. It characterizes our link to the material world of objects as well.

People discover their identities—their self-nesses—in more than just their human relationships. The work people do may be a source of profound satisfaction: a domain in which they become in their own ways authors of a tangible universe of, to them, objects that respond to them. It is Newcomb who seems to me to have the right idea: the A-B relation is not just intersubjectivity that "happens" to be situated with respect to X. The A-X and B-X relations are part of A-B-ness, not incidental to it. We are thoroughly material, as well as spiritual, in our essence as humans (as indeed I think Bakhtin understood).

THE ORGANIZATION AS A BEING: A "NOVEL" IDEA

Bakhtin (1981) begins his essay "From the Prehistory of Novelistic Discourse" with some observations on the nature of the novel, compared with earlier genres such as the epic or tragedy. The existing literature on novels fails, he says, to address what is specific to the novel: "The distinctive features of novelistic discourse, the stylistic *specificum* of the novel as a genre, remained as before unexplored" (1981, p. 42). Perhaps we can discover in his exploration of the novel the "specificum" of modern organization as well.

Bakhtin's answer to his own interrogation is well known. That which is specific to the novel, in contrast to earlier genres, is the dialogic relationship linking the author to the characters in the novel. The novel is characterized by *polyphony:* a multiplicity of voices reflecting a variety of language communities, modes of life, and personality styles. What we end up with, he says, is "a conglomeration of *heterogeneous* linguistic and stylistic forms lacking any real sense of style. It is impossible to lay out the languages of the novel on a single plane, to stretch them out along a single line" (1981, p. 48). There is no "unitary language or style," even though there does exist "a verbal–ideological center." This center is the author, who is found, not at any single one of the novel's language levels, but "at the center of organization where all levels intersect" (1981, p. 49). If the novel differs from earlier genres, it is because it deals with a "reality that is always richer, more fundamental and most importantly *too contradictory and heteroglot* to be fit into a high and straightforward genre" (1981, p. 55). The novel, significantly, "is a comparatively recent genre" (1981, p. 50); in fact, its rise to prominence is contemporaneous with the entry of the West into modernity. The novel, like the society in which it is found, is no longer unicultural.

I suggest that, if we substitute the notion of *organization* (in its modern sense) for *novel*, and members of the organization for the characters, we have in fact described the reality of modern organization as well. The modern organization differs precisely from its earlier prototypes (e.g., a small community of workers, a family enterprise) in its "heteroglossia." The modern organization is also a complex mosaic of more or less interconnected domains of explanation or modes and styles of discourse—Bakhtin's *genres*. Maturana (1997) calls these "cognitive domains," and he sees each as being characterized by its own particular rationality; Lave and Wenger (1991) call them "communities of practice." The authority management claims, with respect to all these other domains of discourse, is not grounded in its greater objectivity or wisdom, nor in its executive efficacy, but in the privileged role it is permitted to play, that of being designated by society to write the story of the organization. The particular relation of character to author, and author to character, is what is specific to the novel; the relation of the multiverse of discursively grounded domains of practice and cognition to the story of the organization is what is specific to the modern organization.

The organization, like the novel, has to be authored if it is to have an objective reality, for both its own members and the public outside it. It needs to be, as Czarniawska (1997) puts it, "narrated." We need to think of the CEO, not as an omniscient hero, but as an author, and an actor, perhaps, but above all a writer. No senior executive, in today's kind of society, can have more than a superficial knowledge of all that occurs in the universe he or she directs. The wise managers are the ones who understand they are not "managing," in the narrow sense, but caught up in a dialogue with the organization and its heterogeneous worlds of meaning. The foolish managers are the ones who imagine that the organization they head is but a passive creation of their conceiving.

Conclusion

I conclude by raising one last theoretical issue. It is related to the intrinsic limitations of any dialogical (or indeed Newcomb-style *A-B-X*) framework of analysis, when translated to the scale of the organization. The problem is this: The corollary of an *I-you* dialogue is a *we-they* nondialogue. That is to say, for every *inclusion* that dialogue effects through the interaction of a first and a second person, co-orienting to a common object, an *exclusion* is ipso facto simultaneously constituted (Latour, 1999). Dialogue creates a relationship, but the effect of relationship is to erect an *inside* and an *outside*. I am particularly sensitive to this consequence of dialogue, precisely because I see it as the dilemma, and challenge, confronting all organization. The organization is a hyper- reality, composed of multiple, more-or-less interconnected, conversations, each of which develops a kind of dialogue specific to it. Yet the organization itself struggles to become a coherent, unified domain of discourse. The "I-you-ness" of the organizational multiversity of local conversations produces a "we-they-ness" that stands in the way of the construction of the identity of the organization as a whole, and gives rise to interdivisional rivalries. Organizations are characterized by internal differences and conflicts, as much as they are by sameness. The image of organization as an irresolvable process of inclusion/exclusion is not what most of the textbooks on organizational theory and practice portray. They tend to focus on a different inside/outside: that which separates the organization from its context. They prefer to portray the manager as omniscient (it is an image that sells books!). Nevertheless, the simultaneous generation of cooperation and conflict in the very act of communicating is something that a great author such as Dostoevsky would always understand, and that Bakhtin theorized. Conflict is, after all, the essence of story.

Note

1. Although Volosinov is listed as the author of this text, many analysts believe Bakhtin was the real author. Because Bakhtin was writing in the heyday of Stalinism, the conditions in which he worked were exceptionally difficult. Occasionally, he seems to have published works that bore others' names.

9

Critical Organizational Dialogue

Open Formation and the Demand of "Otherness"

Stanley Deetz and Jennifer Simpson

The call for dialogue became a core part of our sociality in the later part of the twentieth century, and it clearly continues as a social hope as we confront the problems of a new era. Our contemporary situation is defined by complex tensions that frame the need for dialogue. International conflicts bear on local interests; increased interdependency is met by renewed calls for isolation; recognition and appreciation of pluralism and diversity are coupled with new forms of symbolic and physical violence. Although many still tout the promise of the information age, with the mass reproduction of meaning that new information technologies make possible, the need for discussion and negotiation persists. The struggle of our time is to build the practices of working together. This is the hope of a dialogic theory of communication.

Using the word *dialogue*, rather than simply *communication*, foregrounds specific normative hopes. Dialogue has been useful in drawing together alternative and often more hopeful understandings and practices of communication. The hopes of different conceptions and practices of dialogue are not all the same, however. In the 20th century, three dominant positions on dialogue evolved. The first, a liberal humanist perspective, is rooted in notions of internally located meaning and often grounded in particular interpretations of the works of Maslow (1970, 1973) and Rogers (1965, 1969, 1980) and popular writers like Senge (1990) and Bohm (1996). This position is developed as a normative interaction ideal founded on principles of understanding, empathy, and active listening. Positive communication from this perspective is to find common ground so that a community can comfortably co-exist. The second position, a critical hermeneutic orientation, is reflected in the writing of Gadamer (1975, 1980) and Habermas (1975, 1980, 1984, 1987). This position shifts away from an emphasis on private internal meanings and posits inter-action rather than psychological individuals as the locus of meaning production and negotiation. This perspective gives useful insights and adds a decision-component to dialogue, but it has also been critiqued for its over-reliance on a rational model of civic engagement and deliberation (cf. Young, 1990). Finally, the third model of dialogue, often called postmodern, emerged out of the post-structuralist thinking of scholars such as Bakhtin (1981), Derrida (1973), Foucault (1970), and Levinas (1969, 1985, 1987c). This position emphasizes the role of indeterminacy and "otherness" in reclaiming conflicts, resisting closure, and opening new opportunities for people to be mutually involved in shaping new understandings of the world in which they live and work.

The humanist position has largely become the everyday life, "native," con-ception of dialogue found in basic communication textbooks, personal improve-ment books, and corporate, religious, and community programs. Although many scholars associated with this tradition have developed nuanced theories of dialogue, these nuances are often lost when taken up in native practice. We argue here that the latter two positions, the critical hermeneutic and the post-modern, held in a complementary tension-filled relation, can provide more productive guidance to reforming human interaction and enhancing mutual, free, and open decision making. In our studies and change efforts in organiza-tions, however, the liberal humanist conception of dialogue often stands along-side authority and power relations to thwart this more vibrant form of dialogue. Dialogue requires both *forums*—places for occurrence—and *voice*—the capacity to freely develop and express one's own interests. *Forums* for dia-logue have been developed both in and out of organizational contexts. If the communication practices within them, however, follow from simplistically appropriated liberal humanist conceptions, some expression and sharing of understanding may occur, but *voice* does not.

The everyday conception of dialogue focuses attention on the act of self-expression and the processes by which what one "means" is transferred to others. This orientation presumes that our differences are superficial in contrast to a more essential, precommunicative humanness. With such a view, the self is held as fixed and knowable, and socially produced language and social systems are rendered invisible as mere carriers of meaning. The experi-ences of the moment are treated as "natural" and the constitutive conditions of self-production cannot be seen as politically charged. In practice this gives a false sense of the individual as the originator of meaning and leads to self-expressionism and strategic control of others through expressive acts. The stage is set for control of self and control of others.

In contrast to the common sense view, we develop a concept of dialogic communication that is aimed less at self-expression and more at self-destruction. For growth, differentiation, and progressive individualization of the self to be realized, one must abandon the quest for a unitary self and its control. The point of communication as a social act is to overcome one's fixed subjectivity, one's conceptions, one's strategies—to be opened to the indeterminacy of people and the external environment to form an open redetermination. This we believe is the basis for "voice." Communication in its dialogic form is productive rather than reproductive. It produces what self and other can experience, rather than reproducing what either has. Self-expression is misleading not because people do not or should not try to express their experiences but because such expressions in a dialogic view are the raw material for the production of something new rather than the product of self interests. Process subjectivity becomes possible in the responsiveness to a pull from the outside.

Recognizing "the otherness of the other" breaks a discursive blockage by posing questions to any fixed conception or meaning. In postmodern terminology, otherness deconstructs. The fundamental notion of otherness suggests that any possible label or conception of self, other, and world is capable of being questioned. Perception, as well as conception, is the end product of a conflict, a conflict that can be recovered. This conflict represents a struggle between one's fixed identity and conceptual schemes, and the excess of the other over that. The recollection of this struggle leaves each and every attempt to form an object potentially open to question. Every interaction, thus, holds both the possibility of closure or new meaning—either a reproduction of the dominant socially produced subjectivity or responsiveness to the excess of external events over these conceptions. Developing an appreciation of otherness as a part of dialogic interaction is central to developing a responsibility appropriate to the contemporary age.

Here we wish to focus on communication concepts and practices that facilitate voice. Given the limits of space in this chapter, we sketch more than develop an understanding of dialogue based in a recovery of conflict and a specific understanding of free and open communication. We call the model that we develop here a *politically responsive constructionist theory of communication* because of its grounding in the political realities of a sociohistorical context and its commitment to reformation through mutual constitution. We draw from Gadamer's conception of the "genuine conversation" (1975, 1980) to show why dialogue is based less in attitudes and activities of the self, than in responsiveness to the demands of otherness. We then suggest that Habermas's "ideal speech situation" (1984, 1987; see Deetz 1990, 1992) can provide a heuristic for a process to overcome power relations that leads people to take as their own asymmetrically developed thoughts, feelings, and interests. On the basis of the work of Gadamer and Habermas, we suggest that various forms of invisible discursive closure exist and that these can be overcome. In the context opened by critical communicative practices, otherness can be encountered, indeterminacy recovered, and one's own thoughts, feelings, and interests constructed responsively to the outside. Finally, this chapter provides a discussion of a specific case where an organization attempted to implement dialogue in the face of conflict. In this discussion, we show how at specific moments, encountering "otherness" occurred and productive new understandings emerged, and where dominant views of good communication and dialogue remained a block to community self-determination.

"Otherness" and the Formation of Experience

Our politically responsive constructionist theory of communication begins with the premise that the more interesting processes of communication occur in the production, rather than the reproduction, of specific meanings and experiences. This orientation recognizes that meanings and experiences initially form in the relation between a goal-directed activity and the not-yet-determined stuff of the world including people and events. In these encounters with objects, people, or situations that are "other," both they and we become determined as specific objects, or conceptualized people (Levinas, 1969, 1985, 1987c). Yet, the "others" we perceive are always outcomes of communicative practices situated in specific social–historical circumstances.

Most of our "personal" meanings and experiences are reproductions of earlier formations. These inherited meanings are produced by someone else to serve their purposes in their time and are uncritically taken on as our own. Usually these meanings are those of more dominant groups in which even opposition and conflict are produced in relation to dominant preferences. We are able to understand the distinctions of this versus that, but distinctions that would organize the world differently are hidden and suppressed. Although the reproduced experiences are clearly "ours," they are not formed by us but are borrowed from earlier formative processes that are politically partial.

Most acts of everyday interaction are reproductive in the sense that we trade or share routinized information about what we already "know." Occasionally, though, the routine is radically disrupted and the excess of the other over our determination of it calls out for reconceptualization and redetermination. Otherness is encountered and our experience is transformed from routine to extraordinary and meanings become "ours" in a more radical sense. We reserve the concept *dialogue* to designate the productive (rather than reproductive) communication processes enabling these radical transformations. We believe that this process is what pulls together the great communication theories of dialogue. This is Buber's (1958) encounter with *Thouness* that overcomes calcified understandings of *it,* and Gadamer's (1975) *conception formation* in the great piece of literature or art, for example. *Voice* is grounded in this dialogic open formation.

Embracing this position highlights the dilemma of a dialogic theory rooted in notions of *common ground.* Dialogic models that favor a quest for common ground inherently favor the already-dominant position of institutional privilege. As feminist standpoint theorists have aptly demonstrated, marginalized members of society must be bi- or multicultural. People at the margins must learn not only to navigate their own cultural terrain, but must also be fluent in the workings of the dominant culture. Those in positions of relative privilege, however, can afford to take these workings for granted (see Harding, 1991, 1992; Hartstock, 1998). Calls for "coming together" and "finding common ground" de facto reproduce the status quo because the ground that is common between participants is that of the dominant culture. This inhibits, rather than supports, the radical disruption of self that is central to our productive understanding of dialogue.

Only through our encounter with radical difference does transformation becomes possible, as the taken-for-granted assumptions of dominant ideologies are made visible through juxtaposition with alternative understandings. If we encounter the other in this way, we not only challenge the status quo of existing systems, but also open the door to deeper self-awareness. Otherness may be present either in the concrete person standing there or in the way his or her understanding reopens the things of our world to redetermination. This is the productive potential of dialogue.

A shift in orientation from an understanding of communication as a vehicle for overcoming difference to a process of exploring and negotiating difference fundamentally alters our understanding of the form and function of dialogue and reclaims its transformative potential (see Peters, 1999b, for a detailed history of this difference). Gadamer and Habermas both contribute to our understanding of this process.

Dialogue as a Free and Open Interaction Guided by the "Subject Matter"

Conceptualizing dialogue as a politically responsive constructionist theory of communication shifts our focus to the production of meaning through interaction and away from the strategic reproduction of meaning. Even within the strategy-loaded context of the workplace, communication to express one's "own" (as constructed by others) thoughts and feelings or to strategically influence others can be replaced with communicative attempts to reach greater understanding. In doing this, we foster decisions that enhance creativity and commitment and create opportunity for interlocutors to make specific contributions to mutually determined problems.

Such a conception is grounded in the works of Gadamer and Habermas. Although their positions differ regarding the nature of the dialogic process, they both emphasize continual social formation of consensus in interaction beyond the intentions and opinions of the participants. As developed in many places, this notion of interactionally produced understanding focuses attention on reaching openly formed agreement regarding the subject matter under discussion, rather than on seeking agreement between participants' perspectives (see Deetz, 1978, 1990, 1992).

From this perspective, communication difficulties arise from practices that preclude debate and conflict about values, limit access arbitrarily to communication channels and forums, and involve decisions based on arbitrary authority relations. This perspective suggests a process of preparation and activity to reduce continually all socially determined asymmetries for the interaction as critical to the dialogic process. In the absence of dialogue, communication processes are advanced by power-laden interests that obscure and preclude the demands of otherness. Hence, that which might be contested in interaction is left uncontestable.

The normative preference for this specific form of dialogue is grounded in two ways. First, Gadamer (1975), in developing an ontology of understanding, demonstrated the social character of the formation of experience that precedes each and every expression of it—the hermeneutic situation. Second, Habermas (1979, 1984) and Apel (1979) have shown that the illocutionary structure of discourse demonstrates the types of claims presumed possible in a society and, thus, anticipates the forms of support and dispute if claims are contested. In both cases, the "hermeneutic" and "ideal speech" situation are counterfactual— that is, rarely fully realized—but each is a necessary anticipation even if not achieved. This enables a shift in locus of concern from the individual's point of view and how it is presented to determining whether the interaction includes all relevant positions and interests.

Although many communication studies and native theories of dialogue emphasize what each person has to say about the subject matter, Gadamer focuses on what the subject matter "says" to each. In other words, the imaginary self and world produced in discourse is challenged by the excess of that which the discourse is about over the description of it. The communication question concerns how interaction is to proceed so that this excess is "remembered" or can make its claim.

Gadamer (1975) argued that the ideal is not "self expression and the successful assertion of one's point of view, but a transformation into communion, in which we do not remain what we were" (p. 341). It is not the insides of the other or the self that is to be understood, for either would be covering up the objective demand of the subject matter with one's subjective reaction. Gadamer's claim thus clarifies why a "successful" presentation of one's own meaning can limit rather than aid productive communication. To the extent that the object or "other" is silenced by successful expression, the capacity to engage in reclaiming difference is limited and the conceptual expansion toward a more open consensus on the subject matter is precluded. The otherness before us makes visible the one-sidedness and suppressed conflict in current perceptions and forces us to surrender those perceptions to the development of consensual thought as a new momentary resting place. Levinas (1969) presented the understanding poetically: "The presence of the Other is equivalent to calling into question my joyous possession of the world" (p. 75). Both the loss and the growth are critical to human social conduct.

Although participation in dialogues along the "genuine conversation" mode is possible, such opportunities are relatively rare because of the limitations that daily life imposes both on ourselves and others. Rarely is an experience so powerful that the disciplines, routines of life, and ordinary ways of seeing are spontaneously overcome. Real power relationships, manifested as institutional arrangements and structures of permissible discourse, routinely preclude otherness and block conversation. Although Gadamer recovers dialectics and understanding from modern epistemological domination, he has no politics. A politics requires a more complete analysis of actual communication processes.

Systems of domination usually preclude the genuine conversation. Habermas makes an advance by exploring the nature of interaction and normative hopes in common contexts in which a new consensus does not arise organically out of the interaction. Further, Habermas opens us to the questions of how one can engage the other in such a way that competing claims can be resolved, and illuminates that which allows us to distinguish consensus reached regarding the subject matter from that knowingly or unknowingly produced by authority or relations of power. Because Habermas and others have developed his position in many places, we will be brief.

Essentially, Habermas (1987) argued that every speech act can function in communication by virtue of common presumptions made by speaker and listener. Even if these presumptions are not fulfilled in an actual situation, the common presumptions serve as a base of appeal as the failed conversation itself turns to a special dialogic argumentation to resolve disputed validity claims. Every interaction depends on presumptions made about the identity of participants, the normative rules guiding behavior, knowledge of the external world, and values guiding the interior world. In everyday interaction we express these presumptions to others, but the social, often asymmetrical, conditions of their constitution generally remains invisible. These are the unassessed, unchosen prejudices that stand between us and the specific subject matter at hand. Dialogue, however, provides renewed opportunity for contestation.

Any claim that cannot be brought to open dispute serves as the basis for systematically distorted communication (see Deetz, 1992). Creating situations that come closer to the ideal speech situation helps avoid or overcome such distortions. This conception not only applies to the everyday and ordinary acts of communication but also models the ideal processes by which collective decisions can be made. In this sense, the ideal speech situation acts as a guide to defining institutions and practices that advance participation and democracy (Denhardt, 1981; Mingers, 1980; Ulrich, 1983). Dialogue modeled in this way is central to our moral responsibility to decide what our society will be and what kind of people we will become, and lies at the heart of a productive dialogic process.

The ideal speech situation gives us four basic guiding conditions necessary for free and open participation in negotiating differences (Habermas, 1987). First, the attempt to reach understanding presupposes a symmetrical distribution of the chances to choose and apply speech acts. This specifies the minimal conditions of skills and opportunities for expression, including access to meaningful forums and channels of communication. Such a principle argues against privileged expression forms, routines, and rules that advantage certain experiences, identities, and expressions.

Second, the understanding and representation of the external world needs to be freed from privileged preconceptions in the social development of "truth." Ideally, participants have the opportunity to express interpretations and explanations and to have conflicts resolved in reciprocal claims and counterclaims without privileging particular epistemologies or forms of data. This opens up the possibility for transformation.

Third, participants need to have the opportunity to establish legitimate social relations and norms for conduct and interaction. The rights and responsibilities of people are given in advance neither by nature nor by a privileged, universal value structure, but are negotiated through interaction. The reification of organizational structures and their maintenance without possible dispute and the presence of managerial prerogatives are examples of potential violence in corporate discourse. Acceptance of views because of an individual's privilege or authority or because of the nature of the medium would constitute a possible illegitimate relation. Authority itself is legitimate only if redeemable by appeal to an open interactional formation of relations freed from the appeal to other authorities.

Finally, interactants need to be able to express their own authentic interests, needs, and feelings. This requires freedom from various coercive and hegemonic processes by which the individual is unable to form experience openly, to develop and sustain competing identities, and to form expressions presenting them. Limiting the "other's" right to autonomous definition of self both does violence to the "other" and limits our own capacity for growth.

Gadamer and Habermas each offer much to develop a dialogic conception of communication describing the possibility and conditions for the production of meaning in interaction, and also provide a description of communication problems and inadequacies. In general, most strategic or instrumental communicative acts have the potential to assert the speaker's opinion and to inhibit the quest for understanding regarding the subject matter. In such a case, an apparent agreement precludes the conflict that could lead to a new position of open mutual assent. In cases where the one-sidedness is apparent, usually the processes of assertion/counterassertion and questions/answers are able to reclaim a situation approximating participation.

Humanist conceptions of dialogue offer more complex problems. In many cases, the asymmetries of concern are part of the culture and deeply embedded in socially formed experiences. In these cases, they remain invisible and often naturalized. Superficial equality further supported by warm, caring attitudes and open acceptance may make discovery and contestation of these almost impossible. Attempts to surface these closures and to achieve voice might well be seen as disruptive and violating norms of cooperation and pursuit of commonality. The native dialogic communication model can be used harmfully to silence difference, preclude open dialogue, and support a type of middle class civility in its place. Many workplace participation programs, for example, reduce the very conception of "voice" to merely having a say rather than looking to the social construction of what is to be said or the process of reclaiming a fundamental relation to otherness in order openly to form a position. Difference, representation, and creativity can all be lost when this happens.

The Organizational Context

Communication processes in large organizations provide an interesting site to consider alternative concepts and practices of dialogue. First, globalization of business and the rapid increase in the number of women and various ethnic minorities in the workforce make the active presence of diversity and the need to work with it greater in the workplace than in virtually any other institution in U.S. society. Second, power differences and hierarchical relations are a central and visible part of most large organizations. In this context, much communication is also openly strategic. Yet, here, too, we see widespread direct decision-making distributed across large groups of people more clearly than in any public political process. Further, the forms of interaction in organizations have a bias toward making decisions. Finally, dialogue theories based in liberal humanist principles, following the work of Senge (1990), Bohm (1996), and others, have been actively advanced in many organizations. Our experience in organizations indicates that these perspectives are often appropriated in ways that overemphasize the importance of shared meaning and finding common ground at the expense of encountering difference and mutually constructing understanding. Each of these organizational insights shapes and refines our understanding of dialogic transformation.

WORKPLACE DIVERSITY

Despite gains in the latter half of the 20th century in desegregating public institutions in the United States, the country in many ways remains socially and culturally divided. Native notions of dialogue rooted in understandings of self as fundamentally separate from others have set up an understanding of communication that necessitates a "common ground" from which to build understanding. Although finding common ground may be marginally possible among and between individuals of like mind or like experience, the increasing diversity found in today's organizations points to real problems with this communicative demand in practice. And because segregation and separation are less often present in organizations and more often legally prohibited, organizational members must actively engage and deal with diversity.

Beyond being difficult to *do,* however, organizational dynamics suggest that "coming together" and "finding common ground" may be far less desirable activities than learning to recognize, value, and even celebrate difference. Creativity, member commitment, and customization of products add needed value to organization practices and outcomes. Difference, rather than being a problem, is core to achieving these things. By attending to the centrality of difference in organizations, we can see more clearly that transformation requires not simply a rapprochement of perspective but a more careful examination of a wider range of voices.

POWER AND PARTICIPATION

Although interactions that occur in the private domain are also replete with inequitable distributions of wealth and influence, in organizations these relationships are codified and institutionalized in ways that allow us to focus attention more readily on the dynamic of power. Power distribution differences in organizations draw attention to the dilemma created by a dialogic orientation centered on finding common ground. Because power is never distributed equally and most organizations have massive cultural management programs, what is "common" among stakeholders almost always favors the already privileged position. In emphasizing dialogic processes that encourage "coming together," we lose sight of the uneven ground upon which such a meeting would necessarily take place.

With the increased use of and talk about team decisions, dialogue, and forms of participation generally, alternative ways of communicating have been advanced. Often these alternatives have not been theoretically or empirically investigated, however, and have been presented in a vague unproblematic way as simply "democratic" or participatory communication. Furthermore, these communication practices have often been seen as requiring little training or development. If we build a trusting team, members will communicate well; if we develop participatory attitudes, appropriate skills will spontaneously arise. But all democracies are not alike, and native intuitions and skills can be counterproductive. Anyone hanging around most corporations will hear more complaints about the endlessness and frustrations of meetings than about the lack of opportunity to participate. This results not only from the limited nature of participation tasks but also from the inability to participate *well*. Our biggest task may not be overcoming the autocratic tendencies of many managers and the communication structures, principles, and practices fostered by this, but rather providing new ways to think about and do communication in places where participation is genuinely favored.

Native views of dialogue and communication were never intended to accomplish truly mutual and creative decision-making. Common native understandings are largely based in an 18th century conception of liberal democracy as institutionalized and advanced by Western state institutions. The root conceptions advanced in organizations are the same as the humanist conception of dialogue. Liberal democracy is central to the justification of contemporary forms and institutions of communication. The thin conceptions of communication inherent in this model may account partly for the poor regard people have of political processes and general cynicism in many societies.

Organizations, unlike many other institutions, tend to be less mired in the pretense of naturally occurring discourse because many organizational interactions occur within both sanctioned and unsanctioned strategic space. Although clearly they are filled with forums that do not facilitate voice, including town halls, suggestion boxes, and committees, to name but a few, they are unlike many other social contexts in that they are driven to make decisions rather than simply to vent or recommend. Whether decisions get made by boards, committees, task forces, advisory groups, chairs, managers, executives, or chancellors, the organization has routine and well-defined channels for sanctioning and authorizing those decisions (even if they were initially negotiated around the water cooler, in the rec center, over a power lunch, or on the back nine of a golf course). The ability to make mutually satisfactory decisions together may well be a stronger basis for community than mutual understanding, shared values, or open discussions. Organizations provide a rich context to observe this process.

NATIVE THEORIES OF DIALOGUE

"Dialoguing" about issues is a common catch-phrase for many forms of discourse involving interaction or "coming together." Nevertheless, because of the transformative potential the word invokes, its use often raises expectations of fairness, justice, and equity that may not be readily accomplished by "getting people in a room together." In fact, we find that, for some organizational members, the very invocation of the word *dialogue* is a strong portent of change (Simpson, 2001). The coupling of high expectations with an ill-defined and murky concept, however, increases the likelihood of disappointments, stagnation, and an entrenchment of polarized positions that do not bear out the dialogic promise. Organizations seem to experience this routinely with the use of various humanist-based programs. It may well be that other communities do, too, but we lack the systematic assessment in those contexts that is common to organizational interventions.

Individual organizational actors often subscribe to implicit theories of self and meaning that are rooted in a liberal humanist tradition. This should come as no surprise. Organizational emphasis on individual responsibility and clear, concise presentation of material reinforces notions of autonomous selves with individually formed and internally located meanings. Often, professed "autonomy" is a central feature of advanced control systems in organizations and evidences the absence of voice (see Barker, 1993; Deetz, 1998). The humanist model of communication and identity provides little space for delighting in the difference that makes our encounter with the other rich with possibility. Native theories of dialogue may be one of the greatest threats to productive dialogic encounters.

An Unexpected Organizational Encounter With the Other

A recent study of a large, Western, public university (Simpson, 2001) provides a rich example of how dialogue can be constrained by native theories and how the unexpected intrusion of otherness may establish the conditions for voice. During the course of this study, the institution in question organized a Campus Retreat on Community. We explore how this event, part of a broader initiative to "Build Community" on campus, demonstrates how encounters with dialogic potential that provide space for meeting with and delighting in difference may be manifest in organizational spaces. As Pearce and Pearce (2001) have discovered through their Public Dialogue Consortium, "Public dialogue and participatory democracy are deeply interrelated. The challenge confronting any democratic organization is to balance the needs for efficiency with the structure that not only allows but respects disagreement" (p. 120).

In the two and a half years leading up to the event described below, the campus in question developed many programs and initiatives aimed at fostering a more open, welcoming, and supportive community (Simpson, 2001). Many of the projects of the Building Community Campaign (BCC) offered pronounced examples of the dilemmas and tensions present when sincere efforts to bridge and honor difference collided with socially prescribed understandings of communication and dialogue rooted in expectations of "coming together" and "finding common ground." Although this dilemma was not lost on some members of the group, awareness of it was often eclipsed by a pull, both from institutional forces, and from campaign members, to reach closure, make decisions, and "get things done." In this way, the powerful potential of otherness was at times overshadowed by commonplace understandings of "diversity" and transformative potential was closed off in favor of more expedient action. At times, such as the instance described below, however, the campaign has helped to open spaces ripe with that potential. The following example illustrates how providing a space that allows and encourages expression of difference may also create space for empowering encounters with disagreement that have the potential to allow participants not only to "survive the disgraceful fact of our mutual difference" (Peters, 1999b, p. 31) but also to delight in the insights afforded by that diversity of perspective. As we will see, however, the momentary opening of possibility that occurs here is ephemeral and becomes difficult to sustain as soon as participants return to organizational structures with taken-for-granted norms for interaction.

The Gallery

In January of 2001, the BCC developed a "Gallery" exercise for their second Campus Retreat on Community. During this retreat, approximately 100 students, faculty, staff, and administrators had an opportunity to view 30 posters compiled from words and images taken from newspaper clippings and interviews with campus members and to react by posting notes and responding both to the display and to one another. Sadly, the linear narrative form of this chapter is poorly suited to capturing the dynamic richness of this activity as it unfolded, and part of the uniqueness of this experience was, precisely, the fluid and tactile nature of the exercise. In an interview that preceded the Gallery event, Jackson, an undergraduate student of color on this campus, succinctly captured the commonsense notion that organizational members often have of the dialogic process:

> That's how we deal with things is by sitting down and having meetings, and I'm in my suit and my tie and you're in your suit and your tie and we sit down and, you know, go over a couple of pamphlets and spell out a few point plan and discuss and dialogue.

The Gallery was not that experience of dialogue. The words on the wall as well as the posted-note responses to them became polysemic texts separated from authors and personal authority. The subject matter of the texts remained "other" and evoked responsiveness. As notes were added, no single interpretation remained stable. As individuals returned, their very own statements had shifted in meaning and implored their own rethinking. Simpson (2001) tries to direct our attention to this sense of carnival:

> The room is warm with people. I notice that the poster near the air conditioning is drawing a crowd. As I walk around, I am taken with the many different ways that people are engaging what they see. Their task is to read the quotes, and to respond as they see fit. There is no order to what they see, they simply move from one poster to another as it catches their eye or fancy, or because it has a smaller crowd around it. They will have time later, at dinner, to discuss what they have seen, and what they have felt. . . .
>
> Some participants are very task oriented. They wander the room with their colorful pads of Post-It notes, jotting comments as they go along. Others engage everyone around them. They strike up conversations, share perceptions and stories, and soon the room is a-buzz with conversation. There is another group, though, that seems equally engaged, but much more subdued. They walk quietly, often standing still for long stretches of time, expressions of concern, or deep reflection on their faces. I think about everything I have written about difference in the last few years, and watch attentively as people from all backgrounds, across levels of the organization each engage the writing on the wall in their own way. I will be curious to see what they write. (p. 144)

Later, a senior white male faculty member who participated in the event remarked that the experience was "like being popcorn in a popper": a still silence of hesitation and waiting permeating the air until someone jumped into the fray and others were compelled to follow until, by the end, people were running around trying to find more Post-It notes, so that they could engage yet another idea that had caught their attention. What follows is a condensed and diluted, but nevertheless illustrative, depiction of the event and a reflection on what the experience can teach us about dialogue and its power to transform. Capturing this sense of dialogue can be difficult:

> Afterward, I struggled with how to do justice to this event in my representation. The non-linearity of the event seemed to defy transcription. Comments sometimes referred to both a quotation and a picture on a given poster. Sometimes the comments spoke more to one another as the voices in the room merged with those on the wall and became both a part of and apart from the display. I had no way of knowing in what order some posters might have been viewed or how that might have influenced interpretations. (Simpson, 2001, p. 145)

The example below greatly abbreviates the experience of that evening but provides insight into the dialogic potential of encounters in which difference is not only allowed but also respected and invited. There are many examples that might have been used for this illustration: 30 posters in all, some with multiple quotations or images, and each with multiple posted responses. Due to the space constraints of this chapter, we have selected excerpts from four posters and their responses that, we feel, best capture the cumulative and collective nature of the sense-making process that unfolded throughout this event. Each poster is separated by ********** from the next. Boldface text indicates material that was presented to participants, and *italics* indicate participant responses. Because the experience of this material was not linear or static, we invite you to move around, among and between the posters, as the participants did, and notice how the introduction of new voices shifts earlier interpretations.

****

Everybody is not welcome in this community. Let's get that out on the table, but we know that and we're trying to do something about it and everybody has a part to play in it pretty much. —Female Staff of Color

I appreciate this statement because it is provocative and realistic. I read and hear strategies!

This addresses the issue that we all, each and every one of us, needs to make a commitment to valuing others.

****

I still hear from a lot of people about the insecurity, about the feeling like, you know, from faculty, from young faculty, that they don't know if they are respected here. They don't know if they are safe here. They don't know if they're going to have a job here. They don't know if they're going to get tenure and I think that's like part of it, like the whole process that somebody goes through to be a faculty person just sounds like it's about everything else but building community. —White Female Staff

We all need to feel safe and respected.

What's valued for tenure, eh? It's not about being a community member or even a good teacher. Publish or perish!

Must the pressure to be academically/intellectually "acceptable" necessarily disallow caring, passion, acceptance—community?

****

Do we then lament the fact that we haven't been able to have a lot of senior faculty of color? Well, I can tell you why. It's because nobody cares about them enough, you know, and then after awhile, when nobody pays attention to your

work, when they're not interested in your work, when they don't value it, when evaluation time comes, what do you think happens? We get discouraged. —Female Faculty of Color

The way to being comfortable begins with being uncomfortable.

Unfortunately this attitude then trickles down to the students.

When people who care give up—what have we left to build on?

What will it take to value diverse ways of thinking, approaching research and writing?

We marginalize & devalue topics dealing with multicultural issues—in fact we segregate them. How about integrating diversity into every course in this university?

This is why faculty of color don't stay.

When an entire field of study (i.e. Ethnic Studies or Women Studies) is called into question as a legitimate field for scholarly pursuit—what type of message does this send?

****

What's really missing is caring and generosity. When a faculty, a typical faculty member is approached by a student group or even by an individual student, there's already a kind of tension of an adversarial relationship. —White Male Faculty

This is sad. What a way to start a collegial relationship!

But it is inherently rewarding damn it!

On which side?

Many faculty are generous and caring but reticent to act on these instincts due to the incentive system in place for them.

The stressful academic culture—pressures for achievement for everyone—makes it difficult to find space and time for generosity.

I have found caring and generosity. What is missing is public support for those who are caring and generous.

If faculty were appropriately rewarded for participating in student activities, there might be more willingness (on the part of faculty).

I AGREE. Perhaps "community-building" types of things should be given a little more weight as we make tenure decisions.

****

These brief examples, although oversimplifying a more complex and textured process, provide a glimpse into how the possibility of dialogue may open when we create respectful and delightful opportunities to encounter and engage difference. We suggest that not only is this an important communicative task, but that it is fundamental to a dialogic process rooted in an understanding of historicality and situated, mutually constructed meaning.

Although the nature of the Gallery event challenged and defied neat transcription, its power lay precisely in its capacity to engage a wide range of organizational actors with otherness. As individuals moved through the room and encountered thoughts, ideas, and perspectives that both fit neatly with and deeply challenged previously held conceptions, new meanings and new understandings seemed to emerge, literally, in the writing on the wall. When people responded to the initial quotations and images, the picture of the community that was represented on the walls gained depth and texture. As people's voices intermingled, feelings emerged, ranging from hope and excitement to anger and despair. Along with those feelings, critical organizational issues were named.

The challenge that remained at the end of the night, however, was that, given previously held understandings of communication, dialogue, and action, what had transpired was largely perceived as "just talk" and much of the dinner conversation focused on what "the university" would *do*. As soon as the forum returned to one with clear organizational norms for interaction, many of the items that had been open to contestation in "The Gallery" were once again outside of the ground that was common to participants. Although dinner conversations focused on concerns over minority student and faculty representation on campus and impediments to their recruitment and retention, the solutions offered did not emphasize dialogic models or forums that would permit, encourage, or celebrate continued or deepening encounters with the otherness that had been made visible during the Gallery exercise.

Wrapping Up

Perhaps one of the greatest challenges and most exciting potential contributions before the field of communication today is to recognize the role that we can play in challenging, questioning, and opening to critique those native, commonsense assumptions about communication and dialogue that privilege the self at the expense of the other. Failure to attend carefully to the otherness around us limits our own perspective, produces incomplete and inadequate decision-relevant information, and does violence to those "others" whose positions are often already institutionally and culturally marginalized. Encounters with the other must go beyond notions of exchange, move past understandings of communication as the transmission of internally located meaning, and revitalize conceptualizations of dialogue that recognize the central importance of radical difference to our own capacity for growth in understanding.

Native actors in organizational contexts already believe in dialogue as a powerful tool rich with promise. Yet the commonly held assumptions about what dialogue is and how it happens tend to privilege a "coming together on common ground" perspective that inherently privileges the already dominant set of understandings. From this communicative orientation, those organizational others who must set their perspectives, insights, and understandings aside to "dialogue" on common ground are likely to continue to feel an absence of voice because their issues will always be beyond the scope of the "dialogue."

In our dialogic view, agency is not dependent on a new-found internal will but on a recovery of the demand of otherness or "subject matter," in Gadamer's (1975) sense. Dialogic communicative processes perpetually recover a space for exceeding personal and systemic restraints and distortions. Responsiveness is greatest in chance and transformative events that defy routines and standard recipes. Such chance events make possible reclaimed conflicts and transformations. But openings can also be encouraged, especially in periods of conflict, turmoil, and transition. The production of alternative social memories and counternarratives demonstrates the possibility of new articulations of experience and opens them to a new political understanding. Contemporary everyday conceptions of interacting with others through effective communication are conceptually flawed as a basis for responsibility and responsiveness. Rarely are adequate forums provided and voice is greatly limited. Reclaiming and taking seriously the demand of otherness on dialogic encounters foregrounds an understanding of communication as a productive process grounded in response to particular political circumstances. This, we suggest, holds the greatest potential for recovering voice and the dialogic transformation it invites.

10

Dialectical Tensions and Dialogic Moments as Pathways to Peak Experiences

H. L. Goodall, Jr. and Peter M. Kellett

Into a Dialogue

It was flattering to be asked by Rob, Leslie, and Ken to participate in this volume by offering our views on dialogue. We have been involved in work aimed at understanding and applying dialogue; we have worked together at two universities where our research, teaching, and consulting practices have benefited from friendship and professional collaboration on a number of levels; and we have had—until this chapter emerged as a writing project—a shared set of under-articulated ideas about dialogue that informs our thinking and activities in the world.

So it was that we agreed to respond to this writing opportunity by using it to articulate what has been largely invisible, but thematically present, in our published work, certainly in our thinking, and clearly in our consulting work. In the process of using this opportunity for dialogue to bring those invisible meanings to light, we learned that we were, in fact, ourselves working through a set of dialectical tensions that defined the ways in which our individual work on dialogue speaks to, and through, each other. More important, we learned from and furthered our work by coming to understand that the dialectical

Authors' Note: Special thanks to Alexandra Georgeady for translating the key concepts of this chapter into Greek.

tensions we discovered at the heart of our inquiry also informed how dialogue itself is connected to a broader range of peak human experiences. We believe this insight has profound implications for personal and relational identities as well as for communication practices used to materially manifest them. So, in this chapter, we offer a way of thinking about dialogue as an analogue to other forms of peak experiences and a way to use lessons from those analogues as a feedback loop to help us better understand the dialectical tensions that inform the experiencing of the communicative encounter we know as *dialogue.*

Before we share those insights, and in accordance with the directives given to the contributors to this volume, we will provide brief summary statements of how each of us acquired an interest in dialogue and "where we come from" in our scholarly approach to it.

GOODALL ON DIALOGUE

I had the experience of dialogue long before I ever knew a word for it or read anything philosophical about it. It was late one night back when I was in high school and we had stayed out way beyond when we should have been home, and all we were doing—I swear—was talking. We got into things neither one of us had ever spoken out loud to anyone else, and I know for fact that there were things we talked about that I had not even thought about before. I know my heart was pumping fast, too, and by the time we came to the end of it—more of an arrival than a destination—we were both exhausted but knew we had been somewhere special together. I remember the stars that night, the moon, the feel of the air— everything around us was alive and deeply meaningful. It sounds profoundly silly to say these words, but that's how it was. And I'll never forget it because I've spent so much of my life since then trying to get there again. Trying to find that special place where true communication happens. Probably that is a large reason why I studied communication and why I had so much trouble with what I perceived as the flawed idea of "conversation analysis." For me, conversation was about something a whole lot more meaningful than adjacency pairs and turn-taking. I would learn to call this meaningful conversation "dialogue." And I would learn that it happens not just in talk, but in music, in lovemaking, in communion with nature and Spirit—in a whole lot of what makes this life interesting and memorable.

Goodall approaches dialogue as a privileged communicative form in which organizing ecstatic relational moments, processes, or episodes are themselves part of a much sought-after *community of peak experiences.* These peak experiences are, as Abraham Maslow describes them, "acute identity experiences" (Maslow, 1961, 1962, 1968a, 1968b) that are themselves produced, achieved, recognized, named, and consumed by human beings naturally in search of "something else"—something beyond the stars, if you will—to be gained or learned about the integration of persons, purposes, environments, and the cosmos in everyday life.

Goodall understands dialogue to reflect a definitive human urge to "get beyond" the gray everydayness of relational routines, phatic rituals, and often boring, repetitive, relatively meaningless interpersonal encounters (see Goodall, 1993, 1996, 2000; see also Kellett & Dalton, 2001). This "getting beyond" may be accomplished by "getting into" forms of identity-altering communal and communicative patterns and "acute identity experiences" including music (e.g., Drew, 2001; Eisenberg, 1990; Goodall, 1991, Jourdain, 1998; Miles, 1997), aesthetic moments and artistic and scientific "flow" (e.g., Csikszentmihalyi, 1990; Eisenberg & Goodall, 2001), team sports (e.g., Eisenberg, 1990; Goodall, 1991), hallucinogenic drugs (McKenna, 1993; Myerhoff, 1975), sexual expression and lovemaking (Hite, 1989; Nelson, 1998) and varieties of American spirituality and religion (Bloom, 1992; Goodall, 1996; James, 1902; Kellett, 1993). Gregory Bateson (1972) observes that communication is intimately linked to pattern recognition. To this profound insight, Goodall adds that the connection between dialogue and other forms of peak experiences strikes him as a further reach of that same sentiment.

Goodall believes that the study of communication should be approached as a mystery to be engaged rather than as a problem to be solved, which has led him away from the traditional social sciences and into interpretive ethnography. He uses an "imaginary conversation" among his intellectual heroes to help him construct his theoretical and conceptual understandings of dialogue by reading (among many others) the work of Kenneth Burke (1989) on the relationships of language to symbolic forms, Herbert Blumer (1969) on the relational implications of symbolic interaction, and Mikhail Bakhtin (1981, 1984, 1986) on dialogism.

Goodall's background of exploring how peak experiences create community led us to the idea that dialogic communion may be understood as one manifestation of a *ritual symbolic form* (Burke, 1989; Turner, 1969) as well as a *relational expression* of a fundamental human need to define the unifying and ego-transcending meanings of our identities and the purposes of communication in our lives (Eisenberg, 2001; Goodall, 1996).

Dialogue is routinely conceptualized as "moving through" a communicative process. However, in our view, not enough attention has been given to the ritual symbolic form of this process, which would include proper consideration of *entering, exiting,* and *learning* from dialogic encounters. Because we approach peak experiences as having in common a symbolic form (Burke, 1989), the knowledge of beginnings and endings *as such* serves as important ritual gateways to—and lessons of—dialogic experiences. Additionally, as symbolic forming serves as an inducement to human knowing (Gregg, 1984), an understanding of the context for entering, experiencing the dialectical tensions, exiting, and learning from dialogue is critical to its social construction and experiential outcomes. Just as there are ways of organizing work for flow experiences, coordinating activities for "jamming" experiences, and framing a state of mind and organizing an appropriate context for altered states of consciousness, we believe that there are preparations for dialogue, moods that induce dialogic encounters, and questions that can be used to induce a social context capable of helping people achieve, understand, and learn from dialogic tensions and related peak experiences. However, these characteristics cannot guarantee that persons will reach dialogue any more than the implementation of similar skill sets and conditions guarantee that musicians who play together will experience jamming.

Why not?

The answer, we believe, lies in the necessary and yet paradoxical nature of the inherent in-betweenness of dialectical tensions. These tensions are cocreated and felt by persons who purposefully engage in skillful conversations but who find themselves elevated to dialogue by the interplay of these tensions in and through their communicative exchanges. This brings us to Kellett's investigations of these dialectical tensions.

KELLETT ON DIALOGUE

My archetypal experience of dialogue—and it is one that provides me with a powerful motif for talking about conflict and cooperation today—takes me back to my mother's womb and to one of the most important relationships of my early life. Specifically, as an identical twin, I shared a confined space with another human being exactly the same as myself in most ways. I assume—as I have no memory of the womb-time—that cooperation in that environment was instinctive and unconscious, as it was in the first years of life. We became as close psychically as we were genetically. Through our teens, we would often know what the other was thinking and what he was about to say, and during the college years when we were apart physically, we would instinctively know when the other needed to hear from us. We knew how to play in the moment and how to talk deeply with each other, and we knew our connection was unusual and special. Since the college years, the easy dialogic basis of our relationship has largely gone. There have been moments of dialogue but they are hard to create, and harder to sustain—like synapses that haven't been used for a while, they become harder pathways to reactivate even though you know intuitively that they are still there.

Herein lies my personal experience of moving between effortless dialogue and all the relational peaks that creates, and the difficult discomfort and loss associated with an absence. Dialogue is never far away for us, and yet rarely do we create the pathways that lead to it.

How and why dialogue becomes present and absent in relationships have been the profound questions that have moved my work in communication to focus on conflict, cooperation, and dialogue in relationships, families, workplaces, and communities.

Kellett approaches dialogue in his most recent work as the process of reflective questioning and systemic inquiry through which conflicts can be interpretively understood and the habits of communication through which conflicts can be managed more effectively (Kellett & Dalton, 2001). Dialogue is thus positioned as both the means of analysis and the means of intervention through which an ethos of peacemaking can be nurtured.

Along the pathway between Kellett's early sibling relationship of dialogue and his current interest in peacemaking in a variety of communicative contexts (relationships, families, workplaces, and communities) are a number of key twists and turns through the following deeply significant works on dialogue theory and application. First, and perhaps most significant in shaping Kellett's understanding of the relationship between dialogue and systemic thinking and the reflective questioning that leads to deep learning-based change, is the work on organizational learning (see Senge, Kleiner, Roberts, Ross, & Smith, 1994). As an "Org Comm" guy earlier in his career, this body of theory and lessons from organizational experience proved to be a major turning point in understanding the practicalities and the transformational power of dialogue.

Second, there have been some key scholars who have driven home for Kellett the fact that the quality of communication we practice really counts and does make a difference in the quality of the world we partly create through our everyday negotiations. More specifically, the works of Rapoport (1992), Arnett (1980, 1986), and Cissna and Anderson (1998b) have been important in developing his understanding of the connection between communication and peace, the health of community and relational life that we create through communication, and the way that dialogue leads to constructive relational transformation.

Finally, in shaping his understanding of the microdynamics of how dialogue works as an energizing and energized form of discourse that moves through points of volatility, the dialectical theory work of Baxter and Montgomery (1996) as well as the recent work of Eric Eisenberg (2001) have been crucial.

As a result of these lessons from dialogue scholars, Kellett understands dialogue to be that form of communication that most readily enables people to engage in the systemic questioning that leads to understanding that, in turn, leads to more and richer choices about communication. These communicative choices, in turn, have an impact on our ability to know how to live and work together more productively and peacefully and to pass that knowledge on to others.

In this chapter, Kellett's theoretical and experiential background provides the idea that three dialectical tensions create the points of entry into, shape the experience of, and provide ways of exiting and learning from the peak experience we know as human dialogue. These dialectical tensions are:

1. *Ethos* and *apotelesma*—getting in the spirit *and* knowing you have been there;

2. *Techne* and *mysterion*—skillfully building *and* surrendering to the mystery of dialogue;

3. *Paignion* and *vathis*—being mindlessly playful *and* open to the deeply profound.

Together we agreed to express these tensions in their original Greek formulations to capture their root image and as a respectful nod to the historical grounding of dialogue (*Dialogos*) in ancient Greek thought. Kellett's work also encouraged us to discuss three pathways to peak experiences that are achieved when these dialectical tensions are experienced as moments of balance or fusion through dialogic communication: profound connection, transformational learning, and ego-transcending relational identity.

In sum, our collaboration has led us to see dialogue as a communicative form of peak experience organized by a ritual symbolic form and characterized by three dialectical tensions that occur analogically in other forms of peak human experiences. We believe that experiencing these three dialectical tensions is not only common to the symbolic form of peak experiencing but is also fundamental to achieving the form of peak experience we call *dialogue*. Understanding how these tensions function contributes to our appreciation for how dialogue fits conceptually into the community of peak experiences. As such, the symbolic form of peak experiences can be recognized as an identifiable pattern and personal pathway to authentic community.

What follows in this chapter is an exploratory examination of these three dialectical tensions within the symbolic form of a peak experience. Although these tensions are presented individually and sequentially, they are experienced holistically as an identifiable pattern of experiences that, in essence, shape dialogue. In our view, because these tensions work together as a pattern of experiences to induce a way of knowing and being in the world we call "dialogic," we see the whole structure of dialogic experience as a symbolic form. We conclude with questions that redirect thinking about dialogue and the dialectical practices that induce and shape it.

The Dialectical Tension of *Ethos* and *Apotelesma*: Getting into the Spirit and Knowing You Have Been There

In the communication field—particularly in relational and interpersonal contexts—often we have approached the problem of facilitating dialogue by setting a context or stage in which careful adoption of some specific qualities or strategies that are grounded in a humanistic *ethos* of communication creates the possibility for dialogue to emerge. Creating the right mood, through the spirit that we bring to communication, increases the chances of bringing out the appropriate form of energy that brings us together with others (see Eisenberg, 2001). Specifically, we are thinking here of the triune creed of taking the perspective of other(s), genuinely engaging others, and embracing the possibilities created in communicating with others (Cissna & Anderson, 1998b; Kellett & Dalton, 2001). The simplicity of the creed belies the deep, often structural, challenge of actually practicing such an ethos. Ethos, here, we take to mean the spirit with which we approach communication and the mood that such a spirit creates around us. Rupert Sheldrake (1988) calls this context that we create our "morphic field": the energy field that surrounds each of us and overlaps us with our consociates—others with whom we share existential space and time.

Viewed this way, to enter into dialogue is to engage a goal-directed, strategic set of principles that can create a certain mood and can energize us to broaden and deepen the possibilities for cooperation, peace, conciliation and reconciliation, transformation, and various forms of ecstatic union and communion. By contrast, an alternative form of goal-directed and strategic principles that can create a certain mood for communication is argumentation and its relational partner, debate. However, rather than energizing us toward cooperation, peace, conciliation, or ego-transcending transformation, argumentation energizes us for competition, escalation of conflict, individual victory, and the necessity of a win–lose outcome. Although there are times and places for principled argumentation and debate, we believe that approaching everyday relational communication as having the potential for dialogue is a general, ritual way of approaching our lives that leads to greater awareness, understanding, and knowledge of ourselves and of others.

Disciplinarily, we tend to believe the mythic promise that this deeper understanding of self, other, and context resulting from a dialogic ethos makes us better communicators: We can express, interpret, and share meaning more skillfully. In turn, better communicators probably live richer, more fulfilling, spiritually meaningful, and perhaps more peaceful lives.

The above creed captures the essence of dialogue as an *ethos*. At the same time the principles of this creed offer guideposts for how to promote dialogue—idealized yardsticks—for knowing "where we are" in a relationship so that we can manage the outcomes of our everyday lives more effectively. This idealized yardstick offers a general framework and interpretive assessment tool for not only examining how we match up as relational partners but also for helping us develop questions that get at the pragmatic "whys" of relational communication. For example, why am I in a particular conflict and why will it not move toward peaceful resolution? Why do I have patterns of doing conflict in which I blame others rather than engaging them? By asking these "why" questions, we establish a mental mood, or a context for asking deeper questions: Where do these patterns come from? How do they affect my ability to manage the conflicts that I inevitably move through in my life?

Mental mood and setting lead to reflective questioning, interpretive analysis, and occasional insight. In turn, these "moments of awaking to dialogue" open up possibilities for personal and relational change. Dialogue, then, begins in the way we set the stage for insight—AHA! moments—and the personal and relational transformations that those AHAs make possible (see Kellett & Dalton, 2001). Dialogue, viewed this way, is work: a disciplined set of communication principles and questions that set in place a communicative and reflective path leading to greater insight.

Apotelesma refers to the "reflective intelligence" that means we understand and take seriously the results and implications of our communication. The work we do together brings a dialogic ethos into reality that is balanced and completed by the reflective intelligence to know what that work accomplishes, or has left to accomplish. Knowing that we have "been there" is a reflective sense-making and narrative skill that enables us to articulate, as much as language allows, the experience of dialogic moments. To be able to offer some descriptive account of what it is like—and possibly be able to generalize such experiences to other areas of our lives—is to change the perceptual contours of the everyday based on the dialogic peaks we have constructed and climbed together. For example, we may know that we have been "doing dialogue" when we have more open, reflective, deeper relationships with ourselves and with others, or when we gain a deeper systemic understanding of how we participate in creating the relationships that connect us to the world of others in particularly empathic and creative ways. Becoming smarter at connecting our communication and our behavior—and its underlying spirit—to its results and consequences as they ripple through our lives, we refer to as becoming more *telesmatic*. Being telesmatic increases our opportunities to revisit and repeat our peak experiences.

DIALOGUE AND PROFOUND CONNECTION

The personal and relational experience of dialogue seems frequently to be associated with the words *profound* and *connection*. There seems to be both structural—conceptual and pragmatic—experiential reasons for the coupling of *profound* and *connection* with *dialogue*.

First, from a structural or conceptual view, dialogue, as a form of human communication, is artfully positioned at the upper hierarchical end of a conceptual continuum of relational communicative practices. This conceptual or structural continuum begins with relatively low-level, mindless, and mostly meaningless social exchanges often called *phatic communion,* then displays a preference for ladder-like levels of *ordinary conversation, skillful conversation,* and then *self-disclosure* or *personal narratives,* culminating at the conceptual top-rung of this structural ladder in *dialogue* (Goodall, 2000). Achieving dialogue often results in a deepened sense of connection between oneself and others, between one's self and God, oneself and one's purpose in life, or between oneself and the world that we partly create around us. These profound connections are based on understanding connections between the spirit we bring to communication and the knowledge and learning that results from communication.

Viewed this way, profound connections[1] are both a desirable end-state and an ongoing goal of dialogic talk. It is mindful—we actively seek the profound—but also mysterious in that we often do not know what connections we will make through our talk. While it is happening, we know it is happening, but we do not often know how or why, and as much as we may want it to last forever, it does not, it cannot, and maybe it is just not supposed to.[2] The key is to learn from the connections it brings. It is in this way that for dialogic experiences to feel complete, they must end well: In other words, they must complete some ineffable something that creates in us a sense of an ending, reframing or new beginning—a deep AHA!—or profound connection. When (or shortly after) it is achieved, rounded off, and completed—as is true for a variety of peak experiences—the experience itself may be said to have been profound.

Another way to characterize the structural–conceptual appeal of dialogue as a form of communication is through an appreciation of its (profound) ability to "round off" a desired dialogic experience by fulfilling (or exceeding) the expectations we brought to the exchange. Simply, the profound connections that result from our talk are genuinely profound because they *surprise* us. In this way, experiencing true dialogue seems to respect an Aristotelian preference for dramatic form: There is an initial ritualized period of social exchange during which the participants set up, or create the conditions for, or otherwise enter a dialogic space, followed by a "breakthrough moment" that deeply and meaningfully punctuates the sequence of exchanged talk and silences, which itself is followed by a reentry ritual in which the partners conclude their experience and return to ordinary life as changed, or transformed, persons. The whole of the experience exhibits a formal dramatic structure, and experiencing that form is part and parcel of what makes the dialogic experience feel profound.

One example of how the experience of profound connection as an expression of *ethos* and *apotelesma* finds cultural form includes religious conversion experiences (Kellett, 1993). In such profound changes, converts express a new sense of purpose and new sense of how they should behave to reflect that new spiritual *ethos.* Effective mediation is another example. Here, the participants ideally gain a deeper—more profound—sense of how their behavior helps to create the seemingly intractable conflict, and how they can change that pattern in the future through a cooperative *ethos*. Finally, another example involves the self-help and therapeutic intervention processes in which participants explore the profound connection between their early experiences and current life. The profound connection empowers them to rethink their particular dialectical relationship between *ethos* and *apotelesma*.

The Dialectical Tension of *Techne* and *Mysterion:* The Skills for Building and Surrendering to a Mystery

The second dialectical tension we discuss combines the skillful ability to create dialogic episodes with the artful ability to surrender to dialogue as something that is bigger than what we do—that is, as a process that becomes greater than the sum of the parts. Dialogue requires the skill to push talk forward and the sensibility to allow it to pull us where it will. Dialogue brings our skills to life and also takes on a life of its own.

Dialogue requires us to go beyond skillful discussion (Kellett & Goodall, 1999; Senge et al., 1994). Technique (*techne*) takes us to a depth where we still have a footing in a solid structured process—communication strategies and tactics that help us manage the process once we have created the mood. Yet we have to accept the fluidity—the pull and push, the ebb and flow—of the inherent betweenness in which self and other identities often fuse together. This is the mysterious nature of dialogue (*mysterion*). In dialogue, surrendering to a process that may carry you in a direction that you had not expected is combined with the technique of moving through the inherent ambiguity of the ego-transcending process.

For example, the following tactics combine to offer a technique—*techne*—for both strategically jumping into and surrendering to the mystery—*mysterion*—of dialogic moments and episodes (see Kellett & Dalton, 2001). The first tactic involves creating a spatial container—a "place" communicatively—in which we take the time to allow collaborative–collective thinking to emerge. Second, we engage reflective thinking as an ongoing and thoughtful exchange about the issues we desire to engage and to learn more about. Third, the purpose of our dialogic exchange is to create mutual understanding and the energy for action. Fourth, our mutual understanding involves reflective questioning that releases more possibilities than we knew existed prior to the dialogue. Fifth, our ability to question relies on our ability to listen to and value the issues that can be deep in the subject of our dialogue. Sixth, this spirit of inquiry involves focusing our talk on connections among diverse views, stakes, and interests. Finally, on the basis of the understandings that we create, we should be open to change.

Skills are a necessary but insufficient condition for creating dialogue. Dialogue is more than a system of communication strategies and tactics, although skillful talk used in dialogue requires them at least in part. Dialogue also takes us to a more fluid, more mysterious, less structured place than the rational technique of skillful discussion. Dialogue challenges us to swim with the flow of the talk and trust the fluid context and fluid boundaries of self and other to support a particular type of talk—more fluid and boundary-less, less consciously strategic or stakeholder-based. Our bodies and our talk are required to assume some of the characteristics of fluidity to work within—and perhaps sometimes in spite of— our instincts for grasping the solid ground of technique. The conceptual membrane that our talk "breaks through" becomes the current limit of our collective insight and the assumptions we bring about what is possible for a given context or state that we are talking about. When we combine *techne* and *mysterion,* then the *dia*—the fluid and symbolic "moving between" part of dialogue—is experientially balanced with the more tactile and concrete *logos* part of the ratio—*dia-logos.* When the skillful–tactile and mysterious–fluid are combined, then dialogic breakthroughs are often experienced as deep (or profound) transformational learning.

From a pragmatic–experiential perspective, dialogue is often said to be transformational because it is associated with the emergence of new feelings, understandings, directions, goals, and so forth between the dialogic partners and because this newly achieved learning does not necessarily point to agreement or consensus between the partners. Transformational learning occurs when people engage in deeply skilled talk that moves beyond what is assumed, accepted, or understood to a coordinated sense of something new that would not have occurred to either of them individually without this exchange, this mood, this surrender to the moment.

In dialogue, it is okay to disagree, it is all right to be of different minds, and perfectly normal to sum those experiences by saying you have become "profoundly aware of differences." It is also often the case that dialogic partners discover themselves to be profoundly aware not only of each other and their differences, but also of their surroundings, of nature, of the universe. From such awareness—surely "profound" is the appropriate modifier—there also may come a sense of having arrived at "truth" or "vision." And it is a truth that not only transcends our understandings, but one that also makes us happy. What could be more profound than that? Achieving a transforming vision of who we are or where we are going together—arriving at the truth of our relationship—takes both skill and surrender.

The most obvious cultural form of transformational learning that we have been involved with is in helping companies to manage change through dialogue (see Goodall, 1994; Kellett, 1999). Effective management of change using dialogue necessarily involves the skill to bring the appropriate ritual or symbolic form and interpretive skills to the semistructured conversations that make up the dialogues. At the same time, the challenge is to encourage fluid, open talk in which people both represent their stakes in the change process and allow the talk to take on a life of its own. This is when surrendering to the talk will produce often surprising and largely unplanned results for the change process.

Change dialogues almost always have specific goals in mind and a planned structure or process for achieving those goals. For example, we have used a process we call *narrative recovery technique* (Kellett, 1999) to assist change efforts. We ask each stakeholder to address questions aimed at recovering their personal experience of work. One after another, the personal narratives are given, and a collective narrative that recaptures the personal histories of the company or department is articulated. From this process we locate "gaps" in the narratives and isolate conflicting interpretations, using these openings for dialogue to promote collaborative talk and problem solving. We have yet to use narrative recovery technique without producing unforeseen "AHA!" moments that create a mood for dialogue.

One goal of ours has been to set in place the conditions for collaborative talk that in turn opens possibilities for dialogic exchange. In so doing, the stakeholders have been able to learn about their past in ways that focus on the communication and relational mistakes and problems of the past for the purpose of mending those relationships and finding better ways to deal with each other so these problems are not repeated in the future. Our goal is ultimately to produce a shared vision of the future from the interests and perspectives of multiple stakeholders so that they learn to produce a more inclusive and commonly understood future direction. Furthermore, we use these opportunities with them to build a communication skill set based on principles of dialogue (rather than argumentation and debate, or systematic problem-solving methods). Whatever the specific goals of the change process, bringing stakeholders together in a dialogic process leads to mutual sharing and understanding of experiences that, for most people, have been transformational. Such dialogues help stakeholders to become mindful of connections among organizational events and personal experiences, among communicative practices and relational outcomes, which in turn lead them into deeper awareness of systemic issues. It is through systemic thinking that stakeholders learn to create the changes they desire.

Of course, bringing people together with a goal and the space and time to explore that goal does not mean they are necessarily "doing dialogue." Organizational stakeholders may try instinctively both to reproduce organizational power structures in the change process and to champion their personal stake in the change. Nor is it true that everyone involved in the change process will have AHA! moments or truly engage in dialogue. The key to effective change dialogue is to manage the balance between following the technique of skillfully structured conversations and being open to the mystery of where those conversations go and what decisions are made through them. Easier said than done, but that is always true of achieving dialogue.

The Dialectical Tension of *Paignion* and *Vathis:* Being Mindlessly Playful and Open to the Vastness Beyond

The third dialectical tension is a product of being able to flow in a state of mindless playfulness (*paignion*) while being open to the profound vastness of the broader context of which play can make us aware (*vathis*). More specifically, the idea of being mindlessly playful carries with it the connotations of being in the moment, of focusing on the personally meaningful or truthful aspect of talk—saying what you really want to say and what you feel compelled to say in the moment. Playfulness also carries the connotation of talk that is creative for the sake of responding to the needs of the moment. Examples of talk that may be used to demonstrate playfulness include asking risk-taking questions, using humor to reframe an issue or problem, engaging in wordplay, and creatively misinterpreting intended meanings.

Dialogue also implies reaching a transcendent, egoless state of communication in which there is an appreciation for the fact that in-the-moment playfulness often connects us to the more timeless, enduring, vast sense of the environment and universe beyond ourselves. This connection of creative communication to a deeper and broader, more profound, purpose or meaning is the experience of *vathis.* A simple yet meaningful example of this would be pausing in a good conversation with a relational partner and wondering about all the twists and turns of life (or God's plan as some would narrate this experience) that allowed you to be together in this current moment. The contextualization of the current moment within a much grander purpose or system of connections and possibilities occurs when *paignion* and *vathis* are in balance.

This dialectical experience of being egoless and yet unified has been used to characterize ecstatic religious and spiritual experiences (Bloom, 1992). In fact, some spiritual rituals are used to induce an awareness and personal experience of this sense of connection, including seasonal celebrations and participation in ceremonies, ecstatic dance, and group-based musical performances. But there are also—as Maslow (1968b) points out—many nonreligious personal and relational activities that carry with them a similar pattern of perceived connectedness and egolessness, including meditation, intense lovemaking, aesthetic engagement, sports, and work. By drawing on characteristics of ecstatic religious experience, he found that peak experiences become "a state of mind achievable in almost any activity of life, if this activity is raised to a suitable level of perfection" (Maslow, 1976, p. 179).

Dialogos, Energeia, and *Ekstasis:* Dialogue as the Energy for Ecstasy

Energy (*energeia*), in the atomic sense of the term, comes from one of two sources: fusion or fission. Energy also exists in two states: potential and kinetic. Fusion involves the creation of combinations—or dialectical tensions as we are calling them here—that previously existed as potential energy. Such combinations release energy in that the parts that are being combined react to and play off each other to create new possibilities and hence provide more opportunities to go deeper, to flow with, to learn from, and be transformed by, talk. This, in turn, enriches our storehouse of potential communicative energy. Hence, potential energy is released into kinetic energy and in turn creates more potential than existed before.

Dialogues are exemplars of fusion-based energy. Fusion takes energy to bring the disparate elements together and the skill to direct the energy that such tension creates. Fission involves releasing energy from within a system by the creation of *divisions* between its components. In communication, arguments are exemplars of fission-based energy. Learning to live with the paradoxical nature of dialogue is, we feel, one of the most important keys to connecting dialogue with ecstatic experiences (*ekstasis*).

Energizing paradoxes exist at the point of balance between the fusion of ideas that are pushed together and the fission—or instinct to pull apart—that exists because they are a combinations in opposition. In communication we may call this a "dialectical tension" as the moment when opposing forces inform and shape each other and are understood to be part of the same duality of experience. This is a highly energetic moment in communication. Physical scientists call this state *volatility,* and it is a valuable place to begin dialogue because the point of balance is suffused with both push- (centrifugal) and pull- (centripetal) based energy. The dualities of dialogue, as both strategic ideal and prereflective reality and as both thoughtful and egoless talk, point to the following two main paradoxes.

First, dialogue is both a deeply skillful and mindful form of talk. It is partly about managing the setting and mood and also partly about managing the process. At the same time, dialogue to some extent takes us where it will, often in surprising directions, which requires us to give up control over the process and simply "go with the flow." Managing and surrendering point to both the duality of structure in dialogue and to the communicatively challenging forces to balance in dialogue.

Second, dialogue is partly about outcomes. We want to achieve understandings or goals when we engage each other. We want to change something or learn something, for example. However, we also have to accept that the physical membranes that divide self from other—our skins—must be replaced with a profound sense of connection and unified purpose. We achieve dialogue not when we become self-ish but when we become self-less in the talk. Simply put, to achieve our goals we must let go of our *self* to a large degree and allow the fusion of self and other as *we* to become the primary organic structure out of which dialogic communication emerges. Being both self- and other-centered so that we get what we want challenges us to balance our sense of self and other very carefully. This takes energy and the communicative intelligence to know how to manage relational talk and be managed by that energy through relational talk.

Conclusion: The Dialectics of Dialogue as a Peak Experience

In our view, dialogue is a communicative form of peak experience available to most relational partners willing and skilled enough to undergo the acute identity transformation constituted in the dialectical tensions and pragmatic paradoxes we have described. Essential to the potential for dialogue is the ritual of it: setting the stage and mood for these self-less engagements, surrendering to the mystery as you are performing and reflecting upon it, allowing it to take you with it while you use talk to move it along, attempting to reach a purposeful destination but feeling as though when you get there you have actually arrived somewhere you could not have previously imagined. For those of us who have experienced dialogue, it is hard to say whether it was the process that was the peak experience, or whether the peak experience is where you ended up. Perhaps it is both, simultaneously, and perhaps that, too, is yet another paradoxical feature of the dialectical tensions that shape this ritual symbolic form.

Certainly the relational experience of dialogue, just as the individual peak experience of flow, religious or hallucinogenic ecstasy, jamming, or the sacred, is embodied within a person who interprets it, but it is difficult to say precisely what the "dialogic experience" is. From our conversations with many persons over the years who claim to have experienced dialogue, we can say that beyond the singular word "profound" and various accompanying signifiers that accumulate around the idea of it being a life-changing event, there is a general inability to articulate the dialogic experience. Perhaps the experiencing of it is ineffable, and it is only afterward, in a kind of retrospective sense-making (Weick, 1979), that what we have learned from the experience becomes linguistically entangled with what the experience itself was all about.

This is true for other peak experiences as well. It appears to be a common characteristic of them to be so completely an immersion experience as to be beyond words until well after the peak itself is past. It is as if the ordinary, everyday self left the body (hence, the experience of selflessness) and then returned to that body changed by the extraordinary experience in the dialogic zone, but only vaguely aware of what happened or how, precisely, that deeply felt change actually took place. If, as musicians say, music is what happens between the notes, then perhaps dialogue is what happens between the tensions that outwardly define it.

Notes

1. *Profound* is an important and somewhat problematic term whose synonyms in our standard Microsoft Word 7.0 *Thesaurus* include *thoughtful, deep, reflective, philosophical,* and *insightful.* No study that we are aware of explicates how the experience of being in dialogue facilitates the resulting use of *profound* or *profound connection* to describe it. However, we are confident that all the synonyms listed above do reflect individual meanings and experiences that can be fairly ascribed to what is interpreted as profound about dialogue. Beyond the descriptive implications of the term, we also believe that *profound* implicates issues of personal and relational identity, particularly as they are subject to change based on a dialogic experience and reflection.

2. One of the common characteristics of all peak experiences, as described by Maslow but given further weight by Csikszentmihalyi (1990), Eisenberg (1990), and Myerhoff (1975), is that they cannot be sustained. Individuals and relational partners may experience them—and experience them as profound connections and identity-altering phenomena—but individually and relationally we all return to ourselves from these experiences. Perhaps this is why reflection is a necessary part of the dialogic experience—from reflection we can take stock of "where we have been" and "what we have learned from it."

11

Double Binds as Structures in *Dominance and* of *Feelings*

Problematics of Dialogue

Leonard C. Hawes

I have been working on problems of representation, understanding, suspicion, and vulnerability with respect to dialogue, which I take to mean discourse about differences that threaten the possibility of sustainable inter- dependencies. My interests are both theoretical and practical. Theoretically, I want to explore the subjunctive mood of dialogue, a mood that produces pos- sibility from futility and hopelessness, subjunctivity from victimization and oppression. Practically, I want to represent, to understand, to be suspicious of, and to be vulnerable in ways that more consistently produce possibilities of sustainable, albeit changing and uneven, relationships. "In the end," according to Hammond, Anderson, and Cissna (2003), "dialogue is a human opportunity for discussing or creating truth, and empowering action" (p. 150). My version reads more like this: Dialogue is discourse's desire for discipline and trans- parency. Transparency is approximated to the extent that meta-communicative openings—communicating about current communication patterns, processes, and practices—are available to all participants. Discipline is approximated to the extent that processes and practices for meta-communicating are monitored and enforced. The critical difference between our two definitions of dialogue is the location and figuration of agency. Hammond and colleagues figure agency as an element of individual and collective ingenuity—"a human opportu- nity"—whereas my definition figures agency as an element of discourse—"dis- course's desire." In short, I want to understand in much greater detail how discourse re-distributes human subjectivity and temporality. By discourse I mean language in social practice; theorizing it as desiring-production opens productive ways of solving important limitations of more individualistic and psychological ways of thinking.

Scholarly and practical projects on dialogue and its problems are inter-disciplinary in their reach, but this is not the place for a detailed review of that body of work. Hammond and colleagues (2003) and Arnett and Arneson (1999) review the communication theory literature predicated on the work of Rogers (1980), Buber (1965b), Bakhtin (1981), Levinas (1987b), Gadamer (1980), Kogler (1996), Bohm (1996), and Friedman (1982), among others. Much of the work being done in conflict resolution and cultural studies is informed by the public policy work of Saunders (1999) and Daniels and Walker (2001), the post-colonial studies of Spivak (1987, 1990), the conflict and ethnic studies of Rabie (1994), the work on trauma and memory of Silver and Rogers (2002), the conflict and diversity work of Mindell (1995), the liter-ary criticism of Whitebrook (2001), the feminist theory and criticism of Butler (1997a, 1997b), the psychoanalytic theory and criticism of Volkan (1997), the historical-critical work of Sharp (1973), the analytic philosophy of Rescher (2001), the work on imaginal dialogues by Watkins (1986), and the debates over therapeutic discourse and Socratic dialogue by Maranhao (1986, 1990).

Far from exhaustive, these interdisciplinary influences indicate some-thing of the range of work being done under the sign of dialogue, which has been proposed as a candidate for addressing, if not re-solving, problems that range from mean-spirited conversations in daily life to the ethical dilemmas of institutional life. Less has been written on how to sustain dialogue at the edges of its possibility. For example, when bilateral or multilateral negotia-tions, whether within families or among nation-states, become mired in the emotional, economic, and political violence of embargo, murder, rape, and ethnic cleansing, the question is how to imagine and to put into place the conditions of possibility for dialogue. How are we to know if, when, and how to intervene; what to say and what not to; how to listen; who to address and how to address them; who to include and exclude; and how to negotiate limits and proscribe rules?

I am working both theoretically and practically on dialogue projects involv-ing antagonists and historical enemies who have little or no interest in being in the same place at the same time to talk about anything, much less to talk of building consensus and forging agreements. Even under controlled and civil conditions, dialogue is an assemblage of unstable, nonlinear, and contingent communicative practices that are driven by desire within personal and cultural force fields that range in orderliness from coherence to chaos (Jay, 1993, pp. 84–113). The task is to theorize discursive practices that negotiate *willingness* and *subjunctivity* at the levels of desire, imagination, will, resistance, and reality.

The point in all of this is to implicate theory in practice and to explicate practice as theory—in effect, to put theory into practice in ways that acknowledge and affirm differences and identities and to do so in ways that negate dominant discursive structures *of* feeling and structures *in* dominance. Critical of structuralism's inability to deal with power and hierarchy, Althusser (1969) introduces the term *structure in dominance* to solve the problem structuralist thinking posed for cultural Marxism: namely, to retain structuralism's ability to trace relationships and at the same moment to escape structuralism's inability to rank the differential importance of contradictory historical influences and forces. It is these historical contradictions that devolve into paradoxes and double binds. Dominance can be asserted only on a temporal continuum. Clearly then, "affirming" difference is not, by itself, a sufficient condition to sustain dialogue. The praxiological trick is actually to *assume* more differences and distinctions into dialogue, knowing there are profoundly destabilizing effects of doing so.

Pledging the best of intentions and then for the most part trying to be more tolerant of difference only multiplies cynicism and hatred. From a more inclusively assumptive basis, the next move is actually to *do* more practical and theoretical experimentation at dialogue's impasses. How are we to understand the relations between dialogue and violence? How does dialogue emerge from heteroglossia? How does dialogue reproduce the double binds it works so diligently to solve? How can the edges of communication be approached more imaginatively? Dialogue often dissolves into protracted debates, arguments, fights, and forms of violence if ethnic, racial, and gender identities are at stake. What would productive interventions into such conflicts sound and look like? How are we to address these historically contemporary predicaments in dialogical space and time when factions are suspicious, angry, unheard, and unwilling to listen? Interest-based thinking is not capable, theoretically, of accounting for such identity-based conflicts.

The sounds of dialogue hardening into the fixed positions of assertively avowed identities can be heard whenever self-identified oppression meets *and does not recognize itself* dialectically in the Other of dialogue. Each faction is so consumed by its own history and experience of victimization and oppression that it cannot recognize the other as anything but Other. Williams (1977), for whom such tensions constitute "structures of feeling," argues against social institutions and cultural formations being reduced to the fixed forms of the past, over and against their separation from the present fluidity and intensity of the personal. For dialogue at impasse, what is desired is discursive movement from the fixed forms of the past to more fluid processes of the present. Williams's argument attempts to retain cultural Marxism's analytical and sociohistorical critical methodologies while articulating them with the ways people experience daily life. Structures of feeling are concerned with meanings and values as they are actively lived and felt, with "characteristic elements of impulse, restraint, and tone" (p. 132), which take the material form of spoken discourse. The focus here is on the affective elements of consciousness and relationships—not feeling as against thought, but thought as felt and feeling as thought. Said another way, structures of feeling comprise practical consciousness of a present, living, and interrelated continuity (Williams, 1977, pp. 128–135).

Contradiction, Paradox, Double Bind, and Conflict

Consider the following circumstances: Assume dialogue at impasse at several points along three planes of experience. Along one plane are the oppositions among genres of discourse, particularly between personal narratives and theoretical–critical accounts of discrimination, oppression, victimization, and trauma. Along a second plane are the tensions between lived realities of structural discrimination and the paradoxes of on-going victimization. Along a third plane are the tensions between identity politics and the narrative representations of cultural memory. These planes of experience intersect in ways that challenge and often defeat attempts at dialogue. In such circumstances, discourse can devolve into the double binds of oppressor–oppressed, victim–perpetrator, each side demanding the entitled positions of equality and equity, if not superiority, from the lived experience of scarcity and brutality. These intractable conflicts gravitate around the binaries of race–ethnicity, color–White, male–female, parent–child, sacred–secular, and safety–threat. Occupants of each binary position experience the other as arguing not for equality and equity, as *they themselves* are, but rather for special privilege and elevated rank. Rather than address such conflicts at their respective levels of polemical content—that is, from within the conflicts themselves, as the differences are struggled over during dialogue—I want to shift the level of conceptualization and analysis to processes and patterns of the struggle itself. Such a shift re-frames conflicts and contradictions as discursively interactional paradoxes, or what Gregory Bateson and colleagues called double binds (Bateson, 1961; Bateson, Jackson, & Haley, 1956, 1963; Haley, 1963, pp. 86–116,179–191; Sluzki & Ransom, 1976), and what Joseph Heller (1955) called *Catch-22*.

In dialogue at impasse, in which participants are struggling with double binds, victims and victimizers, oppressors and the oppressed sound increasingly alike in so far as each locates choice, agency, and responsibility in the other, in effect blaming each other as the double bind becomes increasingly entrenched. Defensiveness gets produced in abundance and on all sides in the form of assertiveness, anger, aggression, and intensity. The risk in listening to these conflicting discourses and listening for their *full voices* means understanding their subtleties and complexities. The ethical tensions of such listening and understanding are immense. The threat of hegemonic violence is ever present. Each voice wants to be heard first and to listen later. When unheard, each voice is willing, eventually, to be violent. Willingness to listen is one of many scarce resources, and it usually follows rather than precedes violence, most often through trauma and memory. Listening seldom precedes violence, which usually follows and precedes itself. Listening makes speaking possible, and, insofar as speaking is the onset of conversation, speaking is where the possibilities of dialogue incubate. Ordinary conversations, at whatever level of analysis, are inherently unstable forms of both individual and collective subjectivity whose structures of feeling are reproduced routinely in conversation and usually out of conscious awareness of their structures in dominance. My working definition of dialogue—its desire for discipline and transparency—focuses on the communicative struggle over the politics of meta-communication. Bateson (1972) solved this communicative struggle by putting the entire question of power and contestation into a cybernetic rather than a Cartesian epistemology, which in effect defines dialogue as a discursive response to the double binds of control and power.

The point of departure for Bateson was the concept of logical types from Whitehead and Russell's (1989) *Principia Mathematica,* which emphasized that a class of things at a different level, or logical type, than the members of that class. Of particular interest was the idea that a discontinuity between classes and their members created the conditions of possibility for a paradox to occur in classification. Bateson applied this theory of logical types to human communication and was particularly interested in those moments when humans classify messages such that insoluble interactional paradoxes—double binds— are generated. Bateson was concerned with whether the question of truth and untruth was relevant to the analysis of human communication. His early project focused on analyzing the complex activities in human and animal life in terms of both logical and interactional levels of analysis, with an emphasis on the conflicts that occur between a message and a qualifying message—that is, how one message frames another, which recursively re-frames the first as the next, and so forth.

The necessary ingredients for a double bind are: (a) *Two or more persons,* one of whom is designated initially as the "victim"; (b) *Repeated experience* such that the double bind structures come to be an habitual expectation; (c) *A primary negative injunction* either not to do something for fear of punishment, or to do something for fear of punishment, such that the context of learning is based on avoidance of punishment rather than a context of nurturance; (d) *A secondary injunction conflicting with the first at a more abstract level, and like the first enforced by punishments or signals that threaten survival,* the verbalization of which sounds like "Do not hear this as a punishment," "Do not experience me as punishing you," "Do not submit to my prohibitions," "Do not think of what you must not do," "Do not question my love," and so on; (e) *A tertiary negative injunction prohibiting the victim from escaping from the field*, even though in some cases the escape from the context is made impossible by certain devices that are not purely negative, such as capricious promises of love; and (f) *The complete set of ingredients is no longer necessary when the victim has learned to perceive his universe in double bind patterns*, with the consequence that almost any segment of a double bind sequence is sufficient to interpellate panic or rage (Sluzki & Ransom, 1976, pp. 6–7).

Double bind is Bateson's term for this interactional or communicational paradox. A *contradiction* exists when there is a separating and dividing, when messages qualify each other in conflicting ways at the same logical level. A *paradox*, a particular kind of active doubling—for example, patronizing, sarcasm, cynicism—exists when messages conflict at different logical levels (Sluzki & Ransom, 1976, p. 65). A *double bind* is a particular form of contradictory multiplication; speaking multiple voices is one solution—speaking schizophrenically, or not speaking at all, are more extreme expressions of the oppressions of doubly bound discourse. Double binds take shape when, in addition to messages being paradoxical, there are several levels of injunction *not* to meta-communicate about the paradox. Bateson's reference to "qualifying"—as in, one message or channel qualifies another message or channel in conflicting ways—can be thought of as one among many modes of signification. Channels are levels or strata in universes of discourse, each strata consisting in sliding chains of signifiers in dialectical tension. When imbalanced dialectical relations either are collapsed, denied, or repressed, the risk is doubly bound dialogue and the problem is how to escape or otherwise transform it. These doubly bound circumstances consist in historical patterns of discourse and their encompassing recursive structures of feeling that constitute the material reality within which individuals and collectivities negotiate their lives.

In doubly bound dialogue, each faction or individual feels trapped (which is to say, victimized and oppressed) by the implicit and explicit accusations of the other. In rights-based cultures, each feels wronged. What remains unsaid, as each resists the truths of the other's accusations, is that each is so fearful not only of being what one is accused of, but of actually being one's own accusations of others, that each denies the denial of that knowledge and consciousness, and each continues the pattern of accusation–counteraccusation, often resulting in violence. Each hears the other as being responsible for its lived experience of oppression and counteroppression. Denying the claims and counterclaims of the other is experienced by each as additional oppression and counteroppression, providing additional evidence for the truth of the claims and counterclaims in the first place.

What this punctuation of reality produces is an escalation of accusations, hostility, and violence. Every defense against an offense is itself experienced as an additional offense, for which a defense is both warranted and justified. To name the double bind is to take materially real risks. If one *does not* name oppression when one hears it and lives it, one suffers resentment, shame, rage, trauma, and worse. If one *does* name the oppression and communicates *about* it when one hears it, lives its realities, and pays its prices, one risks being accused by the other of playing the oppression card. Such counterclaims, of course, are heard and experienced by the other as reverse oppression. If, having been accused of racism and oppression, one *does not* name *that* as itself reverse-oppression, one suffers resentment, shame, rage, trauma, and worse. If, on the other hand, the identified oppressor *does* defend against reverse-oppression by naming it when one hears it and lives it, one risks confirming the accusations of oppression the other made in the first place.

Attempts to communicate about such communication is itself heard as even more offense and defense, effectively circumscribing and sealing the full and vicious circle of doubly bound discourse, thereby sabotaging dialogue's possibility. Working within the discursive circle to dis-solve the double bind only worsens it. Determining "who started it" or "where or when it began" are questions for which conventional answers have little or no utility value in terms of facilitating dialogue. Nor do determinations of who is "right" and who is "wrong." Dis-solving doubly bound discourses cannot be accomplished by working only historically (the search for "initial conditions" and their "effects") and epistemologically (the determination of who and what is "right"). The desire for discourse's discipline and transparency requires onto-logical work as well.

For each of the factions, the accusations of oppression are individually and collectively held truths. And so are the counterclaims of reverse oppression by the other faction(s). We now have an assemblage of individually and collec-tively held truths, each framed by the other as implicit or explicit accusations of oppression, which, when taken together, are internally incompatible, falsify-ing the claim to historical and epistemological truth. The problem I am work-ing on is how to dis-solve such doubly bound dialogue.

Structure in Dominance and Fearless Speech

Conventional advice from contemporary advocates of dialogue (e.g., Ellinor & Gerard, 1998, pp. 19–27) is to see the whole among the parts, to see the con-nections among the parts, to inquire into assumptions, to learn through inquiry and disclosure, and to create shared meaning among the many. Notice that such advice presupposes that the parts stand in more or less equal relation to one another; it fails to account for uneven power distribution and the structure in dominance that, according to Althusser (1969), constitutes the unity of the whole. Domination is inscribed in complex wholes; it is the expression of its totality. As Althusser argues, "The complex whole has the unity of a structure articulated in dominance" (p. 202). Following Marx and Mao, Althusser distinguishes between the principal contradiction in any complex process, and the principal aspect in any contradiction. In a complex process such as dialogue, struggling with the vagaries of doubly bound discourse often is the principal contradiction in the complex process of dialogue. The complex process whose unity is expressed in doubly bound discourse is articulated as structure in dominance. The praxiological questions have to do with if, when, and how to transform this structure in dominance. Keep in mind that for Althusser, structure in dominance is the absolute precondition for a real complexity to be a unity and the object of a practice that is capable of transforming a process of such complex unity.

A much less conventional transformative practice is telling the truth about the structures of feeling produced and reproduced by doubly bound dialogues, particularly in the face of the dangers associated with speaking into uneven distributions of power and resources. Such a move, however, is fraught with peril. The aspect of Foucault's genealogical analytic thinking most pertinent to this ethical dilemma is his *problematization* (which Foucault always italicizes) of truth. In *Fearless Speech*, Foucault (2001) traces the concept of *parrhesia* (translated as "frankness in speaking the truth") in ancient Greece from the fifth century B.C. to the beginnings of Christianity, moving from rhetoric, through politics, to philosophy. For Foucault, dialogue is a *parrhesiastic* game, and his genealogical analytic work illuminates the entailments and implications of frankly speaking the truth about the structures of feeling generated by doubly bound structures in discursive dominance.

In Foucauldean terms, the materially real risks a truth-teller (a *parrhesiaste*) assumes are the often life-threatening consequences of breaking the regime of an oppressive double bind by transgressing the negative injunctions against critically meta-communicating on and about the double bind of reciprocal and recursive incongruity, incompatibility, inequality, inequity, oppression, and possible extermination. The individual or faction that *problematizes* a collusive regime of truth—faction A—fears transgressing the negative injunctions of a more powerful individual—faction B—and perhaps others as well, as inherently dangerous, but nonetheless as a necessary and justifiable defense against the offenses of insanity, inequality, inequity, and the oppression of current conditions. At the same time, of course, faction B experiences the transgressed negative injunction(s) not only as bad form and bad faith, but more important as an attack against which a defense is both necessary and justifiable. Faction A, in reactive response, experiences faction B's defensive response not as a defense but rather as itself another offense, another attack that constitutes additional evidence of faction B's apparently willful intention to perpetuate the oppression of faction A, against which, now more than ever, faction A's additional defense is warranted in the face of this mounting offense from faction B.

Foucault argues that what marks the end of pre-Socratic philosophy and the beginning of what has come to be contemporary philosophy is the *problematization* of truth. "What is the importance for the individual and for the society of telling the truth, of knowing the truth, of assuming people tell the truth, and knowing how to recognize them?" (Foucault, 2001, p. 170). The emergent Western critical tradition addresses four interdependent questions: "Who is able to tell the truth, about what, with what consequences, and with what relations to power?" (p. 170). In both classical Greek and Greco-Roman thought and practice, *parrhesia* and dialogue are intimately related. In the Socratic-Platonic tradition, *parrhesia* and rhetoric stand in opposition; rhetoric is the art and practice of monological, suasory discourse whereas *parrhesia* is the art and practice of dialogical questions and answers.

The contradictions of *parrhesia* surface in dialogue today at the intersections of radical democracy (Mouffe, 2000) and an ethic of truths (Badiou, 2001), in which rhetorical persuasion and dialogical inquiry collide. The praxiological problem is how to speak frankly and tell the truth in circumstances in which personal and cultural differences are radically incompatible and resources of all kinds are distributed in wildly uneven ways. The overarching objective is to include and affirm as many incompatible truths as possible. In principle, no differences are too profound to be included, assuming a willingness to participate. In practice, how is it possible to establish a context of proscriptions without crossing over into discourses of prescription? How is it possible to engage radically different identities and at the same time to negate counterproductive values, positions, and interests at the level of desire, imagination, will, resistance, and reality?

Colluding in these doubly bound discursive conditions, knowingly or unknowingly, may feel like the safer course of action, at least in the short term. In the long term, the double bind and its historical, epistemological, and ontological effects become ever more entrenched. Collusion is unconscious if one does not recognize the discursive paradox as a double bind; it is conscious collusion if one does know and still chooses not to transgress the oppressive negative injunctions. Resisting these injunctions and affirming differences are not sufficient; they must be transgressed and named to be addressed and escaped, if only partially and temporarily. Whether conscious or unconscious, resulting conflicts are internalized and externalized, and both spoken and unspoken. The consequences are all too familiar. The discursive structure in dominance is a double bind, and the structures of feeling it authors are variants of reciprocal oppression.

And so it goes. It is the logic of repetition, perpetuation, and escalation. The paradox is that what for faction A is a defense against faction B's offense is for faction B an offense against which faction B's defense is warranted and justified (Watzlawick, Beavin, & Jackson, 1967). What makes this paradox a double bind is that the escalating process itself constitutes the multiple levels of negative injunctions and at the same time functions as the punishment for their transgressions. If either faction meta-communicates about these negative injunctions, the other factions hear it as a further offense, a violation of a sacred covenant against which escalating defense is warranted. Resentment and animosity escalate and eventually both factions (or all factions in a multiparty dialogue) identify themselves as victims of oppression at the hands of the other(s).

Three-Cornered Narratives

Now assume there is an intervention of some sort by a third faction whose job it is to destabilize if not dissolve the worsening double bind that by now may have become an entrenched pattern with a history of contestation, violence, and trauma. If not handled adroitly, all doubly bound factions can unite in turning on and attacking the intervener. The troubling questions have to do with if, when, and how to intervene such that the factions caught up in the double bind identify the intervener as involved but not invested—neither ally, enemy, nor rescuer. Each narrative of oppression represents each of the *other* factions to the double bind as having much more power, many more resources, and an abundance of choices. None of the factions may recognize the conflict as a discursive double bind, and if they do, none is in a position to know what to do except more of the same; to do otherwise is unthinkable (Hawes, 1998). Each faction experiences the circumstances as oppressive, and each identifies the *other* as the oppressor, which effectively positions the intervening faction as a potential rescuer whose role it is to make things right and to ensure that justice is done.

The augmented double bind sets up each faction, including the intervener, to fail and, having failed, to blame the others and to claim the rights, responsibilities, and privileges of the oppressed (minimal power, limited resources, compromised choices, and absolution of accountability). Blaming others constructs a position of oppression, powerlessness, and violation; for the others, it constructs equally one-dimensional positions of responsibility and obligation. The intervener becomes responsible for dis-solving the problem. The victim has the responsibility of feeling powerless, and the oppressor is responsible for carrying the blame and guilt. This three-cornered narrative format represents conflict born of doubly bound discourse in ways that ensure that these reciprocal expectations will be violated and that the narrative cycle of oppression and counteroppression will continue (Cloke & Goldsmith, 2000, pp. 25–29). To the extent that one is positioned narratively *as* and identifies experientially *with* the oppressed, victimized, traumatized position, one is absolved of any responsibility for the problem or its solution. To the extent one is positioned narratively *as* and identifies experientially *with* the oppressor and perpetrator, one is absolved of any responsibility for feelings and emotions, or for the solution, thereby becoming the object of blame and accusation. The only feelings permitted the oppressor are guilt and shame, which must be repressed; they are usually represented instead as righteous indignation. And to the extent that one is positioned narratively *as* and identifies experientially *with* the rescuer, one is absolved of any responsibility for feelings and emotions, or for the conflict and its consequences. And if the solutions fail to materialize, the rescuer becomes repositioned narratively by the oppressed as an oppressor, effectively opening the door for the failed rescuer to identify *as* but not *with* a victim. And this set of reciprocal relations recursively perpetuates the doubly bound patterns of conflict, their narrative representations, and the structures of feeling fed by this doubly bound structure in dominance.

Given that most paradoxes are experienced not from the outside as double binds but from the inside as intractable conflicts, and given that structures of feeling come to be represented narratively, stories afford their tellers the power of formulating both history and memory, and of attributing both causality and responsibility. Stories of conflict told from the position of the oppressor are designed to deny responsibility in an attempt to exchange empathy for sympathy, to exchange the power and accountability of interdependency for the powerlessness and lack of responsibility of dependency. The story of oppression interpellates the story of an oppressor; what narratives of oppression interpellate instead are narratives of denial and defense. Under certain circumstances, these narratives of denial become themselves narratives of even earlier oppression. The story of the oppressed calls for the narrative account of the oppressor; the story of the innocent calls for the story of the guilty; the story of right calls for the story of wrong. In short, accusation calls for confession and apology; it seldom gets either. The advent of truth and reconciliation commissions, victim–offender programs, and war crimes tribunals are initiatives to address the effects of these doubly bound dynamics, each of which shares a common problem.

Implicit in a confession is a request for exoneration and absolution of responsibility for the conflict, its precipitating conditions, and its often-tragic consequences. It is in the interests of both oppressor and oppressed to deny responsibility and to accuse the other(s) of bad faith. The paradox is that a confession, by definition, can never exonerate the confessor, restore the victim, or dissolve the double bind as long as the conditional expectations of exoneration, restoration, and resolution are in place. That is the primary reason why confessional and apologetic practices always already put in place the very conditions that require the reproduction of more extensive confessional and apologetic practices. As long as the implicit expectation of exoneration, restoration, and resolution are in place, the legitimacy of the confession is always already in question.

In addition, if one comments on the questionable legitimacy of the confession and apology, motivated as such commentary often is by the violated expectation of exoneration, restoration, and resolution, such commentary and critique is heard by the oppressed as an accusation by the oppressor—in effect, blaming the victim—which, of course, it often is. And if the oppressed points this out to the oppressor, in effect meta-communicating about the implicit injunction against this very practice, the oppressor hears that critique and commentary as claiming the privileged position of oppression, which, of course, it often is. Heard as an accusation, that meta-communicative critique and commentary becomes one more instance of discursive oppression by the oppressor in the form of bad faith, hypocrisy, and infantilization. Failing, as it must, to produce exoneration, restoration, and resolution, the confessor and apologist becomes, in turn, oppressed by the violation of the implicit expectation of exoneration, and blames the oppressed for counteroppression. Now the confessor and apologist-cum-oppressed expects the oppressor-cum-oppressed to confess and apologize, which, of course, the latter resists, having experienced nothing to confess and apologize for. And even if the oppressed-cum-oppressor were to confess and apologize, it would only re-inscribe this double bind once again.

Let me return now to the narrative pole of the rescuer and raise the ethically troubling question of whose responsibility it is—if, indeed, it is any one faction's responsibility—to dissolve the double bind and thereby resolve the conflict, which may in fact be impossible. The rescuer position, by narrative definition, cannot admit to the possibility of the impossibility of rescue. The rescuer must be undaunted by resistance and negation in discharging its responsibilities, and in doing so, paradoxically and inevitably, it becomes imperialistic, colonialistic, if not fascistic. The more the rescuer accepts responsibility for fixing the problem and resolving the conflict, the more those efforts reproduce the identities of oppressor and oppressed, and the double bind becomes ever more entrenched. This essentialized discursive system becomes, in effect, locked and loaded; neither oppressor or oppressed is willing to identify conflict as a double bind, and all factions resist the meta-communicative identification of the double bind insofar as each faction resists losing its righteously and indignantly coveted self-identified position of oppressed. The question of praxis is: What if anything can be done to transform such double binds to avoid otherwise inevitable escalation?

Re-Figuring Doubly Bound Dialogues

The answer I want to sketch re-figures the problem. Each faction, rather than assuming singular responsibilities for the doubly bound dialogue, instead shares multiple responsibilities for which each has abundant, if radically different, resources. The oppressed is no longer solely responsible for the emotional burden of oppression and trauma, the oppressor is no longer solely responsible for the ethical burden of fault and guilt, and the rescuer is no longer solely responsible for the pragmatic burden of mediation and solution. Rather than assuming that factions negotiate for what they want from conditions of scarcity, assume instead that they negotiate from conditions of multiplicity, which includes both scarcity and abundance. Relative to the other two factions, the oppressed have an abundance of suffering and a scarcity of resources; the oppressors have an abundance of resources and a scarcity of compassion; and rescuers have an abundance of choices and a scarcity of emotionality. This effectively re-figures and multiplies the narratives that each faction relies on to represent their own as well as the others' positions. The discursive task is to somehow redistribute, reintegrate, and transform scarcity and abundance along multiple lines of possibility. Rather than essentializing the three narrative positions that perpetually re-inscribe the double binds, my task is to multiply and diversify those positions. The effects of oppression are in the present and its memories are of the past. The agency of oppression is in the present and unconscious. And rescue from oppression is in the future and abstract. Figuring the double bind in this manner renders it all but insoluble; the oppression is in the indefinite past, the cause is unconscious, and the solution is in the indefinite future. How is it possible to re-figure tense and its memories, agency and its effects, and abstraction and its specificities?

To think into these questions I want to return to the circumstances of the dialogue I sketched earlier, and I want to theorize it outside of the double bind of individual members and factions. The first challenge is to interrupt and destabilize the offensive and defensive narratives that perpetuate this discursive structure in dominance responsible for the structures of feeling that, in turn, feeds it. I suggest that one way of intervening and effectively interrupting a double bind is to ask questions for which the answers are unknown. Think at the level of a system consisting of a series of recursive and discursive practices that, when deployed, return a dialogue, implicitly and explicitly, to questions of *desire* ("What do you want?"), *imagination* ("What would life be like if you had what you want?") *will* ("What are you willing to do to produce what you want?"), *resistance* ("What are you unwilling to do to produce it?"), and *reality* ("So, based on results, what do you want?"). These recursive questions problematize the truth of the answers that keep the double bind locked in discursive space and time and loaded for perpetuation and escalation.

As a system, doubly bound dialogue produces scarcity, resentment, victimization, and violence, which, in turn, reproduce networks of interdependent contradictions and their time-honored, problematic narrative representations that empty the discourse of its articulations of possibility. The discipline of recursively asking questions of desire, imagination, will, resistance, and reality interrupt doubly bound discourse in several counterinjunctive ways. Such questions are a recourse to discourse that displaces desire, extinguishes imagination, transforms will into cynicism and resistance into resentment, and distorts reality's effects. Explicitly questioning desire, imagination, will, resistance, and reality effectively transgresses the negative injunctions against meta-communicating by systematically calling such negative injunctions into implicative and reflexive question. Answers to such questions, formulated as they must be in the first-person present tense rather than the second- or third-person past tense, constitute the possibility of counterdiscourses and counter-memories (Foucault, 1977), effectively turning doubly bound discourse inside out (Deleuze & Parnet, 1987, pp. 1–35). This principled discipline puts into practice counterinjunctions that respond to discourse's desire for transparency. By counterinjunctions I mean injunctions that counter the negative injunctions that keep contradictions and paradoxes locked in doubly bound discursive systems. Consider several of these counterinjunctive practices, which I draw from Haley's (1969) work on the power tactics of Jesus Christ as well as his synthesis of Milton H. Erickson's thought and practice (Haley, 1973, pp. 17–40), from Nisker's (1990) essays on crazy wisdom, as well as from my own experience.

First, following Nietzsche's distinction between active and reactive ways of being in the world as well as his thinking on *ressentiment* and bad conscience (Deleuze, 1983, pp. 111–146), ask questions that encourage others to speak in the first-person, present tense, active voice *for* their structure of feelings, which is to say for the truth of their lived experience, thereby negating the negative injunctions against meta-communicating about doubly bound structures in dominance. The objective is to affirm and encourage active rather than reactive communication (Hawes, 1999, pp. 233–243). When it works, affirmations of structures of feeling and negations of structures in dominance shift agency from "over there" to "right here," from second- and third-person to first-person discourse; they move the discourse from "then" to "now," from past tense to present tense; and they change discourse's voicings from passive to active.

Second, listen carefully to what others are saying in order to understand; disagreeing and debating as forms of resistance are already reactive forces at work. Listen to what others are *not* saying, especially when the impulse to speak is strong. Ask others to do the same. Affirming one's structure of feelings and negating structures in dominance makes interests, values, and beliefs more transparent. When such practices are frustrated, encourage rather than resist others' resistance. Accepting and actively encouraging others' resistance effectively constitutes a paradoxical injunction in which resistance becomes cooperative behavior whereas resisting resistance predictably produces even greater resistance. This practice constitutes an active rather than a reactive form of resistance. Rather than resisting force, accept and encourage it.

Third, characterize the worst alternatives as possibilities rather than threats. Rather than leave the worst-case scenarios critically unexamined, explore their detail instead for possibilities, contingencies, and consequences. The objective here is for all factions to be willing to enlarge the domain of the possible, to consider alternative realities, to initiate new behaviors, and to make more choices, effectively choosing *their own* levels of commitment rather than complying with *others'* dictates. This practice counterposes desire and will by asking about desire and the level of willingness to negotiate the threatening possibilities of worst-case contingencies in order to realize desire. It encourages others to act rather than react in ways that transgress the several levels of injunctions against speaking the truth of lived experience, and in doing so to be both more autonomous and more interdependent in acting *on* and *for* desire.

Fourth, when a dialogue is doubly bound, change metaphors rather than topics. For example, if the faction being accused of oppression resists metacommunicative critique and commentary with counter-accusations, change the metaphor by telling a story about gardening, or hiking, or being a member of a team. By elaborating the team metaphor, for example, the oppressed can talk about different styles of coaching and their very different effects. Resist the temptation to interpret the story. If the metaphor that one faction resists is changed to another metaphor, without making the metaphorical parallels explicit, other factions may make the connections on their own. When and if they do, it is more difficult for them to resist a suggestion or insight that they themselves author, and it is more probable they will appreciate its implications more profoundly. If one metaphor does not work, there are numerous other metaphors to deploy.

Fifth, encourage mistakes and reassessments rather than politeness and cordiality. When a dialogue unfolds rapidly, effortlessly, and cordially, encourage all factions to make mistakes and reassess the integrity of the dialogue. Often, a dialogue proceeds too politely and comfortably, and later, when it encounters contradictions and paradoxes that threaten to double bind its discourse, those contradictions and paradoxes are more likely to be covered over with injunctions against meta-communicating about those conditions, for fear of violating the norms of politeness and cordiality instantiated earlier. Factions become discouraged and dialogue may stall or proceed superficially. They may resist this counterinjunction about mistakes and reassessments by creating some other form of discursive movement.

Sixth, emphasize the positive rather than the negative features of the doubly bound circumstances by assuming that all factions desire growth; factions may demonstrate greater willingness and less resistance if desire is assumed to be affirming as well as negating. Rather than assuming that resistance is evidence of negativity and hostility, assume that there are positive forces that need to be freed for factions to have what they desire. This discursive tactic works best if it is framed in the full light of the severity of the conditions. When communicating about the communicative double binds, it is crucial to acknowledge, in the same moment, the realities of the structure of feelings generated by these particular structures in dominance: their intractability, their historicity, their material and spiritual realities, their differential and uneven intensities, and their effects on all factions. The objective is to articulate a desire for growth with a willingness to speak the truth of lived experience in the face of resistance to the realities of the effects of paradox and double bind. It may be sufficient to acknowledge the other factions for remaining in the dialogue when it would be much easier to leave, or lash out, or worse.

A Parting Thought

My interests in doubly bound dialogue at the edges of possibility are more praxiological than epistemological; I am more interested in counter-intuitive methods of articulating theory and practice than I am in the more intuitive methods of explaining why dialogue becomes doubly bound. The keyword here is *counter-intuitive*. My sketchy discussion of six ways to intervene actively into doubly bound discourse rather than to react against it, and thereby more deeply entrench it, is intended to be provocative rather than definitive. My objective is to theorize and conceptualize counterintuitively, to work inside-out on the problem of doubly bound dialogues that recursively generate conflict. My assumption is that understanding *why* double binds occur in dialogue may be only loosely coupled to *how* to proceed when caught up in them.

Part III

Public Voices in Dialogue

12

Public Dialogue and Intellectual History

Hearing Multiple Voices

Kenneth N. Cissna and Rob Anderson

W e have been studying dialogue together for more than 15 years, creating, off and on, our own dialogue of learning and teaching as we worked. As we briefly summarize our project and its contributions, we also want to discuss *how* we did it and, in so doing, to provide some tentative suggestions regarding how researchers of dialogue might conduct one kind of dialogic research. We are not especially interested in giving advice (for collaboration cannot be bottled and distributed), but it never hurts to be alert to, and aware of, your own processes, even as we attempt to incorporate multiple voices into our research.

The project we describe, which occupied our attention for more than a decade, was a foray into intellectual history and its implications for communication theory and practice: We reconsidered a fascinating public conversation—the participants called it a "dialogue"—that occurred in 1957 between the European, Jewish, existential philosopher Martin Buber and the American humanistic psychologist and psychotherapist Carl Rogers. Our interests in dialogue, though, go back further. Although both of us had read Buber and Rogers and used their ideas in our work much earlier, 1979 might have been the year that we both first wrote, however briefly, about dialogue, Cissna in the context of confirming response in human conversation (Cissna & Sieburg, 1979, p. 16; published as Cissna & Sieburg, 1981, p. 270) and Anderson in a book on interpersonal communication in education (Anderson, 1979, pp. 24–25).

Buber and Rogers developed remarkably similar ideas about human dialogue,[1] and each advanced our understanding of communication and dialogue. However, despite overlapping concerns, the two men met only once, on April 18, 1957, at a University of Michigan conference honoring Buber during his second trip to the U.S. There they attempted to illuminate and compare their approaches to dialogue and did so by engaging in an interpersonal dialogue themselves, on stage and in front of an audience of 400. Over the years, many scholars have commented on the dialogue's historical and conceptual importance, but few have given it the sustained attention that it deserves and invites. We made the Buber-Rogers conversation—their dialogue—the center of our scholarly project.

Martin Buber, the renowned philosopher of dialogue, was one of the most prominent global public intellectuals of the last century. Born late in the 19th century, he published his most important book, *I and Thou*, in 1923 (first printed in the U.S. in 1958), and he spent much of the remainder of his long life (he died in 1965 at age 79) developing the implications of that earlier work for human relationships. By the time of his dialogue with Rogers, Buber was famous for groundbreaking contributions to a half dozen or more scholarly fields. The most complete bibliography of his work (Cohn & Buber, 1980) includes more than 1,400 items in 19 languages. Buber received many honors and was nominated three times for the Nobel Prize for Literature and once for the Nobel Peace Prize. Mikhail Bakhtin, with Buber one of the two leading contributors to dialogic theory in the 20th century, called Buber "the greatest philosopher of the twentieth century, and perhaps . . . the sole philosopher on the scene."[2]

Carl Rogers was also very well known and respected among American psychologists and psychotherapists and was destined to become even more famous—or notorious—for his role in the emerging "third-force" or "humanistic" psychology movement. By the time of their dialogue, he had been elected president of the American Psychological Association and had received its two highest honors (the Distinguished Scientific Contribution Award and the Distinguished Professional Contribution Award). He had introduced a radical rethinking of the processes of psychotherapy and the role of the therapist that he called "client-centered" (Rogers, 1951), and this work had recently garnered him some attention in the national popular print and broadcast media, although he had not yet published the books (e.g., Rogers, 1961) that made him a household name nor done the work facilitating international and intercultural workshops that led to his nomination for the Nobel Peace Prize (Rogers, 1980). To his biographer, Rogers was the "most influential" American psychotherapist (Kirschenbaum, 1979, p. xx), and certainly he was among the most important and influential of American psychologists (cf. Kirschenbaum & Henderson, 1989b, p. xi).

If Buber's concerns were focused on community, value, and cultural expectations, Rogers's were more psychological, in origin at least. Yet both converged in recognizing the importance of relation, what Buber called "the realm of the interhuman." Although neither Rogers nor Buber have been immune from criticism, it is hard to imagine any version of 20th century human studies without their complementary contributions.

Buber and Rogers came to similar interpretations of dialogue from quite different directions. Buber read deeply in philosophy, literature, and social theory; lived under the Nazi regime in Germany; and directly experienced decades of Jewish-Arab tension in Palestine. Rogers was trained in the American social science tradition as a psychologist, psychotherapist, and empirical researcher. Yet, both Buber and Rogers developed their concepts of dialogue in the crucible of immediate interpersonal relationships, through the importance they gave to meeting and understanding others on the others' terms, and by reflecting on their presence in and the effects of those relationships. Although we described Rogers as having a "praxis of dialogue" (Cissna & Anderson, 1990), the term applies nearly as well to Buber, whose "philosophy of dialogue" developed, as Rogers's did, experientially.

Since 1986, our own studies of these two thinkers have explored both the pragmatic and theoretical possibilities for human dialogue, which presupposes, as Buber said, that persons remain thoroughly open to the particular and unique perspectives of their partners. Dialogue does not depend on the intellectually soft expressivism some writers have attributed to humanistic psychology (Hart & Burks, 1972), but rather, on the willingness to assert the validity of one's ground even while confirming the validity of others' essentially different voices. Perhaps the central question for researchers, therefore, is how we can remain open to the full range of these voices, as we sustain a dialogic relationship with the conversational texts we study. We offer here an account, surely one among many, of how this dialogic relation could develop.

Studies of Dialogue

During the past decade, scholars renewed and invigorated their interest in dialogue from a variety of perspectives across the human studies and explored new territory as well. Many of the most influential social theorists in recent years have stressed the concept of dialogue, and the dialogic theories of Mikhail Bakhtin, Martin Buber, and David Bohm, in particular, have influenced numerous interpreters and practitioners. In fields across the human studies, scholars are adopting dialogic perspectives in their work.[3] Practitioners, too, have been exploring dialogue in "learning organizations," "public conversation projects," "national conversations," "neighborhood salons," "national issues forums," "public dialogues," "public journalism," "deliberative democracy" programs, and others. All of these projects rely, to a greater or lesser extent, on dialogue as their key concept.

Dialogue derives from the Greek word *dialogos*—where *logos* can be translated "word" or "meaning" and *dia* means not "two" but "through" or "across" (e.g., Bohm, 1996; Grudin, 1996). We use *dialogue* to refer to both a quality of human relationship and a mutualistic way of thinking about human beings and human relationships. "Dialogue can identify the attitudes with which participants approach each other, the ways they talk and act, the consequences of their meeting, and the context within which they meet" (Cissna & Anderson, 1998b, p. 64). Further, as we wrote recently,

> Dialogue is no calculus for manipulation, although persuasion often happens within its sphere. It depends on respect and a willingness to allow a mutual reality and possibility to unfold, rather than the imposition of opinions and attitudes on the other. (Cissna & Anderson, 2002, p. 57)

The value of dialogue is equally clear: "When a space somehow is cleared for dialogue and when sincere communicators expect and invite it, we glimpse futures that could not have been available or even imagined beforehand" (p. 11).

As Martin Buber put it in 1929, in dialogue, "whether spoken or silent . . . each of the participants . . . has in mind the other or others in their present and particular being and turns to them with the intention of establishing a living mutual relation between himself and them" (1965a, p. 19). In later writing, Buber emphasized three important elements of dialogue: (a) an awareness that others are unique and whole persons, encouraging a turning toward the other and imagining the reality of the other; (b) a genuineness or authenticity that does not mandate full disclosure, but suggests that dialogic partners are not pretending and are not holding back what needs to be said; and (c) a respect for the other that inclines one not to impose but to help the reality and possibility of the other unfold (e.g., 1965b, pp. 85–86). Consistent with Buber's terms, then, dialogic perspectives on communication typically (a) emphasize that meaning, often unexpected meaning, emerges from the encounter between self and other; (b) envision a conception of self as continually emerging in and through relationships with others; and (c) assume that there can be no isolated utterance—that all talk presupposes an ongoing conversation in which one merely participates for a time.

Our Study of the Buber–Rogers Dialogue

In focusing on a particular conversational "text" as a symbolic touchstone for understanding the philosophical and practical possibilities of dialogue, we were following good advice. In a 1984 article charting the existing territory in the interpersonal communication research literature and offering recommendations for future research, Joe Ayres encouraged more and better dialogue studies that accounted for actual talk and seemingly successful communication:

> Additional attention might also be devoted to the identification of dialogic communication characteristics—of particular interest would be analyzing the styles of talk associated with dialogue. . . . The goal of this work would be to search for the existence of genuine dialogue and describe those characteristics that are associated with it. (1984, p. 411)

This is precisely what we attempted to do. The Buber–Rogers meeting was particularly rich because it was metadialogical and reflexive in intriguing ways. Two famous scholars were talking about dialogue, and trying to talk together dialogically. They sought to enact what they were examining.

Our study of this remarkable conversation—including the men, their philosophies, their contexts, their relationship, their influence on each other, and the implications of all of this for contemporary communication theory and practice—developed over a number of years. We began this project somewhat naively, thinking we would study Rogers's conversational style in dialogue. Having earlier written about what we called Carl Rogers's "philosophical praxis of dialogue" (Cissna & Anderson, 1986, 1990), we planned for our next study to analyze a series of public dialogues between Rogers and other public scholars, transcripts of which had been published just after his 1987 death (Kirschenbaum & Henderson, 1989a), and we thought we might learn something worth knowing about how people *do* dialogue, along the lines Ayres suggested, from examining the efforts of Rogers and his partners to engage *in* dialogue. His interlocutors, we noted, seemed like a "who's who" of 20th century social theory; along with Buber, they included anthropologist and systems theorist Gregory Bateson, theologian Paul Tillich, philosopher of science Michael Polanyi, and behavioral psychologist B. F. Skinner. When we were invited early in 1991 to Maurice Friedman's international, interdisciplinary conference on "Martin Buber: His Impact on the Human Sciences," we were in the process of locating tape recordings of the dialogues, and the Buber tape was one we had received already. Although invited "separately or together," we decided to collaborate on what we envisioned would be a short paper on Rogers's dialogue with Buber, which, we thought, later could become part of the larger project we then had in mind. That short paper for Friedman's conference ballooned to 50 pages (Anderson & Cissna, 1991), but it was a while before we fully realized what a sustained project this would become.

We approached this work like rhetorical critics, fascinated by how, in this case, the *coauthors* of this conversation accomplished their task. We began by attempting to validate the text. We read the extant transcripts and compared the two primary and most accessible versions (found in Buber's *The Knowledge of Man* [1965b, pp. 166–184], and in *Carl Rogers: Dialogues* [Kirschenbaum & Henderson, 1989a, pp. 41–63]) with each other and with earlier versions— including the original typescript produced by Rogers. We noted and discussed inconsistencies. We studied the flow of the conversation in great detail, supplementing overt description and critique with informal role-play performances in which each of us assumed the part of Buber or Rogers and played with alternate intonations, inflections, and emphases in order to explore the polysemic possibilities of language choices. This seemed advisable as English was only one of nine languages Buber spoke. Further, as performance theorists Mary Strine, Beverly Whitaker Long, and Mary Frances HopKins (1990) point out, consistent with Barthes (1981), approaching a linguistic message as a finished "work" with stable meanings is not as productive as approaching it as a "text" in the etymological sense—that is, as "a tissue or weave of always potential meanings and values" (p. 184). We believed our informal performances opened out fresh dialogic potential for us in this textual sense.

We learned relatively quickly that the printed transcripts that were available included significant interpretive problems and compromises. After we obtained our first audiotape of their dialogue, we listened to it repeatedly, together and separately, comparing the two primary transcripts to the audio; we eventually decided that we needed to produce our own transcript. Over several years, we returned to the tape, sometimes listening together, more often separately, occasionally playing sections for students and others. Throughout this process, we discussed what was happening in the dialogue, comparing and testing interpretations. Occasionally we counted words (e.g., after we began to produce our own transcript in a computer file, we used the "find" function of our word processing software to identify mentions of various terms and concepts), measured lines of type to determine the amounts of verbal content each contributed, and timed various sections of the dialogue on audiotape. All of this took a number of years, and throughout this period, we continued to develop and refine our transcript of what Buber and Rogers said that evening, hoping to produce a more definitive record on which later scholars could rely.

We began publishing our findings, even as we continued our work. We prepared an essay for the *Journal of Humanistic Psychology* that examined the process of the dialogue (Cissna & Anderson, 1994a). An article in *Human Studies* presented our methodology and our findings about the importance of role, audience, and interpersonal style in the dialogue (Anderson & Cissna, 1996). We published short summaries of our project in Maurice Friedman's *Martin Buber and the Human Sciences* (Cissna & Anderson, 1996) and in the *Person-Centered Review* (Cissna & Anderson, 1997, 1998a). Our transcript of the dialogue with our commentary about both the errors in previous transcripts (there were hundreds, some major) and about some of the interactional features of the conversation appeared in a book-length work (Anderson & Cissna, 1997). Our study in *Communication Theory* examined the extent to which Buber and Rogers agreed about the nature of dialogic moments and applied what we called "the Buber–Rogers position" to post-modern thinking (Cissna & Anderson, 1998b). Our most recent book (Cissna & Anderson, 2002) broadens and applies much of our previous work to the problem of theorizing public dialogue.

To date, our project has, we hope, accomplished six goals. First, we demon-strated the usefulness of close rhetorical or communicative analysis of signifi-cant face-to-face meetings. Although scholars have long been interested in analyzing extended rhetorical texts (usually speeches or documents in contexts of public address, social movement rhetoric, and media criticism), only rarely have they attempted to engage conversational texts in a critical way (see Farrell, 1983; Foss & Foss, 1991; Glaser & Frank, 1982; Sharf, 1979). None of the exist-ing articles that advocate studying conversational texts, however, take dialogue as their central construct.

Second, we deepened the discipline's appreciation for both Buber and Rogers as thinkers and communicators. Although we have identified areas of similarity in their thinking that are often overlooked, their styles as communi-cators in the dialogue were quite different. Rogers, well known as a facilitator, behaved as one. He talked far less than Buber, developed his ideas primarily in order to structure questions for Buber, and often checked his understanding of what Buber said, consistent with his advice about "active listening." His talk was provisional and grounded in his own experience in therapeutic relation-ships. Buber, though, behaved quite differently; his talk emphasized replies, certainty, and reliance on precise terminological distinctions. What we called Buber's "rhetoric of cannot" at times functioned more to correct Rogers than to open a topic for inquiry. Although this rhetorical choice of Buber may seem to undercut the fullest possible sense of mutuality in a public dialogue between communicators of seemingly equal roles, it was consistent with the role defin-itions and expectations described to the principals before this event. Buber expected his work to be the evening's focus (and so did Rogers), and Buber was willing to press his points in order to be understood accurately.

Third, we enhanced a line of scholarly research into this revealing event of dialogue, one in which each man elaborated on ideas not developed elsewhere. For four decades, commentators have used the dialogue to enhance their understanding of Buber's thought, with relatively few using the dialogue to clarify aspects of Rogers's thinking (see Anderson & Cissna, 1997, pp. 2–4; Cissna & Anderson, 2002, pp. 127–134). Previous commentaries have empha-sized their *ideas* rather than their *interaction,* and none have been interested in looking at the dialogue as a coherent conversational accomplishment. Previous commentators seem also to have assumed that the event was a relatively unstructured exchange of ideas between two scholars, and all have relied on an inaccurate transcript of uncertain origin. As noted above, we have shown that the roles Buber and Rogers enacted that evening were "enfolded" into the conversation by explicit design, which greatly influenced and constrained what they did together. Essentially, Rogers was asked by the conference organizers to interview Buber on stage, keeping the focus on the visiting dignitary.

Fourth, we contributed to the scholarly conversation about the theory and practice of dialogue. Our central argument has been that previous commentaries on the dialogue have ignored the particular roles explicitly assigned to Buber (respondent) and to Rogers (interviewer), and also the presence of two non-participating audiences, the 400 not entirely silent participants who were present in Rackham Auditorium that evening and the far larger and more distant potential audience represented by the tape recorder that functioned to preserve their dialogue for the generations. We have shown how audiences and roles (whether explicit or emergent) can function within a theory of dialogue. Because of the demands of having an audience of hundreds of people, organizers of the dialogue created what we called *enfolded roles*—"real but not obvious aspects of the dialogue that exist in the folds of the conversation's process rather than on the surface of its content" (Cissna & Anderson, 2002, p. 160). These roles had a significant impact on the interpersonal styles enacted by Buber and Rogers, yet, nonetheless, dialogue was able to emerge. In addition, although most commentators have described Buber and Rogers as disagreeing sharply, careful analysis reveals a coherent "Buber–Rogers position" in their talk, which we used to suggest how mutuality and—by extension—dialogue are possible, even under unlikely circumstances, in vibrant but brief and transitory moments of meeting.

Fifth, we identified the implications of this conversation for facilitating public dialogue—that is, dialogue available to "listeners" who might not consider themselves direct participants. Although Buber once believed dialogue in public to be impossible—"separated by a chasm," he said, "from genuine dialogue" (1957, p. 113; 1965a, p. 184), he was surprised by how instructive his conversation with Rogers had been, and he changed his mind about the impossibility of public dialogue. Many local, national, and international projects use versions of dialogue to energize public decision making. In our most recent book, we argued that dialogue could enrich the public sphere through a set of *dialogue-productive rhetorics*, which we identified as commons rhetoric, mutuality rhetoric, moments rhetoric, vulnerability rhetoric, praxis rhetoric, and recognition rhetoric (see Cissna & Anderson, 2002, pp. 250–264). These are ways of talking, thinking, and listening that could promote improved public conversation in the new century.

Finally, we demonstrated the value of dialogue in a sustained collaborative scholarly project. Initially, when we began looking at Rogers's five public dialogues, we envisioned writing a single article based on all of them. As the project deepened, so did our collaboration—we hope in ways that mirror the experiences of many other coauthors. We exchanged letters, sketching an idea in one, discussing it in another, and sent drafts of sections of manuscripts and critiques of one another's work back and forth through the mail. We argued some, agreed some, and adjusted some. We talked on the phone, often at length, and occasionally visited each other's homes to work together in more sustained ways. And we had many, many hours of conversation at conventions over the years. More recently, e-mail made conversing at such a distance somewhat easier. We learned to work and write together, dealing with the difficulties of distance and accommodating one another's lives. In the end, we produced a significant body of scholarly work that almost certainly would not otherwise have existed but for our collaboration. Not to be ignored is our having become friends with one another and one another's families, and our having learned a great deal from each other.

The Significance of Public Dialogue

Contemporary life in the late 20th and early 21st centuries is often characterized either by a cynicism that says dialogue is, in fact, impossible and ephemeral, or by a sunny optimism that presumes that dialogue is little more than people being warm and friendly with each other. Buber and Rogers rejected those alternatives, as do we. As they talked together, Buber and Rogers explored the limits, the difficulties, and the conflicts inherent within serious attempts at dialogue, public or otherwise. Their work, and their comments to each other that evening, resound with warnings about contemporary social conditions. Although neither Buber nor Rogers currently enjoys quite the scholarly attention they did in the 1950s and 1960s, both men's work has stimulated an impressive resurgence of academic interest within the past decade.

As we noted above, Buber once thought dialogue in public was not just a difficult challenge for well-meaning interactants but a virtual impossibility—an audience of listeners and onlookers would impede necessarily participants' attempts to hear and respond to each other in genuine and spontaneous ways. On the basis of this one experience with Rogers, however, Buber changed his mind, for he surprised himself by recognizing this as a successful instance of public dialogue. Later, he even directed his editor to remove a paragraph about the impossibility of public dialogue from an important essay when it was reprinted in *The Knowledge of Man* (see Buber, 1965b, p. 184). How he came to change his mind is part of our story, though not a part we have the space to tell here (see especially Anderson & Cissna, 1997; Cissna & Anderson, 2002).

Instances of public dialogue are still rare and therefore important to study. First, access to dialogue in public is a significant challenge of our culture, and the problem of dialogue is likely to become one of the central questions for 21st century communication studies. We live in an increasingly and necessarily pluralized society and in an era of persistent conflicts and disagreements across ethnicity, religion, gender, and sexual preference, as well as ideological, economic, power, and status distinctions. Modern media enable us to transmit messages more efficiently, but communication itself, as we are only too painfully aware, does not automatically improve. Recent controversies swirling around issues of political correctness, abortion, race, censorship, terrorism, and others—far from showing the impossibility of public dialogue—mandate that we learn more about its potential. What are the structures, attitudes, and expectations— in interpersonal relationships and families, in groups and organizations, in neighborhoods and communities, within whole societies and between different peoples and nations—that can facilitate public talking and listening, even when participants do not initially identify with, or even like or respect, the particular persons or positions they confront? Our society abounds with pilot programs of dialogue, large and small. Studies of such efforts as the Buber–Rogers dialogue nearly a half century ago may help inform current projects. The alternative, to concede cynicism, is to risk encouraging the simmering resentments of mutually suspicious groups.

Second, our study—part rhetorical analysis, part intellectual history—is clearly aligned with an emerging tradition of dialogic scholarship concerning the intersection of interpersonal understanding and public controversy. Leaving Buber and Rogers aside, we see many philosophers, social critics, and sociologists grappling with the dilemmas of dialogue (e.g., Gadamer, 1982, 1989a; Grudin, 1996; Habermas, 1990, 1992; Taylor, 1985, 1991b). Political theorists turn to dialogic thought in exploring new approaches to democracy and deliberation, including Bruce Ackerman (1980), Benjamin Barber (1988, 1989), Amy Gutmann (Gutmann & Thompson, 1996), James Fishkin (1991, 1992), and Iris Marion Young (1990). David Bohm (1990, 1996) and others from the scientific community underscore the importance of dialogue. Literary theories such as Bakhtin's (1981, 1984, 1986) dialogism are increasingly persuasive within the social sciences (e.g., Baxter & Montgomery, 1996; Montgomery & Baxter, 1998a; Shotter, 2000). Peter Senge (1990; Kofman & Senge, 1993) and his colleagues (e.g., Isaacs, 1993, 1999; Schein, 1993) stress the dialogic potential of contemporary complex organizations and their management. Nel Noddings's (1984; Witherell & Noddings, 1991a) work in education and a feminine ethic of care is dialogical. Intercultural insights are grounded by a new emphasis on dialogical anthropology (Crapanzano, 1990; Tedlock & Mannheim, 1995). Dialogical and discursive psychology have much to say about the interhuman nature of the person (Cushman, 1995; Sampson, 1993; Shotter, 1995; Smith, Harre, & Van

Langenhove, 1995). Much of the contemporary feminist critique, especially in Black feminist theory (Collins, 1990; hooks, 1994), as well as the neopragmatism of Rorty (1989) and West (1993a), and the rhetorical work in Afrocentric thought (Asante, 1987) have a dialogical basis.

Doing Dialogue Research

Any text, any instance of language, reverberates with a variety of voices. "The speaker" is not the only speaker, for language itself preserves the pluralistic nature of human life. The challenge for dialogue scholars is to keep research into dialogue itself dialogic. Dialogically oriented research cannot become objectified by treating talk as a mere artifact to be analyzed. We cannot (or should not) kill or freeze talk in order to dissect it while it is inert, because then it is not talk any more. Nor can we consider that talk involves only whoever is currently speaking because multiple audiences, present and absent, influence dialogic action as well. Studying talk also involves an awareness of one's own talk, too, for researchers profoundly interact with what they research. "Researchers of dialogue" are, thus, called to be "dialogic researchers" if we are to respect what we study.

On the basis of our own dialogue project, we offer the following tentative suggestions for dialogue research, each of which is simultaneously a reminder of potential dangers and limitations:

First, *recognize that conversations are texts, although not traditionally authored ones.* Conversations are *coauthored* in dialogue, through mutually implicated partners. They arise through conditions of created space, and, as we found with the Buber–Rogers dialogue, are subject to the special demands of role and interpersonal style, of audience (if in public), and surely are subject to other constraints as well.

Researchers should be careful, however, not to impute full intent to each conversational coauthor. Authorship of a conversation belongs, of course, to all of the parties involved, and yet to none of them alone. As Maurice Friedman (e.g., 1955) has reminded us, although one participant might prevent dialogue from occurring, no one person can make it happen.

Second, *conversations are texts that resound with voices beyond those of the coauthors.* Buber spoke from and about others' experiences, as did Rogers. Their utterances were historically situated and represented many unheard persons and groups. Rogers, for example, may have believed that he was speaking for a population of clients whose voices were not sufficiently invited within psychotherapy, and Buber may have believed that he was speaking not only for certain other therapists and clients, but even for a schizophrenic friend, who had not been helped sufficiently by what psychotherapy had to offer.

Researchers might be tempted, though, to "mindread" the central conversation partners, substituting their own interpretations for the interests and motivations of the participants themselves. For example, an earlier draft of this chapter included the phrase "Rogers believed he was speaking for" in the previous paragraph, which was revised to "may have believed." We do know, pretty much, what they both said that night, and from both we have a vast corpus of published work to examine, including some direct and indirect commentary on the dialogue itself. But, we cannot know for sure what was going through their minds that evening.

Third, *researchers interested in dialogue should themselves attempt a dialogic methodology and a dialogic relation to their texts.* We have argued for a coauthored and performative methodology. However, our dialogue was not just with the text—to hear Buber and Rogers hearing each other—but we also sought to hear one another as well. The two of us brought different backgrounds and specializations to this task, as well as significant areas of overlap. Cissna's interests came more from interpersonal communication, communication theory, and applied communication (e.g., 1995; Cissna & Sieburg, 1981), which Anderson complemented with an emphasis on media, rhetoric, and the public sphere (Anderson, Dardenne, & Killenberg, 1994; Killenberg & Anderson, 1989). Our respect for our similarities as well as our differences seemed to serve us well.

The dangers of researchers having this sort of intense involvement with the text and with each other include the temptation of importing contemporary issues into historical texts, believing that Buber and Rogers, for example, were really speaking about postmodernism or other contemporary intellectual trends that were unknown to them. Further, a dialogic involvement with one another requires co-researchers to be willing to state and even argue their own positions and ideas *and* to be open to being influenced by the ideas of the other. Buber made this point rather precisely in the dialogue with Rogers when he explained that as a young man his inclination to meet people dialogically led him "to change if possible something in the other, *but also* to let me be changed by him. . . . I felt I have not the right to want to change another if I am not open to be changed by him as far as it is legitimate" (Anderson & Cissna, 1997, p. 21). Co-researchers too insistent on their own positions may never complete a project together or may even risk destroying their research relationship. Researchers who are too eager to acquiesce to the other's position are almost certain to lose good and creative ideas. Our collaboration is based far more on maintaining a creative tension of openness to change than it is on the mere "feedback mechanisms," "evaluative responses," "an extra pair of eyes," or other clichés sometimes used to describe writers sharing drafts with each other. As Montgomery and Baxter (1998b) wrote of dialogue and collaboration, "Collaborators do not necessarily have to agree; they do have to forge a relationship to produce something that works" (p. 171). Like many of the feminist authors writing about collaboration in Peck and Mink's (1998) *Common Ground: Feminist Collaboration in the Academy,* we, too, have found "that some of our most provocative work has come about as a product of collaboration" (p. 271). Dialogic collaboration must be more than cooperative; it must be deep enough to create some degree of initial turmoil and to allow us to write in a "merged" voice that somehow preserves both of our voices as well (Ede & Lunsford, 1990).

Fourth, *dialogic research involving conversations demands the most accurate transcripts possible in order to preserve the vitality of diverse voices.* Our process of authenticating the Buber–Rogers text led us over a period of years to three tape recordings of their conversation. Comparing the tapes to the extant transcripts convinced us that the number of errors in transcription, interpretation, or editing justified publishing a new transcript (Anderson & Cissna, 1997; see also "Martin Buber and Carl Rogers," 1999). As we were finalizing our first book on the Buber–Rogers dialogue, which contained our new transcript and a commentary on it, we located DeWitt Baldwin, Jr., whose father organized the Michigan conference. He told us of an old reel-to-reel audiotape that he found in the attic among his late father's effects, which he had donated recently to the Humanistic Psychology Archive. That allowed us to obtain a first generation copy of what we believe was the original tape on which the dialogue was recorded, a discovery that helped us—just in time, really—to refine and improve our transcript even further.

Fifth, *dialogue research involving historical conversations is likely to require documentary research.* We spent several very full days together—and additional time for one of us—at the Rogers Collection in the Library of Congress in Washington, D. C., and also at the Rogers Memorial Library at the Center for Studies of the Person in La Jolla, California. We also arranged for representatives to do follow-up research at the Library of Congress, and to conduct research for us at the Martin Buber Archives at the Jewish National and University Library in Jerusalem and at two archives at the University of Michigan. The Director of the Oral History Project and the Humanistic Psychology Archive at the University of California at Santa Barbara copied the Baldwin audiotape for us and reviewed his collection for relevant materials.

Sixth, *dialogue research involving historical texts often calls for original contextual research through interviews.* Some of the dialogic voices we most need to hear come from research-initiated conversations. We interviewed and corresponded with numerous colleagues, friends, and family members of Buber and Rogers as well as others who were involved in planning or who were simply present for their dialogue. As historians understand, recollections, experiences, and evaluations of participants often vary, even contradicting each other in surprising ways. Dialogue itself is ephemeral, shifting, even volatile; no one should be surprised that participants' memories were all these things and more. Researchers interested in instances of public dialogue must be willing both to contextualize their work and to be contingent and tentative about their contextualizations.

Uncritical acceptance of these last three suggestions can also lead researchers astray: The efforts to create the perfect transcript, to explore all of the relevant archives and artifacts, and to obtain every recollection from every possible interviewee can each be so consuming that one risks letting any of those *become* the study. These temptations can be especially vexing if engaging—as we did—an imperfect tape-recording of a 40-year old event, important documents spread widely across two continents, and a fascinating set of potential interviewees, many themselves quite notable intellectuals. Other interesting scholarly projects presented themselves to us from time to time, yet we continued pursuing our primary project, as we never found another as important or compelling.

Conclusion

Our society has too few examples of public intellectuals engaging one another dialogically in public and learning from each other. Similarly, our field has too few examples of sustained, collaborative, critical research projects. Having attempted to examine a fascinating and remarkable instance of the former, we now find to our surprise that we accomplished the latter. Nonetheless, more studies of dialogue—public and private, conversational and mediated, and in varied contexts—are still very much needed. Although we have not investigated any of these in detail, a number of conversations might be approached profitably from a dialogic perspective: the joint appearances of Deborah Tannen and Robert Bly (1993) in which they spoke with each other live on stage about gender, communication, and relationships; Bill Moyers's interviews on public television; Michael Lerner and Cornel West's (1996) private conversation about Jewish–Black relations, which became a public dialogue when published; the public discussion between bell hooks and Cornell West (1991) about relationships between Black men and women (see Malcolm, 2001); and the "rap on race" between Margaret Mead and James Baldwin (1971). Anderson, Dardenne, and Killenberg (1994) examined the journalistic implications of the joint appearance of President Bill Clinton and California Governor Jerry Brown on the Phil Donahue Show in 1992 (pp. 126–130), and recently we turned our attention to examining the relationship between Carl Rogers and B. F. Skinner, who appeared in several rather famous and heated interchanges, yet whose letters reveal a very collegial and even friendly personal relationship. No doubt many other "conversations" of one kind of another might lend themselves to dialogically oriented study.

What began as a modest but intriguing study, followed by an invitation that diverted us temporarily from the path we were pursuing, unexpectedly became (for us, at least) a major road we continued to follow. We found it to be one worth taking. As Paulo Freire says, adapting a proverb by Spanish poet Antonio Machado, "We make the road by walking" (Horton & Freire, 1990).

Notes

1. Others differ with us somewhat about how similar Buber's and Rogers's ideas actually are (e.g., Arnett, 1981, 1982, 1989; Friedman, 1986). For our views, see Anderson, 1982; Cissna & Anderson, 1990, 2002, pp. 54–56, 88–91, 95–96, 115–117, 150–152, 168–169, 272 (n. 8).

2. We found this quotation first in Kepnes (1992, p. 62) and later in Emerson (1997, p. 74, n. 1), both citing the same 1984 Russian language article as the ultimate source. Maurice Friedman's recent study of Buber and Bakhtin, citing the same article, provided a little more context for the quotation. In an interview, Bakhtin is supposed to have said that he thought Buber "the greatest philosopher of the twentieth century, and perhaps in this philosophically puny century, perhaps the sole philosopher on the scene." There were, Bakhtin said, other excellent thinkers, "but Buber is a philosopher. And I am very much indebted to him. In particular for the idea of dialogue. Of course, this is obvious to anyone who reads Buber" (Friedman, 2001, p. 25).

3. For example, at least psychology and psychotherapy, education, composition, sociology, political theory, literary criticism, anthropology, philosophy, journalism, linguistics, management and organizational studies, religion, and of course communication.

13

Race and the
(Im)Possibility of Dialogue

Mark Lawrence McPhail

O n Sunday, September 23, 2001, a cartoon appeared in *The Cincinnati Enquirer's* syndicated series called "Borgman's World" titled "Aftermath." The image depicted two men, one with the word "white" written on his side, the other with the word "black" written on his, sitting atop a pile of rubble that was meant to represent the demolished remains of the World Trade Center. Beneath the image the caption read: "Remind me again what we were arguing about before this happened . . . . ?" (p. F1). In Borgman's world, as in much of the American media, in the aftermath of September 11th, black and white Americans were now united against a foe greater than any domestic dispute that had separated us in the past.

One week later, however, a Cincinnati policeman was found innocent in the shooting death of an unarmed African American youth, and Jim Borgman and the rest of us were reminded again of what black and white Americans have for centuries been arguing about: the worth of an African American life. The incident had led to the violent disturbances that rocked the city several months earlier, disturbances that had their roots in a long tradition of police violence against African American men in the Cincinnati area. A white judge acquitting a white policeman for killing a black man should remind us all that America has a long way to go before even a tragedy as horrific as the events of September 11, 2001, can help us overcome our deeply ingrained divisions and differences, and allow us to efface the significance of race.

Ironically, the social and symbolic realities within which those same divisions and differences are rooted led to the attack on two of the most potent symbols of America's military and industrial power: the historical realities of racial domination and white supremacy. In the hearts and minds of many of the world's peoples of color, America personifies the moral incoherence that has shaped the planet since the 15th century, and it is not difficult to understand how a country that could not hear what we have been arguing about here for over three centuries, what Du Bois (1982) in the last century aptly called "the problem of the color line," would be able to hear the voices of people of color on the other side of the globe. Du Bois believed that the problem of the last century was "the relation of the darker to the lighter races of men in Asia and Africa, in America and the islands of the sea" (p. 45), and as we enter this century it is clear that his words were not only prophetic, but largely ignored. In Borgman's cartoonish black and white world, it would seem that the color line has for all intents and purposes been erased. Indeed, Borgman's deafness and blindness is further complicated by a collective dumbness, a complicity, that characterizes the rhetoric of racism.

Throughout my career I have focused my intellectual efforts on finding a way to transform that complicity into a more coherent understanding of racial difference and identity. In numerous essays, I have drawn upon dialogic approaches to discourse to explore its emergence and submergence in Afrocentric thought (1998a) and contemporary black protest rhetoric (1998b). In both *The Rhetoric of Racism* (1994) and *The Rhetoric of Racism Revisited: Reparations or Separation?* (2002), I theorized a dialogic conception of rhetoric as actively nonargumentative discourse, and further developed this conception of rhetoric in *Zen in the Art of Rhetoric: An Inquiry into Coherence* (1996) in terms of the notion of *dialogic coherence.* I viewed dialogic coherence as a discursive practice that can move us beyond the limits of the color line to, in the words of Jacobson, "that political realm beyond racism that W. E. B. Du Bois significantly called *transcaucasia*" (1998, p. 280). Although once committed to the conviction that nonoppositional discourse might bring us closer to *transcaucasia,* I am no longer convinced that dialogue is an adequate symbolic strategy for dealing with the material realities of race. Indeed, my recent revisiting of the rhetoric of racism (McPhail, 2002) suggests that European and African Americans cannot, when it comes to race, communicate in ways that achieve the major attitudinal dimensions of dialogue: authenticity, inclusion, confirmation, and presentness (Johannesen, 2000, p. 153).

I do not mean that, as individuals, we cannot engage each other dialogically and humanely, but I believe that the symbolic resources of racial essentialism that have framed and constrained our interactions historically limit our collective capacity to do so. This chapter offers an account of the theoretical and practical influences that have reframed my thinking about race and the (im)possibility of dialogue. I begin with an exploration of research on dialogue that addresses issues of race, and I offer a narrative account of an experience that marked the point at which I first began to question the efficacy of dialogue as a transformative practice. I then shift from the personal to the political to offer a case study in the racial resistance to dialogue: the failed nomination and public demonizing of Lani Guinier. Finally, I return to the concerns with which I began this chapter to suggest that the need for dialogue is perhaps greater now than it has ever been before in the history of our nation.

More Than Just Talk:
Dialogue, Race, and Self-Reflexivity

Numerous writers have suggested that dialogic conversations about race have the potential for creating discursive spaces within which self-reflection and transformation can occur and differences of culture and identity can be addressed. In international, national, and local contexts, where these differences often create and sustain barriers and divisions, dialogue has been explored as a way of addressing racial conflict and bringing to the surface the underlying and unconscious motivations that conspire to keep us from moving, in the words of Carl Rogers, "toward greater understanding and greater accommodation to each other, and toward reconciliation" (Whitely, n.d.). Rogers understood clearly the need for a dialogic approach to race in both individual and collective contexts, and advocated and applied it in therapeutic as well as social arenas. "I have learned enormously from the few black-white encounter groups I have facilitated, and have learned that the bitterness and rage which exists can be expressed and prove constructive" (1972, pp. 51–52). One of Rogers's most powerful examples of dialogic encounters between blacks and whites on the subject of race took place in what was one of the most racially divided societies on earth: South Africa. The dialogue was marked by the expression of frustration on the part of Black South Africans of being treated with contempt on the one hand, and being ignored on the other. White South Africans expressed their fear that if the Black majority gained control of the country blacks might do unto whites as had been done unto them. The process, which lasted for about an hour and a half, ended with the participants "speaking to each other individually, and with much more understanding" (Whitely, n.d.). Rogers reports that participants "just kept on talking and talking on stage, talking and talking in the audience. It was the beginning of a dialogue, but it showed that a dialogue could begin and could move toward—could make progress toward better understanding" (Whitely, n.d.). Rogers notes that he received letters from many of the participants "saying how much that experience meant to them," although he offers no indication that the dialogue begun on that day was sustained or continued over time.

An example closer to home of a sustained public dialogue project that addresses racial difference within a community context took place in Baton

Rouge, Louisiana, in 1995. Saunders (1999) offers a compelling case study of an attempt to create and sustain interracial dialogue through a series of town meetings and the creation of a number of civic committees. His study illustrates the difficulties that surface when African and European Americans confront the painful history of racial domination and discrimination that has defined communication and interaction between the two groups since the nation began. He offers an insightful summary of those difficulties in this synopsis of the differences that define the possibilities of dialogue in black and white:

> Some black participants feel that the United States—and perhaps even the dialogue—is not as far along on the issue of race relations as many have hoped or as many observers seem to believe. . . . At the heart of the problem, in the view of these participants, is the denial by many white Americans that racism is a serious problem and their use of a variety of tactical devices to avoid facing up to the reality. (p. 194)

Saunders's discussion of the divisions that mark African and European American perceptions of racial reality reveals the core issues that separate blacks and whites and that undermine the possibility of dialogue on the issue of race: the double-unconsciousness of whiteness and the double-consciousness of blackness.

This dialectical framing of race in the American imagination, which defines relationships between European and African Americans in oppositional, antagonistic, and black and white terms, surfaces in the post-civil rights resistance to racial justice that marks what Aaron Gresson III (1995) calls "the rhetoric of white racial recovery." Gresson argues that contemporary white racial recovery rhetoric reveals an historical amnesia that ostensibly acknowledges the historical realities of racial oppression and discrimination, and yet at the same time diminishes the significance of those realities. Saunders's (1999) observations seem to concur with Gresson's analysis:

> Some white participants feel that they do recognize that racism remains prevalent and is immoral but that black citizens sometimes make the mistake of seeing everything through racial lenses. They acknowledge that African Americans have been grievously wronged in the past and are still being wronged today, but they argue that the only constructive approach is to concentrate on building the future. (p. 195)

The rhetorical tactic of "focusing on the future," like the rhetoric of color blindness, denies the reality of the African American experience, and assumes that white Americans can move forward in their relationships with black people without the moral blindness of the past, and the ethical ignorance it embodied.

This belief, for African Americans, reveals the persistent and pervasive existence of white racism in its most insidious forms. Saunders (1999) gives voice to the frustrations that black Americans feel when confronted with the ethical ignorance of whiteness:

> If ignorance is the result of ignoring persons or things, then black citizens' feelings of being ignored by whites in the United States are largely substantiated. Because they were treated as property for the first 250 years of Western settlement in this North American continent, they are constantly pained at their fellow white citizens' failure to catch up with—and understand—what they speak about with such pain. This presents a challenge of utmost importance for the stability of civil society. (p. 189)

Saunders suggests that the process of dialogue might meet this challenge, and notes that a significant amount of progress in the area of race relations in Baton Rouge resulted from this dialogue on race.

Nonetheless, he also acknowledges that he was unable to "cite highly visible achievements" (p. 195) at the time that he completed his study. Indeed, he suggests at the conclusion of his work that the progress made in the community had not yet achieved in practice the assumptions and principles at the heart of dialogue:

> Having come this far, they seem to stand on the threshold of an opportunity to demonstrate that dialogue can change interracial relationships and that participants in dialogue can together design interactive steps that could engage a whole community at all levels in changing itself. (1999, p. 195)

This dialectic of principle and practice, and the tension between intention and action, emerge persistently in dialogues on race, and appear to be one of the greatest impediments to the achievement of individual or social transformation in the context of black–white relations.

In their essay "More Than Just Talk: The Use of Racial Dialogues to Combat Racism," Joshua Miller and Susan Donner (2000) point to the dialectical character of racial dialogues, their potential to create at one and the same time both self-reflection and projection onto others: "Racial dialogues engage people in a reflective process that responds to their social identities and group affiliations. These allegiances can anchor individuals but also be a source of group conflict" (p. 35). They openly acknowledge the antidialogical character of racial conflict, and the difficulties encountered on both sides of the color line when talking about race. Like Saunders, they offer an actual example of racial dialogue as an engaged and participatory practice. "Everyone had come together to talk about race and racism and there was a focus on self-disclosure and insight, but in the service of taking action, individually and collectively" (pp. 45–46). Although both black and white participants shared a commitment to the process of dialogue, their expectations regarding outcomes revealed some important differences.

Although white participants saw the process of dialogue as inherently important, black participants were concerned ultimately with what the process produced. Whites were "more likely to view racial dialogue as a useful end in and of itself while people of color were more apt to judge it according to whether or not it leads to action" (Miller & Donner, 2000, p. 48). They also point out that dialogue on race may not result in the desired outcomes and may actually inhibit communication:

> Racial dialogues are not risk free. Whites can fear shame and humiliation for say-ing the wrong thing. Conversely, listening to whites' naïve and uninformed per-spective on what constitutes racism and the devastation it wreaks is often a source of frustration and anger for people of color. In racial dialogues this phenomenon is probably unavoidable but comes at a cost. Some people may opt out of them altogether. (p. 48)

Miller and Donner have touched upon the sense of resignation that many African Americans, including myself, have felt when trying to address racial differences in a dialogic and inclusive manner.

Ellinor and Gerard (1998) offer some insights into why this may be the case. As diversity professionals, they are committed to the belief that dialogue is "one way to create a space for the kind of conversation that is needed" (p. 279). In their own work on facilitating diversity in the workplace, they cite one particular story of dialogue between African and European Americans that reveals the ways in which black and whites avoid discussing race even in avowedly dialogical contexts. "This is a story about transformation," they write. "It is a disturbing and a power-ful story. It is the story of a group of people gathered to create a field of inquiry, to explore authentic conversation and collective learning" (p. 279). Their story begins with a group of predominantly white participants and a small number of people of color who attempted to engage in a dialogic process. Soon the issue of race emerged, and the participants engaged in a discourse of avoidance and denial.

The topic of race, Ellinor and Gerard (1998) explain, "was undiscussable. So the energy of the disturbance manifested itself in a discussion about the process" (pp. 279–280). The experience was eventually resolved positively, and candid and frank discussions ensued that dealt with the terrible realities of race and racism, discussions that were framed by compassion instead of denial. "Only great compassion could have provided the space for all of us present to open our hearts, hear, and feel one another's pain and create an opening for new possibilities" (p. 280). Those new possibilities, however, came at a cost:

> The cost of an experience where the only way you are known is through your color and the pain associated with it. The cost of having your greater individuality relegated to a backseat because, first and foremost, people will respond to the color of your skin. (p. 280)

As a "diversity professional," I too have experienced these costs, and in the most unlikely of contexts: a conference on dialogue and self-reflexivity that I attended in 1998.

I was invited to the conference by a colleague who was familiar with my work on dialogue and diversity to speak on the subject of race. During the opening session, each participant was asked to discuss what dialogue meant to her or him, and several commented on the importance of suspending judgment for successful dialogue to occur. When it came my turn to speak, I remarked that the belief that we might be able to suspend judgment was, more or less, a comforting delusion: that dialogue, although potentially transformative, was a difficult and dangerous business, and that although we professed to be committed to its assumptions and practices, we rarely if ever committed ourselves to it fully. In the retrospective space of writing this chapter, I realize that it was at this conference that I first began to rethink my earlier research on rhetoric and race, research that viewed dialogue as a viable discursive strategy for the reconciliation of racial antagonism. From my earliest work on the rhetoric of racism, which called for a nonoppositional approach to language that drew upon the symbolic resources of nonviolence, to my later work on dialogic coherence as a strategy for interrogating and transforming essentialized ways of knowing, I was committed to the conviction that a reconstructed rhetoric could transform race relations. When I arrived at the conference, I was just beginning to question that conviction.

Initially, my questioning of the efficacy of dialogue was motivated more by a need to challenge my colleagues, to test their commitment to keeping the conversation going, than it was by my own lack of conviction. I wanted to problematize dialogue in a way that interrogated many of the divisions and oppositions that had emerged in my own research as well as that which I had read: between rhetoric as a practice of persuasion and dialogue as a nonoppositional discourse; between *yes/and* and *either/or* thinking; and even between the practices of war and peace. I had, in fact, decided to begin my discussion of race and dialogue obliquely, through a discussion of "peace warriorship," a way of defining discourse based upon the Eastern meditative arts of yoga and self-defense. I wanted to suggest that debate and dialogue were not antithetical, but complementary: that one might best achieve the sense of self-confidence and esteem necessary to engage others dialogically if one also possessed the ability to engage them, if necessarily, dialectically. I also wanted to suggest some ways that we might enact dialogue, to get it out of our heads and into our bodies.

I presented these ideas first to a small group of three or four participants, and we talked about the connection between the discursive and martial arts, and how it offered the possibility of theorizing and enacting a transformed understanding of difference and identity. Later that afternoon, I shared with the rest of the participants my thoughts about the relationship between race and dialogue. Because the majority of the conference participants were white, I thought it would be useful to begin the dialogue by discussing whiteness. There is a significant body of research that illustrates how the defense of white privilege results in antidialogical strategies of discourse, including rhetorics of color blindness, white innocence, and reverse racism. Seeing the conference as an opportunity to explore these issues with my European and European American colleagues, I asked the questions, "what does it mean to be white," and "what are the privileges associated with whiteness?" After a long and rather uncomfortable silence, one of the participants said to me, "I knew what we were in for as soon as I saw you." Later in the discussion, another commented that we had "already been over this before," that we no longer needed to talk about race, and that we should "just move on." Later still, a third participant from Europe explained that they "had no race problem" there and that their greatest challenge was dealing with issues relating to immigration and the "influx of foreigners."

The responses of my colleagues were at best puzzling, and at worst troubling. It seemed evident that the woman who "knew what we were in for" knew little or nothing of my work on the subject; that the man who has "already been over this" had not been over any of the contemporary research on race that pointed to the racial reasoning implicit in his resistance; that my European colleague knew nothing of the scholarship produced by his colleagues back home that suggested a clear connection between Europe's "immigrant problem" and its racism. I was saddened by the fact that there seemed to be little interest among my white colleagues to engage self-reflectively in dialogue about race. And to be honest, I was surprised. I had gone to this conference with the conviction that my colleagues, committed as they were to the intellectual exploration of self-reflexivity and dialogue, would be able and willing to discuss the painful and difficult subject of race without the essentializing constraints of prejudgment or prejudice. I had found some of them, instead, unable to suspend their judgments about who I was or what I represented apart from the color of my skin. I left the conference wondering if any type of discourse, nonoppositional or otherwise, was capable of redefining racial realities.

I was confronted with the theoretical possibility, expressed eloquently by Jeanine Czubaroff in her dialogue with Maurice Friedman, that sometimes "even the people who are trying to study dialogue, who are conscious of it, still have a very hard time relating dialogically" (Czubaroff & Friedman, 2000, p. 254). And I was faced with the practical reality of dialogue that Friedman offers in response: that "all sorts of people talk about dialogue, but the way is there in order that you may walk on it, as Buber said. That is the really hard thing to do" (p. 254). My own experience, and my reading of the research on dialogue and race, suggests that our nation's racial problems may be beyond the reach of dialogue, primarily because people of European descent are, collectively, unable or unwilling to listen sincerely to, or to empathize with, people of African descent. Indeed, I have become increasingly less certain of the transformative potential of dialogue, not only because of my intellectual and personal experiences, but because of the concrete cultural and ideological realities that have forced me to reassess and revisit my work on the rhetoric of racism.

The event that most powerfully revealed those realities was the failed nomination of Lani Guinier for Assistant Attorney General for Civil Rights. Guinier was nominated on April 29, 1993, by former President Bill Clinton, and just over one month later, on June 3rd, her nomination was withdrawn after she was publicly ostracized and attacked for her allegedly "antidemocratic" positions and her analysis of America's racial problems. "She is a firm believer in the racial analysis of an irreducible, racial 'us' and 'them' in American society," asserted Abigail Thernstrom. "She stands precisely against everything that Clinton once promised in terms of a new, integrationist approach to civil rights. And she stands for the racial politics that has allowed Republicans to dominate the debate (with a hefty dose of cynicism) for decades" (1993, p. 7). *The New Republic's* condemnation of Guinier was typical of the attacks and accusations that thwarted her nomination ("Withdraw Guinier," 1993) and, like so many others, offered little evidence or substantive support for the claims made against her. Indeed, the case against Lani Guinier was based largely, according to Laurel Leff (1993), on "one paragraph and two footnotes" (p. 3), and overlooked totally her clearly articulated commitment to dialogic approaches to dealing with America's racial problems.

Demonizing Dialogue:
The Strange Case Against Lani Guinier

The failed nomination of Lani Guinier is a case study in white racial recovery and resistance in America. The University of Pennsylvania law professor and former Special Assistant Attorney General was a respected legal scholar and litigator, having lost only two cases in the 7 years that she served with the NAACP Legal Defense Fund. Guinier's views on race are exceptionally well-informed and draw extensively from established scholarship on the issue. Her criticisms of the Reagan administration's dismantling of the protections afforded by the Voting Rights Act seemed prophetic in the wake of the 2000 presidential election, and it was most likely her analysis of the retreat from civil rights initiated during the Reagan years that precipitated the public attacks against her. Guinier challenged the view of a color blind and racially tolerant America that emerged during Reagan's administration, and documented persuasively the continuing existence of racial disenfranchisement and discrimination.

Yet Guinier also expressed an explicit commitment to dialogue: She recalled that in her acceptance speech for the nomination,

> I spoke first of my black father, who had taught me through the stories of his life how to look injustice in the eye and then to fight back. . . . I told how my mother, who is Jewish, had taught me to see the other person's side, how not to internalize criticism as rejection, and how to try to bridge differences with open, frank dialogue and creative compromise. (1998, p. 36)

Her commitment to dialogue is revealed throughout her writings, but this commitment was overshadowed by her critique of the racially destructive policies of the Reagan administration and the continuing existence of racism in American society and politics.

> By choosing to discuss democracy and race at the same time, I immediately became a racial partisan. That made me "too black" for those in the political mainstream, including the press. My ideas challenged the image of a country that has already achieved color blindness. They suggest that there is more work to be done. (1998, p. 292)

Guinier's suggestions, despite their dialogical sentiments, nonetheless were attacked by critics who defined her position within the polarizing divisions of racial reasoning.

Indeed, Guinier exhibited an acute awareness of the fundamental incoherence underlying the attacks launched against her when she wrote: "The irony here is that I am committed to dialogue and I am being silenced" (1998, p. 122). Guinier's critics accused her of being racially divisive and attacked her simply because she argued that racism continues to exist in this country. Thernstrom (1993) asserted that Guinier's "starting point is total distrust of white America," evidenced by the fact that in a scholarly essay she "approvingly quotes two academics who asserted that 'blacks live in a different world than whites'" (p. 18). That Guinier and the "two academics" she cites might actually be correct in their assessment of racial conditions in this country was never given a hearing by her critics. Instead, she was simply dismissed as "extreme, undemocratic, and anticonstitutional" (Will, 1993, p. 78) by those opposed to her nomination and denied the opportunity to defend herself by the very people who nominated her.

The hyperbolic intensity of the discourse surrounding Guinier's nomination, and its underlying appeal to racial fears and stereotypes, was ultimately motivated by a defense of the white racial recovery project that began in the 1980s. Guinier was a critic of the divisive rhetoric and politics of the Reagan administration, which she believed were based "not on consensus but confrontation" (1994, p. 24). The confrontational character of the administration's discourse and deliberations had a particularly destructive effect on black Americans, whose hard-won gains in the areas of civil and voting rights had been eroded under Reagan:

> The polarizing philosophy of the Reagan years affected more than the Administration's enforcement activities. Its legacy, engrafted upon Reconstruction era stereotypes about black elected officials, has perpetuated and accentuated a racially skewed reality in which blacks vote but do not govern, at least in majority white jurisdictions. (Guinier, 1994, p. 30)

Guinier, who carefully documented the undemocratic and exclusivist policies of the Reagan administration, was herself demonized and attacked by her critics as nothing less than an enemy of democracy.

Yet Guinier's "undemocratic" philosophies were grounded in a fundamentally dialogic idea, the idea of a *taking turns*:

> Public dialogue is critical to represent all perspectives; no one viewpoint should be permitted to monopolize, distort, caricature, or shape public debate. We cannot all talk at once, but that doesn't mean only one group should get to speak. We can take turns. (1994, pp. 19–20)

The idea of taking turns is particularly appropriate in a society divided along racial lines, Guinier (1994) suggests, because it "does better than simple majority rule if it accommodates the values of self-government, fairness, deliberation, compromise, and consensus that lie at the heart of the democratic ideal" (pp. 4–5). This is perhaps the most ironic aspect of the attacks against Lani Guinier as undemocratic and anti-American: that her position was grounded in a fundamentally American tradition of democratic government:

> In my legal writing, I follow the caveat of James Madison and other early American democrats. I explore decisionmaking rules that might work in a multiracial society to ensure that majority rule does not become majority tyranny. I pursue voting systems that might disaggregate The Majority so that it does not exercise power unfairly or tyrannically. I aspire to a more cooperative political style of decisionmaking. . . . In looking to create Madisonian majorities, I pursue a positive-sum, taking turns solution. (1994, p. 5)

Guinier's position on the importance of dialogue in the process of communication is unequivocally clear. "Decisionmaking should," she writes, "incorporate a diversity of views to multiply the points of access to government, disperse power, and to ensure a rational, developed dialogue" (1994, pp. 103–104). And yet that clarity was obscured by what the Honorable Paul L. Brady calls "a certain blindness." A federal judge and son of a former slave, Brady believes that "the white majority has willfully blinded itself to the humanity and worth of Americans of African descent in order to preserve the best portion for itself" (1990, p. ix). Guinier would most likely agree with this assessment, as would a large number of African Americans who continue to believe that America has yet to achieve the principles of fairness, justice, and equality as far as its citizens of color are concerned.

Yet this is a message that the majority of Americans of European descent still seem unable or unwilling to hear. And just as there is a certain blindness about race in white America, there appears also to be a certain deafness about dialogue. The strange career of Lani Guinier is a case study in the antidialogical character of whiteness, and it clearly invites not only a revisiting of the rhetoric of racism, but also a rethinking of the possibilities of dialogue. For if, "in dialogue," as Arnett (1986) explains, "each individual must be willing to let the other's stance challenge his or her own, to test ideas, while still affirming the personhood of the challenger" (p. 152), then on the subject of race we are not even close to achieving it. Lani Guinier's understanding of the intersection of race and dialogue offers an important opportunity for all of us who hope to find a way to move beyond oppositionality and the divisions of difference and identity that separate us from our better selves: "Can we get to the point where it's not just about talk, or talking differently, but it's about solving problems differently? Can we get to the point where we can talk to resolve issues, not merely to fight about them?" (Guinier,1996, p. 4). Her words remind us of those of another American of African descent whose commitment to dialogue was unequivocally clear, the late Martin Luther King, Jr., who asked at the end of this life, "Where do we go from here?"

Where Do We Go From Here: Dialogue or "The Fire Next Time"?

On April 16, 1963, the Reverend Dr. Martin Luther King, Jr. offered what continues to be one of the most powerful positive statements on the relationship between race and dialogue, the "Letter From a Birmingham Jail." Early in the letter, King makes specific reference to dialogue and contrasts it with the mono-logic logic of segregation: "Too long has our beloved Southland been bogged down in a tragic effort to live in monologue instead of dialogue" (Quoted in Washington, 1992, p. 87). Later he invokes the words of Martin Buber to empha-size again the divisive and destructive consequences of the South's racial policies:

> Segregation, to use the terminology of the Jewish philosopher Martin Buber, sub-stitutes an 'I-it' relationship for an 'I-thou' relationship and ends up relegating persons to the status of things. Hence, segregation is not only politically, econom-ically and sociologically unsound, it is morally wrong and awful. (p. 89)

Though no longer inscribed in law, the awful consequences of racial segregation and separation continue to undermine the possibility of our achieving the "beloved community" that King hoped for either in this country, or it now seems, on this planet. If dialogue is to have some impact on transforming the problem of the 20th century as we enter the 21st, it will have to produce more than just theory, more than just talk. It will also have to, as King understood, create the possibility of moving beyond words and into action and *praxis*.

The events of September 11th, and the antidialogical rhetorics and politics to which it has given rise, should raise serious concerns for all who are committed to the transformative possibility of discourse and the creation of the "beloved community." The retreat to the I-It relationship that has infected American rhetoric and politics, the unwillingness to explore publicly those events as a consequence of our nation's misdirected policies and priorities, the resistance to self-reflection and its corresponding projection of evil onto the dark skinned "others" of the Middle East, the willingness to curtail civil rights and liberties in the name of security, the persistence of the myth of national unity—all of these keep us segregated from each other, and separated from our better selves. These are the common and special topics of the rhetoric of racism, the doubly unconscious discourse that Du Bois prophetically predicted would shape the relationship of the white and non-white world in the 20th century. This "problem of the color line" continues to divide us as we enter the 21st century, and if it is to be crossed or erased, then we must together come to grips with its fundamentally racial foundations, so that we might in the future, in the aftermath of their destruction, build upon them structures of faith and hope and love that will withstand the fires next time.

"You must put yourself in the skin of a black man," wrote James Baldwin to his white American audiences in *The Fire Next Time,* his 1963 book that took its title from a slave song paraphrasing the apocalyptic prophesies of the Bible. Baldwin's book was a call to dialogue that "sought hope in [the] face of what seems to be the merciless logic of despair," and outlined "the ferment of the present and the possibilities of the future" (Binn, 1963). In closing, and in the spirit of dialogue, I offer the same suggestion to my white American readers: look beyond Borgman's world and try to see the events of September 11 through African American eyes. "I haven't met one black person who was surprised. Like everyone else, they were shocked by the magnitude of it, and appalled by the deaths, but they weren't surprised by the hate and anger that produced it," explains African American writer Walter Mosley. "Black Americans are very aware of the attitude of America toward people who are different, people whose beliefs are different, people of a different colour. We live with that attitude every single day. We know how hated America is" (quoted in O'Hagan, 2002, p. 1).

Mosley's words illustrate the double-consciousness that has shaped the responses of many African Americans to the events of September 11th. "It was a terrible thing, a truly terrible thing, and I don't think that you'll find many black Americans who would agree with the act, but they were not surprised by it the way white America was," Mosley continued. "That is a crucial, and determining difference. It tells you a lot about America, and how it sees itself" (as quoted in O'Hagan, 2002, p. 2). What it may tell us is that, as Lani Guinier and countless others have suggested since the Kerner Commission's report (1968), we continue to live in two Americas, separate and unequal. In one America, the need to talk about race is unnecessary, effectively ended by the events of September 11th, after which we all now stand united. But in the other America, the America of Cincinnati, Ohio, and countless other urban areas, the need to talk about race continues to be a daily fact of life. As Walsh (2001) suggests, "in the midst of an orgy of patriotism and 'national unity,' the declaration of a state of emergency in a major urban center is a more accurate barometer of the real state of social relations in the US" (p. 1).

Walsh (2001) also suggests that the disturbances that rocked Cincinnati in the wake of the acquittal of a white policeman in the shooting death of an unarmed black youth were, like the attacks on the World Trade Center and Pentagon, predictable. Susan Knight, a member of the Greater Cincinnati Homeless Coalition, responded to the events in Cincinnati with words eerily reminiscent of Mosley's: "People were angry but not surprised. Some were crying and others frustrated." She continued:

> Some were saying that the city got everything that it deserved last April. One said this wasn't a matter of police brutality, but the whole city was racist. Someone else mentioned that with events of September 11 there is all this talk of national unity, but don't pretend there is unity in Cincinnati. (quoted in Walsh, 2001)

Nor, according to Mumia Abu Jamal, does it exist in other African American communities. "Cincinnati, sparked by police shootings of a black man, could have happened anywhere in America. The social ingredients are all there, in every major city" (Jamal, as quoted in Nwangaza, 2001, n.p.). Jamal, who currently sits on death row awaiting execution for a crime that he claims that he did not commit, viewed the events in Cincinnati as "a harbinger of things to come. Cincinnati is the fire next time."

That two seemingly unrelated events could have so much in common, could be spoken of in so similar a manner yet with such different motivations, and could offer such different readings of racial reality, may not surprise us, but it should certainly shock, appall, sadden, and awaken us all. But emotional and intellectual responses will not be enough. If we are to stand united in this country, then we must confront our divisions candidly. If we are to heal our communities, then we must first come to grips with the lingering effects of the rhetoric of racism. My own revisiting of that rhetoric has been largely influenced by the work of my colleague and friend Richard Rieke, who over

30 years ago recognized the difficulties of addressing racial difference through discourse. Writing with James Golden, he observed, "the study of the rhetoric of black Americans suggests the possibility that the rhetorical goal—communicating with white men about their beliefs and attitudes regarding black men—may be more a psychiatric than a persuasive problem" (1971, p. 6).

Golden and Rieke's (1971) discussion of the historical failure of white Americans to hear and heed the voices of African Americans is a prophetic commentary on race and the (im)possibility of dialogue:

> When the black speaker tells his white audience to look deep inside their own belief systems and purge their racist ideas, he is confronting the most central, the most ego involving of all attitudes of the listener. The task may require a more intensive effort toward the re-structuring of beliefs, attitudes, and values than can be accomplished through the ordinary channels of communication. (p. 7)

Where ordinary channels of communication have failed, perhaps dialogue can succeed. Yet, if Golden and Rieke are correct, and their observations are supported by much of the emerging research on whiteness, then people of European descent—those who continue to benefit the most from racism—will have to take responsibility for creating the conditions that will make racial reconciliation, and thus dialogue, possible.

Although numerous scholars within the discipline of communication draw upon dialogic conceptions of discourse in the study and analysis of cultural difference and identity, discussions of race by European American scholars writing on dialogue are limited in scope and focus. Some of this research addresses issues of race indirectly, or in relation to parallel discursive practices, but sustained treatments of race in general, and the antidialogical aspects of white racism in particular, are virtually nonexistent. Some limited discussions of race and dialogue can be found in Anderson, Cissna, and Arnett (1994), Arnett (1986), and Cissna and Anderson (2002), but there is little consideration of the ways in which racial consciousness undermines and limits dialogic interaction. Although much of the scholarship on dialogue produced by communication scholars of European descent focuses on the theoretical and philosophical discussions of dialogue's transformative potential, there is no sustained and explicit exploration of how that potential is made impossible by white racism.

Although the absence of such a self-reflexive critique of whiteness may not make fruitful dialogues about race between European and African Americans impossible, I believe that it will make them less likely. Nor do I believe that this is simply a white problem: African and European Americans must continue to communicate with each about what race means for all Americans. In fact, some fruitful conversations have already occurred that have the potential to make dialogue more than just talk. Cornel West in his conversation with Michael Lerner about contemporary relations between Jewish and African Americans, points to the difficulty of dialogues on race, and their importance for our common survival. "Dialogue is a form of struggle; it's not chitchat," notes West. "Create a dialogue that focuses not just on the vulnerability of both groups, but on these larger issues of justice, democracy, and the crisis in our own communities. Then try to hammer out some programs that relate to the everyday lives of these groups" (1996, pp. 266–267). Both West and Lerner have shown through their words and deeds that they are committed to dialogue as a vehicle for transforming the quality of communication and interaction between two groups of Americans who have both suffered from, and struggled with, racism.

But what of those who believe that we just need to move on? Who think that they know what we are in for? Who wonder what it was that we were arguing about before September 11? West's observations are again applicable: We must "engage in conversation that provides an understanding of why we are at an impasse" (1996, p. 267). My own experience, my reading of the research on race and dialogue, and my understanding of the emerging literature on whiteness, have led me to believe that white people of conscience must begin and sustain that conversation in their own communities. And when people of European descent are able and willing to listen to people of African descent with sincerity and compassion, then—and only then—will we be able to engage in dialogue. I conclude with the words of Cornel West, in the hope that they can encourage such conversation among my white friends and colleagues, those students and scholars of dialogue willing to transform words into deed, and discourse into action: "Let us hope and pray that the vast intelligence, imagination, humor and courage of Americans will not fail us. Either we learn a new language of empathy and compassion, or the fire this time will consume us all" (1993b, p. 8).

14

When Is Communication Intercultural?

Bakhtin, Staged Performance, and Civic Dialogue

Mary S. Strine

A cultural domain has no inner territory. It is located entirely upon boundaries, boundaries intersect it everywhere, passing through each of its constituent features. The systematic unity of culture passes into the atoms of cultural life—like the sun, it is reflected in every drop of this life. Every cultural act lives essentially on the boundaries, and it derives its seriousness and significance from this fact. Separated by abstraction from these boundaries, it loses the ground of its being and becomes vacuous, arrogant; it degenerates and dies.

—Mikhail Bakhtin (1990, p. 274)

Widespread interest in multicultural issues in communication studies hinges on several basic, often unexamined assumptions: that cultural diversity is an irrefutable condition of contemporary social life, that cultural identity and difference are preconditions rather than consequences of communicative interaction, and that communication properly undertaken leads to a level of understanding that bridges cultural differences. It follows from this line of thinking that through the cultivation of effective communication practices inherent cultural differences between people can be dissolved, or at least, transcended with more open, even-handed, and productive civic dialogue[1] as the desired outcome. Yet, the historical persistence, even escalation, of seemingly intractable intercultural conflicts on regional, national, and global scales belies this linear progression. Intercultural divisions are as often intensified as overcome through increased communicative interaction between people. Whether communicative practices reduce or reinforce cultural divisions is dependent on the specific contexts or social situations to which they give rise. In this chapter, I argue that cultural identity and difference are fundamentally boundary phenomena, constituted and sustained relationally in the interactive verbal processes through which they achieve meaning and resonance.

The work of negotiating boundaries that intercultural communication entails has been the animating focus of the ongoing documentary theater project of African American playwright and actor Anna Deavere Smith, founding director of Harvard's Institute on the Arts and Civic Dialogue. Two of Smith's award-winning one-woman performance pieces that are a part of this project are based on tape recordings of personal interviews she conducted in the immediate aftermath of the 1991 Crown Heights, Brooklyn, riots and the 1992 Los Angeles riots. Her scripting, staging, and subsequent videotaping of the transcribed interview narratives serve as pointed illustrations of how cultural identity and difference emerge interactively in dialogue with others.

Previously I have used Bakhtin's theoretical perspective to explore dialogical dimensions of performance studies scholarship (Strine, 1986; Strine, Long, & HopKins, 1990), and to illuminate dialogical aspects of poetic practice (Strine, 1989). Drawing upon Bakhtin's dialogic theory of language and culture, I build upon that earlier research in several ways: First, I develop an understanding of cultural identity as relational, interactive, and as caught up in the expressive enactments of persons who, especially under conditions of social conflict, negotiate the boundaries of their cultural identities. Second, I apply that fluid and open-ended conception of cultural identity to an examination of the dialogic dimensions of Smith's documentary theater project. Finally, I suggest ways that Smith's boundary work functions to enrich the possibilities of civic dialogue.

Cultural Identity as Dialogic Process

Unlike the popular conception of dialogue as verbal interaction aimed at overcoming differences within the public arena or striving for consensus through conversation, dialogism—the preferred term for Bakhtin's theory (Hirschkop, 1992, 1999; Holquist, 1990)—emphasizes the relational nature of self-understanding and the necessity of interaction between inherently different persons or perspectives for dialogic exchange to occur. According to Bakhtin (1984), *to be* means *to communicate. . . .* To be means to be for another, and through an other, for oneself. A person has no sovereign territory, [s]he is wholly and always on the boundary, looking inside [her-]himself, [s]he looks into the eyes of another or with the eyes of another. (p. 287)

As Bakhtinian scholar Michael Holquist (1990) explains, dialogism depends on a relation between fundamentally dissimilar persons, perspectives, or viewpoints; dialogic relations sustain and build upon the mutuality and interanimation of differences (p. 40).

Dialogism is rooted in a communication-centered understanding of language, society, and culture that stresses their dynamic interdependence. From this view, the operative unit of language in everyday life, as in literary–artistic expression and in culture generally, is the speech utterance-in-context. Utterances arise and have meaning in response to the social context in which they occur and are always in some sense understood as answers addressed to others who are part of that context. As such, utterances are the material expression of their speakers' positions in the social arena and are conveyors of particular worldviews or social ideologies. Vocal intonation—the attitudinal, evaluative dimension of an utterance—individuates a speaker's contribution to the social dialogue, implicates him or her ethically as an active participant in shaping the situational context, and marks the boundary between self and other in the process. Put simply, intonation functions pivotally as the medium and means whereby self-understanding and social values inform one other, and cultural identity and difference are performatively clarified (Volosinov, 1973, p. 102).[2]

Viewed from the perspective of dialogism, cultures cohere and are distinguishable from one another principally through the organizing effect of speech genres, the recurring historical forms that verbal interactions take among cultural members (Hirschkop, 1999, p. 10). Bakhtin (1986) conceptualizes speech genres as relatively stable yet flexible patterns of verbal interchange that originate in the communicative interactions of everyday life and also organize represented or mediated social interactions circulating among cultural members in the realms of art, literature, science, government, religion, and so forth. Speech genres, both face-to-face and mediated forms, designate particular patterns of intonation, ways of seeing and interpreting reality, structuring principles of discourse, and types of social relationships that such patterns of interaction enable and promote (pp. 60–102).

Bakhtin's life-long interest in heteroglossia, the representation of discourse as multivoiced and irreducibly plural in meanings and values, and especially with novelistic genres, those representational forms that are most open and responsive to other genres and to diversified styles and viewpoints, stems from his desire to expand creatively the scope of real-world public dialogue.

By arguing for the inclusion of secondary speech genres as distinctive "voices" in the public dialogue, his aim was to extend the range and inclusiveness of intercultural exchange. For example, Bakhtin (1981) characterizes his vision of the ideal, community-affirming, public dialogue as occurring in an inter-generic, intertextual, intercultural world: "I imagine this whole to be something like an immense novel, multi-styled, mercilessly critical, soberly mocking, reflecting in all its fullness the heteroglossia and multiple voices of a given culture, people and epoch" (p. 60).

Bakhtin's preoccupation with novelistic genres as the discursive forms best able to represent a culturally diversified public sphere reflects his understanding of the limits of face-to-face public dialogue under real-life conditions of unequal opportunity and uneven power relations. Novelistic discourse functions as an important supplement to actual public dialogue precisely because it can accomplish what the unmediated language of face-to-face social interaction alone cannot; that is, it can reflexively imbue ordinary language with sociohistorical significance and depth of meaning lacking in the discourse of everyday life, thereby heightening social consciousness (Hirschkop, 1992). Moreover, when presented with inventive artistry to a culturally diverse public, novelistic discourse promotes the revitalization of civic dialogue by providing a critically distanced, intersubjective space for imaginatively confronting, clarifying, and working through real-world issues and intercultural conflicts (Hirschkop, 1999).

Documentary Theater as Dialogized Performance

On the Road: A Search for American Character, Smith's title for her ongoing documentary theater project of which the much acclaimed *Fires in the Mirror: Crown Heights, Brooklyn and Other Identities* (Smith, 1993) and *Twilight: Los Angeles, 1992* (Smith, 1994) are key parts, began in the early 1980s as an attempt to accomplish what traditional theater cannot: to explore the interdependent relationship between speech and identity in ordinary individuals' struggles to come to terms with volatile social issues in America, in particular, and with changes in the meaning of racial identity, shifts in interethnic alliances, and increasing intercultural conflicts. In her words, "I wanted to know, What is the relationship of language to identity? What does language, the way we render language, tell us about who we are? What does it tell us on an individual level? What does it tell us on a societal level?" (Smith, 2000, p. 49). The project is propelled by the conviction that empathically inhabiting another's speech pattern through performance leads not only to a felt understanding of that person's individuality and viewpoint but to a fuller realization of one's self in relation to others as well. Smith (1993) explains:

To develop a voice one must develop an ear. To complete an action one must have a clear vision. Does the inability to empathize start with an inhibition, or a reluctance to see? Do racism and prejudice instruct those inhibitions? (p. xxviii)

The project's primary function, then, unlike that of traditional theater, is to create a public forum for intercultural dialogue, drawing together persons who would not otherwise be assembled so that cultural identities and differences might be openly explored, at times renegotiated, and "unlikely connections" might be forged (p. xxxviii).

From the interview process through rehearsals, staged performances, and videotapings, Smith's performance project has been thoroughly dialogized. She begins work on each stage production by conducting and tape recording in-depth interviews with a wide spectrum of persons directly and indirectly affected by the social issue or interracial conflict on which that particular production focuses. With each interview, she attempts "to create an atmosphere in which the interviewee would experience his or her own authorship" (Smith, 1993, p. xxxi) so as "to get at those moments when people are themselves, becoming themselves in language" (Smith, 2000, p. 52), thereby discovering something unique and vital about him- or herself in the process of telling his or her story. Smith develops her one-woman staged performances from verbatim transcripts of those interviews she feels are the most expressive and revealing of ethnic identity formation. Dramaturges—consultants representing the different ethnic groups depicted in each production—assist her throughout the rehearsal period with outside perspectives, intensive interrogations, and critiques so as to sharpen her characterizations and help her to resist stereotyping. Staged performances and video-screenings are often followed by active audience participation in discussion of the production and its ramifications for improving interethnic and intercultural community relations. Notably, Smith's vision of American character as always in a state of formation and transition emerges from this interactive, open-ended process. Her depiction of cultural identity as always in struggle for unity-in-difference distinguish her performance project. Smith explains:

My sense is that American character lives not in one place or the other, but in the gaps between places, and in our struggle to be together in our differences. It lives not in what has been fully articulated, but what is in the process of being articulated, not in the smooth-sounding words, but in the very moment that the smooth-sounding words fail us. (Smith, 1993, p. xli)

Exploring the Boundaries of Identity and Difference

Smith's (1993) first major performance piece, *Fires in the Mirror: Crown Heights, Brooklyn and Other Identities*, explores the deep-seated interracial conflict between two relatively isolated and marginalized ethnic communities living in the Crown Heights section of Brooklyn, New York, that erupted into a riot in August 1991. These distinct communities consist of Blacks, including African Americans and Caribbean immigrants, many without U.S. citizenship, and Lubavitchers, members of an Hasidic Jewish sect that had fled Nazi Germany during World War II. Interrracial violence was sparked when a car in the motorcade of the Hasidic Rebbe, the Lubavitchers' spiritual leader, ran a red light, hit another car, and jumped the curb, striking and killing Gavin Cato, a 7-year-old Black boy from Guyana, and seriously injuring his cousin Angela with whom he was playing on the sidewalk. Rumors spread quickly within the Black community that a Lubavitcher-owned ambulance service had arrived early at the scene and assisted the driver and his passengers but not the children. Later that day a group of Black youths attacked Yankel Rosenbaum, a 29-year-old Hasidic scholar visiting from Australia, stabbing and killing him. Three days of rioting followed, exacerbated by polarizing media coverage, as Blacks stormed Lubavitcher headquarters, burned Lubavitcher business properties, and clashed with police; in turn, Lubavitcher patrols and Brooklyn police retaliated with what many saw as excessive force, beating Black reporters and indiscriminately detaining young Blacks for days as a "preventative measure" (The Crown Heights Conflict, 1993, pp. 4–5). In the aftermath of the riots, Smith interviewed members of both the Black and the Lubavitcher communities as well as persons indirectly affected by the interracial turmoil. She chose 26 of these interviews for characterization in her staged presentation, and 19 for her film adaptation.[3]

Smith's overriding interest in how cultural identities take shape interactively informs the selection and progression of characterizations in *Fires in the Mirror*. In her introduction to the printed play script, Smith reflects: "In America, identity has always been negotiated. To what extent do people who come to America have to give up something about their own identities to conform to an idea of what an American is? Crown Heights, Brooklyn, was the most graphic display I had witnessed of the negotiation of identity" (Smith, 1993, p. xxxiii). The first characterization in the performance piece, based on an interview with African American playwright, poet, and novelist Ntozake Shange, explicitly highlights this identity theme:

> It's a psychic sense of place
> it's a way of knowing . . .
> I am part of my surroundings
> and I become separate from them
> and it's being able to make those differentiations clearly
> that lets us have an identity

and what's inside our identity

is everything that's ever happened to us.

(Smith, 1993, p. 3)

Assuming that cultural identity and difference are constructed dialogically rather than being essential characteristics of persons, most of the interview narratives reveal how everyday social practices and social occasions mark identity and difference separating Blacks and Lubavitchers. Religious and dietary practices, in particular, are shown as root causes of ethnic division within the Crown Heights community. For example, a number of interviews are shown taking place over food or drink, dramatizing the ordinary but important socializing that is accomplished in having coffee or sharing a meal. Minister Conrad Mohammed, New York minister for the Honorable Louis Farrakhan, and Michael S. Miller, executive director of the Jewish Community Relations Council, are interviewed while having coffee; Henry Rice, a Black Crown Heights resident, is interviewed over lunch; Rosalyn Malamud, a Lubavitcher Crown Heights resident, offers Smith food and coffee during her interview; and Sonny Carson, a Black community youth activist, is interviewed while he is eating in an upscale restaurant in Brooklyn.

Carson expresses his passionate solidarity with the Black uprising in Crown Heights and his seething resentment toward Jews and the political establishment. Referring to the police assistance in handling traffic for Lubavitcher religious services and in curbing Black rioters, he confides with resentment:

It is just getting intolerable for me to continue to watch

this small

arrogant

group of people continue to get this kind of preferential treatment. . . .

I have no reason to be eagerly awaiting the coming

together of our

people.

They owe me first.

(Smith, 1993, pp. 104–105)

As if in dialogic response, Rabbi Shea Hecht, a Lubavitcher spokesperson, explains during his interview that mutual respect between Lubavitchers and Blacks, encouraged by the Rebbe, need not imply interethnic socialization or even understanding:

What the Rebbe is talking about is that,

that common denominator that we're all Children of God. . . .

But that does not mean that I have to invite you to my

house for

dinner,

because I cannot go back to your home for dinner,

because you're not gonna give me kosher food. . . .

It's not just a question of buying certain food,

it's buying the food,

preparing it a certain way.

We can't use your dishes, we can't use your oven.

(Smith, 1993, pp. 110–111)

Another seemingly intractable boundary linking yet dividing the two ethnic groups emerges in the different narrative logics that come into play as interviewees reconstruct events surrounding the riots, a division deeply embedded in their parallel and, at times, interwoven histories of oppression. For many Blacks, perception of events was framed within the continuing history of racial oppression beginning with slavery; Lubavitchers typically perceived the riots as the result of virulent anti-Semitism echoing the Holocaust. For example, Rabbi Joseph Spielman, spokesperson for the Lubavitcher community, recalls the events leading to Gavin Cato's death as a tragic, unavoidable accident and the retaliatory murder of Yankel Rosenbaum as an act of wanton violence against Jews (Smith, 1993, pp. 67–73). In contrast, the Reverend Canon Doctor Heron Sams, pastor of St. Mark's Church in Crown Heights, assigns blame for the death of Gavin Cato and the violence that followed to unnecessary speeding by the Rebbe's motorcade and to the Lubavitchers' inflated self-importance and disregard for the larger Crown Heights community, and the death of Yankel Rosenbaum to unfortunate but understandable retaliation (pp. 74–77).

The multivoiced image of intercultural conflict in Crown Heights becomes dramatically resonant in the fluid progression of these personal narratives. Several narratives convey the lived tensions—the choices, constraints, and contradictions—of negotiating cultural identity and difference with particular clarity, such as those of Michael S. Miller who attended Gavin Cato's funeral as representative of the Lubavitcher community, and Richard Green, director of the Crown Heights Youth Collective. Miller's account of the funeral is inflected with conflicting feelings of sorrow at the Cato family's loss of their young son, outrage at the political cast of the funeral service, anger at the overt anti-Semitic heckling of the gathering crowd, and righteous determination to defend the Lubavitcher community against Black violence. Miller recalls:

> Not only
> were there cries of, "Kill the Jews" . . .
> there were cries of, "Heil Hitler."
> There were cries of, "Hitler didn't finish the job."
> There were cries of,
> "Throw them back into the ovens again." . . .
> The hatred is so
> *deep seated*
> and the hatred knows no boundaries.
>
> (Smith, 1993, pp. 86–87)

Green, however, recasts the riots and the apparent anti-Semitic hatred that fueled them in terms of the mounting rage of economically disenfranchised and socially marginalized Black youth. He illuminates another aspect of intercultural conflict in Crown Heights thereby introducing a new perspective in the ongoing civic dialogue:

> Those young people had rage out there. . . .
> And they're not angry at the Lubavitcher community
> they're just as angry at you and me,
> if it comes to that. . . .
>   They have no
> role models,
> no guidance. . . .
> So when they see the Lubavitchers
> they don't know the difference between "Heil Hitler"
> and, uh, and uh, what ever else. . . .
> When you ask 'em to say who Hitler was they wouldn't
> even be able
> to tell you.
> Half of them don't even know.
>
> (Smith, 1993, pp. 117–120)

Fires in the Mirror powerfully dramatizes the ethnic, religious, and socioeconomic boundaries that divide Lubavitchers and Blacks in Crown Heights.

In her next major performance piece, Smith attempts to cross boundaries and bridge differences that lead to intercultural conflict.

Blurring Boundaries and Negotiating Differences

The second major one-woman production in Smith's (1994) performance project, *Twilight: Los Angeles, 1992,* documents the variable and shifting character of cultural identity in multiethnic South Central Los Angeles in the aftermath of the April 1992 riots. The background of the riots can be summarized as follows: In March 1991, Los Angeles police officers beat, subdued, and arrested Rodney King, a Black man being pursued for speeding. A resident in the area captured the beating on videotape and distributed it to the news media. King was subsequently released from custody due to insufficient evidence, and four white police officers were formally charged with felony assault for the beating. Following the April 1992 Simi Valley trial and acquittal of the four police officers on all but one count of excessive force, South Central Los Angeles exploded with the worst riots in U.S. history: three days of violent civil upheaval that left 51 people dead—26 of them African American, 14 Latino or Latina, 8 Caucasian, 2 Asian, and 1 unknown—and over $1 billion in property damage. Roughly 90% of Korean-owned businesses in South Central Los Angeles were damaged or destroyed (Rogow & Smith, 2001, p. 2). Basing her script once again on interviews she conducted with persons involved in or affected by the riots as well as several supplementary commentaries by scholars with unique perspectives on the changing cultural landscape in the U.S., Smith created a one-woman staged performance that explores the sociopolitical landscape of South Central Los Angeles, particularly the boundaries on which cultural identity and difference were being negotiated in post-1992 Los Angeles. Smith conducted over 200 interviews; 25 were represented in the staged performance.[4]

The title *Twilight* orients this performance piece in decisive ways. Smith takes her title from one of her interviewees, Twilight Bey, a former Los Angeles gang member and organizer of a gang truce. With soft-spoken assurance, Twilight Bey explains the association he makes between his chosen street name and his self-identity:

> Twilight
>
> is
>
> that time
>
> between day and night.
>
> Limbo,
>
>> I call it Limbo. . . .

I affiliate darkness with what was first
because it was first,
and then relative to my complexion.
I am a dark individual,
and with me stuck in Limbo,
I see darkness as myself. . . .
[I]n order for me to be a, to be a true human being
I can't forever dwell in darkness,
I can't forever dwell in the idea,
of just identifying with people like me and understanding me
and mine.

(Smith, 1994, pp. 254–255)

In his interview, cultural theorist Homi Bhabha reflects upon the condition of liminality, "the moment of ambivalence and ambiguity" that twilight implies. Bhabha draws several implications of a twilight perspective for making sense of the social upheaval in South Central Los Angeles:

That fuzziness of twilight
allows us to see the intersections
of events with a number of other things that daylight
obscures for us. . . .
We have to interpret more in
twilight,
we have to make ourselves
part of the act,
we have to project more. . . .
The thing itself in twilight
challenges us
to
be aware
of how we are projecting onto the event itself.
We are part of
producing the event.

(Smith, 1994, pp. 232–233)

Together, Bey's and Bhabha's characterizations provide a framework for understanding the intercultural nuances—the boundaries, alliances, and intersections suffusing speech and character—at the heart of Smith's documentary performance project.

The legal system becomes a powerful institutional boundary that personal narratives frequently use to mark cultural identity and difference. In the course of their narratives, many persons of varying socioeconomic status, profession, race, or ethnic background position themselves in relation to the tactical operations of the Los Angeles Police Department, the courts, and the legal establishment generally. Some of those interviewed define themselves in opposition to the police. For example, Latino sculptor and painter Rudy Salas expresses enduring hatred for what he sees as an oppressive white police establishment (Smith, 1994, pp. 1–7). And Theresa Allison, African American mother of a gang truce leader and founder of Mothers Reclaiming Our Children (Mothers ROC), a grassroots activist organization formed to protect minority youth against the police violence, shows indignation at what she sees as the Los Angeles Police Department's blatant abuse of power:

> They used to take our kids
>
> from one project
>
> and drop 'em into another gang
>
> zone and leave 'em in there
>
> and let those guys kill 'em
>
> and then say it's a gang-related thing,
>
> hear me?

(Smith, 1994, p. 38)

Implicit ties to the legal justice system supporting white, middle class identity and privilege are explicitly foregrounded in many of the personal narratives. For instance, Jason Sanford, a young athletic white man speculates during his interview that, had he been arrested for speeding, he would not have been beaten like Rodney King simply because of his neat Caucasian appearance:

> Even the times that I have been arrested
>
> they [the police] always make comments . . .
>
> You look like an all-American white boy.
>
> You look responsible.

(Smith, 1994, p. 22)

Several white interviewees who were not directly threatened by the turbulence emphasize that their normal way of life and sense of well-being were deeply shaken during the riots in the absence of accustomed police control. For example, an anonymous Hollywood agent recalls during his interview that, on hearing about the rioting in South Central Los Angeles, his affluent social set retreated en masse to the Grill, a trendy show business restaurant in Beverly Hills:

> There was an incipient panic—
> you could just feel—
> the tension
> in the
> restaurant. . . .
> I was almost thinking: "Did I deserve this,
> do I, do I deserve it?"
> I thought me, personally—no,
> me, generically,
> maybe so.

(Smith, 1994, pp. 134–135, 139)

However, the clearest and most devastating illustration of how white, middle-class identity relies unthinkingly on its ties to the legal justice system for support occurs when those ties were abruptly severed. A profound sense of betrayal by government officials, the justice system, and the general public coupled with extreme anxiety and self-doubt over political identifications that followed the Simi Valley verdict emerge during one anonymous white male juror's painful recollection:

> And this reporter said,
> "Why are you hiding your heads in shame? Do you know
> that buildings
> are burning
> and people are dying in South L.A.
> because of you?" . . .
> And watching on the TV
> and seeing all the political leaders,
> Mayor Bradley
> and President Bush,
> condemning our verdicts. . . .
> We [the jurors] just feel like we were pawns that were thrown away by
> the system.

(Smith, 1994, pp. 71–72)

But the response that jurors found most distressing was the identification of their verdicts with the values of white racist sympathizers. In utter dismay, the anonymous juror confides:

> One of the most disturbing things . . .
> was a letter from the KKK
> saying,
> "We support you, and if you need our help, if you want to
> join
> our organization, we'd welcome you into the fold."
> And we all just were:
> No, oh!
> God!
>
> (Smith, 1994, p. 73)

Many of the interviewees' responses to the riots were enfolded within personal narratives in which they situate themselves and the rioters differentially in relation to the traditional American success story; that is, they believe that hard work should lead to success within the American system of free enterprise and fair play. In her interview, Judith Tur, a white reporter for the Los Angeles News Service, justifies her outrage and disgust at what was happening during the riots in these terms:

> But what's happening in South-Central now,
> I think they're really taking advantage. . . .
> Let them go out and work for a living.
> I'm sick of it.
> We've all had rough time in our life.
> I've had major rough time. . . .
> But I would never think of going on welfare.
> I would never think of robbing a market,
> holding
> somebody at gunpoint.
>
> (Smith, 1994, pp. 97–98)

Similarly, Mrs. Young-Soon Han, a Korean American and former liquor-store owner, expresses bitterness and indignation that she and other hard-working Korean Americans were victimized in the riots and seemingly denied access to American justice in the aftermath:

Until last year
I believed America is the best.
I still believe it. . . .
Then a couple of months ago
I really realized that
Korean immigrants were left out
from this
society and we were nothing . . .
Okay, Black people
   probably
believe they won
by the [second] trial? . . .
Justice was there. . . .
Then where is the victims' rights?
They [black people] got their rights.
By destroying innocent Korean merchants.

(Smith, 1994, pp. 245–247)

Most telling, two vivid and opposing images of the future of multiethnic culture and intercultural relations in post-1992 Los Angeles are depicted in *Twilight*: Reginald Denny, a white truck driver viciously attacked and critically injured during the riots, and Paul Parker, chairperson of the Free the LA Four Plus Defense Committee, who has been working full time on behalf of Black civil rights. Both men envision having a special room in their future homes that commemorates the riots and preserves their meaning for posterity. Denny's emotional distancing from his near-fatal attack and warm feelings of solidarity with the four Blacks who saved him as well as others who supported him during recuperation led him to a buoyantly optimistic even celebratory image of what his future room would be like:

It's gonna be a happy room. . . .
Of all the crazy things that I've got,
all the,
the
love and compassion
and the funny notes
and the letters from faraway places,

just framed, placed,

framed things,

where people will walk in

and just have a good old time in there.

It'll just be

fun in there . . .

and there won't be

a color problem

in this room.

(Smith, 1994, pp. 110–111)

In sharp contrast, Parker's vision for his commemorative room reflects his firm belief that the riots were a vindication of Black oppression, and his righteous anger at continuing discriminatory treatment of Blacks by the Los Angeles Police Department, the legal system, and the news media:

When I finally get my house I'm gonna have just one room

set aside.

It's gonna be my No Justice No Peace room.

Gonna have up on the wall No Justice,

over here No Peace,

and have all my articles

and clippings and, um,

everything else.

I guess so my son can see,

my children can grow up with it.

Know what Daddy did.

(Smith, 1994, p. 177)

Documentary Theater as the Site of Civic Dialogue

Smith's purpose with each of her performance pieces is to create an aesthetically framed social context for exploring her interviewees' characters and worldviews. Using their own language and speech patterns so as to represent them with utmost clarity, truthfulness, and immediacy, Smith's goal is to generate an open and inclusive civic dialogue that is not otherwise possible.

Her one-woman performances are staged with a minimum of suggestive props, changes in costume, and shifts in staging. In both the live and filmed versions, she presents her interviewees' narratives as if directly addressing her audience, in effect, placing the audience in the position of interlocutor.

Her intention is not simply to impersonate the various characters that she performs; rather, she aims to communicate the palpable tension, in her words, in "the gap between the real person and my *attempt* to seem like them. I try to close the gap between us, but I applaud the gap between us. I am willing to display my own *unlikeness*" (Smith, 1993, pp. xxvii–xxviii). The gap that Smith alludes to here makes her characterizations internally dialogized and motivates the deep empathic listening on the part of Smith's audiences essential to renewed civic dialogue (Schechner, 1993). And it is in this gap between the persons she performs, her self as the performer, and her audience, that Smith's performances are most critically reflexive, interventionist, and insightful.[5]

Through the staged performance event and the subsequent discussion it provokes, an improvised public, imaginatively focused in its social reflexivity, is formed (Warner, 2002). Audience members drawn together in their difference—intersecting lines of race or ethnicity, class, gender, and subject position—are encouraged to respond reflectively to Smith's varied characterizations, to think collectively about the causes of social conflict, and to engage one another, opening new possibilities for understanding identity and difference, self and other. Drama critic Janelle Reinelt argues that Smith's greatest achievement in her one-person performances is her evocative demonstration of this "process of bridging differences." As Reinelt (1996) explains,

> the relationship between interviewer and speaker is mobile—it changes—and since the audience is positioned in the direct address sequence to "be" Smith, they are positioned to *experience the activity of bridging, working with difference*. This effect is the most radical element of Smith's work—it engages the spectator in radical political activity to the extent that the spectator grapples with this epistemological process. (p. 615; emphasis added)

Smith's continuing effort to revive civic dialogue through staged performances that invite thoughtful audience participation,[6] implicating audience members imaginatively in the boundary work of bridging cultural differences and of negotiating identity in difference, resonates fully with Bakhtin's conception of an inclusive, community-affirming public sphere. Moreover, Smith's one-woman performances based on interviews surrounding important social issues serve as a forum for meaningful intercultural dialogue and as rehearsals in the performance of responsible, multicultural citizenship.

Notes

1. Civic dialogue here refers to public discussion among persons who are fundamentally different about issues of common concern.

2. Bakhtin is often credited with texts published under the name V. N. Volosinov.

3. *Fires in the Mirror* was first presented at the Joseph Papp Public Theatre as part of the George C. Wolfe Festival of New Voices in December 1991. Its official public opening was held at the New York Shakespeare Festival, where it ran between May and August 1992. Subsequent performances were presented at the American Repertory Theatre in Cambridge, Massachusetts; the McArthur Theatre in Princeton, New Jersey; Brown University; Stanford University; the Brooklyn Academy of Music; and the Royal Court Theatre in London, among others. In 1992, Smith received a Drama-Logue Award, an Obie Award, a Drama Desk Award, and a Pulitzer Prize nomination for *Fires in the Mirror*. An adapted version of the play was filmed for the PBS American Playhouse series in 1993 (Fortis & Wolfe, 1993). Discussion in this chapter is based on the printed text. Excerpts are reprinted with the kind permission of Random House, Inc.

4. *Twilight: Los Angeles, 1992* premiered at the Mark Taper Forum in Los Angeles in May 1993 and ran until July 1993. It was subsequently presented as a work in progress at the McArthur Theatre, Princeton, New Jersey in 1993. It opened in New York at the Joseph Papp Theatre as part of the 1994 New York Shakespeare Festival. In 1993, Smith received a Tony Award, an Obie Award, a Drama Desk Award, and an Outer Circle Critics Award for *Twilight*. A film adaptation of the play was produced for the PBS Stage on Screen series in 2001 (Smith, Swerdlow, & Levin, 2001). Discussion in this chapter is based on the printed text. Excerpts are reprinted with the kind permission of Random House, Inc.

5. For an incisive explanation of the interventionist potential of artistic performance and performance studies scholarship, see Conquergood (2002).

6. Because of the resounding public support for *Fires in the Mirror* and *Twilight*, the Institute on the Arts and Civic Dialogue was established in 1997 as a 3-year experiment at Harvard University with Anna Deavere Smith as its founding director. The Institute was funded by a $1.5 million challenge grant from the Ford Foundation with the following goals: "to explore ways to add an artistic component to the nation's conversation about differences that counteract the media's oversimplification of complex issues . . . and to use the arts to locate a middle ground in debates that frequently are divided along strict lines" (Institute on the Arts and Civic Dialogue, 1998). Assisted by its joint sponsors, the American Repertory Theatre and the W.E.B. Du Bois Institute for Afro-American Research, the Institute was charged with promoting "artistic collaboration and discovery while exploring issues of race, identity, diversity, and community" (Institute on the Arts and Civic Dialogue, 1998).

15

Media Studies and the Dialogue of Democracy

John J. Pauly

Though dialogic approaches have widely influenced the study of communication, they have left a fainter mark on studies of the mass media. I propose to investigate the reasons for this neglect. The indifference, truth be told, has flowed in both directions. For much of the 20th century, media scholars focused on matters of institutional structure, regulation, policy, economics, law, ideology, and effect. These traditions of research implicitly positioned dialogue as an epiphenomenon, a soft social process less constraining, explanatory, or decisive than the hard architecture of political economy, social structure, and cognitive disposition. Dialogue studies, for their part, have often treated the mass media as an iconic Other, the very embodiment of the impersonal social relations that undermine mutuality. The media, in their noisy ubiquity, have been imagined to crowd out and devalue the truly human.

The cultural turn of the last 20 years has opened a different moment, however, in which media and dialogue scholars might make common cause. The critical versions of media studies continue to insist that powerful structures restrain and determine our forms of communication (and a troubled world offers up ample evidence for their gloomy predictions). But hope finds voice, too. Scholars in both traditions seek reasons to imagine more fluidly responsive, decent, just, and participatory modes of human action. And the two have come to recognize shared assumptions. Both believe, after all, that humans "word" the world together, that our sense of self is emergent and contingent, and that our persistent, existential struggle, as creatures, is simply to make sense.

My chapter traces this trajectory of indifference and rapprochement. I want to explain why media and dialogue studies for so long neglected each other, and why, today, they increasingly find themselves in each other's company. I use my own work in journalism studies to illustrate the process by which media scholars have reframed older questions in ways that dialogue scholars might find resonant. In particular, I reference the ongoing debate over public journalism as an example of how media studies has incorporated insights familiar to dialogue scholars. And I close with ideas about how dialogue scholars might treat the media as a legitimate object of study—that is, as something more than an emblem of their discontent.

Dialogue and the Problems of Scale

Before I explore what has kept dialogue and media studies apart, let me debunk the stereotype that we sometimes imagine divides the two, so that we might consider other realms of difference. If we ask, "What is it about the media that discourages dialogue?" the conventional answer might be "Everything." Dialogue values face-to-face communication and cultivates one-on-one encounters, even when conducted in groups. The media feel like one-to-many; the message goes out to the audience members as a group, but they do not talk with one another. Dialogue is direct, a person-to-person encounter. The media are, well, mediated; they rely on technology rather than interpersonal commit-ment as their mode of connection. Dialogue values depth in the relations it fosters. The media settle for shallowness; they measure their own success in size and wealth of the audience gathered rather than personal transformation achieved.

The scale of the media arouses special concern. How does one encourage mutuality, active listening, and responsiveness among newspaper, magazine, radio, movie, and television audiences that range from the thousands to the tens of millions? Scholars have often judged such gatherings as incapable of producing dialogue (e.g., Bellah, Madsen, Sullivan, Swidler, & Tipton, 1985; Ellul, 1985; Kaplan, 1994; Postman, 1985). This judgment resonates with a longstanding commonplace of American and European thought that inter-prets large-scale media as emblems of a mass society (Bramson, 1961). Older terms like *mass communication* may wither year by year, but the concept per-sists. Indeed, the phrase *the media* still denotes much the same set of social practices as *mass* once did. When they talk about "the media," most Americans mean massive, heavily capitalized, technologically sophisticated, professionally managed, star-driven systems of communication. They think of the company newsletter, parish bulletin, video yearbook, pizza delivery flyer, yellow pages, personal website, wedding DJ, or small scholarly journal as something else—as means of communication, but not media. Even when we apply the term *alter-native media* to smaller systems that audiences invest with special significance, we imagine them as an alternative to the extensive technologies, permanent organizations, market relations, and professional expertise of "the media."

Do the terms *media* and *dialogue* mark incommensurable modes of communication? Perhaps they simply respond to different scholarly questions. For example, technology plays a more obvious role in media studies. Scholars attend closely to the making of such products as news stories, television programs, movie soundtracks, and magazine advertisements. Dialogue requires little technology, but it does depend upon cognate forms of social organization that Lewis Mumford (1952) used to call *technics*—the ordering practices that bind groups with art, language, ritual, and work, even in the absence of machines. Scholars often take for granted the technics of dialogue. In public deliberation projects, for example, the expertise of white-collar professionals has created the occasion, format, and ground rules for dialogue. Before participants speak one word, others have spent weeks or months setting the stage for their conversations. Projects such as the National Issues Forums (Mathews, 1994; Pearce & Littlejohn, 1997, pp. 169–180) employ expert moderators; planners who use phone, Internet, and fax to arrange housing, travel, and food; and scholars and journalists who write and assemble the preliminary materials. The forums, in other words, capitalize the speech of ordinary citizens in the same ways that universities routinely capitalize the speech of their professors. Further, such forums regulate the style of talk (especially if participants prove too performative or agonistic), and they train moderators to forestall eruptions of incivility.

Thus it seems improbable, to me at least, to think of dialogue as a pure, natural, uncorrupted realm that we enter once we shed the artifice of the media. Dialogue is every bit as "made" as any technology. Any attempt to divide technology from technics, to place the machine on one side and the human on the other, misses how we actually live. Nor can we easily discover, in modern societies, a domain of autonomous, genuinely personal experience that stands apart from our involvement with media. Participants come to dialogue with sensibilities and knowledge shaped by their use of mass-produced books, movies, and magazines as well as by ever-more years of formal education. The fact that participants *talk about* their experience as uniquely and authentically personal does not diminish this point. Manufactured knowledge and experience now speaks through all of us.

That is our dilemma, as creatures. We live in a world of widely circulated, objectified symbolic forms whose very existence testifies to their weight and importance. We wonder about our place in that world, suspecting that it makes us more than we make it. Our problem is not merely epistemological—a philosopher's debate about what we know and how—but painfully spiritual, for our sense of ethics depends upon retaining some sense of moral agency. My own conception of dialogue emerges from just such dilemmas of modern experience. I think of dialogue as a fine word for humans' deep, persistent, and self-reflexive attempts to come to terms with the world and one another. Scholars' descriptions of dialogue—as immediacy of presence, mutual implication, vulnerability, genuineness (Cissna & Anderson, 1994a, pp. 13–15)—emphasize that our very humanness is at stake. Whether we believe in a god or dogma matters not; neither theism nor atheism gets us off the hook. The best we do is talk our way through uncertainty and chaos.

I study the mass media because, improbably enough, they offer themselves as an apt object with which to contemplate modernity and its paradoxes (Jensen, 1990). In their form as well as their content, media render the social order visible and public, as cultural studies so often suggest. They also offer us moral dramaturgy—forms of symbolic action by which groups fashion themselves. This is a way of seeing the world that I learned from my teachers, James Carey and the late Al Kreiling, and that they learned, in large part, from pragmatist philosophers such as John Dewey, William James, and George Herbert Mead; sociologists such as Charles Horton Cooley, Robert Park, and W. I. Thomas; and assorted eccentrics such as Lewis Mumford, Kenneth Burke, and Hugh Duncan. These intellectuals were among the first to understand that the radical uncertainty of modernity demands a dialogic response. When change puts group identity in play, individuals must renegotiate their relations with an ever wider array of disparate others. They turn to the mass media to discover new styles of identity, in the process finding new occasions for symbolic display and conflict.

Above all, thinkers in this tradition feared the eclipse of the public, democracy's privileged representation of its shared civic life. Mary Ryan (1997) has posed the issue succinctly:

> Was it possible for so diverse a people, with such different beliefs and competing interests, to mold themselves into one public, even a harmonious circle of publics? Would the decentralized practices of democratic associations create pandemonium or a working coalition? Can a public composed of men and women separated by their different resources and flagrant inequities operate in a truly democratic manner? (p. 17)

American pragmatists, symbolic interactionists, and cultural critics believed that dialogic communication offered an answer. Carey (1997) finds a powerful example of their hopes for democracy in the work of John Dewey. For Dewey, Carey argues, "Communication was an ethical principle. Whatever inhibited communication, whatever inhibited the sharing, widening, expansion of experience was an obstacle to be overcome" (p. 31). Despite its limitations and anomalies, this faith in the power of human connectedness and civic life has animated my research, and constitutes my own deepest commitment to dialogue.

The Dominant Traditions of Media Research

What ultimately divides dialogue and media are the contrasting intellectual traditions from which each has grown. Philosophy gave birth to dialogue studies; our converging interests in political theory, ethics, and hermeneutics have nurtured it; and our experience with professionally managed talking therapies have lent it a familiar form. Media studies owes much more to history, law, and the social sciences. Discourse about the media has taken shape at different sites and moments. The field emerges not as a theory of language and thought, but as a running commentary on historically specific experiences of republican government, machine technology, free markets, immigration, leisure and entertainment, war, and social reform. In media studies, theory and practice often prove indistinguishable. Professional, academic, critic, and aficionado share the same podium. Media studies, as a field, offers a palimpsest of memory, law, canon, and custom on which every policy, narrative form, cultural conflict, and organization has left its mark. These discursive habits are particularly visible in three theoretical traditions that have shaped the field: liberal traditions of free expression, the political economy of media organizations, and the sociology of audiences.

Centuries-old debates over free expression have set the terms with which we continue to understand the significance of the mass media. Free speech, assembly, and press began as practical political accomplishments—attempts to wrest from crown and church the conditions of one's own making. The incompleteness of the liberal revolution—its slowness to recognize all the forms of humanness—does not dampen its reverberations. Unrestrained voice continues to serve as a universally recognizable signature of human freedom. (Does this story not animate our hopes for dialogue, too?) Jürgen Habermas (1989) has famously theorized this history as an invitation to a public sphere, an imagined civil order governed by uncoerced discourse, reason, and law. The new forms of political organization—citizenship and parliaments and parties and constitutions—made this moment palpable but did not exhaust its meaning. Implicit in the ideal of free expression was a new conception of social and moral identity—a sense that humans would no longer be considered fallen creatures, and society could be understood as the group life that humans choose rather than inherit (Unger, 1987). Even marginalized groups such as African Americans have turned to print and publication to fix their place in history and compel others to recognize their presence (Gates, 1990).

I have told the story this way to emphasize the moral dramaturgy associated with free speech. Unrestrained voice intoxicates us with the possibilities of human liberation. Not surprising, then, that the media have worked so hard to forge themselves into emblems of that freedom and guardians of its traditions.

The exercise of free speech and press has proved so incendiary that it has often incited violence, including mobbing of editors, duels, destruction of newspaper offices, press sabotage, and the assassination of reporters (Nerone, 1994). Today, the media invoke the rhetoric of freedom to describe their every adaptation to changing markets and mores. Thus we commonly hear that the press is the only business specifically protected by the constitution (because its freedom matters so much to us), that television viewers freely choose which programs to watch, that objective reporting encourages a free flow of ideas, and that the public interest is served best when media corporations are left to compete with one another in a free market. In each case, media organizations trade on the rhetoric of freedom, whether or not their behavior actually encourages human liberation.

The second literature I wish to reference, on media economics and organizational structure, considers the material conditions of human symbol-making, describing all the ways that modern societies industrialize, bureaucratize, and capitalize their cultural practices. The earliest accounts of media organizations grew out of political economy and the study of law and regulation. Such institutional approaches often interpreted media systems as the lengthened shadow of a nation's political ideology. For instance, the widely influential *Four Theories of the Press* (Siebert, Peterson, & Schramm, 1956) categorized each nation's press system by its commitment to authoritarian, classical liberal, or social responsibility principles. As commentators have noted (Nerone, 1995), *Four Theories* too easily fit its conceptual categories to the political commonplaces of the Cold War. Nonetheless, this approach governed studies of the international press and broadcasting for many years, and critical theories of media still assume that ideological and market forces ultimately determine media performance.

Like the free expression tradition, scholarship on media organizations works with historically specific referents. In the 19th century, for example, the United States and Europe steadily diverged in their organization of telegraph and telephone systems, after starting with similar postal systems. In Europe, the national post offices absorbed the telegraph and telephone into their state monopolies, in part to guarantee access for military purposes. The United States forthrightly committed itself to an expensive, universal, federal postal system as an indispensable infrastructure of republican government (John, 1995; Kielbowicz, 1989). But in 1844, Congress refused Samuel Morse's offer to sell his telegraph patents to the American government (Thompson, 1947). The development of the telegraph as a private system would inflect Americans' approach to every subsequent electrical and electronic technology. The debate over each new invention—telephone, radio, sound recording, television, satellite— would rehearse similar choices. Today we ask whether privately owned portals and content providers should be allowed to structure public access to the

Internet, a system originally sponsored by agencies of the U.S. government. And Europeans ponder the consequences of allowing satellite television providers to compete with state-supported broadcasting systems.

I have noted that for many years scholars interpreted media organizations as the projection of a nation's political and economic beliefs. Since the 1970s, however, studies of media organizations have taken a different turn. Without fully renouncing institutional approaches, scholars have studied media organizations as dynamic systems, responsive to external market pressures, of course, but also driven by internal routines, divisions of labor, technologies, and professional values. Production studies typically focus on the routine manufacture of media artifacts rather than the creation of artistically exceptional single works. They interpret each media product as a remnant left by the organization's practices, a trace of the bureaucratic negotiations that produced it. This approach allows greater weight to professional values, noting their intersection with organizational roles, routines, budgets, and production practices. One can find dozens of examples of this approach applied to journalism alone (e.g., Darnton, 1990; Ericson, Baranek, & Chan, 1989; Fishman, 1980; Gans, 1979; Schudson, 2003; Soloski, 1997; Tuchman, 1978). But one also finds similar studies of music (Faulkner, 1971; Peterson, 1997), television entertainment (Cantor, 1971; Elliott, 1972; Gitlin, 1983), movies (Powdermaker, 1950), magazines (Lutz & Collins, 1993), advertising (Arlen, 1980; Hirota, 1988), and public relations (Jackall, 1988).

Dialogic theory offers little that resembles this literature on political economy and organizational bureaucracy. In a sense, dialogue hopes to escape the sociological by emphasizing the emergent and wondrous over than the normal and routine. That is also why scholars committed to political economy or production approaches may find dialogic models unconvincing. The problem is not so much that dialogue studies are indifferent to questions of power—a charge recently addressed by Hammond, Anderson, and Cissna (2003). Intellectual sensibility, and self-styling, divide the traditions. Scholars who study media organizations believe that claims about economics and organizational structure always dwarf other forms of explanation. Political economy, in particular, prides itself on maintaining a tone of *realpolitik*. In the work of scholars such as Robert McChesney (1993, 1999; McChesney & Nichols, 2002), Nicholas Garnham (1990, 2000), or Noam Chomsky (2002; Herman & Chomsky, 1988), economics and ideology always count for more than culture, interaction, narrative, interpretation, or dialogue.

From the perspective of dialogue studies, this must seem a domineering conception of the real. It identifies power as the key issue—perhaps the only real issue—that media scholarship should address. Political economy declares life's material demands as inescapable, and its existential demands as evanescent. When scholars do examine the talk that occurs within media organizations, they typically study it instrumentally, as a behavior that helps the organization perform its tasks. The dozens of newsroom studies, for example, rarely treat journalists' discourse as self-reflective or ethical (e.g., Bowers, 1998). The working assumption of production studies, true enough, is that media work is hectic and stressful. Participants meet their deadlines only by relying upon standard routines, quick decisions, and taken-for-granted conceptual categories. But ultimately media professionals talk in order to complete their tasks, rather than to discover something about themselves or others.

It is in the third literature, audience studies, that media scholars discover reasons to consider a more dialogic approach. Since the early 20th century, social scientists have been interested in audiences—who they are (both demographically and existentially), what they read and watch, how they use media, how they learn. Commercial media have found it advantageous to answer such questions to measure and package their audiences for advertisers (Converse, 1987). One gets a rough sense of the audience literature by putting its keywords—effects, information, and culture—in historical progression (Carey, 1989, pp. 37–68). From the 1920s to the 1950s, behavioral studies of media effects on attitude, opinion, and behavior dominated. In the 1950s and 1960s researchers began employing cognitive approaches to study learning, framing, and agenda-setting. By the 1970s cultural approaches emerged to account for the media as forms of sense-making. All three approaches continue to coexist today, capitalized and encouraged by different professional and academic constituencies.

Despite their obvious and much-studied differences, each of these paradigms hopes to understand the relation of content and audience. Behaviorists treat content as the stimulus that produces an audience response; cognitivists, as a conceptual frame that reorganizes the audience's mental schema; and culturalists, as a symbolic world that invites play and identification or, in critical versions, sutures the audience to ideology. In each case, media content leads to something. It influences consumer buying, changes our vote, makes a lifestyle attractive, frames our conception of political issues, establishes our common sense about the world, or offers narratives that render experience intelligible. Cultural studies has a special stake in such work, for content offers the audience symbolic models of reality. In content, cultural studies discovers stories about how we live, including any number of dark tales of juvenile delinquency, sexual crossings, ethnic conflict, consumer ecstasy, violence, and propaganda.

I do not intend to survey the sprawling landscape we have come to call cultural studies, or to track its numberless progeny. Let me briefly note, however, two related areas of media studies, not so easily categorized, where one finds strong dialogic influences. One school, following the lead of Marshall McLuhan (1951, 1962, 1964) and Walter Ong (1967, 1977, 1982), has come to be known as "medium theory" or "media ecology." It explores the ways in which different media physiologically and psychologically engage their audiences (e.g., Gozzi, 1999; Meyrowitz, 1985; Postman, 1985, 1992; Strate, Jacobson, & Gibson, 1996). Another school, even more loosely assembled, uses contemporary literary criticism to describe the audience's co-construction of media texts. Television scholar Horace Newcomb (1984) was one of the first to use Bahktin and Volosinov to describe how media texts engage audiences. The work of John Fiske (1987, 1989a, 1989b) would similarly theorize the audience's interactive relation to television and other forms of popular culture. And in the 1990s scholars would apply postmodern perspectives to new electronic media (Poster, 1990, 2001), often searching for signs of community in cyberspace (Jones, 1995, 1997, 1998; Marcus, 1996; Smith & Kollock, 1999).

Media studies such as these have readily incorporated dialogic insights. But many media scholars also consider such work somewhat tangential to their concerns, unless it also engages questions of economics, history, law, and organizational structure. Nonetheless, cultural approaches, broadly considered, have fundamentally altered the field. Many media scholars now acknowledge the centrality of human symbol-making, treat reality as co-constructed and emergent, and recognize the multiplicity and fluidity of the self. Theoretical purists will still find reasons to disagree, of course. Cultural studies may protest that dialogic theory's invitation to escape sociological reality prevents us from confronting the institutional forces that constrain us. And dialogic theory might understandably weary of the cultural studies two-step: its habit of paying lip service to a theoretically fluid, socially constructed reality, but always discovering a determinative ideological order that disciplines the play of meaning.

Journalism and the Dialogue of Democracy

I want to scout a small corner of media scholarship—journalism studies— where I have tried to blend the concerns of cultural studies and dialogic theory. My research has focused on the meaning and significance of journalism's talk about itself, its public, and the polity it serves. Over and over, the profession has metonymically reimagined its public, variously invoking it as audience, market, and community. Each attempt to name journalism's purpose casts public life in a different light. If we describe journalism as information, we are inviting citizens to consider newsreading a civic duty. If we believe that publicity is journalism's source of power, we expect reporters to expose the dark corners of public life to scrutiny. If we think of news as little more than gossip, we will expect little of it. However we conceptualize journalism, we are likely to fall back upon one or another cognate of dialogue. We may consider journalism a form of access, deliberation, or dialogue (Heikkilä & Kunelius, 2002), but it is all still talk.

My writings explore the meanings of our talk about journalism. For example, what do we learn about the profession's ethos by studying the way it demonizes outlaws like Rupert Murdoch (Pauly, 1988), or the public journalism advocates within its ranks (Pauly, 1999), or its lackadaisical readers (Pauly, 1991b)? How does the profession's talk about itself reveal the social commonplaces it holds dear (Pauly & Eckert, 2002)? How does a newspaper assess the difference it has made in the life of a community (Pauly, 2003b)? How have movements within the profession, such as the New Journalism (Pauly, 1990), compelled journalists to reconsider their relations with subjects, sources, and readers? And what have such movements signified to readers, student journalists, and disaffected professionals (Pauly, 1998a)? By what metaphors should we understand the profession's work and the social relations it forges? Is journalism an information utility? A form of storytelling answerable only to the narrative instincts of reporters? Or a moral spectacle? What does it mean when journalism talks about itself as an art form (Pauly, 2003a)? Or an undeveloped medium for social dialogue (Pauly, 1994)? What might we learn from exceptional writers, such as Jane Kramer, who have consistently imagined their work in different terms (Pauly, 1995, 1998b)? And how might the methods of cultural studies help us analyze what and how journalism has signified (Pauly, 1989, 1991a; Jensen & Pauly, 1997)?

The debate over public journalism aptly illustrates the possibilities and difficulties of applying dialogic concepts to media studies. The term *public* (or sometimes *civic*) *journalism* refers to a movement in the 1990s to reconnect news organizations, especially daily newspapers, to the communities they served. In cities like Wichita, Kansas; Charlotte, North Carolina; and Columbus, Georgia, journalists began experimenting with election coverage, but soon opened their pages to wider-ranging discussions of community life, crime, race relations, and city planning. These public journalism projects, as they came to be known, created new rituals of involvement such as community forums, focus groups, and neighborhood pizza parties. Looking back at this history, Rosen (1999, p. 262) has identified four key traits that he thought had characterized the movement: It addressed people as citizens rather than consumers, it helped them act upon not just learn about community problems, it took some measure of responsibility for public discourse, and it recognized that journalism must "help make public life go well" if it hoped to earn the attention and respect of citizens.

I would add one other trait. Public journalism prospered because it recognized that public discourse about press performance had changed. Professional and public dissatisfaction with coverage of the 1988 and 1992 elections provided the immediate impulse to change, but the steady, long-term decline in prestige and centrality of the daily newspaper also opened editors and reporters to ideas they had rejected in the past. The testimony of highly regarded former reporters like Paul Taylor and Richard Harwood underscored the seriousness of the crisis. The movement found prominent and successful spokesmen in successful and respected small-city newspaper editors—most notably Davis "Buzz" Merritt, Jr., of the *Wichita Eagle* and Cole Campbell of the *Norfolk Virginian-Pilot* and later the *St. Louis Post-Dispatch*. Their enthusiasm and friendship lent credibility to the work of Jay Rosen, a professor at New York University, who would spearhead the movement. Rosen drew heavily on a rich body of theoretical writings on journalism by James Carey, first of the University of Illinois and more recently at Columbia University. But Rosen also found imaginative ways to translate that literature for a professional audience, even when his elisions frustrated both professional (Corrigan, 1999) and academic critics (Glasser, 1999b). The movement garnered strong support from the Knight, Kettering, and Pew foundations, helping Rosen earn a hearing for his ideas at industry forums such as the Poynter Institute and the American Press Institute. Representatives of those institutions, such as David Mathews, Ed Fouhy, Jan Schaeffer, and Roy Peter Clark, found ways to hook public journalism to their groups' agendas.

The scholarly response to public journalism demonstrates the ways in which media studies habitually resists dialogic approaches. The book created out of a 1996 Stanford University conference on "The Idea of Public Journalism" (Glasser, 1999b), features a number of hard-nosed critiques of the movement. Barbie Zelizer (1999) writes that she appreciates the idea of public journalism but thinks it has failed to connect itself to the larger professional community and its history. John Peters (1999a) argues that public journalism does not recognize that "dialogue is a form of communication whose form is organically connected to scale." The dream of democracy as a "grand dialogue of all citizens," he writes, is "flawed in compelling ways" (p. 104). Michael Schudson (1999) argues that the communal habits encouraged by public journalism are not adequate to public life, where citizens must "work out problems among people with few shared values, little trust, and a feel of anxiety and enmity" (p. 131). Following Nancy Fraser and Todd Gitlin's criticisms of a unitary public sphere, Ted Glasser (1999a) faults public journalism's quest to create a common discursive space in which all citizens might meet to discuss public affairs. All these criticisms, well-grounded and reasonable, position dialogue as an improbable and unworkable ideal, certainly as something less politically decisive than professional norms (Zelizer), historical precedent (Peters), institutional structure and procedural rules (Schudson), or group interests (Glasser).

This battle over public journalism matters because it broaches larger political questions. From a dialogic perspective, we might ask what we should call "the between" in a nation of citizens? A stage for the performance of group interests? A forum for policy discussion and ideological dispute? A market for the exchange of information? A meeting that makes the town visible to itself as a political entity? Schudson (1997) has noted the ubiquity of one particular metaphor—conversation—in the work of many contemporary thinkers, from Habermas to Bruce Ackerman, Richard Rorty, Hans-Georg Gadamer, and Michael Oakeshott. Recognizing that dialogue and conversation may not describe exactly the same activity, I want to compare Schudson's position with that of his most eloquent interlocutor, James Carey. I have chosen Schudson and Carey because of their prominence and influence in American media studies. They both frequently write about the role of journalism in democracy, and they regularly read and comment on each other's work. Most important, for my purposes, neither takes a purely dialogic stance. Theirs is not a pro-and-con argument, but rather a struggle to imagine how or why one might incorporate dialogue into our theories of democracy.

Schudson (1997) begins by distinguishing two types of conversation that he thinks we have conflated. Sociable conversation, he says, "has no end outside itself" (p. 299). It honors the pleasure of social interaction. Problem-solving conversation, he says, "finds the justification of talk in its practical relationship to the articulation of common ends" (p. 300). This second sort of conversation creates the space for public reasoning, deliberation, and persuasion. It is not an easy space to manage, as it turns out. The possibility of embarrassment keeps many from speaking out, even when given the chance (here he borrows from Jane Mansbridge's [1980] study of actual participation in New England town meetings). In homogeneous settings, shared values and a sense of trust may encourage speech. In heterogeneous settings—that is, exactly the sort found in modern democracies—the risks are higher and the rewards more uncertain. Schudson argues that only social and political norms, conventions, and resources that stand apart from conversation make democracy possible. To make conversation work, we must create "ground rules designed to encourage pertinent speaking, attentive listening, appropriate simplifications, and widely apportioned speaking rights" (p. 307). Deliberation also depends upon inscription—the power of print and broadcast materials to fix and disseminate a record.

Schudson's training as a sociologist shows in this argument, as does his early, and lately renewed, interest in political science. By his account, society operates more powerfully than culture, enabling and constraining members' performances. He considers conversation as one mode of democracy, but certainly not its essence. As in his book *The Good Citizen* (1998), he stresses the importance of social institutions embedded in particular histories, and this emphasis distinguishes him from scholars educated more exclusively in communication traditions. A few years ago I suggested to Schudson that, for all his work in media and communication, he seemed to be seeking something more than a purely communicative perspective. He agreed, saying that he wanted communication *and* something else. In the essay on conversation, his emphasis on sociological context leads him to conclude that sometimes the requirements of democracy may trump those of conversation. The moment may come, he writes, when we need to call a strike or demonstrate or cease speaking or invite conflict, if only to affirm for others the depth of our convictions (Schudson, 1997).

One can read this argument on conversation as a reply to Habermas's (1989) conception of a public sphere. Schudson has spelled out his objections elsewhere, too—in his essay "Was There Ever a Public Sphere?" (Schudson, 1995, pp. 189–193) and in his recent book on the sociology of news (Schudson, 2003). But media scholars have interpreted the conversation essay as a friendly and spirited, if direct and deadly serious, challenge to Carey's writings about democracy and public life. Indeed, Schudson acknowledges that "In communication studies, James Carey has been especially eloquent in placing conversation at the center of public life and the restoration of a public at the heart of the contemporary task of democratic society" (Schudson, 1997, p. 298).

It is not so easy to summarize Carey's work, filled as it is with complexly nested arguments, subtle turns of phrase, and literary allusion. But Carey (1997) himself has provided the following summary in his second collection of essays:

> Communication understood as a metaphor of ritual and conversation encourages, even requires, a primitive form of equality because conversation must leave room for response as a condition of its continuance. Conversation enforces a recognition of others in the fullness of their presence. In conversation we must deal with the full weight of words for they put not only our minds but also our bodies in play and at risk. Therefore, to speak conversationally is not only to invite *and* require a response, but to temper of necessity our criticisms and alienations, our objections and differences, with expressions, implicit and explicit of solidarity and mutual regard. (p. 315)

Carey believes that journalism necessarily plays a special role in any free society—a role bequeathed to it by historical circumstance and custom. "Journalism is central to our politics," he writes, "to the power of the state, to our capacity to form livable communities, indeed to our survivability as a democratic community" (p. 330). The purpose of public journalism, he writes, is "nothing less than the re-creation of a participant, speaking public, ritually formed for democratic purposes, brought to life via conversation between citizen journalists and journalist citizens" (p. 338).

Stated so broadly, Carey's concepts of conversation, public, and journalism may seem vulnerable to Schudson's theoretical objections and historical evidence. But Carey insists that he means to identify the communicative practices by which individuals and societies have imagined the *possibilities* of human freedom. He and Schudson tend to choose different representative anecdotes. Schudson stresses the persistence of social structure, custom, and routine, and the historically specific ways in which new structures, customs, and routines emerge. Carey emphasizes moments of disruption and rebirth.

Thus he discovers inklings of public life in the debates over the United States constitution, in the *samizdat* (i.e., clandestine literature) and coded fictions of Eastern Europeans, in John Dewey's response to Walter Lippmann, and, as noted above, in public journalism. In the spirit of Dewey and the Canadian economist Harold Adams Innis, Carey understands conversation as the oral tradition's stand against military adventurism, imperial technology, arrogant professionalism, and unencumbered markets. And he values the pedestrian everydayness of that tradition. Like Mumford, whose work he read closely in the 1960s and 70s, he considers the city a humanly made container that lends shape and resonance to public life. This, I suspect, is one of the things he admires about public journalism: its plain commitment to making cities work.

It is worth noting that neither Schudson nor Carey foregrounds dialogic theory. Carey's defense of conversation, quoted above, certainly acknowledges the importance of mutuality and positive regard. And yet one feels in Carey's position the strong hand of the free expression tradition. What he describes as conversation can seem like alternating speaking performances, tempered by friendship and civility. He almost never draws upon relational or interpersonal thinkers, preferring to keep company with historians, legal scholars, sociologists, anthropologists, and economists. And despite his commitment to hope, possibility, and choice, he readily acknowledges the weight of history. Schudson's perspective seems, at first glance, unfriendly to dialogic theory. Within his liberal worldview, rules, procedures, and structures matter more than communicative form. As a writer, he comes across as more argumentative and less playful, less willing to entertain whimsical or expressive meanings. He loves to debunk commonplaces. Nonetheless, his writings contain charming moments of personal revelation. In the conversation essay, for example, he argues that "the romance of conversation" does not acknowledge that many people (himself included) are slow to speak and do not enjoy deliberative discourse or large gatherings. And in his fine book on the history of citizenship, which defends a limited, monitorial conception of citizenship against communitarian calls for more political participation, he opens with a description of himself as an election volunteer at his local polling place in California.

Many media scholars operate with similarly mixed commitments and purposes, making it unlikely that dialogic theory will ever displace the dominant traditions of media research. But might dialogue play a larger role than it has in our discussions of the media? Let me briefly note four areas where media studies would profit from closer relations with dialogic theory.

First, the question of how the media represent the forms of human talk remains relatively unexplored. Do the media promote or hinder dialogue by the way they represent our processes of conversation, argument, and discourse? Our cinematic images of human talk, for example, model an apparent preference for the impassioned speech, the burble of young love, the gossip of the high school cafeteria, and the argument that explodes into a fight. How should a society committed to dialogue use popular culture to represent its forms of talk?

Second, dialogic theory might usefully counterbalance the powerful bureaucratic routines and professional norms that govern media production. Public journalism has demonstrated that media professionals begin to think differently about their work when steadily confronted with the perspectives of citizens who stand outside their work routines. Might media organizations consciously create more occasions for dialogue—times and places set aside for nonroutine talk? Are media professionals capable of suspending their professional habits long enough to probe more deeply the social and political implications of their work?

Third, dialogic theory offers an alternative conception of who human beings are. Without insisting on a priori normative beliefs, it entertains the possibility of creaturely solidarity. In this it differs from the oversocialized conception of human nature found in the social sciences. Media studies, especially in its critical modes, too easily codes and categorizes individuals in terms of social structure, group standpoint, and presumed position in hierarchies of power. Dialogue hopes for a more fluid, less structured space for human interaction. It imagines vulnerability and openness as virtues, a sign of our shared existential condition.

Finally, dialogic theory offers perhaps our best grounding for the study of media ethics. Cliff Christians (1977, 1988, 1991, 1995, 1997, 2000; Christians, Ferré, & Fackler, 1993; De Lima & Christians, 1979) has read and published extensively in this vein, pursuing insights from a wide range of social philosophers, including Jacques Ellul, Martin Buber, Charles Taylor, Paulo Freire, and Ivan Illich. His work, steadily deepened over the past 20 years, has had a profound influence on scholarship in media ethics. From such seeds new work has sprung, such as James Ettema and Theodore Glasser's (1998) exemplary study of investigative journalists, which combines ethics and organizational analysis. Work on practical and applied ethics by mainstream philosophers has been moving in this same direction (e.g., May, 1996), foregrounding communication practices and identifying responsiveness to others as the indispensable requirement of ethical behavior.

A commitment to dialogue promises practical as well as theoretical consequences. Consider, one last time, the state of American journalism. In the aftermath of the events of September 11, Barbie Zelizer and Stuart Allan (2002) solicited and published essays on press performance by an array of scholars, including Rosen, Carey, and Schudson. Wisely and perceptively, the authors describe how the profession responded to the crisis, often with renewed enthusiasm and sense of purpose. And yet I saw and heard something different. On that blindingly clear fall day, journalism hesitated in the face of terror and trauma, uncertain of what to do or say, even as armies of reporters and editors were gearing up for lavish, heroic feats of reportage. Dave Eason (1990) has noticed a similar uncertainty in the work of New Journalists such as Joan Didion, Michael Herr, Hunter Thompson, and Norman Mailer. These reporters felt that the enormity of cultural change and political upheaval in the 1960s had outrun their ability to tell stories in the usual way. Might we consider journalists' narrative failure, in such circumstances, a form of radical honesty? Or even a democratic virtue?

Didion (2003) has recently noted the differences between the responses of citizens and the political establishment (including journalists) in the weeks after September 11. On a West Coast book tour that fall, Didion said her audiences "recognized that even then, within days after the planes hit, there was a good deal of opportunistic ground being seized under cover of the clearly urgent need for increased security." Washington, she wrote, "was still talking about the protection and perpetuation of its own interests." And her listeners' response? "These people got it. They didn't like it. They stood up in public and they talked about it" (p. 54). Under such dire circumstances, citizens turned immediately to talk. But were their institutions listening? All too quickly, reflection yielded to retribution. At such moments, dialogue hopes to call us to our better nature, as creatures, as simply human beings. Conceived as a dialogic institution (Anderson, Dardenne, & Killenberg, 1994), journalism might have opened and defended a space for dialogue, where citizens could reflect, speak, and be heard. Journalism could have imagined its charge differently—not to inform, but to do whatever it could to prevent us from forging our portraits of grief into declarations of war.

16

Concluding Voices, Conversation Fragments, and a Temporary Synthesis

Rob Anderson,
Leslie A. Baxter, and Kenneth N. Cissna

A t the end of a lengthy and complex project, we struggled particularly with one decision: How should we conclude the book? Although dialogue itself is to a significant extent ongoing and "unfinalizable," as Bakhtin would say, publishing a book about it is a different story. Readers, being human, reasonably expect some sense of clarity as they turn to the final pages.

Regrettably, perhaps, we will not be able to provide much clarity in the traditional sense; certainly it is impossible to boil down our authors' complex ideas to bullet points. We simply are not aware of tidy or definitive ways to summarize the sprawling dialogue research in communication studies. A conclusion would not be conclusive, but rather might serve as a segue to subsequent voices. We do want to acknowledge that there are many such important voices beyond those represented between this book's covers. Surely they are now exploring fresh questions, considerations, and conflicts that we have not accounted for. (By the way, you know who you are.) In this transitory "conclusion," though, we merely hope to invite further conversation in a somewhat dialogic way; here, we hope to recreate something of the tone and substance of various conversations the three of us had while deciding how to shape the book.

Anthropologist Vincent Crapanzano (1990, 1992), building on ideas similar to Bakhtin's *superaddressee* and sociology's *reference group*, offers the concept *shadow dialogue*, which we have borrowed here. Crapanzano

259

believes that whenever humans communicate, we speak and listen not only to our immediate communication partners, but also with absent voices and persons who may never know of our imaginary invocation of them as auditors and interlocutors. This clearly is a phenomenon to which ethnographic interviewers must be attuned, as their dialogues with interviewees surely stimulate many shadow conversations in which informants' disclosures are also for the benefit of imagined audiences. A shadow dialogue experience, according to Crapanzano (1990), involves

> a position external to the immediate exchange, though never fixed or timeless, that enables [a dialogue partner] to reproduce the exchange and offer an interpretation of it. I should hasten to add that the other participants to the dialogue are also engaged in shadow dialogues that afford them external vantage points and that enable them to reproduce and interpret the dialogue when they choose. (p. 288)

Consistent with Bakhtin, Crapanzano suggests that this inner process occurs constantly as we talk with each other, and notes that something similar also often develops later, as communicators cognitively revisit conversations to make sense of their interactions through more focused "interpretive dialogues" (p. 289). In reconsidering our mutual effects, we are not generalizing, but rather enacting a dialogically concrete inner interplay of voices, however imaginary.

In a sense, this is the move we are about to make, however clumsily, by creating several conversation fragments that take into account other ways to imagine the book, as well as additional external voices, potential positions, and underconsidered themes. We also hope this approach invites extended interpretive dialogues in readers' reactions.

Fragment 1: Common Themes in Dialogic Perspectives

Leslie: Readers might wonder why we chose to organize the book more or less traditionally—by context—rather than by theme. After all, we have several dialogic themes that keep surfacing in multiple chapters.

Ken: We have the theme of *dialogue as creation*. Several of our contributors argue that dialogue is characterized by mystery and surprise, creating something unforeseen. The core idea here is that meaning is emergent, in the moments of meeting between people. You certainly address this in your chapter, Leslie, in your discussion of Bakhtin's dialogue as constitutive, and in the idea that the utterance is located between speakers. Rob and I pick up the same theme in

| | our chapter—both Buber and Rogers emphasize the emergence of meaning in the encounter between self and other. |

Rob: The theme of creation appears in other chapters, too. It's a central theme in the McNamee and Shotter chapter, the contribution by Pearce and Pearce, and the discussion of "peak experiences" by Goodall and Kellett. I think this theme appears, also, in the chapter by Stewart and his colleagues—the intellectual move to dialogue was created out of particular life experiences by the leading dialogic scholars.

Ken: *Dialogue as a conversation of voices in tension* also is a recurring theme in several chapters. Stewart and his colleagues point to the "tensionality" that appears as a common feature in the works of leading dialogic theorists. Leslie, you emphasize this in your discussion of Bakhtin's view that the social world is a contradiction-ridden, tension-filled unity of voices.

Leslie: Yes, but "voice" in two senses—the embodied "voices" of different people, and the verbal–ideological "voices" of different perspectives, values, or ideas. You're right in positioning Bakhtin as centered in conversation—the utterance, as he called it. The utterance isn't owned by one speaker or one voice. Strine's chapter, centered in Bakhtin, also emphasizes the multivocality of the utterance. So does Taylor, in his discussion of similarities and differences between Bakhtin and the *A-B-X* coorientation model.

Rob: And Deetz and Simpson clearly develop this theme in their discussion of discursive formations. Certainly Hawes's chapter, grounded in Bateson's work, emphasizes this theme, too. The tension of voices escalates because of the double binds of interaction. And there's the dialectical tension inherent in the peak experiences discussed by Goodall and Kellett.

Leslie: Although tensionality isn't particularly emphasized in the McNamee and Shotter and Pearce and Pearce chapters, certainly they are also centered in the communicative encounter between people.

Ken: So what we have in this second theme is a number of chapters dealing with the communicative experience, with several of them emphasizing the tensionality between voices.

Rob: A third theme is *dialogue as a relation of self-and-other.* Both the Hyde and Arnett chapters emphasize this theme in addressing the centrality of Other to the human experience. The Buber–Rogers dialogue shows this, and you also address the centrality of the self–other relation in your chapter, Leslie, in your discussion of Bakhtin's dialogism.

Leslie: What I most appreciate about our contributors' thinking on the self–other relation is that they don't gloss the celebration of Other. Truly taking others into account is hard work, rendered through taking him or her seriously.

Ken: And taking the Other seriously involves willingness to disagree with him or her at the same time you are open to change. The McPhail chapter speaks in a very personal way to the challenges of the self–other relation.

Rob: So do the Hawes and Strine essays. None of the authors who speak to this theme suggest that embracing the notion of the Other is somehow a simple undertaking. It is, however, a goal central to our humanity.

Leslie: Although these are the three themes of dialogue woven throughout the book, it should be apparent why we couldn't organize the book around these themes! Most of the chapters address multiple themes. Our chapters can't be pigeon-holed usefully into single themes.

Ken: Of course, the "big" theme shared by all the chapters is *dialogue as difference.*

Rob: The surprise and creativity of dialogue is wrought out of difference. The tensionality of voices is a residual of difference. The communicative encounter is a unity of different voices. And the self–other relation is a dance celebrating difference.

Leslie: I guess this explains the book's title, doesn't it? Dialogue studies create new ways to theorize difference. Certainly, this approach to difference is quite distinct from traditional approaches to conflict, where difference is framed as a problem to be somehow managed or resolved through appropriate conflict management practices that end in consensus. Dialogic communication theory is an effort to reclaim conflict.

Ken: If you couple this with the other dialogic themes we've just been talking about—celebrating otherness, embracing multivocality, legitimating emergent meaning created in the moment, and rejecting finalizability, dialogue theory harkens to many postmodernist themes, doesn't it?

Fragment 2: Postmodern Resonance

Rob: Ken, you and I have speculated that dialogue theorists such as Buber prefigure several contemporary postmodern themes. A postmodern orientation seems to be compatible with a dialogic commitment to creation—the notion that meanings are emergent, contingent, in flux.

Ken: Postmodern thinking also embraces meaning as fragmented, discontinuous, multiple, and dispersed.

Leslie: This is certainly a quality shared with a dialogic perspective. Dialogue involves a multivocality that's often contradiction-ridden—the different voices are crucial. Conceiving of the self not as an autonomous entity but as a relation between self-and-other also parallels the postmodern move to decenter the self.

Ken: Working from postmodern sensibilities, dialogue theorizing recasts subjective experience as a relational process: "self" emerges in the conversation with Other. This, of course, decenters the subject and means that the dialogic self is, of necessity, fragmented and fleeting.

Rob: The postmodern suspicion of "metanarratives"—authoritative discursive structures—is also shared by a dialogic perspective. A metanarrative is what Bakhtin would call a monologue—the dominance of one voice over the muted voices of alternative narratives.

Leslie: Certainly the constitutive view of communication found in dialogue theory parallels the postmodern rejection of the metanarrative of communication as a representational enterprise. Language-in-use is profoundly about creating realities in the moment, not merely representing preformed realities, whether speaker's cognitions or distant objects.

Ken: The postmodern sensibility is also one committed to Otherness, particularly marginalized, subaltern voices. Of course, this is central to the dialogic sensibility, as well.

Leslie: I don't think any of us is arguing that theorists such as Bakhtin and Buber were postmodernists in the sense that this term is usually applied these days. You talked about "prefiguring"—useful language, I think, because it asserts that some of the issues currently labeled as "postmodern" were presaged by earlier dialogic thinkers from the last century.

Ken: The point, I think, is that a productive conversation can develop between dialogic scholars and postmodern scholars—there is a common core of concerns to both traditions.

Fragment 3: Power in
Dialogue and the Power of Dialogue

Rob: There's also a productive conversation to be had between dialogic scholars and those who affiliate with various approaches to the politics of power—feminist theorists and theorists of racism, for example.

Ken: But what do we mean by "power"? Some people refer to "power" as something that is located in individuals (and their related social-group identities); that's one possible definition. From that perspective, it seems to me that the question facing dialogic theorists is how dialogue happens between people who vary in their power—how can voices of those with less power be heard? How can dialogue take place in the presence of social inequality?

Leslie: I think this meaning of power guided McPhail's essay, and can be found in much of race theory.

Ken: Yes, absolutely. Many white Americans deny that racism and other forms of social inequality exist, making dialogue appear seemingly easy—a conversation between different voices but voices thought to be on equal footing.

Leslie: And theorists looking at interracial encounters would urge dialogic scholars to complicate how social inequality affects the nature of dialogue.

Rob: Obviously, the same applies to feminist thinkers. Voice has been one of feminists' central concepts and central concerns. In many contexts, women's voices have been muted and dialogue implies that, necessarily, various and even divergent voices are heard.

Leslie: I think Bakhtin notes inequality of voices when he talks about voices in centripetal–centrifugal flux and his discussion of how speakers use others' voices to promote their own agendas. So there's some recognition that voices are not equal. But he under-theorizes this point, I think.

Ken: I don't think any serious dialogic scholarship suggests that dialogue is free of confrontation and influence. Speakers do have positions, and they voice them—often with passion and commitment. Influence isn't abandoned, but neither is it viewed as a linear process whose goal is to persuade the other to adopt one's own habits of heart and action.

Rob: Yes. Dialogic theorists recognize that influence happens, but it's a mutual form of influence, an emergent influence, anchored in responsiveness to the other's voice.

Leslie: Well, this brings us to a second way to think about power—power as an emergent process of mutual influence. In this second sense, power isn't located in individuals—it's located between persons, in the dialogic emergence that sits in the talk between them.

Ken: Yes, dialogue suggests the possibility for creating something new and surprising. Out of standing your ground and being willing to stick up for what you believe, you give the other the "gift" of your position, but this gift of hearing and seeing isn't intended to silence the voice (and position) of the other.

Rob: Don't some people assume that dialogue comes with a wishy-washy "anything's okay with me" attitude? No wonder there's a cynicism about its potency in human communication. Coupled with giving the other the gift of your position (as strongly as you experience it) is your willingness to be responsive to the corresponding gift that the other gives you, in exposing you to his or her own position. That gift—even after careful listening—could still be solid disagreement.

Leslie: And this is power as emergence—out of the process of each person's "gifting" to the other comes something that wouldn't have been predictable or even possible when the conversation began.

Fragment 4: Locating the Absences

Rob: Although these authors contribute such a wide range of ideas, it seems to me there will inevitably be gaps. For example, the book may underrepresent how dialogue theory could be applied to concrete contexts such as healthcare, education, freedom of expression, and organizational change. Are there other important absences?

Ken: Well, beyond what's been described in the book already, I'm wondering whether, in some way, dialogue scholarship could be framed as engaged scholarship—intended to make a difference in the world. For years, I've been interested in how scholars can conduct concrete and empirically sound research using actual communication encounters instead of just trying to discover attitudes and concerns about those encounters. It's possible that applied communication researchers would find our collection congenial to their interests, but maybe not immediately helpful enough in a practical way. Do we and our authors engage the dialogic aspects of research methodology enough?

Leslie: In some ways, the chapters offer quite a few research implications as the authors discuss their own programs and how they came to conceptualize dialogue as they do. Many of them, too, are self-aware about how their own subjectivities and involvements could have influenced their conclusions. But frankly, readers of these essays could be hard-pressed to construct a clear picture of how dialogic assumptions could inform the research enterprise itself. Now, this could be because no clear picture of this is possible, given the multiplicity of the forms of communication research and its contexts, or it could be so simply because to this point, with notable exceptions, we've seen few efforts to systematize the connections between dialogue and communication research. What do you think?

Ken: I suspect it's the latter. And maybe this involves paying more attention to the point I made earlier about engaged scholarship— whether we are investigating dialogue or anything else. Applying our theories in everyday life and being alert to the consequences is an inherently dialogic process of mutual influences. The lines between researcher and researched get awfully blurry.

Rob: Gadamer helps here, doesn't he? He imagines that truth and factuality are not to be discovered through applying so-called proper methods, but through the constant dialogic testing of observations and prejudices in the context of what we already think we know. Knowledge becomes constantly contingent by our being open to new learning and hearing its voices.

Ken: Right. The reason why it's tough to identify essential differences between those doing the research and those being researched is that we're all—as humans—doing research all the time. Researchers, especially in dialogue studies, aren't the spectators some folks would like to assume we are.

Leslie: Wait a minute, guys. I'm with you generally, but it's surely not that simple. There might be a danger in dismissing methods too readily. Even if I agree that spectatorship is a problem, which I do, that doesn't mean that we don't need carefully constructed methods for observation. Researchers are choosers. For example, even the diffuse and sometimes scattered work of Bakhtin can be turned into a coherent system for approaching texts and digging in—discovering the linguistic resources of dialogue that animate them.

Rob: Agreed. There's a useful tension, isn't there, between probing how complicated something really is, and still wanting to make it accessible? We want both. Researchers respect the complexity, but still have to translate the ideas into action when choosing appropriate methods.

Ken: Leslie mentioned texts a moment ago. When this methodological issue of handling texts comes up, I tend to think about rhetoric and the rhetorical tradition in our field. Does the book probe deeply enough into this tradition? Hyde's chapter approaches dialogic ethics from a rhetorical point of view, but there aren't a lot of scholars who approach dialogue with a rhetorical lens, are there?

Leslie: I think that's true among rhetorical scholars who adopt a traditional conception of rhetoric as persuasion. But there is some exciting dialogic work grounded in Buber and Bakhtin, for example, that is beginning to emerge among rhetorical scholars, especially among those who adopt constitutive approaches to rhetoric. And many feminist rhetorical scholars, it seems to me, draw on assumptions similar to those that ground dialogue scholars.

Rob: A key here seems to be a move away from a conception of communication as one-way influence. Especially in media and public sphere rhetoric, I know Pauly and others would hope to see more studies of deliberation, for example, as a mutual process even if mediated. There have been a few such projects; I'm thinking of the very solid Public Dialogue Consortium work that Pearce and Pearce discuss.

Leslie: There are many "dialogue" movements in the public sphere, but I think it's important to distinguish those in which the term *dialogue* is being used as a mere synonym for *conversation* as opposed to those efforts, like the Public Dialogue Consortium, in which *dialogue* has a particular meaning, grounded in theorists such as those mentioned in this volume.

Ken: I'm attracted to the impulse of the various "dialogue" movements to make a difference in the tenor of public democracy, but I agree with Leslie—just because something is labeled *dialogue* doesn't necessarily make it so, as we and our contributors are using this term.

Leslie: We made an explicit decision in this book to focus on established research programs in dialogue by communication scholars, but we're all aware of the interest in public discourse that cuts across many different disciplines by dialogic scholars who draw on the same theorists we draw from in communication studies—such as the interest from English, political science, theology, and philosophy.

Ken: In editing the book, we never set out to ensure equal coverage for all possible dialogic perspectives, but to invite some scholars who represent dialogue studies in communication to share where their own interests were taking them. I guess we'll hear in the responses from our readers where that approach leads.

References

Ackerman, B. A. (1980). *Social justice in the liberal state.* New Haven, CT: Yale University Press.

Althusser, L. (1969). *For Marx.* London: Verso.

Altman, I., & Taylor, D. (1973). *Social penetration: The development of interpersonal relationships.* New York: Holt, Rinehart & Winston.

Anderson, H. (1997). *Conversation, language, and possibilities: A postmodern approach to therapy.* New York: Basic Books.

Anderson, R. (1979). *Students as real people: Interpersonal communication and education.* Rochelle Park, NJ: Hayden.

Anderson, R. (1982). Phenomenological dialogue, humanistic psychology and pseudo-walls: A response and extension. *Western Journal of Speech Communication, 46,* 344–357.

Anderson, R. (1984). Response to the symposium "Empathic Listening." *Communication Education, 33,* 195–196.

Anderson, R., & Cissna, K. N. (1991). *The Buber-Rogers dialogue: Studying the influence of role, audience, and style.* Presented at the international, interdisciplinary conference "Martin Buber: His Impact on the Human Sciences," San Diego State University, San Diego, CA.

Anderson, R., & Cissna, K. N. (1996). Criticism and conversational texts: Rhetorical bases of role, audience, and style in the Buber-Rogers dialogue. *Human Studies, 19,* 85–118.

Anderson, R., & Cissna, K. N. (1997). *The Martin Buber-Carl Rogers dialogue: A new transcript with commentary.* Albany: State University of New York Press.

Anderson, R., Cissna, K. N., & Arnett, R. C. (Eds.). (1994). *The reach of dialogue: Confirmation, voice, and community.* Cresskill, NJ: Hampton Press.

Anderson, R., Dardenne, R., & Killenberg, G. M. (1994). *The conversation of journalism: Communication, community, and news.* Westport, CT: Praeger.

Anzaldúa, G. (2002). Preface: (Un)natural bridges, (un)safe spaces. In G. Anzaldúa & A. Keating (Eds.), *This bridge we call home: Radical visions for transformation* (pp. 1–5). New York: Routledge.

Apel, K. O. (1979). *Toward a transformation of philosophy* (G. Adey & D. Frisby, Trans.). London: Routledge & Kegan Paul.

Arendt, H. (1959). *The human condition.* New York: Anchor.

Arendt, H. (1968). *Men in dark times.* New York: Harcourt, Brace & World.

Arendt, H., & Jaspers, K. (1992). *Hannah Arendt/Karl Jaspers: Correspondence, 1926-1969* (R. Kimber & R. Kimber, Trans.; L. Kohler & H. Saner, Eds.). New York: Harcourt Brace Jovanovich.

Arlen, M. J. (1980). *Thirty seconds.* New York: Farrar, Straus & Giroux.

Arnett. R. C. (1978). Self-fulfillment and interpersonal communication? *Religious Communication Today, 1,* 23–28.

Arnett, R. C. (1980). *Dwell in peace: Applying nonviolence to everyday relationships.* Elgin, IL: The Brethren Press.

Arnett, R. C. (1981). Toward a phenomenological dialogue. *Western Journal of Speech Communication, 45,* 201–212.

Arnett, R. C. (1982). Rogers and Buber: Similarities, yet fundamental differences. *Western Journal of Speech Communication, 46,* 358–372.

Arnett, R. C. (1986). *Communication and community: Implications of Martin Buber's dialogue.* Carbondale: Southern Illinois University Press.

Arnett, R. C. (1989). What is dialogic communication? Friedman's contribution and clarification. *Person-Centered Review, 4,* 42–60.

Arnett, R. C. (1992). *Dialogic education: Conversation about ideas and between people.* Carbondale: Southern Illinois University Press.

Arnett, R. C. (1997). Therapeutic communication: A moral *cul de sac.* In S. L. Longenecker (Ed.), *The dilemma of Anabaptist piety: Strengthening or straining the bonds of community* (pp. 149–160). Camden, ME: Penobscot Press.

Arnett, R. C. (2001). Dialogic civility as pragmatic ethical praxis: An interpersonal metaphor for the public domain. *Communication Theory, 11,* 315–338.

Arnett, R. C., & Arneson, P. (1999). *Dialogic civility in a cynical age: Community, hope, and interpersonal relationships.* Albany: State University of New York Press.

Arnett, R. C., & Nakagawa, G. (1983). The assumptive roots of empathic listening: A critique. *Communication Education, 32,* 368–378.

Asante, M. K. (1987). *The Afrocentric idea.* Philadelphia: Temple University Press.

Aune, J. A. (1979). The contribution of Habermas to rhetorical validity. *Journal of the American Forensic Association, 16,* 104–111.

Ayres, J. (1984). Four approaches to interpersonal communication. *Western Journal of Speech Communication, 48,* 408–440.

Badiou, A. (2001). *Ethics: An essay on the understanding of evil.* London: Verso.

Bakhtin, M. M. (1965). *Rabelais and his world* (H. Iswolsky, Trans.). Bloomington: Indiana University Press.

Bakhtin, M. M. (1981). *The dialogic imagination: Four essays by M. M. Bakhtin* (M. Holquist, Ed.; C. Emerson & M. Holquist, Trans.). Austin: University of Texas Press.

Bakhtin, M. M. (1984). *Problems of Dostoevsky's poetics* (C. Emerson, Ed. & Trans.). Minneapolis: University of Minnesota Press.

Bakhtin, M. M. (1986). *Speech genres and other late essays* (C. Emerson & M. Holquist, Eds.; V. W. McGee, Trans.). Austin: University of Texas Press.

Bakhtin, M. M. (1990). *Art and answerability: Early philosophical works by M. M. Bakhtin* (M. Holquist & V. Liapunov, Eds.; V. Liapunov, Trans.). Austin: University of Texas Press.

Bakhtin, M. M. (1993). *Toward a philosophy of the act* (V. Liapunov & M. Holquist, Eds.; V. Liapunov, Trans.). Austin: University of Texas Press.

Baldwin, J. (1963). *The fire next time.* New York: Dell.

Barber, B. (1984). *Strong democracy: Participatory politics for a new age.* Berkeley: University of California Press.

Barber, B. (1988). *The conquest of politics: Liberal philosophy in democratic times.* Princeton, NJ: Princeton University Press.

Barber, B. (1989). Liberal democracy and the costs of consent. In N. L. Rosenblum (Ed.), *Liberalism and the moral life* (pp. 54–68). Cambridge, MA: Harvard University Press.

Barker, J. (1993). Tightening the iron cage—Concertive control in self-managing teams. *Administrative Science Quarterly, 38,* 408–437.

Barrett, F. J. (1998). Creativity and improvisation in jazz and organizations: Implications for organizational learnings. *Organization Science, 9,* 605–622.

Barthes, R. (1981). Theory of the text. In R. Young (Ed. & Trans.), *Untying the text: A post-structuralist reader* (pp. 31–47). Boston: Routledge & Kegan Paul.

Bateson, G. (1961). *Perceval's narrative: A patient's account of his psychosis.* Stanford, CA: Stanford University Press.

Bateson, G. (1972). *Steps to an ecology of mind.* New York: Ballantine.

Bateson, G. (1979). *Mind in nature: A necessary unity.* London: E. P. Dutton.

Bateson, G., Jackson, D. D., & Haley, J. (1956). Toward a theory of schizophrenia. *Behavioral Science, 1,* 251–264.

Bateson, G., Jackson, D. D., & Haley, J. (1963). A note on the double bind–1962. *Family Process, 2,* 154–161.

Baumann, Z. (1992). *Intimations of postmodernity.* London: Routledge.

Baxter, L. A. (1987). Symbols of relationship identity in relationship cultures. *Journal of Social and Personal Relationships, 4,* 261–280.

Baxter, L. A. (1990). Dialectical contradictions in relationship development. *Journal of Social and Personal Relationships, 7,* 69–88.

Baxter, L. A., & Braithwaite, D. O. (2002). Performing marriage: The marriage renewal ritual as cultural performance. *Southern Communication Journal, 67,* 94–109.

Baxter, L. A., Braithwaite, D. O., Bryant, L., & Wagner, A. (in press). Stepchildren's perceptions of the contradictions of communication with stepparents. *Journal of Social and Personal Relationships.*

Baxter, L. A., Braithwaite, D. O., Golish, T. D., & Olson, L. N. (2002). Contradictions of interaction for wives of elderly husbands with adult dementia. *Journal of Applied Communication Research, 30,* 1–26.

Baxter, L. A., Braithwaite, D. O., & Nicholson, J. (1999). Turning points in the development of blended families. *Journal of Social and Personal Relationships, 16,* 291–313.

Baxter, L. A., & Bullis, C. (1986). Turning points in developing romantic relationships. *Human Communication Research, 12,* 469–493.

Baxter, L. A., & Bylund, C. (in press). Social influence in close relationships. In J. S. Seiter & H. Gass (Eds.), *Readings in persuasion, social influence, and compliance-gaining.* New York: Allyn & Bacon.

Baxter, L. A., & DeGooyer, D., Jr. (2001). Perceived aesthetic characteristics of interpersonal conversations. *Southern Communication Journal, 67,* 1–18.

Baxter, L. A., Dun, T., & Sahlstein, E. (2001). Rules for relating communicated among social network members. *Journal of Social and Personal Relationships, 18,* 173–200.

Baxter, L. A., & Erbert, L. (1999). Perceptions of dialectical contradictions in turning points of development in heterosexual romantic relationships. *Journal of Social and Personal Relationships, 16,* 547–569.

Baxter, L. A., Mazanec, M., Nicholson, J., Pittman, G., Smith, K., & West, L. (1997). Everyday loyalties and betrayals in personal relationships. *Journal of Social and Personal Relationships, 14,* 655–678.

Baxter, L. A., & Montgomery, B. M. (1996). *Relating: Dialogues and dialectics.* New York: Guilford Press.

Baxter, L. A., & Pittman, G. (2001). Communicatively remembering turning points of relationship development. *Communication Reports, 14,* 1–18.

Baxter, L. A., & Simon, E. (1993). Relationship maintenance strategies and dialectical contradictions in personal relationships. *Journal of Social and Personal Relationships, 10,* 225–242.

Baxter, L. A., & West, L. (in press). Couple perceptions of their similarities and differences: A dialectical perspective. *Journal of Social and Personal Relationships.*

Baxter, L. A., & Widenmann, S. (1993). Revealing and not revealing the status of romantic relationships to social networks. *Journal of Social and Personal Relationships, 10,* 321–338.

Beatty, M. J., Behnke, R. R., & Banks, B. J. (1979). Elements of dialogic communication in Gandhi's second round table conference address. *Southern Speech Communication Journal, 44,* 386–398.

Becker, E. (1973). *The denial of death.* New York: The Free Press.

Beebe, B., & Lachmann, F. M. (2002). *Infant research and adult treatment: Co-constructing interactions.* Hillsdale, NJ: Analytic Press.

Belkin, L. (1999, October 31). Parents blaming parents. *The New York Times Magazine,* 60–67, 78, 94, 100.

Bellah, R. N., Madsen, R., Sullivan, W. M., Swidler, A., & Tipton, S. M. (1985). *Habits of the heart: Individualism and commitment in American life.* Berkeley: University of California Press.

Berger, C. R., & Calabrese, R. (1975). Some explorations in initial interaction and beyond: Toward a developmental theory of interpersonal communication. *Human Communication Research, 1,* 99–112.

Bernasconi, R. (1988). "Failure communication" as a surplus: Dialogue and lack of dialogue between Buber and Levinas. In R. Bernasconi (Ed.), *The provocation of Levinas* (pp. 100–135). London: Routledge.

Bernstein, R. (1986). *Philosophical profiles.* Philadelphia: University of Pennsylvania Press.

Billig, M. (1987). *Arguing and thinking: A rhetorical approach to social psychology.* Cambridge, UK: Cambridge University Press.

Binn, S. (1963). The fire next time. Review of *The fire next time* by James Baldwin. *New York Times.* Retrieved August 30, 2002, from http://partners.nytimes.com/books/98/03/29/specials/baldwin-fire.html

Bloom, H. (1992). *The American religion.* New York: Simon & Schuster.

Blumer, H. (1969). *Symbolic interactionism: Perspective and method.* Englewood Cliffs, NJ: Prentice-Hall.

Boal, A. (1985). *Theatre of the oppressed* (C. & M. McBride, Trans.). New York: Theatre Communications Group.

Bohm, D. (1951). *Quantum theory.* New York: Prentice-Hall.

Bohm, D. (1966). *The special theory of relativity.* New York: W. A. Benjamin.

Bohm, D. (1980). *Wholeness and the implicate order.* London: Routledge.

Bohm, D. (1990). *On dialogue.* Ojai, CA: David Bohm Seminars.

Bohm, D. (1996). *On dialogue* (L. Nichol, Ed.). London: Routledge.

Bohm, D., Factor, D., & Garrett. P. (1991). *Dialogue: A proposal.* Retrieved October 3, 2002, from http://www.infed.org/archives/e-texts/bohm_dialogue.htm

Bohman, J. (1996). *Public deliberation: Pluralism, complexity, and democracy.* Cambridge, MA: MIT Press.

Bonhoeffer, D. (1955). *Ethics* (N. H. Smith, Trans.). New York: Touchstone.

Borgman, J. (2001, September 23). Aftermath. *The Cincinnati Enquirer,* p. F1.

Bormann, D. R. (1980). Adam Muller on the dialogic nature of rhetoric. *Quarterly Journal of Speech, 66,* 169–181.

Bowers, P. J. (1998). *Taylor's practical reason and moral decision-making among journalists.* Unpublished doctoral dissertation, Stanford University.

Brady, P. (1990). *A certain blindness: A Black family's quest for the promise of America.* Atlanta: ALP Publishing.

Braithwaite, D. O., & Baxter, L. A. (1995). "I do" again: The relational dialectics of renewing marriage vows. *Journal of Social and Personal Relationships, 12,* 177–198.

Braithwaite, D. O., & Baxter, L. A. (2002, February). *"You're my parent but you're not my parent": Contradictions of communication between stepchildren and their nonresidential parents.* Paper presented at the annual meeting of the Western States Communication Association, Long Beach, CA.

Braithwaite, D. O., Baxter, L. A., & Harper, A. M. (1998). The role of rituals in the management of the dialectical tension of "old" and "new" in blended families. *Communication Studies, 48,* 101–112.

Bramson, L. (1961). *The political context of sociology.* Princeton, NJ: Princeton University Press.

Bridge, K., & Baxter, L. A. (1992). Blended relationships: Friends as work associates. *Western Journal of Communication, 56,* 200–225.

Brown, C. T., & Keller, P. W. (1973). *Monologue to dialogue: An exploration of interpersonal communication.* Englewood Cliffs, NJ: Prentice-Hall.

Brown, C. T., & Van Riper, C. (1973). *Communication in human relationships.* Skokie, IL: National Textbook.

Bruner, J. (1990). *Acts of meaning.* Cambridge, MA: Harvard University Press.

Buber, M. (1957). Elements of the interhuman. *Psychiatry, 20,* 105–113.

Buber, M. (1958). *I and thou* (2nd ed.; R. G. Smith, Trans.). New York: Scribner.

Buber, M. (1965a). *Between man and man* (M. Friedman, Ed.; R. G. Smith, Trans.). New York: Macmillan.

Buber, M. (1965b). *The knowledge of man: A philosophy of the interhuman* (M. Friedman, Ed.; M. Friedman & R. G. Smith, Trans.). New York: Harper & Row.

Buber, M. (1967a). Hope for this hour. In F. W. Matson & A. Montagu (Eds.), *The human dialogue: Perspectives on communication* (pp. 306–312). New York: Free Press.

Buber, M. (1967b). Replies to my critics. In P. A. Schilpp & M. Friedman (Eds.), *The philosophy of Martin Buber* (pp. 689–744). New York: Open Court.

Buber, M. (1970). *I and thou* (W. Kaufmann, Trans.). New York: Scribner.

Buber, M. (1973). *Meetings* (M. Friedman, Ed.). LaSalle, IL: Open Court Press.

Buber, M. (1991). *Tales of the Hasidim* (O. Marx, Trans.). New York: Schocken Books.

Buber, M. (1996). *Paths in utopia* (R. F. C. Hull, Trans.). Syracuse, NY: Syracuse University Press.

Buber, M. (1998). *The knowledge of man: Selected essays* (M. Friedman, Ed.; M. Friedman & R. G. Smith, Trans.). New York: Humanity Books.

Burke, K. (1989). *On symbols and society* (J. R. Gusfield, Ed.). Chicago: University of Chicago Press.

Burleson, B. R. (1979). On the foundations of rationality: Toulmin, Habermas, and the a priori of reason. *Journal of the American Forensic Association, 16,* 112–127.

Burleson, B. R., & Kline, S. L. (1979). Habermas' theory of communication: A critical explication. *Quarterly Journal of Speech, 65,* 412–428.

Butler, J. (1997a). *Excitable speech: A politics of the performative.* New York: Routledge.

Butler, J. (1997b). *The psychic life of power.* Stanford, CA: Stanford University Press.

Butler, J. (1999). *Gender trouble* (10th anniversary ed.). New York: Routledge.

Bybee, J., & Fleischman, S. (1995). *Modality in grammar and discourse.* Amsterdam: John Benjamins.

Cantor, M. G. (1971). *The Hollywood TV producer: His work and his audience.* New York: Basic.

Carey, J. W. (Ed.). (1988). *Media, myths, and narratives: Television and the press.* Newbury Park, CA: Sage.

Carey, J. W. (1989). *Communication as culture: Essays on media and society.* Boston: Unwin Hyman.

Carey, J. W. (1997). *James Carey: A critical reader* (E.S. Munson & C. A. Warren, Eds.). Minneapolis: University of Minnesota Press.

Casey, D. (1999). Levinas and Buber: Transcendence and society. *Sophia, 38,* 69–92.

Caspary, W. R. (2000). *Dewey on democracy.* Ithaca, NY: Cornell University Press.

Cervenak, S., Cespedes, K., Souza, C., & Straub, A. (2002). Imagining differently: The politics of listening in a feminist classroom. In G. Anzaldúa & A. Keating (Eds.), *This bridge we call home: Radical visions for transformation* (pp. 341–356). New York: Routledge.

Charity, A. (1995). *Doing public journalism.* New York: Guilford.

Chasin, R., Herzig, M., Roth, S., Chasin, L., Becker, C., & Stains, R. R., Jr. (1996). From diatribe to dialogue on divisive public issues: Approaches drawn from family therapy. *Mediation Quarterly, 13,* 323–345.

Chen, K-H. (1987). Beyond truth and method: On misreading Gadamer's praxical hermeneutics. *Quarterly Journal of Speech, 73,* 183–199.

Chevigny, P. (1988). *More speech: Dialogue rights and modern liberty.* Philadelphia: Temple University Press.

Chomsky, N. (2002). *Media control: The spectacular achievements of propaganda.* New York: Seven Stories Press.

Christians, C. G. (1977). Fifty years of scholarship in media ethics. *Journal of Communication, 27*(4), 19–29.

Christians, C. G. (1988). Dialogic communication theory and cultural studies. *Studies in Symbolic Interaction, 9,* 3–31.

Christians, C. G. (1991). Communication ethics. *Communication Research Trends, 11*(4), pp. 1–34.

Christians, C. G. (1995). Communication ethics as the basis of genuine democracy. In P. Lee (Ed.), *The democratization of communication* (pp. 75–91). Cardiff, UK: University of Wales Press.

Christians, C. G. (1997). The common good and universal values. In J. Black (Ed.), *Mixed news: The public/civic/communitarian journalism debate* (pp. 18–33). Mahwah, NJ: Lawrence Erlbaum.

Christians, C. G. (2000). Social dialogue and media ethics. *Ethical Perspectives, 7*(2–3), 182–193.

Christians, C. G., Ferré, J. P., & Fackler, P. M. (1993). *Good news: Social ethics and the press.* New York: Oxford University Press.

Cissna, K. N. (Ed.) (1995). *Applied communication in the 21st century.* Mahwah, NJ: Lawrence Erlbaum.

Cissna, K. N., & Anderson, R. (1986, November). *Empathy, genuineness and communication: The concept of dialogue of Carl R. Rogers.* Paper presented at the annual meeting of the Speech Communication Association, Chicago.

Cissna, K. N., & Anderson, R. (1990). The contributions of Carl Rogers to a philosophical praxis of dialogue. *Western Journal of Speech Communication, 54*, 125–147.

Cissna, K. N., & Anderson, R. (1994a). Communication and the ground of dialogue. In R. Anderson, K. N. Cissna, & R. C. Arnett (Eds.), *The reach of dialogue: Confirmation, voice, and community* (pp. 9–30). Cresskill, NJ: Hampton.

Cissna, K. N., & Anderson, R. (1994b). The 1957 Martin Buber-Carl Rogers dialogue, as dialogue. *Journal of Humanistic Psychology, 34*, 11–45.

Cissna, K. N., & Anderson, R. (1996). Dialogue in public: Looking critically at the Buber-Rogers dialogue. In M. Friedman (Ed.), *Martin Buber and the human sciences* (pp. 191–206). Albany: State University of New York Press.

Cissna, K. N., & Anderson, R. (1997). Carl Rogers in dialogue with Martin Buber: A new analysis. *Person-Centered Journal, 4*, 4–13.

Cissna, K. N., & Anderson, R. (1998a). Correction to: "Carl Rogers in dialogue with Martin Buber: A new analysis." *Person-Centered Journal, 5*, 63–65.

Cissna, K. N., & Anderson, R. (1998b). Theorizing about dialogic moments: The Buber-Rogers position and postmodern themes. *Communication Theory, 8*, 63–104.

Cissna, K. N., & Anderson, R. (2002). *Moments of meeting: Buber, Rogers, and the potential for public dialogue.* Albany: State University of New York Press.

Cissna, K. N., & Sieburg, E. (1979, February). *Interactional foundations of interpersonal confirmation.* A paper presented at the International Communication Association/ National Communication Association Postdoctoral Conference, "Human Communication from the Interactional View," Asilomar, CA.

Cissna, K. N., & Sieburg, E. (1981). Patterns of interactional confirmation and disconfirmation. In C. Wilder-Mott & J. H. Weakland (Eds.), *Rigor and imagination: Essays from the legacy of Gregory Bateson* (pp. 253–282). New York: Praeger.

Clark, A. (1973). Martin Buber, dialogue, and the philosophy of rhetoric. In D. G. Douglas (Ed.), *Philosophers on rhetoric* (pp. 225–242). Skokie, IL: National Textbook.

Clark, K., & Holquist, M. (1984). *Mikhail Bakhtin.* Cambridge, MA: The Belknap Press of Harvard University Press.

Cloke, K., & Goldsmith, J. (2000). *Resolving personal and organizational conflict.* San Francisco: Jossey-Bass.

Cloud, J. (2001, March 19). The legacy of Columbine. *Time*, 32–35.

Cohen, R. A. (1985). Introduction. In E. Levinas, *Time and the other* (R. A. Cohen, Trans.; pp. 1–27). Pittsburgh, PA: Duquesne University Press.

Cohen, R. A. (1998). Introduction. In E. Levinas, *Otherwise than being or beyond essence* (A. Lingis, Trans.; pp. vi–xvi). Pittsburgh, PA: Duquesne University Press.

Cohn, M., & Buber, R. (1980). *Martin Buber: A bibliography of his writings 1897–1978*. Jerusalem and Munich: Magnes Press and K. G. Saur.

Colker, R. (1992). *Abortion & dialogue: Pro-choice, pro-life, & American law*. Bloomington: University of Indiana Press.

Collins, P. H. (1986). Learning from the outsider within. *Social Problems, 23*, 514–532.

Collins, P. H. (1990). *Black feminist thought: Knowledge, consciousness, and the politics of empowerment*. Boston: Unwin Hyman.

Collins, P. H. (1998). *Fighting words: Black women and the search for justice*. Minneapolis: University of Minnesota Press.

Collins, P. H. (2000). Comment on Hekman's "Truth and method: Feminist standpoint theory revisited": Where's the power? In C. Allen and J. Howard (Eds.), *Provoking feminisms* (pp. 43–49). Chicago: University of Chicago Press.

Conquergood, D. (1985). Performing as a moral act: Ethical dimensions of the ethnography of performance. *Literature in Performance, 5*, 1–13.

Conquergood, D. (1988). Health theatre in a Hmong refugee camp: Performance, communication, and culture. *Drama Review, 32*, 174–208.

Conquergood, D. (1991). Rethinking ethnography: Towards a critical cultural politics. *Communication Monographs, 58*, 179–194.

Conquergood, D. (1992). Ethnography, rhetoric, and performance. *Quarterly Journal of Speech, 78*, 80–97.

Conquergood, D. (1998). Beyond the text: Toward a performative cultural politics. In S. Dailey (Ed.), *The future of performance studies: Visions and revisions* (pp. 25–36). Annandale, VA: National Communication Association.

Conquergood, D. (2002). Performance studies: Interventions and radical research. *TDR: The Drama Review, 46*, 145–156.

Converse, J. M. (1987). *Survey research in the United States: Roots and emergence 1890–1960*. Berkeley: University of California Press.

Cook, G. A. (1993). *George Herbert Mead: The making of a social pragmatist*. Urbana: University of Illinois Press.

Cooperrider, D. L., & Whitney, D. (2002). *A positive revolution in change: Appreciative inquiry*. Retrieved December 5, 2002, from http://www.taosinstitute.net/coopwhitney1.doc

Corrigan, D. H. (1999). *The public journalism movement in America: Evangelists in the newsroom*. Westport, CT: Praeger.

Cortese, A. (1990). *Ethnic ethics: The restructuring of moral theory*. Albany: State University of New York Press.

Cox, J. R. (2001). Reclaiming the "indecorous" voice: Public participation by low-income communities in environmental decision-making. In C. Short & D. Hardy-Short (Eds.), *Proceedings of the fifth biennial conference on communication and the environment* (pp. 21–31). Flagstaff, AZ: Northern Arizona University, School of Communication.

Craig, R. T. (1989). Communication as a practical discipline. In B. Dervin, L. Grossberg, B. J. O'Keefe, & E. Wartella (Eds.), *Rethinking communication: Vol. 1. Paradigm issues* (pp. 97–122). Newbury Park, CA: Sage.

Crapanzano, V. (1990). On dialogue. In T. Maranhao (Ed.), *The interpretation of dialogue* (pp. 269–291). Chicago: University of Chicago Press.

Crapanzano, V. (1992). *Hermes' dilemma and Hamlet's desire: On the epistemology of interpretation*. Cambridge, MA: Harvard University Press.

Crenshaw, K., Gotanda, N., Peller, G., & Thomas, K. (Eds.). (1996). *Critical race theory: The key writings that formed the movement*. New York: New Press.

Cronen, V. E. (2001). Practical theory, practical art, and the pragmatic-systemic account of inquiry. *Communication Theory, 11*, 14–35.

Cronen, V. E., & Pearce, W. B. (1985). Toward an explanation of how the Milan method works: An invitation to a systemic epistemology and the evolution of family systems. In D. Campbell & R. Draper (Eds.), *Applications of systemic family therapy: The Milan approach* (pp. 69–86). London: Grune & Stratton.

Csikszentmihalyi, M. (1990). *Flow: The psychology of optimal experience*. New York: Harper & Row.

Cushman, D. P., & Dietrich, D. (1979). A critical reconstruction of Jürgen Habermas' holistic approach to rhetoric as social philosophy. *Journal of the American Forensic Association, 16*, 128–137.

Cushman, P. (1995). *Constructing the self, constructing America*. Reading, MA: Addison Wesley.

Czarniawska, B. (1997). *Narrating the organization: Dramas of institutional identity*. Chicago: University of Chicago Press.

Czubaroff, J. (2000). Dialogical rhetoric: An application of Martin Buber's philosophy of dialogue. *Quarterly Journal of Speech, 86*, 168–189.

Czubaroff, J., & Friedman, M. (2000). A conversation with Maurice Friedman. *Southern Communication Journal, 65*, 243–254.

Dallmayr, F. R. (1984). Introduction. In M. Theunissen, *The other: Studies in the social ontology of Husserl, Heidegger, Sartre, and Buber* (C. Macann, Trans.; pp. ix–xxi). Cambridge, MA: MIT Press.

Daniels, S. E., & Walker, G. (2001). *Working through environmental conflict: The collaborative learning approach*. London: Praeger.

Darnell, D. K., & Brockriede W. (1976). *Persons communicating*. Englewood Cliffs, NJ: Prentice-Hall.

Darnton, R. (1990). Journalism: All the news that fits we print. In *The kiss of Lamourette: Reflections in cultural history* (pp. 60–93). New York: Norton.

Davis, C. (1996). *Levinas: An introduction*. Notre Dame, IN: University of Notre Dame Press.

Deetz, S. (1973a). An understanding of science and a hermeneutic science of understanding. *Journal of Communication, 23*, 139–159.

Deetz, S. (1973b). Words without things: Toward a social phenomenology of language. *Quarterly Journal of Speech, 59*, 40–51.

Deetz, S. (1978). Conceptualizing human understanding: Gadamer's hermeneutics and American communication studies. *Communication Quarterly, 26*, 12–23.

Deetz, S. (1990). Reclaiming the subject matter as a guide to mutual understanding: Effectiveness and ethics in interpersonal interaction. *Communication Quarterly, 38*, 226–43.

Deetz, S. (1992). *Democracy in an age of corporate colonization: Developments in communication and the politics of everyday life*. Albany: State University of New York Press.

Deetz, S. (1995). *Transforming communication, transforming business: Building responsive and responsible workplaces.* Cresskill, NJ: Hampton Press.

Deetz, S. (1998). Discursive formations, strategized subordination, and self-surveillance: An empirical case. In A. McKinlay & K. Starkey (Eds.), *Foucault, management and organizational theory* (pp. 151–172). London: Sage.

Deleuze, G. (1983). *Nietzsche and philosophy.* London: Athlone Press.

Deleuze, G., & Parnet, C. (1987). *Dialogues.* New York: Columbia University Press.

Delgado, R., & Stefancic, J. (Eds.). (1997). *Critical white studies: Looking behind the mirror.* Philadelphia: Temple University Press.

De Lima, V., & Christians, C. (1979). Paulo Freire: The political dimensions of dialogic communication. *Communication, 4,* 133–155.

Denhardt, R.B. (1981). *In the shadow of organization.* Lawrence, KS: Regents Press.

Denzin, N. (2002). *Interpretive interactionism* (2nd ed.). Thousand Oaks, CA: Sage.

Derrida, J. (1973). *Speech and phenomena* (D. B. Allison & N. Garver, Trans.). Evanston, IL: Northwestern University Press.

Derrida, J. (1997). *Of grammatology* (G. C. Spivak, Trans.). Baltimore: Johns Hopkins University Press.

Derrida, J. (1999). *Adieu to Emmanuel Levinas* (P. A. Brault & M. Naas, Trans.). Stanford, CA: Stanford University Press.

Dervin, B., Grossberg, L., O'Keefe, B. J., & Wartella, E. (Eds.). (1989). *Rethinking communication: Vol. 1. Paradigm issues.* Newbury Park, CA: Sage.

Dewey, J. (1927). *The public and its problems.* New York: Henry Holt.

Dewey, J. (1944). *Democracy and education.* New York: The Free Press. (Original work published 1916)

DIA•logos. (2001). *The approach.* Retrieved March 22, 2002 from http://www.thinkingtogether.com/company.html

Dialogue Group. (2002). *The Dialogue Group.* Retrieved March 24, 2002, from http://www.thedialoguegrouponline.com/index.html

Didion, J. (2003, January 16). Fixed opinions, or the hinge of history. *New York Review of Books, 50,* 54–59.

Dixon, N. M. (1996). *Perspectives on dialogue: Making talk developmental for individuals and organizations.* Greensboro, NC: Center for Creative Leadership.

Drew, R. (2001). *Karaoke nights: An ethnographic rhapsody.* Walnut Creek, CA: AltaMira Press.

Du Bois, W. E. B. (1982). *The souls of black folk.* New York: New American Library.

Eaglestone, R. (1997). *Reading after Levinas.* Edinburgh: Edinburgh University Press.

Eason, D. (1990). The New Journalism and the image-world. In N. Sims (Ed.), *Literary journalism in the twentieth century* (pp. 191–205). New York: Oxford University Press.

Ede, L. S., & Lunsford, A. (1990). *Singular texts/Plural authors: Perspectives on collaborative writing.* Carbondale: Southern Illinois University Press.

Eisenberg, E. (1990). Jamming: Transcendence through organizing. *Communication Research, 17,* 139–164.

Eisenberg, E. (2001). Building a mystery: Toward a new theory of communication and identity. *Journal of Communication, 51,* 534–552.

Eisenberg, E. M., & Goodall, H. L., Jr. (1993). *Organizational communication: Balancing creativity and constraint.* New York: St. Martin's Press.

Eisenberg, E., & Goodall, H. L., Jr. (2001). *Organizational communication: Balancing creativity and constraint* (3rd ed.). New York: Bedford/St. Martin's.

Eliot, T. S. (1944). *Four quartets.* London: Faber and Faber.

Ellinor, L., & Gerard, G. (1998). *Dialogue: Rediscover the transforming power of conversation.* New York: Wiley.

Elliott, P. (1972). *The making of a television series: A case study in the sociology of culture.* Beverly Hills, CA: Sage.

Ellis, C., & Bochner, A. (Eds.). (1996). *Composing ethnography: Alternative forms of qualitative writing.* Walnut Creek, CA: AltaMira Press.

Ellul, J. (1964). *The technological society* (J. Wilkinson, Trans.). New York: Anchor.

Ellul, J. (1985). *The humiliation of the word* (J. M. Hanks, Trans.). Grand Rapids, MI: William B. Eerdmans.

Emerson, C. (1997). *The first hundred years of Mikhail Bakhtin.* Princeton, NJ: Princeton University Press.

Ericson, R., Baranek, P., & Chan, J. (1989). *Negotiating control: A study of news sources.* Toronto: University of Toronto Press.

Ettema, J. S., & Glasser, T. L. (1998). *Custodians of conscience: Investigative journalism and public virtue.* New York: Columbia University Press.

Etzioni, A. (1993). *The spirit of community: Rights, responsibilities, and the communitarian agenda.* New York: Crown.

Evans, S. M., & Boyte, H. C. (1992). *Free spaces: The sources of democratic change in America* (Rev. ed.). Chicago: University of Chicago Press.

Farrell, T. B. (1979). Habermas on argumentation theory: Some emerging topics. *Journal of the American Forensic Association, 16,* 77–82.

Farrell, T. B. (1983). Aspects of coherence in conversation and rhetoric. In R. T. Craig & K. Tracy (Eds.), *Conversational coherence: Form, structure, and strategy* (pp. 259–284). Beverly Hills, CA: Sage.

Farrell, T. J. (2000). *Walter Ong's contributions to cultural studies: The phenomenology of the word and I-Thou communication.* Cresskill, NJ: Hampton Press.

Faulkner, R. R. (1971). *Hollywood studio musicians: Their work and careers in the recording industry.* Chicago: Aldine.

Ferguson, M., & Golding, P. (Eds.). (1997). *Cultural studies in question.* London: Sage.

Ferrarotti, F. (1988). *The end of conversation: The impact of mass media on modern society.* New York: Greenwood.

Fisher, B. A. (1978). *Perspectives on human communication.* New York: Macmillan.

Fisher, P. (1998). *Wonder, the rainbow, and the aesthetics of rare experiences.* Cambridge, MA: Harvard University Press.

Fisher, W. R. (1987). *Human communication as narration: Toward a philosophy of reason, value, and action.* Columbia: University of South Carolina Press.

Fishkin, J. S. (1991). *Democracy and deliberation: New directions for democratic reform.* New Haven, CT: Yale University Press.

Fishkin, J. S. (1992). *The dialogue of justice: Toward a self-reflective society.* New Haven, CT: Yale University Press.

Fishman, M. (1980). *Manufacturing the news.* Austin: University of Texas Press.

Fiske, J. (1987). *Television culture.* London: Methuen.

Fiske, J. (1989a). *Reading the popular.* Boston: Unwin Hyman.

Fiske, J. (1989b). *Understanding popular culture.* Boston: Unwin Hyman.

Fletcher, J. (1962). *Moral responsibility: Situational ethics at work.* Philadelphia: Westminster Press.

Forster, E. M. (1989). *Howard's End.* New York: Vintage Books.

Fortis, C. (Producer), & Wolfe, G. C. (Director). (1993). *Fires in the mirror* [Video]. New York: PBS Video.

Foss, K. A., & Foss, S. K. (1991). *Women speak: The eloquence of women's lives.* Prospect Heights, IL: Waveland.

Foucault, M. (1970). *The order of things: An archaeology of the human sciences.* New York: Random House.

Foucault, M. (1977). *Language, counter-memory, practice: Selected essays and interviews* (D. Bouchard, Ed.). Ithaca, NY: Cornell University Press.

Foucault, M. (2001). *Fearless speech* (J. Pearson, Ed.). Los Angeles, CA: Semiotext(e).

Francesconi, R. (1986). The implications of Habermas's theory of legitimation for rhetorical criticism. *Communication Monographs, 53,* 16–35.

Frankl. V. (1974). *Man's search for meaning: An introduction to logotherapy* (I. Lasch, Trans.). New York: Pocket Books.

Fraser, N. (1989). *Unruly practices: Power, discourse, and gender in contemporary social theory.* Minneapolis: University of Minnesota Press.

Fraser, N. (1992). Rethinking the public sphere: A contribution to the critique of actually existing democracy. In C. Calhoun (Ed.), *Habermas and the public sphere* (pp. 109–142). Cambridge, MA: MIT Press.

Fraser, N. (2000). Recognition without ethics. In M. Garber, B. Hanssen, & R. L. Walkowitz (Eds.), *The turn to ethics* (pp. 95–126). New York: Routledge.

Freire, P. (1990). *Pedagogy of the oppressed* (M. B. Ramos, Trans.). New York: Continuum.

Freire, P. (1998). *Pedagogy of freedom: Ethics, democracy, and civic courage.* New York: Rowman & Littlefield.

Friedman, M. (1955). *Martin Buber: The life of dialogue.* Chicago: University of Chicago Press.

Friedman, M. (1965). Introductory essay. In M. Buber, *The knowledge of man: Selected essays* (M. Friedman, Ed.; M. Friedman & R. G. Smith, Trans.; pp. 1–48). New York: Harper.

Friedman, M. (1974). *Touchstones of reality: Existential trust and the community of peace.* New York: E. P. Dutton.

Friedman, M. (1981). *Martin Buber's life and work: The early years 1878–1923.* New York: E. P. Dutton.

Friedman, M. (1982). *The human way: A dialogic approach to religion and human experience.* Chambersburg, PA: Anima.

Friedman, M. (1983a). *The confirmation of otherness: In family, community, and society.* New York: Pilgrim Press.

Friedman, M. (1983b). *Martin Buber's life and work: The later years 1945–1965.* New York: E. P. Dutton.

Friedman, M. (1983c). *Martin Buber's life and work: The middle years 1923–1945.* New York: E. P. Dutton.

Friedman, M. (1985). *The healing dialogue in psychotherapy.* New York: Jason Aronson.

Friedman, M. (1986). Carl Rogers and Martin Buber: Self-actualization and dialogue. *Person-Centered Review, 1,* 409–435.

Friedman, M. (1992). *Dialogue and the human image: Beyond humanistic psychology.* Newbury Park, CA: Sage.

Friedman, M. (Ed.). (1996). *Martin Buber and the human sciences.* Albany: State University of New York Press.

Friedman, M. (2001). Martin Buber and Mikhail Bakhtin: The dialogue of voices and the word that is spoken. *Religion and Literature, 33,* 25–36.

Friedman, P. G. (1978). *Interpersonal communication: Innovations in instruction.* Washington, DC: National Education Association.

Gadamer, H.-G. (1975). *Truth and method* (G. Barden & J. Cummings, Eds. & Trans.). New York: Seabury Press.

Gadamer, H.-G. (1976). *Philosophical hermeneutics* (D. E. Linge, Ed. & Trans.). Berkeley: University of California Press.

Gadamer, H.-G. (1980). *Dialogue and dialectic: Eight hermeneutical studies on Plato* (P. C. Smith, Trans.). New Haven, CT: Yale University Press.

Gadamer, H.-G. (1982). *Truth and method* (2nd ed.; G. Barden & J. Cumming, Trans.). New York: Crossroad.

Gadamer, H.-G. (1985). *Philosophical apprenticeships* (R. R. Sullivan, Trans.). Cambridge, MA: MIT Press.

Gadamer, H.-G. (1989a). Text and interpretation (D. J. Schmidt & R. Palmer, Trans.). In D. P. Michelfelder & R. E. Palmer (Eds.), *Dialogue and deconstruction: The Gadamer-Derrida encounter* (pp. 21–51). Albany: State University of New York Press.

Gadamer, H.-G. (1989b). *Truth and method* (2nd Rev. ed.; J. Weinsheimer & D. G. Marshall, Trans.). New York: Crossroad.

Gadamer, H.-G. (1997). Reflections on my philosophical journey. In L. E. Hahn (Ed.), *The philosophy of Hans-Georg Gadamer* (pp. 555–602). Chicago, IL: Open Court.

Gans, H. (1979). *Deciding what's news: A study of* CBS Evening News, NBC Nightly News, Newsweek, *and* Time. New York: Pantheon.

Gardiner, M. (1992). *The dialogics of critique: M. M. Bakhtin and the theory of ideology.* New York: Routledge.

Garfinkel, H. (1967). *Studies in ethnomethodology.* Englewood Cliffs, NJ: Prentice-Hall.

Garnham, N. (1990). *Capitalism and communication: Global culture and the economics of information.* Newbury Park, CA: Sage.

Garnham, N. (2000). *Emancipation, the media, and modernity: Arguments about the media and social theory.* New York: Oxford University Press.

Gates, H. L., Jr. (1990). The master's pieces: On canon formation and the African-American tradition. *South Atlantic Quarterly, 89,* 89–111.

Geertz, C. (1979). From the native's point of view: On the nature of anthropological understanding. In P. Rabinow & W. M. Sullivan (Eds.), *Interpretive social science: A reader* (pp. 225–242). Berkeley: University of California Press.

Geertz, C. (1983). *Local knowledge.* New York: Basic Books.

Gergen, K. J. (1991). *The saturated self.* New York: Basic Books.

Gergen, K. J. (1994). *Realities and relationships: Soundings in social construction.* Cambridge, MA: Harvard University Press.

Gergen, K. J. (1999). *An invitation to social construction.* Thousand Oaks, CA: Sage.

Gergen, K. J., McNamee, S., & Barrett, F. (2001). Toward a vocabulary of transformative dialogue. *International Journal of Public Administration, 24,* 697–707. Retrieved

November 26, 2002, from http://www.swarthmore.edu/SocSci/kgergen1/web/page.phtml?id=manu23&st=manuscripts&hf=1

Gibb, J. R. (1961). Defensive communication. *Journal of Communication, 11,* 141–148.

Gibbs, N., & Roche, T. (1999, December 20). The Columbine tapes. *Time,* 40–51.

Giddens, A. (1989). The orthodox consensus and the emerging synthesis. In B. Dervin, L. Grossberg, B. J. O'Keefe, & E. Wartella (Eds.), *Rethinking communication: Vol. 1. Paradigm issues* (pp. 53–65). Newbury Park, CA: Sage.

Giffin, K., & Patton, B. (1970). *Fundamentals of interpersonal communication.* New York: Harper & Row.

Gitlin, T. (1983). *Inside prime time.* New York: Pantheon.

Glaser, S. R., & Frank, D. A. (1982). Rhetorical criticism of interpersonal discourse: An exploratory study. *Communication Quarterly, 30,* 353–358.

Glasser, T. L. (1999a). The idea of public journalism. In T. L. Glasser (Ed.), *The idea of public journalism* (pp. 3–18). New York: Guilford.

Glasser, T. L. (Ed.). (1999b). *The idea of public journalism.* New York: Guilford.

Glendon, M. A. (1991). *Rights talk: The impoverishment of political discourse.* New York: Macmillan.

Goffman, E. (1959). *The presentation of self in everyday life.* New York: Anchor.

Goffman, E. (1967). *Interaction ritual.* Garden City, NY: Anchor.

Golden, J., & Rieke, R. (1971). *The rhetoric of black Americans.* Columbus, OH: Merrill.

Goldsmith, D., & Baxter, L. A. (1996). Constituting relationships in talk: A taxonomy of speech events in social and personal relationships. *Human Communication Research, 23,* 87–114.

Goodall, H. L., Jr. (1991). *Living in the rock n roll mystery: Reading context, self, and others as clues.* Carbondale: Southern Illinois University Press.

Goodall, H. L., Jr. (1993). Mysteries of the future told: Communication as the material manifestation of spirituality. *World Communication Journal, 22,* 40–49.

Goodall, H. L., Jr. (1994). *Casing a promised land: The autobiography of an organizational detective as cultural ethnographer.* Carbondale: Southern Illinois University Press.

Goodall, H. L., Jr. (1996). *Divine signs: Connecting spirit to community.* Carbondale: Southern Illinois University Press.

Goodall, H. L., Jr. (2000). *Writing the new ethnography.* Walnut Creek CA: AltaMira.

Goodnight, G. T. (1982). The personal, technical, and public spheres of argument: A speculative inquiry into the art of public deliberation. *Journal of the American Forensic Association, 18,* 214–227.

Gordon, H. (1988). *The other Martin Buber: Recollections of his contemporaries.* Columbus: Ohio University Press.

Gordon, N. (1999). Ethics as reciprocity: An analysis of Levinas's reading of Buber. *International Studies in Philosophy, 31,* 91–109.

Gozzi, R. (1999). *The power of metaphor in the age of electronic media.* Cresskill, NJ: Hampton Press.

Gregg, R. B. (1984). *Symbolic inducement and knowing: A study in the foundations of rhetoric.* Columbia: University of South Carolina Press.

Gresson, A. (1995). *The recovery of race in America.* Minneapolis: University of Minnesota Press.

Gronbeck, B. E., Farrell, T. J., & Soukup, P. A. (Eds.). (1991). *Media, consciousness, and culture: Explorations of Walter Ong's thought.* Newbury Park, CA: Sage.

Grossberg, L. C. (1992). *We gotta get out of this place: Popular conservatism and postmodern culture.* London: Routledge.

Grossberg, L. C., Nelson, C., & Treichler, P. A. (Eds.). (1992). *Cultural studies.* New York: Routledge.

Grudin, R. (1996). *On dialogue: An essay in free thought.* Boston: Houghton Mifflin.

Guinier, L. (1994). *Tyranny of the majority: Fundamental fairness in representative democracy.* New York: Macmillan.

Guinier, L. (1996). Democracy as theater. *Columbia Journalism Review, 34,* 4.

Guinier, L. (1998). *Lift every voice: Turning a civil rights setback into a new vision of social justice.* New York: Simon & Schuster.

Gutmann, A., & Thompson, D. (1996). *Democracy and disagreement.* Cambridge, MA: Harvard University Press.

Habermas, J. (1971). *Knowledge and human interests* (J. J. Shapiro, Trans.). Boston: Beacon Press.

Habermas, J. (1975). *Legitimation crisis* (T. McCarthy, Trans.). Boston: Beacon Press.

Habermas, J. (1979). *Communication and the evolution of society* (T. McCarthy, Trans.). Boston: Beacon Press.

Habermas, J. (1980). *Discourse ethics: Notes on philosophical justification; Moral consciousness and communicative action* (C. Lenhart & S. Weber Nicholson, Trans.). Cambridge: MIT Press.

Habermas, J. (1984). *The theory of communicative action: Vol. 1. Reason and the rationalization of society* (T. McCarthy, Trans.). Boston: Beacon Press.

Habermas, J. (1987). *The theory of communicative action: Vol. 2. Life world and system: A critique of functionalist reason* (T. McCarthy, Trans.). Boston: Beacon Press.

Habermas, J. (1989). *The structural transformation of the public sphere.* Cambridge, MA: MIT Press.

Habermas, J. (1990). *Moral consciousness and communicative action* (C. Lenhardt & S. W. Nicholsen, Trans.). Cambridge, MA: MIT Press.

Habermas, J. (1992). *Autonomy and solidarity: Interviews with Jürgen Habermas* (Rev. ed.; P. Dews, Ed.). London: Verso.

Habermas, J. (1993). *Justification and application: Remarks on discourse ethics* (C. P. Cronin, Trans.). Cambridge, MA: MIT Press.

Habermas, J. (1998). *On the pragmatics of communication* (M. Cooke, Ed.). Cambridge: MIT Press.

Haiman, F. S. (1981). *Speech and law in a free society.* Chicago: University of Chicago Press.

Haley, J. (1963). *Strategies of psychotherapy.* New York: Grune & Stratton.

Haley, J. (1969). *The power tactics of Jesus Christ and other essays.* New York: Avon.

Haley, J. (1973). *Uncommon therapy: The psychiatric techniques of Milton H. Erickson, M.D.* New York: Norton.

Hall, S. (1989). Ideology and communication theory. In B. Dervin, L. Grossberg, B. J. O'Keefe, & E. Wartella (Eds.), *Rethinking communication: Vol. 1. Paradigm issues* (pp. 40–52). Newbury Park, CA: Sage.

Halliday, M. A. K., & Hasan, R. (1989). *Language, context, and text: Aspects of language in a social-semiotic perspective.* Oxford: Oxford University Press.

Hallin, D. C. (1985). The American news media: A critical theory perspective. In J. Forester (Ed.), *Critical theory and public life* (pp. 122–146). Cambridge, MA: MIT Press.

Hammond, S. C., Anderson, R., & Cissna, K. N. (2003). The problematics of dialogue and power. *Communication Yearbook, 27,* 125-157.

Hand, S. (Ed.). (1989). *The Levinas reader.* Cambridge, MA: Blackwell.

Hanssen, B. (2000). Ethics of the other. In M. Garber, B. Hanssen, & R. L. Walkowitz (Eds.), *The turn to ethics* (pp. 127–179). New York: Routledge.

Haraway, D. (1988). Situated knowledges: The science question in feminism and the privilege of partial perspective. *Signs, 14,* 575–599.

Harding, S. (1991). *Whose science? Whose knowledge? Thinking from women's lives.* Ithaca, NY: Cornell University Press.

Harding, S. (1992). Rethinking standpoint epistemology: What is "strong objectivity?" *Centennial Review, 36,* 437–470.

Harding, S. (1998). *Is science multicultural?* Bloomington: University of Indiana Press.

Hardt, H. (1992). *Critical communication studies: Communication, history, and theory in America.* London: Routledge.

Hart, R. P., & Burks, D. M. (1972). Rhetorical sensitivity and social interaction. *Speech Monographs, 39,* 75–91.

Hartsock, N. (1983). The feminist standpoint: Developing the ground for a specifically feminist historical materialism. In S. Harding & M. B. Hintikka (Eds.), *Discovering reality* (pp. 283–310). Boston: Ridel.

Hartstock, N. C. M. (1998). *The feminist standpoint revisited and other essays.* Boulder, CO: Westview Press.

Haspel, K. C. (2001). *Not just "hot air": Talk of personal experience on news talk radio as collaborative and critical engagement in the public sphere.* Unpublished doctoral dissertation, Rutgers University, New Brunswick, NJ.

Hawes, L. C. (1977). Toward a hermeneutic phenomenology of communication. *Communication Quarterly, 25,* 30–41.

Hawes, L. C. (1998). Becoming other-wise: Conversational performance and the politics of experience. *Text and Performance Quarterly, 18,* 273–299.

Hawes, L. C. (1999). The dialogics of conversation: Power, control, vulnerability. *Communication Theory, 9,* 229–264.

Heany, T. (1995). *Issues in Freirean pedagogy.* Retrieved October 3, 2002, from http://nlu.nl.edu/ace/Resources/Documents/FreireIssues.html

Heidegger, M. (1949). *Existence and being* (D. Scott, R. F. C. Hull, & A. Crick, Trans.). South Bend, IN: Henry Regnery.

Heidegger, M. (1959). *An introduction to metaphysics* (R. Mannheim, Trans.). New Haven, CT: Yale University Press.

Heidegger, M. (1962). *Being and time* (J. Macquarrie & E. Robinson, Trans.). New York: Harper & Row.

Heidegger, M. (1966). *Discourse on thinking* (J. M. Anderson & E. Hans Freud, Trans.). New York: Harper & Row.

Heidegger, M. (1968). *What is called thinking?* (J. G. Gray, Trans.). New York: Harper & Row.

Heidegger, M. (1969). *Identity and difference* (J. Stambaugh, Trans.). New York: Harper & Row.

Heidegger, M. (1971a). *On the way to language* (P. D. Hertz, Trans.). New York: Harper & Row.

Heidegger, M. (1971b). *Poetry, language, thought* (A. Hofstadter, Trans.). New York: Harper & Row.

Heidegger, M. (1972). *On time and being* (J. Stambaugh, Trans.). New York: Harper & Row.

Heidegger, M. (1977). Letter on humanism (F. A. Capuzzi & J. G. Gray, Trans.). In D. F. Krell (Ed.), *Basic writings* (pp. 193–242). New York: Harper & Row.

Heidegger, M. (1993). *Basic concepts* (G. E. Aylesworth, Trans.). Bloomington: Indiana University Press.

Heikkilä, H., & Kunelius, R. (2002). *Access, dialogue, deliberation: Experimenting with three concepts of journalism criticism.* Retrieved March 3, 2003, from The International Media and Democracy Project Web site, http://www.imdp.org/artman/publish/article_27.shtml

Heller, J. (1955). *Catch-22.* New York: Dell.

Herman, E. S., & Chomsky, N. (1988). *Manufacturing consent: The political economy of the mass media.* New York: Pantheon.

Heschel, A. J. (1951). *Man is not alone: A philosophy of religion.* New York: Noonday Press.

Heyerdahl, T. (1960). *Aku-Aku: The secret of Easter Island.* New York: Pocket Books.

Hirota, J. M. (1988). *Cultural mediums: The work world of "creatives" in American advertising agencies.* Unpublished doctoral dissertation, Columbia University, New York.

Hirschkop, K. (1992). Is dialogism for real? *Social Text, 10,* 102–113.

Hirschkop, K. (1999). *Mikhail Bakhtin: An aesthetics for democracy.* New York: Oxford University Press.

Hite, S. (1989). *The Hite report.* New York: Dell.

Hoerl, K. (2002). Monstrous youth in suburbia: Disruption and recovery of the American dream. *Southern Communication Journal, 67,* 259–275.

Holquist, M. (1981). Glossary. In M. M. Bakhtin, *The dialogic imagination: Four essays by M. M. Bakhtin* (M. Holquist, Ed.; C. Emerson & M. Holquist, Trans.; pp. 423–434). Austin: University of Texas Press.

Holquist, M. (1986). Introduction. In M. M. Bakhtin, *Speech genres and other late essays* (C. Emerson & M. Holquist, Eds.; V. W. McGee, Trans.; pp. ix–xxiii). Austin: University of Texas Press.

Holquist, M. (1990). *Dialogism: Bakhtin and his world.* New York: Routledge.

Homer. (1996). *Odyssey* (R. Fagles, Trans.). New York: Penguin Books.

Honneth, A. (1996). *The struggle for recognition: The moral grammar of social conflicts* (J. Anderson, Trans.). Cambridge, MA: MIT Press.

hooks, b. (1994). *Teaching to transgress: Education as the practice of freedom.* New York: Routledge.

hooks, b., & West, C. (1991). *Breaking bread: Insurgent Black intellectual life.* Boston: South End Press.

HopKins, M. F. (1989). The rhetoric of heteroglossia in Flannery O'Connor's *Wise Blood. Quarterly Journal of Speech, 75,* 198–211.

Horton, M., & Freire, P. (1990). *We make the road by walking: Conversations on education and social change* (B. Bell, J. Gaventa, & J. Peters, Eds.). Philadelphia: Temple University Press.

Howe, R. (1963). *The miracle of dialogue.* New York: Seabury Press.

Husserl, E. (1962). *Ideas: General introduction to pure phenomenology* (W. R. B. Gibson, Trans.). New York: Collier.

Hycner, R. (1991). *Between person and person: Toward a dialogical psychotherapy.* Highland, NY: The Gestalt Journal Press.

Hyde, M. J. (1993). Medicine, rhetoric, and the euthanasia debate: A case study in the workings of postmodern discourse. *Quarterly Journal of Speech, 79,* 347–363.

Hyde, M. J. (1994). The call of conscience: Heidegger and the question of rhetoric. *Philosophy and Rhetoric, 27,* 374–396.

Hyde, M. J. (2001a). *The call of conscience: Heidegger and Levinas, rhetoric and the euthanasia debate.* Columbia: University of South Carolina Press.

Hyde, M. J. (2001b). Defining "human dignity" in the debate over the (im)morality of physician-assisted suicide. *Journal of Medical Humanities, 22,* 69–82.

Hyde, M. J. (2001c). Hermeneutics. In T. O. Sloane (Ed.), *Encyclopedia of rhetoric* (pp. 329–337). New York: Oxford University Press.

Hyde, M. J. (2002a). The interruptive nature of the call of conscience: Rethinking Heidegger on the question of rhetoric. In M. B. Matustik & W. L. McBride (Eds.), *Calvin O. Schrag and the task of philosophy after postmodernity* (pp. 253–269). Evanston, IL: Northwestern University Press.

Hyde. M. J. (2002b, July). *The rhetoric of social death: The controversy over the flying of the confederate battle flag in South Carolina.* Paper presented at the Fifth Conference of the International Society for the Study of Argumentation, Amsterdam, Netherlands.

Hyde, M. J. (in press-a). The gift of acknowledgment. In R. E. Ramsey (Ed.), *Experiences between philosophy and communication: Engaging the philosophical contributions of Calvin O. Schrag.* Albany: State University of New York Press.

Hyde, M. J. (in press-b). Rhetorically, we dwell. In M. J. Hyde (Ed.), *The ethos of rhetoric.* Columbia: University of South Carolina Press.

Hyde, M. J., & Rufo, K. (2000). The call of conscience, rhetorical interruptions, and the euthanasia debate. *Journal of Applied Communication Research, 28,* 1–23.

Hyde, M. J., & Smith, C. R. (1979). Hermeneutics and rhetoric: A seen but unobserved relationship. *Quarterly Journal of Speech, 65,* 347–363.

Hyland, D. A. (1968). Why Plato wrote dialogues. *Philosophy and Rhetoric, 1,* 38–50.

Institute on the arts and civic dialogue: Project goals. (1998, November 30). Retrieved October 28, 1999 from http:arts-civic.org/goals.html

Isaacs, W. (1993). Taking flight: Dialogue, collective thinking, and organizational learning. *Organizational Dynamics, 22,* 24–39.

Isaacs, W. (1999). *Dialogue and the art of thinking together: A pioneering approach to communicating in business and in life.* New York: Doubleday.

Jackall, R. (1988). *Moral mazes: The world of corporate managers.* New York: Oxford University Press.

Jacobson, M. (1998). *Whiteness of a different color: European immigrants and the alchemy of race.* Cambridge, MA: Harvard University Press.

James, W. (1902). *The varieties of religious experience.* New York: Longman, Green.

James, W. (1975). *Pragmatism: A new name for some old ways of thinking; and, the meaning of truth.* Cambridge, MA: Harvard University Press.

Jansen, S. C. (1983). Power and knowledge: Toward a new critical synthesis. *Journal of Communication, 33*(3), 342–354.

Jay, M. (1993). *Force fields: Between intellectual history and cultural critique.* New York: Routledge.

Jensen, J. (1990). *Redeeming modernity: Contradictions in media criticism.* Newbury Park, CA: Sage.

Jensen, J., & Pauly, J. J. (1997). Imagining the audience: Losses and gains in cultural studies. In M. Ferguson & P. Golding (Eds.), *Cultural studies in question* (pp. 155–169). Thousand Oaks, CA: Sage.

Johannesen, R. L. (1971). The emerging concept of communication as dialogue. *Quarterly Journal of Speech, 57,* 373–382.

Johannesen, R. L. (1975). *Ethics in human communication.* Columbus, OH: Charles E. Merrill.

Johannesen, R. L. (2000). Nel Noddings's uses of Martin Buber's philosophy of dialogue. *Southern Communication Journal, 65,* 151–160.

John, R. R. (1995). *Spreading the news: The American postal system from Franklin to Morse.* Cambridge, MA: Harvard University Press.

Johnston, P. (1993). *Wittgenstein: Rethinking the inner.* London: Routledge.

Johnstone, H. W., Jr. (1978). *Validity and rhetoric in philosophical argument: An outlook in transition.* University Park, PA: The Dialogue Press.

Jones, S. G. (Ed.). (1995). *CyberSociety: Computer-mediated communication and community.* Thousand Oaks, CA: Sage.

Jones, S. G. (Ed.). (1997). *Virtual culture: Identity and communication in cybersociety.* Thousand Oaks, CA: Sage.

Jones, S. G. (Ed.). (1998). *CyberSociety 2.0: Revisiting computer-mediated communication and community.* Thousand Oaks, CA: Sage.

Jost, W., & Hyde, M. J. (1997). Rhetoric and hermeneutics: Places along the way. In W. Jost & M. J. Hyde (Eds.), *Rhetoric and hermeneutics in our time* (pp. 1–42). New Haven, CT: Yale University Press.

Jourard, S. (1971). *The transparent self.* New York: Van Nostrand Reinhold.

Jourdain, R. (1998). *Music, the brain & ecstasy: How music captures our imagination.* New York: Avon.

Jung, H. Y. (1990). Bakhtin's body politic: A phenomenological dialogics. *Man and World: An International Philosophical Review, 23,* 85–99.

Kaid, L. L., McKinney M., & Tedesco, J. (2000). *Civic dialogue in the 1996 presidential campaign: Candidate, media, and public voices.* Cresskill, NJ: Hampton Press.

Kaplan, A. (1994). The life of dialogue. In R. Anderson, K. N. Cissna, & R. C. Arnett (Eds.), *The reach of dialogue: Confirmation, voice, and community* (pp. 34–46). Cresskill, NJ: Hampton Press.

Katz, A. M., Conant, L., Inui, T., Baron, D., & Bor, D. (2000). A council of elders: Creating a community of care. *Social Science and Medicine, 50,* 851–860.

Kearney, J. (2002). *The Heyerdahl solution: Remaking social work practice.* Unpublished manuscript, University of Sunderland, Sunderland, UK.

Keepin, W. (1993). *Lifework of David Bohm: River of truth.* Retrieved August 27, 2002, from the Satyana Institute Web site, http://www.satyana.org/thml/bohm.html

Kegan, R., & Lahey, L. L. (2001). *How the way we talk can change the way we work.* San Francisco: Jossey-Bass.

Keller, E. F. (1985). *Reflections on gender and science.* New Haven, CT: Yale University Press.

Keller, P. W. (1981). Interpersonal dissent and the ethics of dialogue. *Communication, 6,* 287–304.

Keller, P. W., & Brown, C. T. (1968). An interpersonal ethic for communication. *Journal of Communication, 18,* 73–81.

Kellett, P. M. (1993). Communication in accounts of religious conversion: An interpretive phenomenological account. *Journal of Communication and Religion, 16,* 71–81.

Kellett, P. M. (1999). Dialogue and dialectics in managing organizational change: The case of a mission-based transformation. *Southern Communication Journal, 64,* 211–231.

Kellett, P. M., & Dalton, D. G. (2001). *Managing conflict in a negotiated world: A narrative approach to achieving dialogue and change.* Thousand Oaks, CA: Sage.

Kellett, P. M., & Goodall, H. L., Jr. (1999). The death of discourse in our own chatroom: "Sextext," skillful discussion, and virtual communities. In D. S. Slayden & R. K. Whillock (Eds.), *Soundbite culture: The death of discourse in a wired world* (pp. 155–190). Thousand Oaks, CA: Sage.

Kelley, H. H., Berscheid, E., Christensen, A., Harvey, J. H., Huston, T. L., Levinger, G., et al. (Eds.). (1983). *Close relationships.* New York: Freeman.

Kellner, D. (1995). *Media culture: Cultural studies, identity and politics between the modern and the postmodern.* London: Routledge.

Kelly, A. (1995). Reciprocity and the height of God: A defense of Buber against Levinas. *Sophia, 34,* 65–73.

Keltner, J. (1970). *Interpersonal speech-communication: Elements and structures.* Belmont, CA: Wadsworth.

Kepnes, S. (1992). *The text as thou: Martin Buber's dialogical hermeneutics and narrative theology.* Bloomington: Indiana University Press.

Kerner, O. (1968). *Report of the national advisory commission on civil disorders.* Washington, DC: Government Printing Office.

Kielbowicz, R. B. (1989). *News in the mail: The press, post office, and public information, 1700–1860s.* New York: Greenwood Press.

Kierkegaard, S. (1999). *Provocations: Spiritual writings of Kierkegaard* (C. E. Moore, Ed.). Farmington, PA: The Plough Publishing House of The Bruderhof Foundation.

Killenberg, G. M., & Anderson, R. (1989). *Before the story: Interviewing and communication skills for journalists.* New York: St. Martin's Press.

Kingwell, M. (1995). *A civil tongue: Justice, dialogue, and the politics of pluralism.* University Park: Pennsylvania State University Press.

Kirsch, M. (2001). *Queer theory and social change (opening out).* New York: Routledge.

Kirschenbaum, H. (1979). *On becoming Carl Rogers.* New York: Delacorte Press.

Kirschenbaum, H., & Henderson, V. L. (Eds.). (1989a). *Carl Rogers: Dialogues— Conversations with Martin Buber, Paul Tillich, B. F. Skinner, Gregory Bateson, Michael Polanyi, Rollo May, and others.* Boston: Houghton Mifflin.

Kirschenbaum, H., & Henderson, V. L. (Eds.). (1989b). *The Carl Rogers reader.* Boston: Houghton Mifflin.

Kline, S. L. (1979). Toward a contemporary linguistic interpretation of the concept of stasis. *Journal of the American Forensic Association, 16,* 95–103.

Kofman, F., & Senge, P. M. (1993). Communities of commitment: The heart of learning organizations. *Organizational Dynamics, 22,* 5–22.

Kogler, H. H. (1996). *The power of dialogue: Critical hermeneutics after Gadamer and Foucault.* Cambridge, MA: MIT Press.

Krippendorff, K. (1989). On the ethics of constructing communication. In B. Dervin, L. Grossberg, B. J. O'Keefe, & E. Wartella (Eds.), *Rethinking communication: Vol. 1. Paradigm issues* (pp. 66–96). Newbury Park, CA: Sage.

Labov, W., & Fanshel, D. (1977). *Therapeutic discourse: Psychotherapy as conversation.* New York: Academic Press.

Laing, R. D. (1969). *Self and others* (2nd ed.). New York: Penguin.

Lanigan, R. L. (1977). *Speech act phenomenology.* The Hague: Martinus Nijhoff.

Lanigan, R. L. (1984). *Semiotic phenomenology of rhetoric.* Washington, DC: University Press of America.

Lanigan, R. L. (1988). *Phenomenology of communication: Merleau-Ponty's thematics in communicology and semiology.* Pittsburgh, PA: Duquesne University Press.

Lasch, C. (1979). *The culture of narcissism: American life in a time of diminishing expectations.* New York: W. W. Norton.

Latour, B. (1987). *Science in action: How to follow scientists and engineers through society.* Cambridge MA: Harvard University Press.

Latour, B. (1999). *Politiques de la nature: Comment faire entrer les sciences en democratie* [*The politics of nature: How to introduce the sciences into democracy*]. Paris: Editions la Decouverte.

Latour, B., & Woolgar, S. (1986). *Laboratory life: The construction of scientific facts.* Princeton, NJ: Princeton University Press.

Lave, J., & Wenger, E. (1991). *Situated learning: Legitimate peripheral participation.* Cambridge, UK: Cambridge University Press.

Lawton, P. N. (1976). Love and justice: Levinas' reading of Buber. *Philosophy Today, 20,* 77–83.

LeBlanc, A. N. (1999, August 22). The outsiders: How the picked-on cope—or don't. *The New York Times Magazine,* 36–41.

Leff, L. (1993). From legal scholar to quota queen: What happens when politics pulls the press into the groves of academe? *Columbia Journalism Review, 32,* 36–41.

Lerner, M., & West, C. (1996). *Jews & Blacks: Let the healing begin.* New York: Grosset/Putnam.

Levinas, E. (1969). *Totality and infinity: An essay on exteriority* (A. Lingis, Trans.). Pittsburgh, PA: Duquesne University Press.

Levinas, E. (1978). *Existence and existents* (A. Lingis, Trans.). The Hague: Martinus Nijhoff.

Levinas, E. (1981). *Otherwise than being or beyond essence* (A. Lingis, Trans.). Hague: Martinus Nijhoff.

Levinas, E. (1983). Beyond intentionality (K. McLaughlin, Trans.). In A. Montefiore (Ed.), *Philosophy in France today* (pp. 100–115). Cambridge, UK: Cambridge University Press.

Levinas, E. (1984a). Ethics of the infinite. In R. Kearney (Ed.), *Dialogues with Contemporary continental thinkers: The phenomenological heritage* (pp. 49–70). Manchester, UK: Manchester University Press.

Levinas, E. (1984b). Martin Buber, Gabriel Marcel, and philosophy. In H. Gordon & J. Bloch (Eds.), *Martin Buber: A centenary volume* (pp. 305–321). New York: KTAV.

Levinas, E. (1985). *Ethics and infinity: Conversations with Phillipe Nemo* (R. Cohen, Trans.). Pittsburgh, PA: Duquesne University Press.

Levinas, E. (1987a). *Collected philosophical papers* (A. Lingis, Trans.). The Hague: Martinus Nijhoff.

Levinas, E. (1987b). *Outside the subject.* Stanford, CA: Stanford University Press.

Levinas, E. (1987c). *Time and the other* (R. Cohen, Trans.). Pittsburgh, PA: Duquesne University Press.

Levinas, E. (1991). *Otherwise than being or beyond essence* (A. Lingis, Trans.). Dordrecht, the Netherlands: Kluwer.

Levinas, E. (1996). *Proper names* (M. B. Smith, Trans.). Stanford, CA: Stanford University Press.

Levinas, E. (1998). *Of God who comes to mind* (B. Bergo, Trans.). Stanford, CA: Stanford University Press.

Levinas, E. (1999). *Alterity & transcendence* (M. B. Smith, Trans.). New York: Columbia University Press.

Levy-Bruhl, L. (1926). *How natives think* (L. A. Clare, Trans.). London: George Allen and Unwin.

Lipari, L. A. (November, 2001). [*Diversity, ethics, and the other: Articulating philosophical perspectives for communication studies*]. Presentation at the annual meeting of the National Communication Association, Atlanta, GA.

Luft, J. (1969). *Of human interaction.* Palo Alto, CA: National Press.

Lumsden, S. (2000). Absolute difference and social ontology: Levinas face to face with Buber and Fichte. *Human Studies, 23,* 227–241.

Lutz, C. A., & Collins, J. L. (1993). *Reading* National Geographic. Chicago: University of Chicago Press.

Lyons, J. (1977). *Semantics* (Vol. 2). Cambridge, MA: Cambridge University Press.

Lyotard, J.-F. (1984). *The postmodern condition: A report on knowledge* (G. Bennington & B. Massumi, Trans.). Minneapolis: University of Minnesota Press.

MacIntyre, A. (1998). *A short history of ethics: A history of moral philosophy from the Homeric age to the twentieth century* (2nd ed.). Notre Dame, IN: University of Notre Dame Press.

Madison, D. S. (1999). Performing theory/embodied writing. *Text and Performance Quarterly, 19,* 107–124.

Madison, D. S. (in press). Critical ethnography: Performance, protest, and the meaning of home. In N. Denzin & Y. Lincoln (Eds.), *Handbook of qualitative research* (3rd ed.). Thousand Oaks, CA: Sage.

Makay, J. J., & Brown, W. R. (1972). *The rhetorical dialogue: Contemporary concepts and cases.* Dubuque, IA: William C. Brown.

Malcolm, N. (2001, November). *An analysis of audience influence on the hooks-West dialogue.* Paper presented at the National Communication Association convention, Atlanta, GA.

Manning, R. J. S. (1993). *Interpreting otherwise than Heidegger: Emmanuel Levinas's ethics as first philosophy.* Pittsburgh, PA: Duquesne University Press.

Mansbridge, J. (1980). *Beyond adversary democracy.* New York: Basic Books.

Maranhao, T. (1986). *Therapeutic discourse and Socratic dialogue: A cultural critique.* Madison: University of Wisconsin Press.

Maranhao, T. (Ed.). (1990). *The interpretation of dialogue.* Chicago: University of Chicago Press.

Marcus, G. E. (Ed.). (1996). *Connected: Engagements with media.* Chicago: University of Chicago Press.

Marcus, G. E., & Fischer, M. M. J. (1986). *Anthropology as cultural critique: An experimental moment in the human sciences.* Chicago: University of Chicago Press.

Markham, A. (1998). *Life online: Researching real experiences in virtual space.* Walnut Creek, CA: AltaMira Press.

Markova, I., & Foppa, K. (Eds.). (1990). *The dynamics of dialogue.* New York: Springer-Verlag.

Martin Buber and Carl Rogers [dialogue] (K. Cissna & R. Anderson, Transcribers & Eds.). (1999). In J. B. Agassi (Ed.), *Martin Buber on psychology and psychotherapy: Essays, letters, and dialogue* (pp. 246–270). Syracuse, NY: Syracuse University Press.

Maslow, A. (1961). Peak-experiences as acute identity experiences. *American Journal of Psychoanalysis, 121,* 254–260.

Maslow, A. (1962). Lessons from the peak-experiences. *Journal of Humanistic Psychology, 2,* 9–18.

Maslow, A. (1964). *Religions, values, and peak experiences.* Columbus: Ohio State University Press.

Maslow, A. (1968a). Music education and peak-experiences. *Music Educators Journal, 54,* 163–171.

Maslow, A. (1968b). The farther reaches of human nature. *Journal of Transpersonal Psychology, 1,* 1–9.

Maslow, A. (1970). *Motivation and personality* (2nd ed.). New York: Harper & Row.

Maslow, A. (1973). *The farther reaches of human nature.* New York: Viking Press.

Maslow, A. (1976). *Religions, values and peak-experiences.* New York: Penguin Books.

Mathews, D. F. (1994). *Politics for people: Finding a responsible public voice.* Urbana: University of Illinois Press.

Matson, F., & Montagu, A. (Eds.). (1967). *The human dialogue: Perspectives on communication.* New York: Free Press.

Maturana, H. (1990). *Emociones y lenguaje en educacion y politica* [*Emotions and language in education and politics*]. Santiago, Chile: Dolmen Ediciones.

Maturana, H. (1997). *La objetividad: Un argumento para obligar* [*Objectivity: A compelling argument*]. Santiago, Chile: Dolcen Ediciones.

Maturana, H. R., & Varela, F. J. (1980). Autopoiesis: The organization of the living. In H. R. Maturana & F. J. Varela (Eds.), *Autopoiesis and cognition: The realization of the living* (pp. 59–140). Boston: D. Reidel.

Matustik, M. B. (2001). *Jürgen Habermas: A philosophical-political profile.* New York: Rowman & Littlefield.

May, L. (1996). *The socially responsive self: Social theory and professional ethics.* Chicago: University of Chicago Press.

McCarthy, T. (1979). Translator's introduction. In J. Habermas, *Communication and the evolution of society* (pp. vii–xxiv). Boston: Beacon.

McChesney, R. W. (1993). *Telecommunications, mass media, and democracy: The battle for the control of U.S. broadcasting, 1928–1935.* New York: Oxford University Press.

McChesney, R. W. (1999). *Rich media, poor democracy: Communication politics in dubious times.* Urbana: University of Illinois Press.

McChesney, R. W., & Nichols, J. (2002). *Our media, not theirs: The democratic struggle against corporate media.* New York: Seven Stories.

McGuire, M., & Slembek, E. (1987). An emerging critical rhetoric: Hellmut Geissner's Sprechwissenschaft. *Quarterly Journal of Speech, 73,* 349–400.

McKenna, T. (1993). *Food of the gods: A search for the original tree of knowledge.* New York: Bantam.

McKeon, R. (1957). Communication, truth and society. *Ethics, 67,* 89–99.

McLuhan, M. (1951). *The mechanical bride: Folklore of industrial man.* New York: Vanguard Press.

McLuhan, M. (1962). *The Gutenberg galaxy: The making of typographic man.* Toronto: University of Toronto Press.

McLuhan, M. (1964). *Understanding media: The extensions of man.* New York: New American Library.

McMillan, J., & Hyde, M. J. (2000). Technological innovation and change: A case study in the formation of organizational conscience. *Quarterly Journal of Speech, 86,* 19–47.

McNamee, S. (2002a). The social construction of disorders: From pathology to potential. In J. D. Raskin & S. K. Bridges (Eds.), *Studies in meaning: Exploring constructivist psychology* (pp. 143–168). New York: Pace University Press.

McNamee, S. (2002b). Appreciative inquiry: Social construction in practice. In C. Dalsgaard, T. Meisner, & K. Voetmann (Eds.), *A symphony of appreciation: Development and renewal in organisations through working with appreciative inquiry* (pp. 110–129). Copenhagen: Danish Psychology Press.

McNamee, S., & Gergen, K. J. (1999). *Relational responsibility: Resources for sustainable dialogue.* Thousand Oaks, CA: Sage.

McPhail, M. (1994). *The rhetoric of racism.* Lanham, MD: University Press of America.

McPhail, M. (1996). *Zen in the art of rhetoric: An inquiry into coherence.* Albany: State University of New York Press.

McPhail, M. (1998a). From complicity to coherence: Rereading the rhetoric of Afrocentricity. *Western Journal of Communication, 62,* 114–140.

McPhail, M. (1998b). Passionate intensity: Louis Farrakhan and the fallacies of racial reasoning. *Quarterly Journal of Speech, 84,* 416–429.

McPhail, M. (2002). *The rhetoric of racism revisited: Reparations or separation?* Lanham, MD: Rowman and Littlefield.

Mead, M., & Baldwin, J. (1971). *A rap on race.* Philadelphia: Lippincott.

Mehrabian, A. (1981*). Silent messages: Implicit communication of emotions and attitudes* (2nd ed.). Belmont, CA: Wadsworth.

Menand, L. (2001). *The metaphysical club: A story of ideas in America.* New York: Farrar, Straus, and Giroux.

Merleau-Ponty, M. (1968). *The visible and the invisible.* Evanston, IL: Northwestern University Press.

Meyrowitz, J. (1985). *No sense of place: The impact of electronic media on social behavior.* New York: Oxford University Press.

Meyrowitz, J. (1994). Medium theory. In D. T. Crowley & D. Mitchell (Eds.), *Communiction theory today* (pp. 50–77). Stanford, CA: Stanford University Press.

Miles, E. (1997). *Tune your brain: Using music to manage your mind, body, and mood.* New York: Berkeley Publishing Group.

Miller, J., & Donner, S. (2000). More than just talk: The use of racial dialogues to combat racism. *Social Work with Groups, 23,* 31–53.

Mills, C. W. (1940). Situated actions and vocabularies of motive. *American Sociological Review, 5,* 439–452.

Mindell, A. (1995). *Sitting in the fire.* Portland, OR: Lao Tze Press.

Mingers, J. (1980). Towards an appropriate social theory for applied systems thinking: Critical theory and soft systems methodology. *Journal of Applied Systems Analysis, 7,* 41–49.

Minister, K. (1991). A feminist frame for the oral history interview. In S. Gluck & D. Patai (Eds.), *Women's words: The feminist practice of oral history* (pp. 27–41). New York: Routledge.

Mishler, E. G. (1986). *Research interviewing: Context and narrative.* Cambridge, MA: Harvard University Press.

Montgomery, B. M., & Baxter, L. A. (Eds.). (1998a). *Dialectical approaches to studying personal relationships.* Mahwah, NJ: Lawrence Erlbaum.

Montgomery, B. M., & Baxter, L. A. (1998b). Dialogism and relational dialectics. In B. M. Montgomery & L. A. Baxter (Eds.), *Dialectical approaches to studying personal relationships* (pp. 155–183). Mahwah, NJ: Lawrence Erlbaum.

Morson, G. S., & Emerson, C. (1990). *Mikhail Bakhtin: Creation of a prosaics.* Stanford, CA: Stanford University Press.

Mouffe, C. (2000). *The democratic paradox.* London: Verso.

Mulhall, S. (1990). *On being in the world: Wittgenstein and Heidegger on seeing aspects.* London: Routledge.

Mumford, L. (1952). *Art and technics.* New York: Columbia University Press.

Murphy, J. W., & Pilotta, J. J. (1983). *Qualitative methodology, theory and application: A guide for the social practitioner.* Dubuque, IA: Kendall/Hunt.

Myerhoff, B. (1975). Organization and ecstasy: Deliberate and accidental communitas among Huichol Indians and American youth. In S. Moore & B. Myerhoff (Eds.), *Symbol and politics in communal ideology* (pp. 33–67). Ithaca, NY: Cornell University Press.

Nelson, S. (1998). Intersections of *eros* and ethnography. *Text and Performance Quarterly, 18,* 1–21.

Nerone, J. (1994). *Violence against the press: Policing the public sphere in U.S. history.* New York: Oxford University Press.

Nerone, J. (Ed.). (1995). *Last rights: Revisiting* Four Theories of the Press. Urbana: University of Illinois Press.

Newcomb, H. M. (1984). On the dialogic aspects of mass communication. *Critical Studies in Mass Communication, 1,* 34–50.

Newcomb, T. (1953). An approach to the study of communicative acts. *Psychological Review, 60,* 393–404.

Nisker, W. (1990). *Crazy wisdom.* Berkeley, CA: Ten Speed Press.

Noddings, N. (1984). *Caring: A feminine approach to ethics and moral education.* Berkeley: University of California Press.

Nwangaza, E. (2001). People of Cincinnati protest against police murders. *Flame.* Retrieved June 18, 2003, from http://www.fantompowa.net/Flame/cincinnati.htm

O'Hagan, S. (2002). Time for a new Black power movement. *Guardian Unlimited.* Retrieved August 30, 2002, from http://www.guardian.co.uk/usa/story/0,12271,776439,00.html

Oliver, R. T. (1973). *Communication and culture in ancient India and China.* Syracuse, NY: Syracuse University Press.

Ong, W. J. (1958). *Ramus, method, and the decay of dialogue.* Cambridge, MA: Harvard University Press.

Ong, W. J. (1967). *The presence of the word: Some prolegomena for cultural and religious history.* New York: Simon & Schuster.

Ong, W. J. (1977). *Interfaces of the word: Studies in the evolution of consciousness and culture.* Ithaca, NY: Cornell University Press.

Ong, W. J. (1982). *Orality and literacy: The technologizing of the word.* London: Methuen.

Ott, H. (1993). *Martin Heidegger: A political life.* San Francisco: Basic Books.

Palmer, P. J. (1983). *To know as we are known.* New York: HarperCollins.

Palmer, P. J. (1998). *The courage to teach.* San Francisco: Jossey-Bass.

Park-Fuller, L. M. (1986). Voices: Bakhtin's heteroglossia and polyphony, and the performance of narrative literature. *Literature in Performance, 7,* 1–12.

Patton, B., & Giffin, K. (1974). *Interpersonal communication.* New York: Harper & Row.

Pauly, J. J. (1988). Rupert Murdoch and the demonology of professional journalism. In J. W. Carey (Ed.), *Media, myths, and narratives: Television and the press* (pp. 246–261). Newbury Park, CA: Sage.

Pauly, J. J. (1989). New directions for research in journalism history. In L. Caswell (Ed.), *Guide to sources in journalism history* (pp. 31–46). Westport, CT: Greenwood.

Pauly, J. J. (1990). The politics of the New Journalism. In N. Sims (Ed.), *Literary journalism in the twentieth century* (pp. 110–129). New York: Oxford University Press.

Pauly, J. J. (1991a). A beginner's guide to doing qualitative research in mass communication. *Journalism and Mass Communication Monographs, 125,* 1–29.

Pauly, J. J. (1991b). Interesting the public: A brief history of the newsreading movement. *Communication, 12,* 285–297.

Pauly, J. J. (1994). Making the news relevant to democracy. In R. Anderson, R. Dardenne, & G. Killenberg, *The conversation of journalism* (pp. vii–xvii). Westport, CT: Praeger.

Pauly, J. J. (1995). [Review of the book *Whose art is it ?*] *Critical Studies in Mass Communication, 12,* 488–490.

Pauly, J. J. (1998a). Finding ourselves in the New Journalism: A struggle for meaning in a chaotic time. *Media Studies Journal, 12,* 142–147.

Pauly, J. J. (1998b). Jane Kramer. In A. J. Kaul (Ed.), *Dictionary of literary biography— American literary journalists, 1945–1995* (Vol. 185, pp. 138–148). Detroit: Gale Research.

Pauly, J. J. (1999). Journalism and the sociology of public life. In T. Glasser (Ed.), *The idea of public journalism* (pp. 134–151). New York: Guilford.

Pauly, J. J. (2003a). Recovering journalism as a democratic art. In J. Harper (Ed.), *Media, profit and politics: Competing priorities in an open society* (pp. 18–32). Kent, OH: Kent State University Press.

Pauly, J. J. (2003b). *What it means when a newspaper dies.* Manuscript submitted for publication.

Pauly, J. J., & Eckert, M. (2002). The myth of "the local" in American journalism. *Journalism and Mass Communication Quarterly, 79,* 308–324.

Pearce, K. A. (2002). *Making better social worlds: Engaging in and facilitating dialogic communication.* Redwood City, CA: Pearce Associates.

Pearce, K. A., & Pearce, W. B. (2001). The Public Dialogue Consortium's school-wide dialogue process: A communication approach to develop citizenship skills and enhance school climate. *Communication Theory, 11,* 105–123.

Pearce, W. B. (1989). *Communication and the human condition.* Carbondale: Southern Illinois University Press.

Pearce, W. B. (1993). Achieving dialogue with "the other" in the postmodern world. In P. Gaunt (Ed.), *Beyond agendas: New directions in communication research* (pp. 59–74). Westport, CT: Greenwood.

Pearce, W. B. (1994). *Interpersonal communication: Making social worlds.* New York: HarperCollins.

Pearce, W. B. (1995). Creating places for dialogic argument in the national conversation. In S. Jackson (Ed.), *Argumentation and values* (pp. 242–249). Backlick, VA: Speech Communication Association.

Pearce, W. B. (1999). *Using CMM: The coordinated management of meaning.* Redwood City, CA: Pearce Associates.

Pearce, W. B., & Conklin, R. F. (1979). A model of hierarchical meanings in coherent conversation and a study of indirect responses. *Communication Monographs, 46,* 75–87.

Pearce, W. B., Cronen, V. E., & Conklin, R. F. (1979). On what to look at when studying communication: A hierarchical model of actors' meanings. *Communication, 4,* 195–220.

Pearce, W. B., Harris, L. M., & Cronen, V. E. (1981). The coordinated management of meaning: Human communication in a new key. In C. Wilder-Mott & J. Weakland (Eds.), *Rigor and imagination: Essays from the legacy of Gregory Bateson* (pp. 149–194). New York: Praeger.

Pearce, W. B., & Littlejohn, S. W. (1997). *Moral conflict: When social worlds collide.* Thousand Oaks, CA: Sage.

Pearce, W. B., & Pearce, K. A. (2000). Combining passions and abilities: Toward dialogic virtuosity. *Southern Communication Journal, 65,* 161–175.

Peck, E. G., & Mink, J. S. (Eds.). (1998). *Common ground: Feminist collaboration in the academy.* Albany: State University of New York Press.

Penman, R. (2000). *Reconstructing communicating: Looking to a future.* Mahwah, NJ: Lawrence Erlbaum.

Peters, J. D. (1999a). Public journalism and democratic theory: Four challenges. In T. L. Glasser (Ed.), *The idea of public journalism* (pp. 99–117). New York: Guilford.

Peters, J. D. (1999b). *Speaking into the air: A history of the idea of communication.* Chicago: University of Chicago Press.

Peterson, R. A. (1997). *Creating country music: Fabricating authenticity.* Chicago: University of Chicago Press.

Pickering, A. (1995). *The mangle of practice.* Chicago: University of Chicago Press.

Pilotta, J. J. (Ed.). (1982). *Interpersonal communication: Essays in phenomenology and hermeneutics.* Washington, DC: University Press of America.

Pilotta, J. J., & Mickunas, A. (1990). *Science of communication: Its phenomenological foundation.* Hillsdale, NJ: Lawrence Erlbaum.

Postel, D. (2002, June 7). The life and the mind. *The Chronicle of Higher Education,* A16–A18.

Poster, M. (1990). *The mode of information: Poststructuralism and social context.* Chicago: University of Chicago Press.

Poster, M. (1995). *The second media age.* Cambridge, UK: Polity.

Poster, M. (2001). *What's the matter with the Internet?* Minneapolis: University of Minnesota Press.

Postman, N. (1985). *Amusing ourselves to death: Public discourse in the age of show business.* New York: Viking.

Postman, N. (1992). *Technopoly: The surrender of culture to technology.* New York: Knopf.

Poulakos, J. (1974). The components of dialogue. *Western Journal of Speech Communication, 38,* 199–212.

Powdermaker, H. (1950). *Hollywood, the dream factory: An anthropologist looks at the movie-makers.* Boston: Little, Brown.

Powell, J. (1969). *Why am I afraid to tell you who I am?* Chicago: Argus.

Prosser, M. H. (1978). *The cultural dialogue: An introduction to intercultural communication.* Boston: Houghton Mifflin.

Pruyn, F. (2000). *Infinite potential: The life and times of David Bohm.* Retrieved August 27, 2002, from http://www.theosophy-nw.org/thesnw/science/sc-pruyn.htm

Public Conversations Project. (2002). About PCP. Retrieved March 24, 2002, from http://www.publicconversations.org/Pages/aboutpcp.html

Public Dialogue Consortium. (2002). About the PDC. Retrieved March 24, 2002, from http://www.publicdialogue.org/pdc/index.html

Rabie, M. (1994). *Conflict resolution and ethnicity.* Westport, NY: Praeger.

Rapoport, A. (1992). *Peace: An idea whose time has come.* Ann Arbor: University of Michigan Press.

Rawlins, W. (1992). *Friendship matters: Communication, dialectics, and the life course.* New York: Aldine de Gruyter.

Real, M. R. (1989). *Super media.* Newbury Park, CA: Sage.

Reinelt, J. (1996). Performing race: Anna Deavere Smith's *Fires in the Mirror. Modern Drama, 39,* 609–617.

Rescher, N. (2001). *Paradoxes: Their roots, range, and resolution.* Chicago: Open Court.

Ricoeur, P. (1991). *From text to action: Essays in hermeneutics, II* (K. Blarney & J. B. Thompson, Trans.). Evanston, IL: Northwestern University Press.

Ricoeur, P. (1995). Emmanuel Levinas: Thinker of testimony. In *Figuring the Sacred: Religion, narrative, and imagination* (M. L. Wallace, Ed.; D. Pellauer, Trans.; pp. 108-128). Minneapolis, MN: Fortress Press.

Rieff, P. (1990). *The feeling intellect: Selected writings.* Chicago: University of Chicago Press.

Risser, J. (1997). *Hermeneutics and the voice of the other: Re-reading Gadamer's philosophical hermeneutics.* Albany: State University of New York Press.

Rogers, C. R. (1951). *Client-centered therapy: Its current practice, implications, and theory.* Boston: Houghton Mifflin.

Rogers, C. R. (1961). *On becoming a person.* Boston: Houghton Mifflin.

Rogers, C. R. (1965). *Client-centered therapy: Its current practice, implications and theory.* Boston: Houghton Mifflin.

Rogers, C. R. (1969). *The freedom to learn.* Columbus, OH: Charles E. Merrill.

Rogers, C. R. (1972). Some social issues which concern me. *Journal of Humanistic Psychology, 12,* 45–60.

Rogers, C. R. (1980). *A way of being.* Boston: Houghton Mifflin.

Rogow, F., & Smith, A. D. (2001). *Twilight Los Angeles: Discussion guide.* San Francisco: American Documentary.

Rorty, R. (1967). *The linguistic turn.* Chicago: University of Chicago Press.

Rorty, R. (1979). *Philosophy and the mirror of nature.* Princeton, NJ: Princeton University Press.

Rorty, R. (1989). *Contingency, irony, and solidarity.* Cambridge, UK: Cambridge University Press.

Rosen, J. (1999). *What are journalists for?* New Haven, CT: Yale University Press.

Rosengren, K. E. (1989). Paradigms lost and regained. In B. Dervin, L. Grossberg, B. J. O'Keefe, & E. Wartella (Eds.), *Rethinking communication: Vol. 1. Paradigm issues* (pp. 21–39). Newbury Park, CA: Sage.

Rossiter, C. M., Jr., & Pearce, W. B. (1975). *Communicating personally: A theory of interpersonal communication and human relationships.* Indianapolis, IN: Bobbs-Merrill.

Ryan, M. P. (1997). *Civic wars: Democracy and public life in the American city during the nineteenth century.* Berkeley: University of California Press.

Sacks, H., Schegloff, E. A., & Jefferson, G. (1974). A simplest systematics for the organization of turn-taking for conversation. *Language, 50,* 696–735.

Sacks, O. (1985). *The man who mistook his wife for a hat.* London: Duckworth.

Safranski, R. (1998). *Martin Heidegger: Between good and evil.* Cambridge, MA: Harvard University Press.

Sahlstein, E., & Baxter, L. A. (2001). Improvising commitment in close relationships: A relational dialectics perspective. In J. H. Harvey & A. E. Wenzel (Eds.), *Close romantic relationships: Maintenance and enhancement* (pp. 115–132). Mahwah, NJ: Lawrence Erlbaum.

Sampson, E. E. (1993). *Celebrating the other: A dialogic account of human nature.* Boulder, CO: Westview Press.

Saunders, H. H. (1999). *A public peace process: Sustained dialogue to transform racial and ethnic conflicts.* New York: St. Martin's Press.

Schechner, R. (1993). Anna Deavere Smith: Acting as incorporation. *TDR: The Drama Review, 37,* 63–64.

Schein, E. H. (1993). On dialogue, culture, and organizational learning. *Organizational Dynamics, 22,* 40–51.

Schiffrin, D. (1987). *Discourse markers.* New York: Cambridge University Press.

Schrag, C. O. (1969). *Experience and being.* Evanston, IL: Northwestern University Press.

Schrag, C. O. (1986). *Communicative praxis and the space of subjectivity.* Bloomington, IN: Indiana University Press.

Schudson, M. (1995). *The power of news.* Cambridge, MA: Harvard University Press.

Schudson, M. (1997). Why conversation is not the soul of democracy. *Critical Studies in Mass Communication, 14,* 297–309.

Schudson, M. (1998). *The good citizen: A history of American civic life.* New York: Free Press.

Schudson, M. (1999). What public journalism knows about journalism but doesn't know about "public." In T. L. Glasser (Ed.), *The idea of public journalism* (pp. 118–133). New York: Guilford.

Schudson, M. (2003). *The sociology of news.* New York: Norton.

Schultz, E. A. (1990). *Dialogue at the margins: Whorf, Bakhtin, and linguistic relativity.* Madison: University of Wisconsin Press.

Schutz, A. (1966). *Collected papers III: Studies in phenomenological philosophy* (I. Schutz, Ed.). The Hague, Netherlands: Martin Nijhoff.

Schutz, W. C. (1960). *FIRO: A three-dimensional theory of interpersonal behavior.* New York: Holt, Rinehart & Winston.

Scott, M. D., & Lyman, S. (1968). Accounts. *American Sociological Review, 33,* 46–62.

Searle, J. (1969). *Speech acts: An essay in the philosophy of language.* London: Cambridge University Press.

Sedgewick, E. (1990). *Epistemology of the closet.* Berkeley: University of California Press.

Seikkula, J. Aaltonen, J., Alakara, B., Haarakangas, K. Keranen, J., & Sutela, M. (1995). Treating psychosis by means of open dialogue. In S. Friedman (Ed.), *The reflecting team in action* (pp. 62–80). New York: Guilford Press.

Senge, P. M. (1990). *The fifth discipline: The art and practice of the learning organization.* New York: Doubleday.

Senge, P. M., Kleiner, A., Roberts, C., Ross, R. B., & Smith, B. J. (1994). *The fifth discipline fieldbook.* New York: Doubleday.

Shands, H. C. (1971). *The war with words: Structure and transcendence.* The Hague: Mouton.

Sharf, B. F. (1979). Rhetorical analysis of nonpublic discourse. *Communication Quarterly, 27,* 21–30.

Sharp, G. (1973). *The politics of nonviolent action.* Boston: Porter Sargent.

Shaull, R. (1990). Foreword. In P. Freire, *Pedagogy of the oppressed* (M. B. Ramos, Trans.; pp. 9–14). New York: Continuum.

Sheldrake, R. (1988). *The presence of the past: Morphic resonance and the habits of nature.* New York: Times.

Shotter, J. (1980). Action, joint action, and intentionality. In M. Brenner (Ed.), *The structure of action* (pp. 28–65). Oxford, UK: Basil Blackwell.

Shotter, J. (1984). *Social accountability and selfhood.* Oxford: Basil Blackwell.

Shotter, J. (1991). Wittgenstein and psychology: On our "hook up" to reality. In A. P. Griffiths (Ed.), *The Wittgenstein centenary essays* (pp. 193–208). Cambridge, UK: Cambridge University Press.

Shotter, J. (1993a). *Conversational realities: Constructing life through language.* London: Sage.

Shotter, J. (1993b). *Cultural politics of everyday life: Social constructionism, rhetoric, and knowing of the third kind.* Toronto, Ontario, Canada: Toronto University Press.

Shotter, J. (1995). Dialogical psychology. In J. A. Smith, R. Harrè, & L. Van Langenhove (Eds.), *Rethinking psychology* (pp. 160–178). London: Sage.

Shotter, J. (2000). Inside dialogical realities: From an abstract-systematic to a participatory-wholistic understanding of communication. *Southern Communication Journal, 65,* 119–132.

Shotter, J. (2003). "Real presences": Meaning as living movement in a participatory world. *Theory & Psychology, 13,* 435–468.

Siebert, F. S., Peterson, T., & Schramm, W. (1956). *Four theories of the press: The authoritation, libertarian, social responsibility, and Soviet communist concepts of what the press should be and do.* Urbana: University of Illinois Press.

Sieburg, E. (1985). *Family communication: An integrated systems approach.* New York: Gardner.

Sigman, S. J. (1995). Toward study of the consequentiality (not consequences) of communication. In S. J. Sigman (Ed.), *The consequentiality of communication* (pp. 1–14). Hillsdale, NJ: Lawrence Erlbaum.

Sillars, A. L. (1974). Expression and control in human interaction: Perspective on humanistic psychology. *Western Journal of Speech Communication, 38,* 269–277.

Silver, S. M., & Rogers, S. (2002). *Light in the heart of darkness: EMDR & the treatment of war and terrorism survivors.* New York: Norton.

Simpson, J. L. (2001). *The making of multivocal culture: Building community on a university campus.* Unpublished doctoral dissertation, University of Colorado, Boulder.

Sluzki, C. E., & Ransom, D. C. (1976). *Double bind: The foundation of the communicational approach to the family.* New York: Grune & Stratton.

Smith, A. D. (1993). *Fires in the mirror: Crown Heights, Brooklyn and other identities.* New York: Anchor Books.

Smith, A. D. (1994). *Twilight: Los Angeles, 1992.* New York: Anchor Books.

Smith, A. D. (2000). *Talk to me: Listening between the lines.* New York: Random House.

Smith, A. D. (Producer), Swerdlow, E. (Producer), & Levin, M. (Director). (2001). *Twilight Los Angeles* [Video]. New York: PBS Video.

Smith, B. H. (1997). *Belief and resistance: Dynamics of contemporary intellectual controversy.* Cambridge, MA: Harvard University Press.

Smith, C. R. (1985). Martin Heidegger and the dialogue with being. *Central States Speech Journal, 36,* 256–269.

Smith, C. R., & Douglas, D. G. (1973). Philosophical principles in the traditional and emerging views of rhetoric. In D. G. Douglas (Ed.), *Philosophers on rhetoric: Traditional and emerging views* (pp. 15–22). Skokie, IL: National Textbook.

Smith, D. (1987). *The everyday world as problematic: A feminist sociology.* Boston: Northeastern University Press.

Smith, J. A., Harrè, R., & Langenhove, L. V. (Eds.). (1995). *Rethinking psychology.* London: Sage.

Smith, M. A., & Kollock, P. (Ed.). (1999). *Communities in cyberspace.* New York: Routledge.

Snyder, I. (1996). *Hypertext: The electronic labyrinth.* Melbourne, Australia: Melbourne University Press.

Soloski, J. (1997). News reporting and professionalism: Some constraints on the reporting of the news. In D. Berkowitz (Ed.), *Social meanings of news: A text-reader* (pp. 138–154). Thousand Oaks, CA: Sage.

Spano, S. (2001). *Public dialogue and participatory democracy: The Cupertino community project.* Cresskill, NJ: Hampton Press.

Spender, D. (1985). *Man made language* (2nd ed.). Boston: Routledge.

Spivak, G. C. (1987). *In other worlds: Essays in cultural politics.* London: Methuen.

Spivak, G. C. (1990). *The post-colonial critic: Interviews, strategies, dialogues* (S. Harasyn, Ed.). London: Routledge.

Steiner, G. (1967). *Language and silence: Essays 1958–1966.* New York: Atheneum.

Steiner, G. (1989). *Real presences.* Chicago, IL: University of Chicago Press.

Stern, D. (2002). *The first relationship: Infant and mother.* Cambridge, MA: Harvard University Press.

Stewart, J. (Ed.). (1973). *Bridges not walls: A book about interpersonal communication.* Reading, MA: Addison-Wesley.

Stewart, J. (1978). Foundations of dialogic communication. *Quarterly Journal of Speech, 64,* 183–201.

Stewart, J. (1994). Foreword. In R. Anderson, K. N. Cissna, & R. C. Arnett (Eds.), *The reach of dialogue: Confirmation, voices, and community* (pp. i–xi). Cresskill, NJ: Hampton Press.

Stewart, J. (1995). *Language as articulate contact: Toward a post-semiotic philosophy of communication.* Albany: State University of New York Press.

Stewart, J. (Ed.). (1996). *Beyond the symbol model: Reflections on the representational nature of language.* Albany: State University of New York Press.

Stewart, J., & D'Angelo, G. (1975). *Together: Communicating interpersonally.* Reading, MA: Addison-Wesley.

Stewart, J., & Zediker, K. (2000). Dialogue as tensional, ethical practice. *Southern Communication Journal, 65,* 224–242.

Stone, D., Patton, B., & Heen, S. (1999). *Difficult conversations: How to discuss what matters most.* New York: Viking.

Strate, L., Jacobson, R., & Gibson, S. B. (Eds.). (1996). *Communication and cyberspace: Social interaction in an electronic environment.* Cresskill, NJ: Hampton Press.

Streeck, J. (1994). Culture, meaning, and interpersonal communication. In M. L. Knapp & G. R. Miller (Eds.), *Handbook of interpersonal communication* (2nd ed., pp. 286–322). Thousand Oaks, CA: Sage.

Strine, M. S. (1986). Between meaning and representation: Dialogic aspects of interpretation scholarship. In T. Colson (Ed.), *Renewal and revision: The future of interpretation* (pp. 69–91). Denton, TX: NB Omega.

Strine, M. S. (1988). Performance and critical theory: Negotiating the tensions between art and everyday life—A response. *Literature in Performance, 8,* 35–38.

Strine, M. S. (1989). The politics of asking women's questions: Voice and value in the poetry of Adrienne Rich. *Text and Performance Quarterly, 9,* 24–41.

Strine, M. S., Long, B. W., & HopKins, M. F. (1990). Research in interpretation and performance studies: Trends, issues, priorities. In G. M. Phillips & J. T. Wood (Eds.), *Speech communication: Essays to commemorate the 75th anniversary of the Speech Communication Association* (pp. 181–204). Carbondale: Southern Illinois University Press.

Study Circles. (2002). Who we are. Retrieved March 24, 2002, from http://www.studycircles.org/pages/who.html

Suurmond, J. J. (1999). Beyond Buber: Gestalt therapy in the light of Levinas. *The Gestalt Journal, 22,* 65–87.

Tallon, A. (1978). Intentionality, intersubjectivity, and the between: Buber and Levinas on affectivity and the dialogical principle. *Thought, 53,* 292–309.

Tannen, D. (1989). *Talking voices: Repetition, dialogue, and imagery in conversational discourse.* Cambridge, UK: Cambridge University Press.

Tannen, D. (1998). *The argument culture: Moving from debate to dialogue.* New York: Random House.

Tannen, D. (1999). *The argument culture: Moving from debate to dialogue.* New York: Ballantine.

Tannen, D., & Bly, R. (1993). *Men & women: Talking together* [Videorecording]. New York: Mystic Fire Video.

Taylor, C. (1985). *Human agency and language.* Cambridge, UK: Cambridge University Press.

Taylor, C. (1991a). The dialogical self. In D. R. Hiley, J. F. Bohman, & R. Shusterman (Eds.), *The interpretative turn* (pp. 304–314). Ithaca, NY: Cornell University Press.

Taylor, C. (1991b). *The ethics of authenticity.* Cambridge, MA: Harvard University Press.

Taylor, C. (1995). *Philosophical arguments.* Cambridge, MA: Harvard University Press.

Taylor, J. R. (1993). *Rethinking the theory of organizational communication: How to read an organization.* Norwood, NJ: Ablex.

Taylor, J. R., Groleau, C., Heaton, L., & Van Every, E. J. (2001). *The computerization of work: A communication perspective.* Thousand Oaks, CA: Sage.

Taylor, J. R., & Van Every, E. J. (2000). *The emergent organization: Communication as its site and surface.* Mahwah, NJ: Lawrence Erlbaum.

Taylor, M. C., & Saarinen, E. (1994). *Imagologies: Media philosophy.* London: Routledge.

Tedlock, D. (1983). *The spoken word and the work of interpretation.* Philadelphia: University of Pennsylvania Press.

Tedlock, D., & Mannheim, B. (Eds.). (1995). *The dialogic emergence of culture.* Urbana: University of Illinois Press.

Teens may have hinted at massacre in class. (2002, March 30). *Winston-Salem Journal,* p. A2.

The Crown Heights conflicts: Background information. (1993). *Fires in the mirror: Essays and teaching strategies.* Boston, MA: WGBH Educational Print and Outreach.

Thernstrom, A. (1993). Guinier miss. *The New Republic, 208,* 16–19.

Theunissen, M. (1984). *The other: Studies in the social ontology of Husserl, Heidegger, Sartre, and Buber* (C. Macann, Trans.). Cambridge, MA: MIT Press.

Thomlison, T. D. (1975). The necessary and sufficient characteristics of dialogic communication: The dialogic process equation. *Journal of the Illinois Speech and Theatre Association, 29,* 34–42.

Thomlison, T. D. (1982). *Toward interpersonal dialogue.* New York: Longman.

Thompson, R. L. (1947). *Wiring a continent: The history of the telegraph industry in the United States, 1832–1866.* Princeton, NJ: Princeton University Press.

Todorov, T. (1984). *Mikhail Bakhtin: The dialogical principle* (W. Godzich, Trans.). Minneapolis: University of Minnesota Press.

Tournier, P. (1957). *The meaning of persons.* New York: Harper & Row.

Tuchman, G. (1978). *Making news: A study in the construction of reality.* New York: Free Press.

Turner, V. (1969). *The ritual process: Structure and anti-structure.* Ithaca, NY: Cornell University Press.

Tyler, S. A. (1987). *The unspeakable: Discourse, dialogue, and rhetoric in the postmodern world.* Madison: University of Wisconsin Press.

Ulrich, W. (1983). *Critical heuristics of social planning: A new approach to practical philosophy.* Bern, Switzerland: Haupt.

Unger, R. M. (1987). *Social theory, its situation and its task.* New York: Cambridge University Press.

Voegelin, E. (1987). *Order and history: Vol. 5. In search of order.* Baton Rouge: Louisiana State University Press.

Voegelin, E. (2000). *Order in history: Vol. 18. In search of order.* Columbia: University of Missouri Press.

Volkan, V. (1997). *Blood lines: From ethnic pride to ethnic terrorism.* Boulder, CO: Westview Press.

Volosinov, V. N. (1973). *Marxism and the philosophy of language* (L. Matejka & I. R. Titunik, Trans.). Cambridge, MA: Harvard University Press.

Volosinov, V. N. (1976). Discourse in life and discourse in art. In V. N. Volosinov, *Freudianism: A Marxist critique* (I. R. Titunik & N. H. Bruss, Eds.; I. R. Titunik, Trans.; pp. 93–116). New York: Academic Press.

von Bertalanffy, L. (1968). *General systems theory.* New York: Braziller.

Walsh, D. (2001). State of emergency declared after acquittal of Cincinnati cop who shot youth. Retrieved August 30, 2002, from http://www.wsws.org/articles/2001/sep2001/cinc-s28.shtml

Warner, D. (1996). Levinas, Buber and the concept of otherness in international relations: A Reply to David Campbell. *Millennium: Journal of International Studies, 25,* 111–128.

Warner, M. (2002). *Publics and counterpublics.* Cambridge, MA: MIT Press.

Warnke, G. (1987). *Gadamer: Hermeneutics, tradition, and reason.* Stanford, CA: Stanford University Press.

Washington, J. M. (Ed.). (1992). *Martin Luther King, Jr., I have a dream: Writings and speeches that changed the world.* San Francisco: HarperCollins.

Watkins, M. (1986). *Invisible guests: The development of imaginal dialogues.* Hillsdale, NJ: Analytic Press.

Watzlawick, P., Beavin, J. H., & Jackson, D. D. (1967). *Pragmatics of human communication: A study of interactional patterns, pathologies, and paradoxes.* New York: Norton.

Watzlawick, P., Weakland, J. H., & Fisch, R. (1974). *Change: Principles of problem formation and problem resolution.* New York: W. W. Norton.

Webb, E. (1981). *Eric Voegelin, philosopher of history.* Seattle: University of Washington Press.

Weick, K. (1979). *The social psychology of organizing* (2nd ed.). Reading, MA: Addison-Wesley.

Wenzel, J. W. (1979). Jürgen Habermas and the dialectical perspective on argumentation. *Journal of the American Forensic Association, 16,* 83–94.

Werner, C., & Baxter, L. A. (1994). Temporal qualities of relationships: Organismic, transactional, and dialectical views. In M. L. Knapp & G. R. Miller (Eds.), *Handbook of interpersonal communication* (2nd ed., pp. 323–379). Thousand Oaks, CA: Sage.

Wertsch, J. V. (1991). *Voices of the mind: A sociocultural approach to mediated action.* Cambridge, MA: Harvard University Press.

West, C. (1993a). *Keeping faith: Philosophy and race in America.* New York: Routledge.

West, C. (1993b). *Race matters.* Boston, MA: Beacon Press.

Whitebrook, M. (2001). *Identity, narrative and politics.* London: Routledge.

Whitehead, A. N., & Russell, B. (1989). *Principia mathematica.* London: Cambridge University Press.

Whitely, J. (n.d.). Facilitating peace: Insights from three experiences. Interview with Carl R. Rogers. Retrieved August 30, 2002 from http://www.ucf.ics.uci.edu/zencin/peace2/interviews/rogers-facilitating.html

Will, G. (1993). Sympathy for Guinier. *Newsweek, 121,* 78.

Williams, P. (1992). *The alchemy of race and rights.* Cambridge, MA: Harvard University Press.

Williams, R. (1977). *Marxism and literature.* Oxford, UK: Oxford University Press.

Winch, R. F. (1958). *Mate selection: A study of complementary needs.* New York: Harper & Row.

Withdraw Guinier. (1993). *The New Republic, 208,* 7.

Witherell, C., & Noddings, N. (1991a). Prologue: An invitation to our readers. In C. Witherell & N. Noddings (Eds.), *Stories lives tell: Narrative and dialogue in education* (pp. 1–12). New York: Teachers College Press.

Witherell, C., & Noddings, N. (1991b). *Stories lives tell: Narrative and dialogue in education.* New York: Teachers College Press.

Wittgenstein, L. (1921). *Tractatus logico-philosophicus.* London: Routledge and Kegan Paul.

Wittgenstein, L. (1963). *Philosophical investigations* (G. E. M. Anscombe, Trans.). Oxford, UK: Basil Blackwell.

Wold, A. H. (Ed.). (1992). *The dialogical alternative: Towards a theory of language and mind.* London: Scandinavian University Press.

Wood, J. T. (1997). Diversity in dialogue: Commonalities and differences between friends. In J. M. Makau & R. C. Arnett (Eds.), *Communication ethics in an age of diversity* (pp. 5–26). Urbana: University of Illinois Press.

Wright, R. (1994). *The moral animal: Evolutionary psychology and everyday life.* New York: Vintage.

Yankelovich, D. (1991). *Coming to public judgment: Making democracy work in a complex world.* Syracuse, NY: Syracuse University Press.

Yankelovich, D. (1999). *The magic of dialogue: Transforming conflict into cooperation.* New York: Simon and Schuster.

Young, I. M. (1990). *Justice and the politics of difference.* Princeton, NJ: Princeton University Press.

Zelizer, B. (1999). Making the neighborhood work: The improbabilities of public journalism. In T. L. Glasser (Ed.), *The idea of public journalism* (pp. 152–172). New York: Guilford.

Zelizer, B., & Allan, S. (Eds.). (2002). *Journalism after September 11.* New York: Routledge.

Index